UNDERSTANDING SOCIAL LIFE

AN INTRODUCTION TO SOCIAL PSYCHOLOGY

UNDERSTANDING SOCIAL LIFE
AN INTRODUCTION TO SOCIAL PSYCHOLOGY

PAUL F. SECORD
Queens College
City University of New York

CARL W. BACKMAN
University of Nevada, Reno

DAVID R. SLAVITT
Cambridge, Massachusetts

McGRAW-HILL BOOK COMPANY

New York   St. Louis   San Francisco   Auckland   Düsseldorf
Johannesburg   Kuala Lumpur   London   Mexico   Montreal   New Delhi
Panama   Paris   São Paulo   Singapore   Sydney   Tokyo   Toronto

This book was set in Baskerville by Rocappi, Inc.
The editors were Richard R. Wright, Janis M. Yates,
and David Dunham; the designer was J. E. O'Connor;
the production supervisor was Leroy A. Young.
Kingsport Press, Inc., was printer and binder.

The photographs in this book were conceived and
taken by Julie Low, except where otherwise credited.

Cover photograph by Burk Uzzle. Used with the permission
of Magnum Photos, Inc.

301.1
Se 2u
123240
nov.1982

UNDERSTANDING SOCIAL LIFE
AN INTRODUCTION TO SOCIAL PSYCHOLOGY

1 2 3 4 5 6 7 8 9 0   KPKP   7 9 8 7 6

Library of Congress Cataloging in Publication Data

Secord, Paul F
    Understanding social life.

    Bibliography: p.
    Includes indexes.
    1. Social psychology.   I. Backman, Carl W.,
joint author.   II. Slavitt, David R., date,
joint author.   III. Title.
HM251.S42   301.1   75-25870
ISBN 0-07-055917-1

CONTENTS

PREFACE

This book presents the elements of social psychology in a brief form suitable for either a one-quarter or a one semester course. Its brevity is such that instructors who wish to do so may supplement their favorite topics. Every effort has been made to present ideas lucidly and with a minimum of jargon, without at the same time sacrificing some technical concepts that we consider to be valuable aids to understanding social behavior. Emphasis is upon ideas rather than the details of methodology or experimentation.

The book is interdisciplinary, emphasizing the important contributions of both psychology and sociology to social psychology. These two disciplines emphasize somewhat different areas within the field and differ in their approaches, but typically we have presented multiple viewpoints on particular topics or problems and have attempted to integrate the diverse contributions into a coherent pattern of explanation.

Inevitably, some topics are either not covered at all or are covered only briefly in a short book. Our choice of topics has been guided by what has received the most attention in the research literature and by what social psychologists consider to be of central interest. This suggests an inevitable comparison between the present text and the second edition of Secord and Backman's *Social*

Psychology, published in 1974. The present text has been completely rewritten, expressly to meet several purposes: (1) to communicate the material clearly and in an interesting manner at the beginning level of two- or four-year colleges, (2) to considerably shorten the amount of material presented and topics covered, (3) to reduce the direct reliance on research literature, emphasizing instead concepts and ideas in social psychology, and (4) to update those few areas where critical reconceptualizations or crucial experiments have brought about substantial changes. To capture and hold the reader's interest, we give numerous examples which illustrate how social psychological ideas apply to everyday life and experience. Photographic illustrations are also included to enhance interest.

Instructors who wish to teach social psychology in a comprehensive manner at an intermediate or advanced level will probably prefer the second edition of *Social Psychology* to the present brief text. But those who prefer a short, less demanding text may wish to use this brief edition.

We owe special thanks to Julie Low, who provided the ideas for the illustrations, as well as the photographs themselves. We also thank Myra Ferree, who wrote the Instructor's Manual.

Paul F. Secord
Carl W. Backman
David R. Slavitt

UNDERSTANDING SOCIAL LIFE

AN INTRODUCTION TO SOCIAL PSYCHOLOGY

ONE

INTRODUCTION

Human activity is largely social. Individuals do little in total isolation from other persons; most behavior is jointly enacted. Most people live in family units; they work in organizations of some size; they play in the company of each other. This social activity is the focus of the social psychologist. Unlike general psychologists, who often study single individuals in the isolation of the psychological laboratory, social psychologists study the behavior of individuals who are interacting with each other. Or if they do focus on single individuals, it is only in a social context or situation (for example, the individuals studied might be asked to describe their feelings about other people who are not present). The work of sociologists, on the other hand, transcends the individual; often sociologists are interested in the nature of social institutions, like the school or the family, or in characteristics of society, like its stratification into social classes. Their emphasis is on the general characteristics of these institutions or the patterned structures of society apart from the participating individuals.

NATURE OF SOCIAL INTERACTION

People behave differently in the presence of other persons from the way they behave when alone. They anticipate that others will react to their actions in various ways—approving or disapproving, agreeing or disagreeing, cooperating or competing, and they temper their behavior accordingly. But more than that. Under ordinary circumstances, interaction flows smoothly. This occurs because each party anticipates how the other will react, and knows how he in turn will respond. And this knowledge is only possible when both parties share the same definitions of their own and each other's acts, as well as a common understanding of the structure of their relation.

When this shared understanding is lacking, interaction produces surprise, dismay, disgust, anger, or other disruptive feelings. When two men in our society are introduced, each extends his hand and expects the other to extend his hand. But if one of the men is from a society where the handshake is not known as a symbol of greeting, this action is likely to falter. The horseplay of adolescents similarly displays the underlying normal expectation in the surprise the other party experiences when one who extends his hand suddenly jerks it away at the last minute. Or worse, when the hand of a practical joker is grasped, and a concealed buzzer goes off.

People are gregarious. (Magnum Photos, Inc.; photo by Burk Uzzle)

Communication through the handshake as a standard form of greeting.

Our *mutual expectations* govern much of our everyday behavior, and they must be identified if social behavior is to be understood. Social psychology deals with expectations of this kind in several different contexts; the concept will be encountered again and again throughout this book.

PERSONALITY, SOCIAL, AND CULTURAL SYSTEMS

The behavior of individuals in interaction may be analyzed in terms of three systems: the personality system, the social system, and the cultural system. Analysis in terms of *personality* considers properties of individuals such as attitudes, traits, feelings, habits, needs, and motives, as well as the way in which the individual conceives of himself and the world around him. Such analysis emphasizes the differences between one individual and another, and attempts to identify the distinguishing characteristics of a person, whether they be attitudes, motives, habits, or whatever. Social psychologists have given only limited attention to personality; more often they try to identify the characteristics of social interaction in terms intended to apply to everyone in our society or in similar societies. Usually, too, whenever possible, they favor characterizing attributes of individuals in terms of the regular structure or processes of social interaction rather than as inherent properties of the individuals themselves. The simplest example of this comes from treatments of delinquency and crime. While psychiatrists sometimes see delinquent or criminal behavior as a product of the individual's own characteristics, social psychologists are more apt to emphasize the role of societal factors in producing such behavior. A fragmentary glimpse of such factors from the point of view of a prisoner who was recently shot to death in an attempted bank robbery is provided by some notes he left behind:

> I remember things. Like being hit with a bed slat at the Children's Center in Lauren, Md. . . . like being beaten at the National Training School for Boys. . . . Prison became a habit. I knew damn little of the outside world. I didn't know how to live on the streets. All I had known for most of my life was crime and prison. A .38 and armed robbery, at that point in my life, seemed to be a logical, if frightening, step in my career as a convict. . . . It occurred to me that when most people leave prison, they do so with a sense of shame because society has branded them as second-class citizens. And society treats them as second-class citizens for the rest of their lives, beginning as soon as they hit the street. . . . They get hustled and pushed around, and 8 out of every 10 ex-cons soon become prisoners all over again. (*Boston Globe,* Feb. 24, 1975)

Chapter 15 will show how personality and social systems interact to produce and maintain one's identity and its corresponding behavior, while Chapter 16 will emphasize the role of societal factors in producing and maintaining deviant identities, like those of "criminal" or "mental patient."

Analysis in terms of the *social system* focuses on relations among persons. Typically, each person is thought of as occupying one or more positions in these relations. Associated with each position are expectations as to how a person in that position should think, feel, and act toward other members. Such systems have a certain persistence over time, and each instance of them has much similarity to other instances. An example is the nuclear family, containing the positions of father-husband, mother-wife, son, daughter. Individuals in these positions are expected to behave in certain ways, not only by other members of the family, but also by people outside the family but having some relation to it. Much of the behavior of the members of a social system is a function of the structure of the system, consisting of the sets of expectations for the various positions. Thus, mothers in many families behave in similar ways toward their children because of the constraints placed upon them by expectations which they share mutually with other family members and with outsiders related to the family.

That most of us do have definite expectations as to how a mother and a child should behave is shown by a study of overprotective mothers and their children. Consider, for example, the following excerpts from two cases of boys, aged eight and thirteen. Most of us will consider the behaviors to be gross violations of our normal expectations.

CASE 1 (MALE, 8 YEARS)

Excessive contact: When he was an infant mother could never leave him for an instant. . . . Has been sleeping with him the past six months because he has called her. . . . Mother says they are attached together like Siamese twins.

Prolongation of infantile care: Mother dresses him every day, takes him to school every morning and calls for him every afternoon. . . . Mother still goes to the bathroom with him and waits for him. . . .

Prevention of independent behavior: He has one friend whom mother takes him to see every two weeks. Mother does not allow him to help in housework for fear he'll fall and break a dish, etc.

Maternal control: Mother must have a light burning for him until he falls asleep. He goes to bed at 10 P.M. Mother always gives in to him; does everything for him; is dominated by him. He spits at her and strikes her.

CASE 2 (MALE, 13 YEARS)

Excessive contact: Mother has slept with him the past three years. Up to age 7, she never let him go out with any adult (even father) except herself.

Prolongation of infantile care: When the patient is disobedient she puts him to bed in the afternoon, even now. She still prepares special food for him when he refuses to eat. She still sits by and coaxes.

Prevention of independent behavior: Mother delayed his schooling until he was seven because she did not like him to leave her. . . . She kept him from having friends or learning bad things from other children. When he was sent to camp at 14, the mother visited him on the second day, found that his feet were wet and took him home.

Maternal control: General obedient, submissive response to maternal domination. Uses aggressive methods to maintain his dependency on the mother, insisting she walk to school with him, etc.[1]

The most direct discussion of role expectations and social systems appears in Chapters 13 and 14 but such systems are brought in at many other points to help explain the nature of social interaction.

Central to analysis in terms of *culture* are the agreed-upon ideas about the social and the nonsocial world. These include complex systems of beliefs as well as the values that members of a society place upon various kinds of activities. The juvenile gang is unknown in some societies, a fact which suggests that certain aspects of our culture are relevant to gang formation. These include belief patterns favoring late marriage, which leave a large number of males unaffiliated, and the complex technological nature of employment in our society, which prevents the early entrance of a sizable number of young males into adult employment.

Psychologists as psychologists are concerned primarily with analysis in terms of individual behavior; sociologists as sociologists are interested primarily in analysis of the social system. Anthropologists are concerned with cultural sys-

[1] Reprinted by permission from D. Levy. *Maternal overprotection*. New York: Columbia University Press, 1943, pp. 28, 30.

tems. Social psychologists, however, while using as basic data the behavior and characteristics of individuals, try to understand individual behavior in terms of variables from all three systems. While analysis in each of the systems is kept distinct, individual behavior provides the focal point for relating the systems to each other.

Thus, certain aspects of the personality of individuals may result from properties of the social system. When the social system called the *family* is structured in a certain way, for example, it produces individuals who are strongly motivated to achieve wealth, success, and status in a society. Such ambitions become characteristics of the individuals whose nature has been shaped by their family. When the family is structured in other ways, it produces a much weaker need for achievement. The examples of overprotective mothers just discussed, as well as other research, suggest that children treated in this way will be excessively passive and lacking in independence. At the same time they will show little consideration for others and will expect to be catered to.

In a similar way, certain personality variables may affect the functioning of social systems. For example, the personality makeup of members of individual families produces marked variation in the functioning of this social system. Passive, timid, sickly children are more apt to elicit overprotective behavior from their mothers. Or, women who rebel against the traditional role of wife and mother may deviate markedly from the expectations normally associated with such positions. Finally, families in a whole society may be structured so as to encourage strong needs for achievement in children, because such behavior is related to the central values of the culture of the group. For the most part, social psychology deals in this fashion with the interplay between personality, social system, and, to a lesser extent, culture.

PLAN OF THE BOOK

Chapter 2, which follows, discusses the mechanisms by which infants and children learn to become adult participants in our society. The family plays a vital role in this process, although recent research has shown that play and other interaction with peers is of crucial importance if development is to proceed normally. Our examples of overprotective mothers illustrate how these "socializing" processes may go awry and produce adults who have problems in relating to other people or in learning to be independent. Chapter 3 continues the discussion of socialization in an attempt to show how children eventually learn to control their own behavior, and how they develop moral values which they use as a guide. Chapter 4 attempts to identify the sources that lead to two different social motives: aggression and achievement. Both of these are highly prevalent in our society, and it is therefore important to understand what creates them.

Chapters 5 and 6 turn to a different topic, how we come to know and to evaluate people. It is impossible to react to each person in all his individuality;

people are too complex. So children gradually learn to put people into categories: they type them. This makes it easier for the children to know how to act toward other people—whether to anticipate having fun or to be afraid, for example. Chapter 6 continues with a discussion of some of the complexities in presenting ourselves so as to create a certain impression, or in determining another person's intentions or responsibilities for an action.

Liking, friendship, and love is the subject matter of Chapter 7. Attraction between people is central to human society; it is the basis of the family, of friendships, of politics, and it plays an important part in business and work. It is the glue that holds groups together, and its polar opposite, hostility or rejection, creates many of the problems of society. The chapter tries to provide insights into the factors that create and maintain attraction.

Chapter 8 deals with social power. Its concern is with understanding how one individual gains and maintains power over another person—power that enables him or her to influence that person. Like attraction, social power is central to the functioning of all human groups. The last part of this chapter deals with strategies and tactics for manipulating power—for increasing it or for resisting its exercise. While Chapter 8 focuses on the conditions that give one individual power over another, and on how these conditions change, Chapter 9 approaches the problem of influence from another perspective, that of considering what goes on in individuals when people try to influence them. What happens when they are confronted with an inconsistency between their beliefs and their behavior? How effective are threats or appeals to fear, as used in the mass media, such as advertisements?

Chapter 10 describes the nature of human groups, showing how they are self-maintaining, and how the processes that go on in them have a patterned character. Such patterns or structures are based upon attraction, social power, status, or communication. Chapter 11 introduces social norms and explains how groups control their individual members. A theory of social control within groups identifies the conditions that produce strong or weak conformity to the norms of the group, and discusses the context in which deviations from these norms are permitted. Chapter 12 demonstrates how leadership and group morale can be understood in terms of group structure and process.

The role of institutions in human behavior is brought out in Chapters 13 and 14, which deals with social roles and social systems, already briefly discussed in this introductory chapter. Chapter 15 is an intensive discussion of the interplay between individual and group, with emphasis on the development in the individual of a concept of self, a sense of identity. This vital property of individuals grows out of their participation in social life, out of the ways in which other persons see and behave toward them, and their reactions toward these other persons' definitions of them. This same theme is carried further in the final chapter, showing how an interplay between individual and societal forces can produce a sense of a deviant identity, such as that of a "criminal" or a "mental patient," and how, once established, such identities are frequently perpetuated.

TWO

LEARNING
TO
BE HUMAN

A student asked to make observations as if she were a boarder in her own home wrote the following report:

A short, stout man entered the house, kissed me on the cheek and asked, "How was school?" I answered politely. He walked into the kitchen, kissed the younger of the two women, and said hello to the other. The younger woman asked me, "What do you want for dinner, honey?" I answered, "Nothing." She shrugged her shoulders and said no more. The older woman shuffled around the kitchen muttering. The man washed his hands, sat down at the table, and picked up the paper. He read until the two women had finished putting the food on the table. The three sat down. They exchanged idle chatter about the day's events. The older woman said something in a foreign language which made the others laugh.[1]

As Harold Garfinkel puts it, given the impersonal viewpoint of a boarder, behavior was described without reference to the identity of the persons and their relations to each other and to the larger setting of the family as well as its history. The strangeness of the description, given that the observer was a daughter talk-

[1] Reprinted by permission from H. Garfinkel. *Studies in ethnomethodology*. Englewood Cliffs, N.J.: Prentice-Hall, Inc., 1967.

ing about her father and mother, reveals that we ordinarily take many aspects of social interaction for granted. They only come to our attention when someone behaves in a way that violates these deeply embedded, background contexts. *Socialization* is the process of learning to behave within such frameworks and contexts.

The term *socialization* used to be applied only to the development of children into adults and was nearly synonymous with *upbringing*. But socialization does not stop at a given age. It continues through our adult lives, and is a process particularly evident in any new situation—in a new grade, a new school, a new business organization. We learn how to act and react. We learn to anticipate how other persons will behave, and we learn that they expect us to behave in certain ways toward them. Socialization is the modification of one's attitudes and behavior to conform to the expectations of people with whom one interacts. It involves learning to categorize other persons as well as oneself, and it extends to moral values and standards.

Two aspects of socialization distinguish it from other kinds of changes in behavior. First, only developments of attitude and behavior through *learning* are relevant. Other changes, such as those resulting from growth, are not part of the socialization process. Second, only changes of behavior and attitude having their origins in *interaction with other persons* are products of socialization. The interaction can be direct and intimate, as in adopting a roommate's choice obscenities, or indirectly, as through movies or books or television.

Socialization should not be viewed as molding a person to a standard social pattern. Even different individuals in the same family are treated quite differently by other members. One child may be favored, another slighted. Moreover, individuals react to pressures in different ways. So their ultimate character and nature is a joint product of socialization pressures and their reactions to them. Consequently, socialization can produce distinctive differences among persons, as well as similarities among members of a given group, class, region, or nation.

Socialization generally centers on four sets of processes. These are:

1 Social learning mechanisms such as imitation, identification, and role learning.
2 The establishment of internal or moral controls and other cognitive processes such as the *self* concept.
3 The development of various social behavior patterns such as dependency, aggression, and achievement.
4 The influence on social behavior exerted by groups and institutions, such as ethnic units and the family.

The first of these processes, social learning mechanisms, underlies all the others. Understanding how social learning occurs is fundamental to socialization. Although our knowledge on this topic is far from complete, there are many suggestions about patterns of social learning. We will discuss some of the more important of these in the present chapter.

ELEMENTARY SOCIAL LEARNING

Among the competing theories of learning, one of the most viable and popular is the *radical behaviorism* of B. F. Skinner.[2] Skinner's ideas have been applied to a wide variety of learning problems under the rubric of behavior modification. Radical behaviorism starts with an easily identifiable response—a rat pressing a lever, or a pigeon pecking at a marked spot on the wall of his cage. The three important elements associated with making this response are (1) the occasion on which the response occurs, (2) the response itself, and (3) the action of the environment on the organism after the response has been made.

The relation among these three elements is referred to as *contingencies of reinforcement*. Reinforcement is any action of the environment that changes the response—or changes the probability that it will occur again. Contingencies that strengthen the response are called positive reinforcement—food pellets for rats or pigeons, or candy, money, praise, or social approval for people. Negative reinforcement, or avoidance learning, is more complicated. It strengthens an act which avoids an unpleasant contingency. Each time a rat jumps over an electrified grid to avoid a shock or each time a child tells a lie to escape being spanked, the act of jumping or lying is strengthened.

The occasion on which the response occurs is often marked by some special feature of the situation called a *discriminative stimulus*. Thus, a rat in a box may learn to press its lever to get its food pellet only when the light is on. The light is the discriminative stimulus. Or a child may learn only to ask her mother for cookies when her mother is smiling and in a good mood. There, the smile, the body attitude, the tone of voice of the mother are all discriminative stimuli.

Responses are strengthened or weakened according to the contingencies of reinforcement which, in radical behaviorism, are considered a sufficient explanation for the learning of any particular action. If the individual can be shown to learn or unlearn a particular action as a result of alterations in the reinforcement contingencies that are in effect, that is held to be both a sufficient and complete explanation of the learning. There is no need to invoke reasons or motives which consider the individual's view of what took place. All such attempts are superfluous to radical behaviorism.

Some acts are undoubtedly learned as a result of the way in which contingencies of reinforcement are arranged, either accidentally or by design. Certainly such learning has been repeatedly demonstrated in the laboratory both with animals and children. Our knowledge of positive reinforcement can be applied

[2] Skinner, 1969.

fairly readily when animals or children perform acts that we would like them to repeat. But another kind of learning is perhaps more complicated—learning to inhibit, suppress, or *not* perform a particular act. Such learning is commonplace in childhood. Parents try to eliminate undesirable behaviors from their children's repertoire. Generally, some form of aversive stimulation or punishment is involved in the suppression of acts, although positive reinforcement may also play a role. A child learns not to belch at the dinner table, the behavior being suppressed by a look, a frown, a joke. More serious behavior is often discouraged by strong action in the form of punishment.

Does punishment work? Many people believe in its effectiveness—for children, for employees, for criminals, who are spanked, docked, locked up. The idea is that either aversive stimulation or removal of positive contingencies will eliminate undesirable behavior. Punishment may not necessarily establish other, more desirable behavior, but in combination with positive reinforcement it may be effective in suppressing behavior. But often punishment may be completely ineffective in eliminating some behavior, and may sometimes produce other undesirable effects.

A popular position with psychologists for the past twenty or thirty years has been that although punishment may temporarily suppress a particular behavior, it does not permanently weaken the motivation to perform that action. More recently, it has been established that punishment is not necessarily temporary in its effect. In some situations, punishment can be remarkably potent.[3]

For instance, high-intensity punishment is more effective in suppressing acts than low-intensity, and punishment which immediately anticipates an act or immediately follows it is more effective than delayed punishment. Immediacy also increases the effectiveness of positive reinforcement. These facts have been demonstrated in laboratory experiments,[4] where essential conditions can be established, but in everyday situations, the circumstances necessary for punishment to be effective are often lacking or are impossible to establish.

Richard Solomon and his associates demonstrated that punishment is especially effective if it is combined with reinforcement for doing something other than the punished act.[5] They punished beagle dogs by swatting them on the snout with a rolled-up newspaper as soon as they touched horsemeat, and, at the same time, offered them dry food pellets (positive reinforcement). After thoroughly learning to avoid the horsemeat, the dogs were placed in the test room without the experimenter present and given a choice of horsemeat and a few food pellets. Compared with dogs who had simply been punished but not reinforced, and who ate when they were given the chance later, these dogs avoided the horsemeat for about two weeks, even though they became ravenously hungry within five days and did not receive sufficient dry food to maintain their weight.

[3] Church, 1963; Solomon, 1964; Aronfreed, 1968; Parke, 1970.
[4] Aronfreed, 1968.
[5] Solomon, 1964.

What this demonstrates is that the simple negation of behavior is less effective than a combination of negation of one kind of behavior and reward for some other, related action. The avoidance of punishment positively reinforces the act that successfully avoids the punishment. A dog given an intense shock following a warning signal will very soon learn to leap over a barrier into a shock-free compartment as soon as he hears the warning signal. When the shock apparatus is turned off, the dog will continue to make the same jump to the safe area hundreds of times.

The strength of this learning was dramatically demonstrated by taking a dog trained this way and trying to teach it *not* to jump.[6] The "safe" part of the cage was now electrified and the old shock area disconnected. The dog kept right on jumping for a long time, despite the fact that he received a shock each time.

The experiment with the beagles also showed some dramatic effects of delaying punishment. In addition to the dogs who were *immediately* punished for just *touching* the horsemeat, and who consequently avoided it for about two weeks after punishment stopped, other dogs were punished five seconds after starting to eat the meat, and still others fifteen seconds after. Later, these dogs did not show as strong a resistance to temptation. Those whose punishment was delayed for five seconds avoided the meat for about ten days during the test session, while those with the fifteen-second delay began eating it as early as the second day of the test session.

These investigators point out that in the delay groups, the punishment occurred *after the dogs had eaten some horsemeat and while they were still eating.* This had important and dramatic effects upon their later eating behavior in the test session. These dogs ate fearfully, snatching some food, running away, furtively approaching the food again, gulping more, and slinking away again. The dogs who had been punished only for *touching* the food did not behave this way while eating when they had finally broken the taboo. Their *approach* to the food, however, was furtive and similar to that of the other dogs.

The interpretation given by the investigators to these findings was that punishment establishes an association between each specific learning situation and its consequences. Thus, the dogs immediately punished for *touching* the meat learned to be afraid of approaching or touching it, but since they were never punished while actually eating it they did not display fear at that time. The delay groups, on the other hand, were punished while eating the meat, so they learned to be fearful both while approaching *and* while eating it. The investigators note that many life situations with human beings involve punishment that is delayed so that the individual is engaging in the forbidden act when he or she is punished. In fact, punishment at the moment of initiation of an act is relatively rare. Thus, we might expect that the effects of the punishment (fear and other emotional states) would become associated with the act itself. Extending this idea further, punishment delivered after an act has been completed is apt to produce

[6] Aronfreed, 1968.

associations between fear and whatever stimuli are present *after* the completion of the act. For example, the mother who warns her child that he will be punished when his father comes home may merely be teaching him to be afraid of his father's homecoming.

The application of these kinds of experiments to life situations is in part speculative. Naturally we would not want to perform such experiments with children. The point is to try to imagine how analogous avoidance-learning situations might operate in situations outside the laboratory. Any action that avoids punishment would tend to be reinforced. Of course, this may mean that the forbidden action is not performed; but it may also reinforce some undesirable act, such as lying. Denial and lying could even become the habitual learned behavior. This process will be discussed and extended in the next chapter when we take up the development of cognitive, or moral, controls.

The avoidance of punishment seems simple enough, but there is an interpretation which goes beyond radical behaviorism and considers the state of mind of the subject. The apprehension or anticipation of punishment is *anxiety*. In children, punishment may lead to the control of behavior by a two-part process involving reinforcement conditioning.[7] First, anxiety is conditioned to the performance of the punished act or to elements associated with it so that, as the act is repeated, the various painful consequences induced by the socializing agent arouse anxiety each step of the way. Repeated punishments eventually produce conditioned associations between the anxious state and the mere *idea* of performing the act. The second part of the process is the anxiety reduction that attaches to nonpunished acts that replace the punished ones.

Eventually, in the absence of the socializing agent, the arousal of anxiety prevents the occurrence of the punished act, which is replaced instead by acceptable acts. This interpretation in terms of anxiety, which is an inner state, goes beyond radical behaviorism. It does not, however, necessarily involve thought and reason—for example, judgments of the act as wrong or immoral.

The question is how a child is socialized, how he learns to behave this way rather than that. The influences upon the child are complicated, not always entirely consistent, and frequently not deliberate or planned. Parents and teachers do not behave like clinical investigators—which is, no doubt, a good thing. But the instrumentalities of rearing and training have in them combinations of punishment and reward, the arousal and the reduction of anxiety, and, eventually, the application of reason, justification, and explanation. Punishment may consist of the simple withdrawal of affection or the deprivation of pleasurable activities. ("Go to your room!") Or, when the child substitutes the approved behavior for the disapproved one, the substitution can be reinforced by restoring the previously withdrawn affection or pleasurable activity. ("You can come out now, and have a cookie!")

[7] Aronfreed, 1968.

While it is often possible to debate whether a particular kind of behavior has been learned simply through reinforcement or through thought and reason, it does seem that at least some acts and some inhibition of acts can be learned solely through reinforcement contingencies. Justin Aronfreed has noted that much behavior is inhibited under conditions where, after the habit has been learned through reinforcement, there is no visible external surveillance nor is there any discernible cognitive or moral control.[8] For example, a pet dog that has been housebroken does not soil the rug even when his owner is out of the house. And children can be taught to inhibit various behaviors even before they possess the rudimentary use of language.

Outside the laboratory it is difficult to isolate the instrumentalities of socialization. One study, for instance, examines mothers' views of their own effectiveness in socializing their children.[9] The mothers who said that they combined physical punishment of aggressive behavior with extensive use of reasoning reported that their children were less aggressive than did mothers who used physical punishment alone. But this finding is difficult to interpret. Certainly mothers who use punishment without reason and explanation are providing models for the very aggressiveness they are trying to curb. And the reasonable, explaining mothers were manifesting tolerance and affection at the same time as they were talking and explaining. But quite possibly the mothers who valued reason and communication also placed a higher value on nonviolence and would therefore report that their children were less aggressive, even when they weren't.

We have very little information concerning the use of punishment in natural settings.[10] What kinds of punishments are used, and how often, relative to other techniques for control? We don't really know what kinds of punishments are most effective—and it isn't so simple to discover as one might assume. For example, repeated low-intensity punishment following the performance of an act will often *increase* the probability that it will reoccur![11] One explanation for this is that very mild punishment makes an act stand out and be remembered and emphasizes its importance without acting as a deterrent to repeating it.

We may also ask whether socializing agents especially favor using punishment for certain types of transgressions. How do the child's reactions to the punishment affect its future use? Often such reactions are disruptive and interfere with learning desirable behaviors. They may also adversely affect the relationship between parent and child. And what is the context in which the punishment is administered? Is it applied in an overall atmosphere of acceptance by the parent of the child? Or does the child feel totally rejected? Or is punishment the only time when the child really feels that the parent is paying attention to him or her? Much more research needs to be done in natural settings to answer questions of this kind.

[8] Aronfreed, 1968.
[9] Sears, Maccoby, and Levin, 1957.
[10] Aronfreed, 1968; Parke, 1970.
[11] Aronfreed, 1968.

Summary: Elementary Social Learning

Socialization is the modification of one's attitudes and behavior to conform to the expectations of the people with whom one interacts. It involves learning the background contexts in which social behavior takes place and the categories of persons with whom one interacts. It also involves the social roles one learns, the moral standards and values one acquires, and the views of oneself—the sense of identity—that one adopts. Much of this kind of learning is subtle and complicated.

In this section we have discussed more elementary forms of learning various behaviors. In this elementary learning, inner mental states and more explicit thoughts and feelings are not thought to play much part. Here, behavior is thought to be contingent upon the kind of reinforcement it receives. Behavior followed by positive consequences appears to be readily learned. Negative consequences, like punishment, are more complicated. Punishment results in suppression of behavior only under certain conditions, most notably when it is combined with reinforcement for some desirable act which is a substitute for the forbidden behavior. When a substitute act successfully avoids the punishment, that act is reinforced and learned—even if it, too, is undesirable. Thus, parents who use punishment may inadvertently be reinforcing undesirable acts that substitute for the forbidden act. Punishment may have other undesirable consequences, such as interfering with learning desirable acts and damaging the relationship between parent and child.

LEARNING FROM MODELS

Human beings often model their behavior after another person. Human beings act like other human beings, and they learn how to do this by observing others of their kind. This kind of learning has been called *modeling,* or *imitation,* or *observational learning.* Observations may be direct, or indirect—through books, films, and television. The models may be fictional, as when a small boy tries to be like Peter Pan or The Lone Ranger. Sometimes the observer immediately enacts the modeled behavior, but more often it is not enacted until later.

For this reason, conventional learning theory is not particularly helpful in explaining the way models and modeling work. Nearly always, conventional learning research has used situations where the learners can be directly observed, situations where they are enacting observable behavior. But imitation requires learning the model's behavior without immediately enacting it, and remembering it so that it can be performed later. This is a nontraditional learning situation. The more recent trend toward studying memory and learning within the same conceptual and experimental framework hopefully will eventually help to explain modeling.[12]

[12] Kintsch, 1970.

For better or worse, television is one important source of socialization influences.

Only in recent years has explicit attention been given to learning through the imitation of models. There is no general agreement about how best to conceptualize this kind of learning. There are a number of competing points of view. One of them that seems relatively comprehensive, and the one we offer here, is that of Albert Bandura.[13] This discussion will suggest the elements of the modeling process, but we must leave for future research the problem of specifying the exact mechanisms that underlie modeling. Bandura suggests that modeling requires four related processes. Individuals, he says, must *attend* to the behavior of the other person, must *remember* what they have observed, must have the *capability* to perform the remembered behavior, and must have the *motivation* to enact the behavior.

Obviously, the first requirement is that an individual *attend* to the behavior of a model. If Harry does not see what Barry is doing, doesn't notice it in the first place, Harry is not going to learn a whole lot from Barry. Attention, of course, is selective, and one pays more attention to models that may be useful or attractive or which are somehow obtrusive. Television commercials frequently try to combine these qualities, showing an attractive woman with a headache in a particularly grating or vulgar commercial (in which, say, her whole forehead turns into a sink drain, opens, and clears her sinuses).

[13] Bandura, 1969, 1971.

Imitation, or modeling. (Photo Researchers, Inc.; photo by Erika)

The behavior, once noticed, must be *remembered*. We remember things, however, in a variety of ways. There are verbal memories, and there are images. There are also kinesthetic memories by which we imitate a particular walk or attitude of the head, remember how that feels, and can reproduce the feeling by reproducing the posture. Information which can be coded verbally can be even more greatly refined. Often we translate images into words for precision, reducing the welter of impressions of an automobile journey to "turn right at the second traffic light and then left after crossing the railroad tracks," and so on.

Not only must individuals attend to a model and remember the behavior, they must also have the *capacity* to perform that behavior. To attend a performance of a concert pianist is one thing; no amount of attention and memory will enable just anyone in the audience to sit down at the Steinway and actually play the way the pianist did. Or even play at all. There are always more people in the stands of a stadium than down on the field playing the game.

A great performance, in the concert hall and on the football field, may be inspiring. And there may be members of the audience who are *motivated* at least to try to imitate the kind of behavior that has so much impressed them. They may start to work, practice, practice, practice, and find reinforcement at various stages along the way as they develop proficiency. Traditional learning theory suggests that learning only takes place in the presence of reinforcement. Bandura suggests that *imitative learning* can on occasion occur without reinforcement. People may observe, code, and retain patterns of behavior that can be reproduced at a later time even when they are not rewarded. But he recognizes that the process may sometimes involve subtle forms of reinforcement that are difficult for the individual to remember or for the researcher to detect.

Much of the early theorizing and research on modeling or observational learning centered on the motivation underlying the choice of a particular model. Psychoanalytic theory offered two types of motivation for identification with a model—the nurturing relationship of the child with the mother, and the relationship of anxiety generated by the Oedipal rivalry with the father (for a boy) or the mother (for a girl).

The nurturing relationship is that of the child during its first year of life with the mother who gives, but who also sometimes holds back, affection and support. The resulting threat of loss of love and its accompanying anxiety was thought to motivate the child to *introject* the behavior and attributes of the mother, incorporating her behavior into its own personality. These ideas were subsequently reformulated in terms of learning theory. One such formulation was that of R. R. Sears, who argued that as a result of a warm, nurturing relationship, the child acquires a dependency need.[14] When the mother, in her attempts to train the child, withdraws affection, the result is frustration of the dependency need, moving the child to imitate or role play the mother's behaviors. The relation among nurturance, withdrawal of love, the development of dependency, and identification, or modeling, was also employed to explain the development of cognitive, or moral, controls. The child was supposed to be learning not only behavior but standards of conduct as well.

But this plausible formulation may not be correct. In later work, Sears and his colleagues found reason to doubt that the frustration of dependency needs was a crucial determinant of identification.[15] A study by others found that aggressive responses were imitated regardless of the degree of a model's nurturance.[16] Another study suggested that nurturing by the adult diminished the degree to which the child adopted high standards of achievement.[17] Apparently, children were afraid that adopting high standards might involve the risk of failure, embarrassing or shaming them.

The second theory of identification with a similar psychoanalytic origin emphasized anxiety reduction as the motivation underlying identification—the classical Oedipal complex. The male child is afraid of castration because of his incestuous desires for the mother. So he reduces his anxiety by identifying with his father, tries to be like his father, tries to *be* his father. A rich, venerable theory,

[14] Sears, 1957.
[15] Sears, Rau, and Alpert, 1965.
[16] Bandura and Huston, 1961.
[17] Bandura, Grusec, and Menlove, 1967.

but it has been difficult to demonstrate that identification with one's father results from resolving Oedipal feelings, and it is not at all clear why copying the behavior of a threatening competitor would reduce anxiety. The evidence for the theory is clinical and anecdotal,[18] and Bandura argues further that identification with an aggressor might well raise instead of lower anxiety.[19]

The difficulty is that one would like to find a way of reconciling Freudian theory and learning theory and coming up with some model that can be verified. One attempt to do this suggests that it is not the anxiety reduction of the classical psychoanalytic roles of mother and father and child, but rather that these figures translate themselves as instrumentalities of learning into a configuration of envy and vicarious gratification on the part of the child.[20] The supposition is that the child models his behavior after powerful adults because they are able to obtain envied rewards. Or, taking it another way, others have speculated that the child identifies with the controller of resources. Further along the spectrum, away from psychoanalysis and closer to reinforcement theory, there is the suggestion that the selection of a model may be in large part determined by the consequences of the model's behavior both for him or her and for the observer. There are possible models among those who are aggressive, or who have high power and status, or who are nurturing. But individuals are apt to choose what works. Thus, in the case of models who have status and power, individuals see that the behavior of such models is frequently rewarded and that reproducing such behavior is likely to have very favorable consequences. This would be especially true in situations in which the individual lacks confidence in his own choice of appropriate behaviors.

The diversity and complexity of human behavior is such that it is especially difficult to tell why and how individuals select models for learning modes of behavior. One might assume that persons of low self-esteem and self-confidence would be more susceptible to modeling influences. Frequently, this is the way it actually happens—children learn from adults, students from teachers, novices from experts. But it is frequently a more delicate and subtle arrangement. Ezra Stotland has conducted a series of studies suggesting that similarity between model and learner may be a factor in the choice.[21] Stotland believes that identification based on similarity occurs when persons conceive of themselves and another individual as having some trait in common and further perceive that the other individual has some additional trait. They then believe themselves to have the second trait—at least potentially—and behave in such a way as to realize it. These two traits may not be meaningfully related. There does not need to be any motive for the identification. The model need not be an object of affection or fear. The similarity between the model and the learner may be entirely in the mind of the learner. But if a child perceives himself to be a nifty quarterback, a

[18] Freud, 1946; Bettelheim, 1943.
[19] Bandura, 1969.
[20] Whiting, 1960.
[21] Stotland, 1961.

Playing the role of cowgirl.

new Joe Namath, he may adopt Namath's white football shoes. It may also work the other way, in which consumers are invited to try Noxema shave cream and establish an identification with Broadway Joe—that may extend to his reputed success with women.

Still, the research is not conclusive. There are studies that support Stotland's theory of model selection based upon similarities, and there are other investigations in which it seems that individuals imitate the behavior of dissimilar models.[22]

Discussions of model selection used to be more or less limited to parents—which fitted in with the psychoanalytic approach. Social psychologists neglected extrafamilial models. But in our society, children have a wide choice of possible models, and must often depend on people other than those in their immediate family. They have age-mates, older children, teachers, scout leaders, coaches, rock stars, motion picture and television personalities, characters from fiction.

[22] Jakubczak and Walters, 1959; Bandura and Kupers, 1964; Hicks, 1965; Epstein, 1966.

They can learn whatever they want, whatever is rewarded, whatever is useful, and they sometimes do so in strange, quirky ways. The research has raised some interesting questions; it has not yet provided all the answers about who and how and why.

Summary: Learning from Models

Children learn to act like human beings by observing other human beings, or their representations in fictional media. This kind of learning is termed *modeling, imitation,* or *observational learning.* Such learning has only recently begun to be studied in its own right; it is more complicated than most kinds of learning that take place in the laboratory. Modeling requires that the learner attend to the behavior of the model, remember what he has observed, have the capability of performing the behavior, and the motivation to enact it.

Factors that lead to choice of one model rather than another are not entirely clear. Affection for a potential model, especially when that affection is occasionally withdrawn, has been thought to create dependency on that person, and produce some imitation. But recent research questions this idea. Another suggestion was that when there are some threatening aspects of relating to a potential model, imitation may be a way of reducing the anxiety that is aroused. It is hard to see why this should happen. Still another possibility is that observation of a model receiving coveted rewards may lead the observer to copy the rewarded behavior. Several experiments support this idea. Finally, some experimental evidence suggests that being similar to another person in one or more respects, whether or not one is aware of it, may produce some imitation.

LEARNING SOCIAL ROLES

Learning via contingencies of reinforcement suggests a mechanical type of learning, learning bits and pieces of behavior in a chancy fashion. Learning through modeling suggests acquiring somewhat larger, more meaningful patterns of behavior. Another form of learning that is apt to consist of even larger, integrated, internally consistent patterns of behavior is *role learning.* A *social role* consists of the patterns of behavior that are expected of a group of persons who fall into a particular category, or position. The individual in the role category is a *role player,* or *actor.* Traditionally, a woman who is a mother is expected to nurture and care for her children, to guide them, to correct and direct their behavior. These expectations are held by her husband, her children, her neighbors, her own mother and father, the community at large, and even the state, which has the power to take a child away from parents who grossly abuse their role.

We have expectations about individuals who occupy highly visible occupational categories, such as public school teachers, ministers, pediatricians, psychiatrists, congressmen, taxi drivers, waiters, policemen, and airline stewardesses.

Reversal of traditional sex-role model.

We also have expectations concerning people in defined age-sex categories, such as "small boy," "small girl," "young man," "young woman," "old man," and "old woman." And the "small boy," discovering what is expected of him, learns to be a "small boy." He does not remain one forever, but must learn to give up lollipops and perhaps take up cigars by the time he becomes an "old man."

A part of socialization, then, consists of learning about role categories and expectations for the behaviors appropriate to them. These expectations are shared by both the actors within the categories and those in related ones, called *role partners.* Examples of related role categories include mother and child, teacher and student, doctor and patient. Actors come to feel that they have a *right* to expect certain behaviors of their partners, and that they have an *obligation* to behave toward their partners in particular ways.

Role learning includes learning to behave, feel, and see the world in a manner similar to other persons in the same category. Fellow actors in the same role category as oneself share a set of attitudes and behavior about themselves and about the world. The hospital intern, for instance, learning the role of the physician, comes to view nurses, patients, orderlies, and technicians as other doctors view them. Similarly, the fledgling thief learns from his more professional associates ways of viewing both the police and his victims (they are suckers, marks, and dupes). The role aspirant acquires attitudes and develops patterns of behavior that are shared by more experienced actors in the role. To return to hospital interns, they learn the attitudes of physicians toward disease, death, and the uncertainties of medical knowledge, and develop a toughness without which they might not be able to function.

There are penalties, or sanctions, for deviation from accepted role expectations. These may be direct and explicit, as when a child says, "I hate my sister!" and is scolded and punished for so doing. Or they may be subtle and indirect, in the form of a vague dissatisfaction with a role player without quite knowing why. Part of role learning is the incorporation and internalization of pride, approval, shame, disgust, and guilt, which are the punishment and reward instruments of role playing, and which contribute toward the shaping of behavior. To say that a certain kind of behavior is "unprofessional" is to condemn it.

Most roles require learning specific skills and techniques. The more sophisticated the role, the more complicated the techniques. These skills and techniques go beyond the requirements of the tasks inherent in the role and include matters of style and tone. All math teachers, for example, must learn the multiplication table and much more, but they must also learn how to be teachers, how to stand up in front of a class and get children to sit still, pay attention, and not throw erasers. Role playing may also include learning how to insulate oneself against the perversity and demands of those outside the role. Those who work at soda fountains learn to talk in code as a protection against the hungry herds at rush hour and the dehumanization of the frenzied activity. Sample codes are: "Draw three," for three cups of coffee; "eighty-six," for "we're out of it and have no more"; or "hold the fruit," for no onions on it.

Beyond the norms and the skills, there is finally an identity, an idea of oneself, so that the role learner comes to define himself as an actor of the role, acquiring the esteem and the self-esteem of the role category. Using our interns once more, they know how little they know. On the other hand, the nurses, patients, and other doctors call them "doctor," and they come to feel themselves as "doctors."

Role learning includes all the social learning principles discussed so far and also some to be explained later in this book. These principles combine to structure the behavior of group members in a manner appropriate to their role categories. A deeper understanding might be gained by setting up a greatly simplified example of the role-learning process and noting ways in which the conception is *not* adequate to describe what seems to happen.

One such example of the process is that of the old hand teaching the novice, the master teaching the apprentice, the teacher teaching the student. This model emphasizes *direct instruction,* but neglects other processes of social learning. A lot of

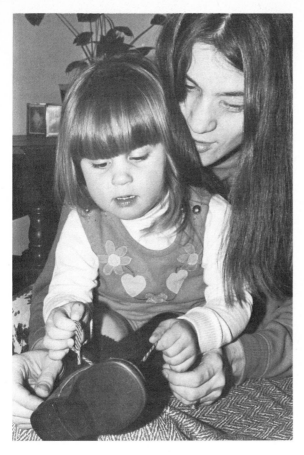

Direct tuition: learning to tie shoelaces.

the learning goes on through *practice,* often in the absence of a teacher. Also, learning occurs as a result of encountering and solving real problems which are inherent in the role. Our interns, for example, may learn through rueful experience with patients that they must make their instructions absolutely clear and must emphasize their importance, if patients are to follow them.

The teacher-student relation seems to distort the process by making the teacher active and the learner relatively passive. In fact, however, the learner is active, *choosing* ways of playing a particular role from a permissible range of expectations, or from a variety of models in the role. Furthermore, there is considerable *negotiation*—as between children and their parents—as to which role is actually appropriate. Remember the way in which children continually renegotiate bedtimes, stretching them later and later. The teacher-student relationship also seems to leave out one's fellow actors, who often contribute much to role learning. One learns from one's classmates as much as one learns from one's teacher—different things, maybe, but just as real. Fellow actors serve as sources of reward, as instructors, and as models.

Finally, the teacher-student idea implies a more orderly series of lessons than experience actually offers. The world is a teaching machine, but weird and repetitive and tricky. It starts teaching before you have even registered. Those interns had been learning about the role of the physician from the time they were first taken to their pediatricians, as infants. Who knows what they remember? The needle, probably, because sometimes injections hurt. But mommy was very respectful to the pediatrician. And he or she wore a nice white coat. And often made one feel better. Much of this may register, and be filed away.

Another way to understand role learning is to consider some of the factors that help or hinder it. Some of these factors have to do with the features of the role itself; others are a part of the broad social setting in which it is to be played; and, by way of logical completeness, still others have to do with the individual who is learning it.

Probably the role itself carries with it a degree of ease or difficulty which depends on the *clarity* of its demands. Some roles are clear and definite, and therefore, easier to learn. Others are more complicated in what they require. Some of this clarity or complexity arises from the degree of *consensus* with which society views the role. It used to be much simpler—even if less desirable or less fair—to know what was expected of a woman in our society. Females now have greater aspirations and greater opportunities than they once did, but there is less consensus about the female role, and each girl must create her own identity and choose her models as she grows into a womanhood that is evolving. The prospect is for a richer and a better life, but creating it is a problem that her grandmother did not have to face. Her grandmother's roles were clearer, and there was a great deal of consensus about what was expected of her, what she should expect of herself. Similarly, there can be a confusion of roles that arises from a lack of consensus among the role partners. A mother who treats her daughter sometimes as a grown woman and sometimes as a child is not being clear in her demands. A son who is treated by his father as an adult and by his mother as a baby is getting contradictory messages and will find it difficult to act in a role which is badly defined because of lack of agreement among role partners. This is a distant view of what can be a painful situation, but the abstract statement is as clear as the role is not and is therefore easier to learn from and to understand.

The business of passing from childhood to adulthood is further complicated by the changes in role, some of which are in themselves confusing—even without the contradictions of inconsistent parents or of a society in the process of evolution and change. Military cadets passing from one class to the next, or students turning into graduate teaching-fellows, face difficulties that come up because of inconsistencies and discontinuities between the expectations of the successive positions they must assume. Nurses, for instance, begin as students with a view of their profession as a humanitarian, nurturing activity—a matter of helping patients. And of course it is. But after a year or two of training, the young student nurses will see their roles in terms of specific skills in much the same way that professional nurses do. As with our interns, the change in emphasis is necessary to provide a degree of emotional protection and to keep the continual confrontation with sickness and death from being too depressing and becoming disabling to the curers—but the emotional distance and the attitudes of professionalism must be learned, and at least some of the naive compassion must be *unlearned.* Although there isn't any direct evidence, it is reasonable to assume that the greater the difference between the lay conception of the role and the role expectations of those already in the role, the more difficulty there will be for aspirants in learning the role.

The structure of society does not necessarily make role passage more difficult. For many roles, it smooths the way. For example, children's play anticipates the elements of roles that they will later enact. They play house, taking the role of parents as well as children. A child may learn something of the nursing role by playing nurse. In the Boy Scouts or Girl Scouts, first-aid techniques may be learned that are appropriate to paramedical roles. In many instances, being a role partner to an actor facilitates learning that individual's role. For example, all of us know something about the bedside manner of the physician from having been patients.

A lot depends on the role itself, what it demands and what it proposes to include. Some roles are fairly limited, others more pervasive and general. Nuns' and priests' roles pervade their entire lives, require a long period of training and socialization, and are more demanding than those of, say, carpenters, whose roles are segregated from other aspects of their lives and can be learned in a much shorter period. Not that we are belittling carpenters. Most occupational roles are quite narrowly limited.

Some roles are in themselves rewarding, and therefore are positively reinforcing. Age roles, for example, can be positively reinforcing—or, in some instances, negatively. The child may be highly motivated to adapt to the role of an adult, there being more freedom in the adult's role. On the other hand, with a society that places so much emphasis on youth, there is a negative reinforcement in the transition from mature man or woman to old man or woman. And we see some middle-aged people fighting against it and losing gracelessly.

Much role learning is institutionalized, and the individual may even be deliberately manipulated to intensify learning. Military training is role teaching, and the learner is deliberately maneuvered into a position in which there are relatively few choices. In the 1940s, Coast Guard cadets were *desocialized,* and for the first two months the new "swab" was not allowed to leave the base nor to have any contact with noncadets. All clues to previous social position were suppressed so that interaction in terms of those earlier role categories could be discouraged. Discussion of wealth or family background was taboo. Money from home was forbidden. The role of the cadet was supposed to supersede other roles the individual had learned to play.[23]

Most socializing situations do not work through isolation and desocialization, but through *intensification*. Medical interns are not cut off in the way the Coast Guard "swabs" were, but the demands of their work are such that they have no time for anything else. They hardly have time to sleep. And such monopolization strengthens the new role behavior and helps to weaken the old. Relatively exclusive interaction within the new group fosters the growth of each member's dependency on it for satisfaction of needs, and this in turn increases the group's cohesiveness and its influence on each of the members.

Rituals and ceremonies are another instrumentality for role learning and socialization. Graduations, initiations, bar-mitzvahs, confirmations, weddings, all emphasize the attractiveness of the new role and the lower status of the old. The *rite of passage* is significant both for the individual whose status is changing, and for those others who may be in the audience. In most cases, the members of the privileged group beam with pleasure, and the nonmembers feel *status envy*. The worth of the new status may be increased by the discomforts experienced by the learner during hazing, exams, the hunt in the plains for the lion skin, or whatever.

It can be fairly said that the more rigorous the ordeal in these rites of passage, the greater the emphasis on the contrast between the old role and the new, and the higher the value the group assigns to the new role. In undergoing the ordeal, the neophyte signals agreement with this high valuation, and is inclined to maintain that valuation if only because so much has already been invested in the effort to assume the new role. These ordeals can be primitive or sophisticated. Running for public office involves a campaign that one might construe as an ordeal. Aside from the risk of losing, there is all that travel, all those hands to shake, all those speeches to make. . . .

In role learning, there is often an intermediate figure between master and apprentice, teacher and student. There is the slightly older peer, the more advanced learner, who can be an important resource to the neophyte. These near-peers mediate between the two positions, can be a source of friendship and emotional support, can offer encouragement, and can be, in their own way, effective models. Eldest children, for example, learn from their parents, but younger children learn from their parents and also from older siblings.

Summary: Learning Social Roles

Learning a social role is learning the expectations and behavior patterns that are associated with categories of persons occupying a particular position or place in a

---

[23] Dornbusch, 1955.

social relation. A family, for example, has the basic positions of *mother, father, son, daughter,* and so forth. Both the members of the family and the people outside it expect certain behaviors of people in each of these family positions. Growing children learn not only what is expected of them, but also of the other members of the family. Expectations for their behavior change as they pass through the various life stages, such as infant, small girl, adolescent girl, young woman, mature woman, and old woman. Each of these stages is considered a different life role, which has to be learned. Learning takes place not only through observation of models, but also through practice and through playing opposite another role— a patient may learn something about the occupational role of doctor through being a patient. Roles are learned more readily when their expectations are clearly defined and there is agreement about them among different people.

In this chapter we have discussed social learning in terms of contingencies of reinforcement, learning from models by imitation, and learning the larger patterns that we call social roles. In the next chapter we will take up another important process in the shaping and controlling of behavior—the individual's own thoughts and feelings—his conscience or moral sense.

THREE

COGNITIVE AND MORAL CONTROLS

When Pinocchio was tempted, puzzled, confused, or uncertain, he was instructed to give a little whistle, at which point an elegant cricket named Jiminy would appear, and J. C. would function as Pinocchio's conscience. This represents a considerable advance from the use of the nose as a contingent reinforcer. You remember about the nose. When Pinocchio told a lie, his nose would grow. A huge, monstrous lie, and the nose would really pop out there, sprout into branches, replete with a nest of singing birds. That was negative reinforcement, intended to shape up truthfulness. In fact, the whole progress of the story was from the simplicities of reinforcement contingencies to the development of *internal* or *cognitive* controls. By *cognitive*, we mean thoughts or ideas or knowledge.

It is sometimes difficult to sort out what kinds of behavior may be learned through simple reinforcement or through cognitive controls, or through a combination of both. Clearly, at least some acts, or the inhibition of some acts, are learned through reinforcement contingencies alone. Aronfreed's dog does not go on the rug, remember, and Aronfreed is probably right in suggesting that there is no discernible cognitive or moral control at work. In much the same way, children learn to inhibit various behaviors even before they have a rudimentary sense of language. And even after the child—or the adult—has a full command of language, some behavior is still learned through reinforcement contingencies. Children punished for their choices of attractive toys during experiments in which no explanations or further reasons were given later showed suppression of the punished behavior—even when they were apparently free of any surveillance or risk of punishment.

The contribution of a "moral prohibition" to control of behavior was demonstrated in a laboratory situation with children in the first and second grades.[1] There was a training session and a test session. During the training session, the children were subjected to a variety of treatments intended to inhibit them from touching or picking up certain toys. Two intensities of punishment— weak and strong—were used. The punishments were timed at two different intervals following the forbidden act—early and late. And two rationales—a weak one and a strong one—were used to prohibit the act. The weak prohibition given to one of the groups was that if a child picked up or touched certain toys that shouldn't be played with, a buzzer would sound. The other children, receiving the strong prohibition, were told:

> . . . some of these toys you should not touch or play with because I don't have any others like them. And if they were to get broken or worn out from boys playing with them, I wouldn't be able to use them any more. So for that reason I don't want you to touch or play with some of these toys. And if you pick one of the toys you're not supposed to touch or play with, I'll tell you and you'll hear a buzzer.[2]

In addition, if a child picked up one of the forbidden, attractive toys, after the buzzer went off the experimenter said, "No, that one might get broken."

After the training session, the children were left alone with the toys they had been punished for choosing. Figure 3-1 graphs the results. Those who had been given a rationale for not playing with some of the toys showed less disobedience than did the others. The relation between the rationale and the timing of the punishment also reveals an interesting fact. Without a rationale, delayed punishment was not as effective as early punishment. But with the rationale, delayed punishment was also effective. This suggests that the rationale helps to bridge the delay between the commission of the deed and the punishment, making the punishment more effective than it otherwise would be.

Another study turned the screws even tighter, and used a rationale that focused on the child's intention rather than the deed, with the phrase, "No, you should not have *wanted* to pick up that thing."[3] This was also successful in producing inhibition, and in supporting the idea that linguistic prohibitions can

[1] Parke, 1970.
[2] Reprinted with permission from R. D. Parke. The role of punishment in the socialization process. In R. A. Hoppe, G. A. Milton, & E. C. Simmel (Eds.), *Early experiences and the processes of socialization*. New York: Academic Press, Inc., 1970. P. 92.
[3] Aronfreed, 1965.

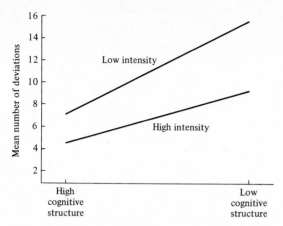

Figure 3-1   Effects on deviation produced by cognitive structure and intensity of punishment. The minimum number of deviations (touching forbidden toys) is produced by high intensity of punishment and a strong cognitive structure. Reprinted by permission from R. D. Parke. The role of punishment in the socialization process. In R. A. Hoppe, G. A. Milton, & E. C. Simmel (Eds.), *Early experiences and the processes of socialization.* New York: Academic Press, Inc. 1970. P. 95.

operate to inhibit behavior. In this chapter, we try to identify the factors that are important requisites if children are to develop internal controls to guide their behavior, and are to be amenable to reason, somebody else's or even their own.

EFFECTS OF DEPRIVATION AND ISOLATION

Attachment to and affection for one or more socializing agents in childhood is crucial to normal development. These attachments create incentives for the child to behave in a way that will get approval and affection. Once such an attachment is formed, and language develops, the socializing agent can use disapproval and withdrawal of affection to create feelings of right and wrong, of guilt and shame. Conversely, unless there is some connection with another person—some acceptance by other persons that is vitally important—children will have little motivation for modifying their behavior. And the first requirement for the development of this kind of dependency on another person is, obviously, that the other person must be there. And most of the time, he or she is.

What happens, though, when there is no mother, not even a surrogate, when a child is raised, say, in an institution without the warmth and the relationship that most children have with a mother? Apparently this constitutes a great handicap to growing up normally. In two different cases of extreme isola-

Attachment to a parent is basic to socialization.

tion, mothers kept their infant daughters in solitude, in a secluded room, over a period of years, giving them only enough attention to keep them alive.[4] When discovered around the age of six, both children were extremely retarded, infantile. Neither could talk. One couldn't walk. They both showed fear of strangers and an inability to form a relation to other persons. Ultimately, one was placed in an institution for retarded children where she died at an early age. The other girl achieved a normal level of development, which indicates the importance of early experience, but also the flexibility of human beings.

Take a less extreme situation—that of children in institutions in which individual attention from adults was extremely limited. Studies of such children[5] find less extreme but significant physical and social retardation. Moreover, older children who have spent their early years in an institution exhibit more problem behavior, more demands for attention, and more aggression. They are retarded

[4] Davis, 1947.
[5] Spitz, 1945, 1946; Spitz and Wolfe, 1946; Dennis and Najarian, 1957.

in speech development, mental development, and educational performance. Children of similar background who spent their early years in a foster home instead of an institution did not show these forms of retardation.[6]

Back in the laboratory, the same kinds of suggestions come from work with animals. Raise an animal in isolation, deprive it of a mother, of a peer group, of all sensory experiences, and you get an abnormal animal. That's clear enough, but which conditions are responsible for the negative effects? Several have been proposed:

1 The absence of a mother or mother substitute distorts or prevents later relations to others.
2 Restricted sensory stimulation interferes with the formation of perceptual categories, symbols, and concepts.
3 A restricted environment prevents the organism from learning how to profit from experience.
4 During the critical period of infancy, restricted stimulation and experience will not allow for normal development.

These suggestions are not mutually exclusive. In fact they may all be operative. The traditional view has been that it is the strong attachment of the child to the mother that is crucial in producing adequate socialization. This strong attachment has been suggested as the source of the child's dependency upon the mother's approval and affection. Effects of isolation or deprivation have been assumed to come from the lack of such dependency. This view is changing to emphasize other conditions as well. The recent position is that we ought to separate stimulus deprivation from maternal deprivation. This is tricky because they often coincide, but when they are successfully separated, the results are different.

Another kind of distinction that some investigators have been making has to do with when the isolation and deprivation occurred and how long it lasted.[7] How old was the child? How long was he isolated and deprived? How do you separate the long-term effects from the immediately obvious ones? Maternal deprivation before six months of age seems to result in few observable effects at the time but apparently interferes with the development of the ability to form close relationships with others in later life. Separation from the mother in middle infancy may result in heightened dependency—anxiety, fear, and withdrawal. Later on, the child will seem to be more concerned with attachment to others.

Children institutionalized during early infancy, where they suffer reduced stimulation, appear to suffer fewer immediate effects than those institutionalized after six months when strong dependency on the mother has been established. The first instance is deprivation alone, and the other is loss and deprivation. On the other hand, when the children who were institutionalized come back out,

[6] Goldfarb, 1943a, 1943b.
[7] Bronfenbrenner, 1968.

those who had been deprived in middle or late infancy, the traumatized losers, seem to recover rapidly, while those institutionalized very early show effects that persist for some time. How long? It depends on the behavior in question. Early writers viewed the effects of early deprivation as relatively long lasting or even as permanent, but later studies suggest this may not be the case—particularly for intellectual or language abilities or for serious psychopathology. Whether there are milder effects that persist without utterly crippling is still an open question.

As a matter of fact, there is some question as to whether dependency is a clearly identifiable, unified behavior pattern.[8] Dependent behavior at one point in a child's life is different from behavior at another stage. Various behaviors which are called dependency are not always found together in the same child. Attention seeking, for instance, and a desire to be physically near the mother are both dependent actions, but one often occurs without the other.

Summary: Effects of Deprivation and Isolation

Attachment to and affection for one or more socializing agents in childhood is crucial to normal development. These attachments create incentives for the child to behave in a way that will win approval and affection. While the mother is usually the most important agent, relations with peers are also essential to normal development. Children under extreme isolation for a long period suffer considerable damage both emotionally and in learning ordinary human skills, damage that may not be reparable. Institutionalized children suffer less severe, but appreciable, loss.

DEVELOPMENT OF AFFECTIONAL SYSTEMS

Is the mother the key to socialization? It's a good question. There are lots of good questions about how and why patterns of love and dependency develop, and about what happens if they don't. Inasmuch as any answer is likely to have certain political implications, or at least to offer some suggestions about how our societies ought to be ordered, the answers to these questions are likely to be subjects of disputes.

Take, for instance, the idea that the attachment to the mother is the key to socialization of the child. If that suggestion is true, then there are all sorts of conclusions we might draw about child care centers, women's careers, and the way we live or ought to live. But the picture is much less clear than we might like. The laboratory work of the Harlows on affectional systems in monkeys suggests that there is a series of related attachments which we must understand in order to talk about the nature of socialization.

[8] Maccoby and Masters, 1970.

Mother-child affectional system.

The Harlows have distinguished five relatively distinct affectional systems in primates.[9] These are:

1   The mother-infant affectional system
2   The reciprocal infant-mother system
3   The age-mate (or peer) system
4   The heterosexual affectional system
5   The paternal affectional system

The behaviors acquired in the development of *each* system are a part of normal social growth, and development in one system facilitates development in other systems. The security provided in the infant-mother system provides a confidence which the infant must have in order to explore the surrounding animate and inanimate environment, and this exploration is vital for the growth of the peer affectional system. A monkey deprived of contact with its mother and reared with a cloth dummy instead will grow up to be incapable of having sexual relations with other monkeys (the heterosexual system). Even attempts to train the males of this group by using especially experienced females failed to enable them to function normally. It is not clear whether affectional systems must be learned in a certain order but it does seem that all five are necessary for normal behavior and development.

The way the Harlows went about their study of the affectional system in monkeys was to deprive the young monkeys of normal interaction with their mothers in one of three ways: (1) raising them in total isolation, (2) bringing

[9] Harlow and Harlow, 1965, 1966.

Peer affectional system.

them up with dummy surrogate mothers covered with terry cloth and equipped with bottles and nipples, or (3) letting them grow up with age-mates only. When the monkeys reared in any of these ways were later placed together with normally reared age-mates, they were found to be retarded in the way they related to them. Eventually, they did work out adequate social adjustments, but it took time, and the Harlows inferred that normal mothering is important to the normal development of peer relations.

In another study, monkeys given normal mothering but deprived of interaction with age-mates suffered severely retarded development. The several affectional systems are all important and influence each other. The Harlows write:

> In designing our original studies, we tended to contrast the relative importance of mother-infant relationships as opposed to infant-infant affectional relationships in the socialization process. We are now convinced that this is the wrong way to look at these social forces. Both normal mothering and normal infant-infant affectional development are extremely important variables in the socialization of rhesus monkeys and presumably of the higher primates. These variables are interactive, and either variable may not of necessity socially destroy an infant monkey if it is subsequently allowed to lead a normal or more or less normal life, but there can be no doubt that

the easier and safer way to become a normal monkey is to learn to love and live with both mothers and age mates.[10]

It seems reasonable to assume that children, too, need a mother or mother-surrogate, and they also need to play with other children, if they are to experience normal development. The implications of this finding are that, through future research, we need to find out precisely what it is that children get out of being with a mother and what they get out of playing with other children that is so vital to their development. Probably the sense of security and emotional support that a mother provides is crucial. Exactly what play with peers provides is not so clear at this point.

Summary: Development of Affectional Systems

Studies in which rhesus monkeys were raised under different conditions of deprivation suggest that as many as five different relational systems are important for normal development: (1) mother-infant system, (2) infant-mother system, (3) peer system, (4) heterosexual system, and (5) paternal system. Each of the systems is associated with certain kinds of behaviors and with the development of a particular kind of attachment. Interference with any of the systems appears to result in striking disabilities in the adult monkey, who appears far from normal. It seems likely that socialization of human beings is equally, if not more, complex.

DEVELOPMENT OF MORAL CONTROLS

You see them all the time on television programs and in the movies—the people who appear to be normal, who behave in ways that are entirely acceptable most of the time, but who have no moral sense whatever, and, when it seems useful or convenient, do not hesitate to kill. And it is tough to catch these people because, without any sense of guilt, they do not panic, do not break under questioning, do not show any irregular responses on the lie detector's graph paper.

These conscience-free characters are not merely fictional, but have their counterpart in real life, although there are relatively few of them. They represent the extreme case of the failure of moral control, and perhaps the clearest and most dramatic example of how very important moral values and their proper development are to society and its members. Without these moral controls, society would be either unworkable or a living nightmare—a dog-eat-dog environment in the worst possible sense. Perhaps such characters are as close to the

---

[10] Reprinted by permission from H. F. Harlow and M. K. Harlow. The affectional systems. In A. M. Schrier, H. F. Harlow, and T. Stollnitz (eds.), *Behavior of nonhuman primates.* Vol. 2. New York: Academic Press, Inc., 1965. P. 272.

vision of evil as we can get. So the development of moral controls that keep most people from falling into that inhuman state is of supreme importance.

We have already noted that attachment to or love for a socializing agent is of critical importance to the development of moral controls, and constitutes a first step. The work with monkeys by the Harlows suggests that other affectional systems may also be relevant, but a socializing agent with some authority appears to be crucial. This is brought out in two theories of moral development, proposed by Jean Piaget and by Lawrence Kohlberg.

Moral Stage Theories

Both these men see the child as moving through a series of stages as a result of the unfolding of cognitive capacities, a process which is partly due to maturation or biological growth, and partly due to the kinds of experiences with the environment that normally accompany growing up. We will discuss Piaget's views first.

Piaget thought of this process as a series of steps from a state of moral absolutism to a morality based upon mutual agreement.[11] The authority of the parents sets the first stage. Behaviors are totally right or wrong, and rules are sacred and unalterable. Acts are right or wrong depending on the seriousness of their consequences, whether they conform to the rules, and whether or not they are punished. The child believes in *immanent justice:* violations are followed by accidents or misfortunes willed by not just the parent, but by nature itself—by God! Spill your milk, and you're going to stub your toe.

In the more advanced state, rules are established through social agreement between the participating parties and may be modified for good reason. Diverse views of right and wrong are acknowledged, and a major consideration is whether or not the deed was performed intentionally. Punishment is not ordained by some impersonal entity or diety. It can be negotiated, and it will be adjusted to meet the magnitude of the misdeed. It may also be relevant punishment involving restitution or retaliation.

The transition from the first to the second stage is made possible by the growth of cognitive capacities that move children away from (1) a state of egocentrism in which they naively assume that others view events the same way they do, and (2) a state, called *realism* by Piaget, where children confuse objective and subjective reality (for instance, think their dreams are actually occurring). What such a shift requires is the development of the idea that one is a distinct person with individual views and feelings that may be different from those of other people. Piaget emphasizes the way in which interaction with peers helps this development, this understanding of the identity and limits of the self, and the beginnings of the identity of others.

Commenting on Piaget's scheme, Martin Hoffman suggests that as children grow older they attain more and more equality with parents and with older

[11] Piaget, 1932.

children, and as this happens the authority of elders is reduced[12] and their respect for themselves and for their peers grows. They are better able to interact with other people and to arrive at cooperative agreements about rules. Instead of coming from absolute authority, rules come to be understood as the outcome of negotiation.

The second, more complicated process that Hoffman points out involves interacting with other people in terms of roles so that growing children have opportunities to assume the roles of other people. This role taking enables them to see similarities and differences between themselves and others, to understand how they feel, and how the world appears to them. What this wider view does is to change morality from a judgment based entirely on overt behavior and its outcome to an evaluation that considers intention and responsibility as basic.

Kohlberg has advanced a more elaborate conception of moral development that has three levels.[13] Each level has two stages. His ideas were developed by presenting ten hypothetical moral dilemmas to a wide variety of people in our society and in other societies, and asking them to tell in their own words how the dilemma should be resolved, and why. He then developed a systematic way of coding the kinds of answers people gave. This enabled him to identify the dominant themes in moral judgments, and to arrange them according to stage of development. Consider, for example, the following dilemma:

> In Europe, a woman was near death from cancer. One drug might save her, a form of radium that a druggist in the same town had recently discovered. The druggist was charging $2,000, ten times what the drug cost him to make. The sick woman's husband, Heinz, went to everyone he knew to borrow the money, but he could only get together about half of what it cost. He told the druggist that his wife was dying and asked him to sell it cheaper or let him pay later. But the druggist said, "No." The husband got desperate and broke into the man's store to steal the drug for his wife. Should the husband have done that? Why?[14]

Answers to questions raised by this moral dilemma will contain certain themes identified by the coding system. This particular dilemma has two especially prominent themes: the *motives* of the husband and the *consequences* of his actions, as well as several others to be mentioned shortly. The way in which these themes are handled determines the moral level and stage of the judgments for that answerer. This is illustrated below.

Kohlberg's three moral levels are the following:

Level I. Moral value resides in external, quasi-physical happenings, in bad acts, or in quasi-physical needs rather than in persons and standards.

[12] Hoffman, 1970.
[13] Kohlberg, 1969.
[14] Reprinted with permission from L. Kohlberg. Stage and sequence: The cognitive-developmental approach to socialization. In D. A. Goslin (ed.), *Handbook of socialization theory and research*. Chicago: Rand McNally & Company, 1969. P. 379.

In stage 1 at this level, badness is judged by focusing upon the irrelevant physical form of the act (such as the amount of physical damage). For example (quotations are from Kohlberg[15]):

"He shouldn't steal the drug, it's a big crime. He didn't get permission, used force and broke and entered. He did a lot of damage, stealing a very expensive drug and breaking up the store, too."

In stage 2, the physical consequences are ignored in favor of a human need. For example:

"It's all right to steal the drug because she needs it and he wants her to live. It isn't that he wants to steal, but it's the way he has to use to get the drug to save her."

Level II. Moral value resides in performing good or right roles, in maintaining the conventional order and the expectancies of others.

In stage 3 at this level, the action is evaluated according to the type of motive or type of person likely to perform the act. For example:

"He should steal the drug. He was only doing something that was natural for a good husband to do. You can't blame him for doing something out of love for his wife, you'd blame him if he didn't love his wife enough to save her."

In stage 4, an act is always or categorically right or wrong, regardless of motives or circumstances. For example:

"It's a natural thing for Heinz to want to save his wife but it's still always wrong to steal. He still knows he's stealing and taking a valuable drug from the man who made it."

Level III. Moral value resides in conformity to shared or shareable standards, rights, or duties.

In stage 5 at this level, the legal or principled necessity not to make exceptions to rules is held to, but the mitigation of blame because of motive is recognized. For example:

"You can't completely blame someone for stealing but extreme circumstances don't really justify taking the law in your own hands. . . . The end may be good, but the ends don't justify the means."

In stage 6, the rightness of an act follows from general self-chosen moral principles and not from motives. For example:

"This is a situation which forces him to choose between stealing and letting his wife die. In a situation where the choice must be made, it is morally right to steal. He has to act in terms of the principle of preserving and respecting life."

The themes of motive and consequence are not the only ones. In the examples given, rights of possession and property, and concern for welfare of other persons are important. Kohlberg identifies twenty-five different themes that he

[15] Kohlberg, 1969.

uses in coding moral judgments. Other important themes involve punishment, responsibility, conscience, justice, and so on. Each of these themes may be involved in moral dilemmas.

Kohlberg thinks of the six stages as progressing to higher and higher levels of moral development, with stage 6 representing the highest. But this is not clearly the case. Even in his stage 2 example, the answer displays altruism in recognizing that the husband wants to save his wife—he isn't stealing for himself. This same principle appears in stage 6, only the language is more elegant. His stage 5 example is also controversial. Does a stubborn adherence to the letter of the law really represent so high a *moral* value?

William Alston, a philosopher, has also questioned whether these stages show progression from a low to a high order of morality.[16] Some philosopher theologians, he argues, offer moral arguments at the level of stage 4. Is their morality not of the highest order? Alston notes that Kohlberg's studies are more at the level that children and adults habitually *use* in moral reasoning, and that the level at which they are *capable* of reasoning is not assessed. Another rather serious shortcoming pointed out by Alston seems to be the emphasis on cognition at the expense of affect (feeling). Many serious thinkers have felt that morality is based more on feeling than on knowledge and reasoning. A moral act is one that feels right and good; an immoral act is one that arouses guilt or shame. Another critical review of Kohlberg's work has found both serious fault with his coding system for assigning stages to moral reasoning, as well as a variety of other technical faults.[17]

Yet the works of Piaget and Kohlberg are pioneer attempts to study an aspect of experience that has been neglected by psychologists. The two theories are useful in describing features of the growth of moral controls. Even though they may be wrong in some respects, the broader outlines of their view of moral development seem consistent with much of what we know about morality and behavior. They do not say very much, however, about the conditions under which the stages develop, or about special circumstances that arrest development at some particular stage. We turn to this question in the remainder of the chapter.

The theories of Piaget and Kohlberg suggest a number of tentative generalizations that might be made concerning the development of moral controls. Moral controls appear to evolve along with more general cognitive development, possibly in a stagelike sequence. The earliest stages involve dependence on authority as well as on the physical effects of the world on an individual. Later there is some understanding of the relativity of moral values—an appreciation of the fact that they can be seen from the point of view of the other person. This apparently comes about through assuming the roles of other people through play and other means. At the same time, this perspective allows some recognition of

[16] Alston, 1971.
[17] Kurtines and Greif, 1974.

the role of motives—of intention and responsibility in contributing to the moral value of an act. At a higher level, moral value resides in shared standards, agreed-upon norms. The highest level involves choosing to agree or disagree with such standards, rather than to conform for conformity's sake alone. This characterization is highly tentative; much more research is needed.

Social Learning Mechanisms and Moral Controls

In the previous chapter, social learning mechanisms were offered as partial explanations of the process by which the untutored infant turns into a decent, responsible adult. While such mechanisms may play an important part in the socialization process, they do not seem sufficient to account for the development of moral controls. Contingencies of reinforcement may be largely responsible for toilet training and a variety of other childhood inhibitions, but such contingencies need not involve thought and reason; hence, they could not account for such feelings as guilt and shame.

In the past, a popular explanation of the development of conscience was in terms of imitation and modeling. A crucial factor in this line of thinking was the strength of dependency and its role in inducing the child to identify with his parents. Identification was offered as one of the possible intervening ways in which the child who felt anxiety about the loss of love was motivated to reproduce the parents' behavior and to adopt their standard of conduct. But experimental evidence has failed to find associations between the extent of identification with parents and such supposed consequences as resistance to temptation, feelings of guilt, and behavior patterns modeled after the parent identified with.[18] If the theory were correct, it would require that children who strongly identify with their parents have stronger consciences than those who identify less strongly—and this does not seem to be true.

Learning from models does not seem to play a major role in the development of moral controls. Various studies looked for effects of observing a model's behavior on resistance to temptation,[19] on the inhibition of aggression,[20] on self-improved performance standards resulting in self-denial,[21] and on deferment of gratification.[22] Little was found. In fact, there was a contrary effect. Role models seemed more effective at breaking down controls than in building them up. Role models can open up possibilities, can break down, weaken, or entirely remove controls that had been there before.[23] Children who were allowed to observe another child playing with prohibited toys without being punished more often played with the prohibited toys themselves.

[18] Bandura and Walters, 1963; Sears, Rau, and Alpert, 1965.
[19] Walters, Leat, and Mezei, 1963; Walters and Parke, 1964; Stein, 1967.
[20] Bandura, Ross, and Ross, 1963b; Bandura, 1965.
[21] Bandura and Kupers, 1964; Bandura and Whalen, 1966; Mischel and Liebert, 1966; Bandura, Grusec, and Menlove, 1967.
[22] Mischel, 1965; Bandura and Mischel, 1965.
[23] Hoffman, 1967.

Quite possibly this experimental work may be inconclusive—it's tough in a laboratory to get sufficiently strong motives for identification. Strangers used as models in experiments surely have less influence than parents. And although some naturalistic studies also cast doubt on explanations of internal controls in terms of identification, it might be that the idea has validity in some cases and under certain conditions. The definitive studies remain to be done.

Childrearing Practices and Moral Development

Another approach to understanding moral development examines childrearing practices and their effect. Three kinds of discipline in childrearing have been identified:[24] *power assertion* techniques (the parent punishes the child either physically or through deprivation); *withdrawal of love* (the parent shows disapproval of the child); and *induction* (the parent gives explanations and reasons for wanting the child to change behavior, particularly in terms of the consequences of the behavior for the child, the parent, or for other persons).

And what kind of discipline works? Martin Hoffman reviewed the evidence to find out which form had the greatest effects on internalization, on resistance to temptation, guilt feelings, independence from external sanctions, and the acceptance of responsibility for one's own conduct.[25] But the evidence was not entirely consistent. Several findings were obtained for mothers only. Power assertion by the mother was found to be *negatively* related to moral development. Withdrawal of love and affection related positively but infrequently to moral development. Induction and the expression of affection were positively related to internalization, but not always, and the correlation was not strong enough to produce firm conclusions. Few relationships appeared between moral development and the father's style of discipline, except that in homes where the father was absent, boys showed a lower level of moral development.

Hoffman has analyzed these disciplinary techniques further and offers several opinions. He suggests that induction is superior to love withdrawal and power assertion because it most often generates the right amount of emotional feeling in children, making them desire approval from a parent. Power assertion arouses anger and resentment, emotions too strong to allow for caring about approval. Love withdrawal usually also arouses too much emotion.

Hoffman reasons that in any disciplinary encounter all three techniques are present in some mix, and that in different disciplinary encounters the mix varies. Power assertion, love withdrawal, and induction are all being exercised, but in varying strengths. Where power assertion predominates, a lot of anger is generated in children. They feel frustrated not only about the forbidden action, but also in their need for independence. Not only will they feel anger and frustration, but they will see in the parent a model for the direct discharge of anger, and an object for their own anger. It also follows that power assertion focuses children's

[24] Hoffman and Saltzstein, 1967.
[25] Hoffman, 1967.

Withdrawal of love: scolding and banishing to room.

Induction as a socializing technique: giving reasons for behaviors and their consequences.

attention on the consequences of their behavior for themselves, rather than the consequences for other people. Avoiding the punishment is primary.

Similarly, withdrawal is apt to arouse too much emotion, and the higher the level of affection to which the child has been accustomed, the more bereft the child will feel at the withdrawal. The better the relationship has been, the more powerful the emotions that can be aroused by withdrawal of love.

Induction is less likely to arouse anger, fear, or feelings of loss. It also has the advantage of identifying specifically what is wrong with children's behavior and showing how it might be corrected. When induction involves pointing out the consequences of children's behavior for others, it may improve their ability to empathize—to imagine the lives of those others, to experience vicariously their discomfort and to connect that discomfort to their own behavior that was responsible for it. Thus, theoretically at least, it should relate to conscience formation.

The infrequent and inconsistent correlation between love withdrawal and moral development seems to contradict much of the earlier thinking about moral development, particularly the idea that it results from dependency and identification. Another study suggests that while withdrawal of love may not be related to the strength of internal controls, it may account in part for variations in the manner in which these controls operate.[26]

Two groups of seventh-grade children were separated on the basis of story-completion tests designed to tap two qualities of moral judgment. These two types were *humanistic-flexible* and *conventional-rigid.* The humanistic-flexible children were more aware of the consequences of an action for other persons, and

[26] Hoffman and Saltzstein, 1967.

were more likely to take extenuating circumstances into account in judging the morality of the act. Such children were relatively tolerant and accepting of their own impulses. Their story completions suggested that they were high on guilt and other indexes of internalization, but could still contemplate, in fantasy, acts which violated their moral standards. Clearly, their impulses were not under rigid control.

The conventional-rigid children, on the other hand, were more likely to give a legal or religious basis for moral judgments, and to ignore extenuating circumstances. This is consistent with the Freudian notion that guilt depends less on the consequences—the harm actually done—than on the awareness of unacceptable impulses. These children avoided expressing such impulses, even in fantasy. In that way they avoided moral conflict. Another word describing the mechanism they used is, of course, *repression.*

What is especially significant about this study is that parents of these two types of children were found to use different combinations of disciplinary techniques. Both groups of parents were alike in expressing considerable affection for their children and in frequently using induction. But compared to the humanistic-flexible group, parents of the conventional-rigid children used more love withdrawal and less power assertion as disciplining techniques. Combined with considerable affection and frequent induction, this would be expected to elicit strong guilt about hostile and other impulses, eventually leading to strong inhibition or repression of such feelings.

Parents of humanistic-flexible types used power assertion more often and love withdrawal less often than parents of conventional-rigid children. Such usage is apt to account for greater awareness of consequences of acts for other persons. The less frequent use of love withdrawal would account for the more moderate conscience and for greater flexibility in considering extenuating circumstances.

Clearly, common sense prescriptions like "spare the rod and spoil the child" are mostly wrong. The use of power assertion techniques (including punishment) depends upon what else is done. Their use may often produce undesirable hostility and resentment. But in the context of this study, their use led to recognizing the consequences of acts for the welfare of other persons. And using love withdrawal instead of power assertion created what was probably too rigid a conscience, with too much guilt. The popularity of the love withdrawal technique as an instrument of discipline may have had undesirable consequences for middle-class American families. If the views here are correct, the possible consequence of love withdrawal, which was in vogue a generation ago, may be an overly rigid and guilt-ridden generation.

Summary: Development of Moral Controls

A socializing agent with authority, to whom the child becomes attached, is crucial in the development of moral controls. Both Piaget and Kohlberg have offered stage theories of moral development. Piaget sees the child moving through a series of steps from moral absolutism—where behaviors are either right or wrong and judged according to their consequences—to a final stage where morality is based upon shared or mutual agreement. Kohlberg proposes a similar progression, but attempts to identify a larger number of stages in between the first and last. At the present state of knowledge, it is not entirely clear that these are distinct stages, nor is it clear that they represent a progression from a lower to a higher state of morality. Moreover, these stages are based upon children's reasoning processes, with insufficient attention to their moral *feelings.*

Learning through reinforcement contingencies alone does not seem sufficient to explain the development of moral controls. Moral controls seem to have considerable cognitive content, as well as associations with guilt and other emotions. The once popular idea that moral views were learned by children through a process of taking the views of the parents with whom they identify has not found much support in experimental evidence. Role models, in fact, under certain circumstances, appear to be more effective in breaking down some controls than they are in building them up. If a model displays some behavior contrary to a moral principle, identification with the model can lead to adoption of similar behaviors.

Three kinds of discipline in childrearing have been identified: power assertion techniques—the parent punishes the child either physically or through deprivation; withdrawal of love—the parent shows disapproval of the child; and induction—the parent gives explanations and reasons for wanting the child to change behavior, particularly in terms of the consequences of the behavior for the child, the parent, or for other persons. Induction appears to be superior to love withdrawal and power assertion because it most often generates the right amount of emotional feeling in children, making them desire approval from a parent. Power assertion arouses anger and resentment, emotions too strong for them to care about approval. Love withdrawal most often arouses too much emotion. In any disciplinary encounter, all three techniques are present in some mix, which varies with different situations. Considerable use of induction and love withdrawal combined with affection appears to produce rigidity and excessive guilt in children. Considerable use of induction with less love withdrawal and more power assertion in a context of affection produces more flexible children with less guilt and more awareness of the feelings of other persons.

FOUR

SOCIAL
MOTIVATION

Not only in social psychology but in everyday language as well, one way of thinking about sets of behaviors enacted by a single individual is to concentrate upon the direction that all the members of a given set have in common. Can we find a set of behaviors that has the same general tendency and direction and that seems to accomplish a certain end? And can we discern another set that points in a different direction, and has a different goal? We recognize such sets in our daily lives. A set of this kind that has a common goal can usually be identified as a social motive.

Examples of social motives that particular individuals exhibit are self-preservation, acquisitiveness, gregariousness, aggression, and achievement, to name a few that have been considered important. We will deal only with the last two, to illustrate social psychological thinking about motivation.

Aggressive behaviors and achievement behaviors are widespread in modern societies. The most extreme form of aggression, war, has been characteristic of human behavior for thousands of years, and now threatens to destroy civilization. At the individual level, aggressive behaviors range from physical violence to malicious gossip, and they all have in common the desire to hurt someone. Achievement behaviors range from striving for success in a career to playing to win a hand of bridge or a round of golf. Achievement becomes so important to some individuals that the loss of a lifetime career results in severe distress or depression, and sometimes even suicide. Moreover, achievement is highly valued in our own American society.

Because aggressive behavior is often a social problem, and because the motivation to achieve is important to success in our society, we will discuss how these motives are established, how they are weakened or intensified, and the conditions under which they find expression in behavior.

ACQUIRED DRIVES

Until recently, one of the most firmly established ideas in psychology has been that motives are established through classical conditioning. It was long thought that most motives that are not obviously biological were learned in the *service* of primary or biological drives, such as hunger or thirst. For instance, when given food, a hungry infant typically sees the mother's face and its expressions and hears her voice when he or she is given food. The satisfying response the infant experiences when sucking upon her nipple or the bottle, brought on by the unconditioned stimulus (milk), could become conditioned to the various stimuli associated with the mother. Thus, the child would eventually experience a similarly satisfying response upon the mere sight of the mother or the sound of her voice. By extending the idea to include other experiences in which the mother is associated with the satisfaction of biological drives, the development of affection and love for her could be explained.

It was also recognized quite early that instrumental or operant conditioning could similarly explain some acquired drives. Edward Chace Tolman, for example, pointed out that social drives could develop in the course of satisfying primary drives.[1] In seeking to satisfy hunger or physical comfort, an individual could learn to become acquisitive—to want to acquire materials that would satisfy more basic needs. Or, in some societies, the individual might achieve the same end through cooperative behavior, and would therefore learn to be cooperative and gregarious. This fits the operant learning paradigm because food-seeking or physical-comfort behavior produces consequences that are reinforcing.

Perhaps the best example of acquired motivation is the desire for money. In itself, paper money has no value. But people will do many things in exchange for it. Because the spending of money is reinforcing (through the acquisition of desired objects or services), money itself has become a *secondary reinforcer*—it can be used to reward behavior. This entire system of conceptualizing motivation in terms of primary and secondary drives and primary and secondary reinforcers was at one time the key model in understanding animal and human motivation.

But consider whether the concept of "secondary drive" fits the drive concept, and whether a "secondary reinforcer" is, indeed, a reinforcer. If the desire for money is a drive, then its lack should stimulate a person to get some, in the same way that the lack of food prods an individual to search for some. Once the

[1] Tolman, 1932.

money is obtained, the drive should be reduced (as in the case of food). And whatever was done to get it should be reinforced—should occur more frequently in the future.

Common sense observations do not agree with these stipulations. Many people who obtain money do not then relax until they run out of it again. Some, indeed, may escalate their efforts to get more of it once they have their first few dollars. They may adopt some entirely new and different behavior for getting it, and never repeat the behavior that was supposedly reinforced.

Many psychologists with a stimulus-response approach to understanding behavior firmly believe that an originally neutral stimulus may acquire, through conditioning, the power to reinforce behavior. They cite experiments to support their belief. But more recent experimentation has cast doubt on the meaning of such experiments and suggests that such stimuli do not acquire an automatic reinforcing power, but rather serve simply as a source of information—in the same sense that a paper dollar is known to be exchangeable for some desired item. If paper dollars suddenly became permanently worthless, they could no longer be used to reward people for their work or services. This is a cognitive, or information, interpretation instead of a conditioning one, and is more suitable to social-psychological explanations.

Langdon Longstreth has summarized the evidence for the concept of secondary reinforcement in both animal and human learning.[2] He makes three telling points against it. The first two are self-evident, but the third needs some explanation. First, he notes that many studies which have attempted to establish a stimulus as a secondary reinforcer have failed to do so. Second, he states that in some studies a neutral stimulus that has been paired with a rewarding one has not only failed to become a positive reinforcer in itself, but has actually acquired negative reinforcing power, thus making the response that it follows *less* likely to occur again.

His third point is that in some of the experiments the neutral stimulus (which supposedly became a reinforcer) was visible *before* the participant responded to it, making it possible that the stimulus served as *information* to elicit the response, but not to reinforce it. According to the conditioning interpretation, excited *responses* exhibited by the hungry infant who sees the bottle have been connected through experience to the stimulus of the bottle of milk. A cognitive or information interpretation of this would be that the infant recognizes the bottle as a sign that he or she is going to be fed—there is no mechanical connection between stimulus (the bottle) and response (the excited acts), and the bottle does not become a "secondary reinforcer." In many of the experiments reviewed by Longstreth, including the widely cited studies in which chimpanzees worked for poker chips that could be put into vending machines, the results can be reinterpreted as a function of the information value of the stimuli used, rather than of an acquired "reinforcing power."

[2] Longstreth, 1971.

It seems doubtful, then, that any motives should be labeled "secondary drives." Unlike primary drives, such motives do not have states of deprivation which are relieved by "reinforcement." Moreover, the idea that some stimuli become "secondary reinforcers" through association with primary reinforcers is a dubious one. Such stimuli (like money) do not function in the same way as known reinforcers (like food). It is probably their information value, their value as signals, that makes them functional in motivation.

Two broad questions need to be answered with respect to any social motive. First, why do different people show different intensities of a particular motive? What is it about one's personal history or one's makeup that makes one more aggressive than another person, less acquisitive, or more gregarious? Second, why does one society—or other category of people—exhibit stronger motivation in some particular activity than other societies do?

Although the comparison of societies or cultures is primarily the work of the anthropologist, social psychologists are interested in differences among individuals in their social motives, and in differences among various categories of people. In fact, of central importance is the interplay between the individual and the subgroups to which he belongs, as this interplay bears on the development or modification of social motives. This is the kind of interaction referred to in the introductory chapter as that occurring between personality and social system. As we will see, the learning of social motives and their expression appears to result from such interplay. The socialization mechanisms discussed in Chapter 2—such as modeling, or imitation, and role learning, as well as tuition, or direct instruction—are primarily responsible for the development of aggressive, or achieving, behavior.

AGGRESSION

A behavioral act which has as its intent to harm or to injure someone, either physically or otherwise, is usually labeled as aggressive. At the extreme, aggression may be so disguised that the perpetrator of an aggressive act may not be consciously aware of his intent. Some of our aggressive acts are direct and violent, while others may be sly and indirect. Some are accompanied by rage; others are done coldly and without apparent emotion. The infant's action patterns are primitive and direct and bear little resemblance to the complicated end product of twenty or thirty years of socialization. It may be that the primitive rage of an infant is unlearned, but the intent and form of aggression in the socialized adult are definitely learned. As Sears, Maccoby, and Levin have suggested, this learning falls into the following pattern.[3] The child experiences discomfort which initially leads to rage and to behaviors that evoke discomfort in other persons. These behaviors also frequently lead others to unintentionally reward him by

[3] Sears, Maccoby, and Levin, 1957.

Aggression

relieving his discomfort. In time, the infant learns that the expression of aggression is likely to bring about rewarding behavior from other persons. Thus, the young child who throws temper tantrums does so to get his or her way.

These investigators go on to suggest that aggressive acts eventually become satisfying in themselves—implying that aggression is established as an acquired motive. They cite conditioning mechanisms of the sort we have criticized in the preceding section. It seems unnecessary to assume that people engage in aggression for its own sake, but rather that they perform aggressive acts whenever they achieve some end, or purpose. Especially important in this process are the conditions under which the aggression occurs.

The Social Context of Aggression

Early research on the determinants of aggression was guided by the notion that the strength of aggression was a function of the degree of frustration experienced.

The first studies seemed to support this notion.[4] More recent evidence suggests that the relation between frustration and aggression is not so direct.

First, it has become clear that frustration does not always lead to aggression. Leonard Berkowitz, in a recent assessment of the status of the frustration-aggression idea, has provided an analysis of the nature of frustration and has identified some of the conditions under which frustration leads to aggression.[5] Frustration is thought to arise as a result of the blocking, or nonconsummation, of an anticipated state of affairs. The anticipated state is important in understanding the conditions under which a situation is experienced as frustrating, and thus liable to result in aggression. The individual has to *expect* success in reaching the desired end state in order to feel frustrated when blocked. It is an *arbitrary* interference with an ongoing action leading to a goal that is frustrating. Where blocking of an act is nonarbitrary, as when encountering a natural barrier, frustration may not occur since success was not necessarily expected.

Pigeons who had learned to expect food on a regular basis whenever they repeatedly pecked a key became aggressive, attacking another pigeon, when the experimenter stopped giving them food for their pecking responses.[6] Human beings similarly led to anticipate a given *level* of reward react with aggression when that level is not forthcoming, even if the level received is greater than it has been in the past but is still not up to that expected. Students of revolution, as Berkowitz notes, have long been aware that revolutionary outbreaks are apt to occur during periods of rising expectations (frequently stimulated by an increase in the level of experiencing rewards). A study applying the frustration-aggression hypothesis to countries undergoing modernization indicated that as people experienced rising levels of education and food consumption, political instability increased.[7] This study supports the view that it is the frustration of expectations that produces aggressive behavior.

Two conditions may prevent aggression from occurring even when an individual has been frustrated in trying to reach some goal. Many forms of aggression carry strong social sanctions; their enactment leads to disapproval or punishment. Parents rarely allow children to behave aggressively toward members of the family—especially toward the parents themselves. So children learn to inhibit this form of behavior, and frustrations created by the parents often do not produce an aggressive act with the parents as target. The other condition preventing aggression involves learning to perform some act that is *incompatible* with aggression. Children learn, for example, that they can seldom successfully carry out a difficult task if they explode in helpless rage when the task frustrates them. So they learn to persevere, trying new approaches to complete the task.

One way to produce more aggressive behavior is by lowering established

[4] Dollard, Doob, Miller, et al., 1939.
[5] Berkowitz, 1969.
[6] Azrin, Hurchinson, and Hake, 1966.
[7] Feierabend and Feierabend, 1966.

inhibitions. In an experiment,[8] some male college students were given several treatments intended to anger them, while others were given nonfrustrating control treatments. The treatments included creation of a frustrating atmosphere by (1) being put to work on an insoluble jigsaw puzzle and (2) being insulted by a confederate of the experimenter after trying to do the insoluble puzzle, and creation of a nonfrustrating atmosphere by (3) being put to work on an easily soluble puzzle and not being insulted. Following the task experience, each student viewed a movie of a violent boxing match, or one of an exciting but nonviolent foot race. Since boxing is a socially sanctioned form of aggression, it was expected to lower inhibitions.

When the film was over, the participants in the experiments were given an opportunity to electrically shock the persons they had met earlier—the confederates of the experimenter. This was done under the guise of a learning experiment with electric shocks used as punishment for mistakes. The intensity of the shock administered by a participant was taken as a measure of aggressiveness.

The results were that those who had not been given the frustrating tasks, even after seeing the aggressive fight film, did not give appreciably more intense shocks than those seeing the foot-race film. But those who saw the fight film *and* who had been frustrated by the insoluble task, along with those who were also insulted, did give more intense shocks than those who were frustrated and insulted but who saw only the foot-race film. So it seems that the fight film induced a readiness for aggression that was called out if the individual was frustrated or insulted or both. In sum, it appears that greater aggression can be produced by a combination of anger-arousing frustration along with a lowering of inhibitions produced by modeling aggression in a socially approved context. This fits most gang-violence situations, where the act of some member of a rival gang induces anger, and the retaliating aggression is sanctioned by the offended gang.

Further research by Berkowitz and his associates has illustrated another condition that affects the probability of aggression in response to frustration—the presence of aggressive cues.[9] Stimuli that have become associated with aggression or with frustration elicit aggression in frustrating situations. For instance, the mere presence of a gun or other weapon of violence in a laboratory has, in some experiments, been associated with the delivery of more intense shocks. Aggression can occur in the absence of such cues, but these cues somehow increase the probability of its happening.

The idea that stimuli associated with aggression can elicit aggressive behavior has been tested in a number of ways. There have been pistols and rifles displayed on a nearby table—and participants gave stronger shocks.[10] There have been boxing films shown in which the name of the boxer who received the

[8] Geen and Berkowitz, 1967.
[9] Berkowitz, 1970.
[10] Berkowitz and LePage, 1967.

beating was the same as that of the confederate who insulted the participant— and the participant administered more shocks when the names were the same. In some way, then, the cues encourage aggression.

Direct Learning of Aggression

Not only can frustration occur without aggression, but the frustration-aggression hypothesis has had to be modified in the direction of allowing for aggression without prior frustration. Aggressive behavior can be learned through the same processes of social learning as can other behaviors, described in Chapter 2. Children may learn aggression when the contingencies of reinforcement are suitably arranged. It is not the intention of mothers to reward such behavior, but by continuing to be the source of frustration and by giving such positive rewards as picking the children up and soothing them when they behave aggressively, they foster the continuance of aggression. As the children grow older, tolerant or permissive attitudes toward aggression will allow the continued expression of aggression.

Direct tuition—instruction or encouragement—may also foster aggression. A number of studies show that where parents approve of aggression against age-mates, it will occur.[11] Finally, the processes of role learning and identification are consistent with the findings that parental aggression in the form of punishment of the child—particularly physical punishment—is associated with high aggression on the part of the child. As Sears, Maccoby, and Levin point out in summarizing their research on aggression and its control: "When the parents punish—particularly when they employ physical punishment—they are providing a living example of the use of aggression at the very moment they are trying to teach the child not to be aggressive." The most peaceful homes, they suggest, are those in which parents rely on nonpunitive forms of control; the homes where the children show angry, aggressive outbursts are likely to be those in which the parents have a tolerant or careless attitude toward such behavior and where they use it to punish aggressive behavior—or both.[12]

Whether aggressive behavior is considered good or bad depends both upon the type of behavior and the group to which an individual belongs. Killing or maiming people is considered good by most members of a society if the people so affected are their enemies in a war. As long as such values prevail, that kind of aggressive behavior is no mystery at all. It is valued, encouraged, and reinforced by society. Individuals who conform are rewarded; those who resist and object are apt to be punished. This example at the societal level is comparable to the example mentioned earlier of parents who encourage their children (especially boys) to be tough fighters in relation to other boys. Direct instruction and encouragement is the mechanism operating here. The idea put forth by an occasional

[11] Davis and Dollard, 1940; Lesser, 1952.
[12] Reprinted by permission from R. R. Sears, E. E. Maccoby, and H. Levin. *Patterns of child rearing.* New York: Harper & Row, Publishers, Incorporated, 1957. P. 266.

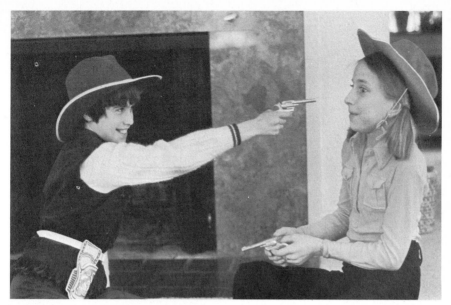

Playing at aggression with toy weapons.

psychoanalyst that we have war because human beings have an instinct for destruction or aggression is sheer nonsense as an explanation of war.

This suggests a point that is worth underscoring. Aggression often is exercised in the service of other needs or motives, as Otto Kleinberg has noted.[13] War often has an economic base, or sometimes a religious one. Kleinberg reports that an Iroquois Indian chief proposed to a neighboring ruler that their young men be allowed to have a little war. On the second chief's refusal, the Iroquois chief asked, "With whom can my children play?" War raids for profit are characteristic of many primitive societies—to say nothing of modern societies. In Aztec Mexico religious factors were responsible for the major part of warlike behavior. One of the important beliefs was that the gods would die if deprived of food, and that the only satisfying nourishment consisted of human hearts. One report states that when the great temple of Huitzilopochtli was dedicated in 1486, the chain of sacrificial victims stretched out for two miles—over 70,000 captive warriors of rival nations.[14]

Prestige, pride, self-esteem, glory, can all produce aggressive behavior. A psychological analysis of Adolf Hitler suggests that glory was one of the prominent motives operating in his attempt to establish Germany as a superstate during World War II.[15] Closer to home, similar motives operate in youth gangs,

[13] Kleinberg, 1954.
[14] Kleinberg, 1954.
[15] Langer, 1972.

where killing or injuring a rival gang member is a symbol of pride or status, like the notch in the gun of the Western gunfighter. Finally, we should also note that society or other subgroups can channel or restructure behavior that might ordinarily take the form of direct aggression. Indians of the Northwest Coast settled disputes through the potlatch system. Instead of fighting, individuals gave feasts in which they tried to give away or destroy as much of their property as possible. This shamed their enemies, who lost status in the community unless they retaliated in kind. Eskimos, who are especially unwarlike, settle quarrels by composing satirical songs mocking their enemy and challenging them to public singing contests.[16] Some rivalries in our own society may be settled through sporting contests or through a boxing contest in which the rules prevent any serious injury.

Summary: Aggression

Aggression is a behavioral act which has as its intent the harm or injury of someone, either physically or otherwise. There is little satisfactory evidence that it is a motive in its own right. Instead, such behavior depends upon various aspects of social learning and on the social context in which it occurs. Arbitrary blocking of expectations is frustrating, and under some circumstances results in aggression. Various inhibitory factors can be learned which prevent aggression from occurring, even in a state of frustration. Tolerance of aggression and stimulus cues previously associated with aggression can lower such inhibitions. Much aggression is directly learned, through instruction, encouragement, and support. Finally, aggression may often occur because it is a way of satisfying other needs.

ACHIEVEMENT MOTIVATION

People differ in the extent to which they try to achieve some standard of excellence in their work or other activities. At one extreme, some people set high standards for themselves, strive to achieve them, and respond with much feeling to success or failure in meeting them. At the other extreme, some people are unlikely to set such standards, exert little effort, and are indifferent to success or failure. These two kinds of people are said to differ in *achievement motivation*. This behavior has been investigated extensively in recent years. Generally, it has been measured either in terms of some behavioral index of achievement, or in terms of achievement themes found in stories told by individuals in response to viewing a series of pictures.

The research on achievement motivation has led to one of the few examples of a precise mathematical formula of motivational phenomena. We will try to explain this theory in words. The interested reader can find a brief summary in more mathematical terms,[17] or a more complete presentation.[18]

[16] Kleinberg, 1954.
[17] Secord and Backman, 1974.
[18] Atkinson and Feather, 1966.

Achievement motivation: studying for an "A" grade.

Jack Atkinson and Norman Feather have suggested that in situations calling for behavior which is to be evaluated against some standard of excellence, the behavior is a function of the following two constructs: (1) the tendency to approach success, and (2) the tendency to avoid failure.[19] People differ in the emphasis they place on these constructs. Some are more afraid of failure, others are more optimistic about success.

An individual's behavior in a given activity can be predicted from the importance to him of success and of failure. The tendency to approach success or avoid failure can each be calculated for an individual from the following three elements:

1 The strength of motives to succeed (or to avoid failure).
2 The probabilities that a given act will result in success (or failure).
3 The incentive value attached to success (or failure) in that activity.

Thus, the hope of success is a function of the strength of the motive to succeed, the probability that one will succeed, and the value of success in that activity. The greater the magnitude of these three elements, the greater the hope of success. The last two of the three elements can be related to the difficulty of

[19] Atkinson and Feather, 1966.

the task. The easier the task, the greater will be the probability of success. But the more difficult the task, the greater the value attached to succeeding. One takes more pride in accomplishing a difficult task than an easy one. So as the probability of success goes up, the incentive value goes down.

The fear of failure is also a function of three elements: the strength of the motive to avoid failure, the probability that one will fail, and the negative value or costs attached to failing. The higher the magnitude of these three elements,

Achievement motivation: striving to score. (Rapho/ Photo Researchers, Inc.; photo by Bruce Roberts)

the greater the fear of failure. The negative value or cost of failing is greater when the task is easy. It is more embarrassing and thus more costly psychologically to fail an easy task than a hard one.

If we were to use the mathematical formula for achievement motivation and to assign values to the elements described here, we would find that the hope of success is greatest for tasks of moderate difficulty, especially where the motive to achieve is strong. The same thing is true of the fear of failure—it is strongest for tasks of intermediate difficulty. The essential reason for this conclusion lies in the reciprocal relation between probability of success (or failure) and the value of success (or cost of failure). As one goes up, the other goes down. When such extreme values are multiplied, the product is lower than it is for two moderate values. For example, $0.1 \times 0.9 = 0.09$, while $0.5 \times 0.5 = 0.25$. Thus, one gets higher motive values when the components are moderate.

Whether or not an individual will attempt a task is a joint function of the hope of success and the fear of failure. The calculated values of these two functions vary for different individuals, because some may be strongly motivated to succeed, while others may be strongly motivated to avoid failure. Based on our reasoning so far, we may make the following predictions. Where an individual is strongly motivated to succeed and has little fear of failure, he will most readily attempt tasks of intermediate difficulty. He would gain little satisfaction from easy tasks, and might not succeed with difficult ones. Just the reverse is true of individuals with a strong fear of failure and a weak motivation for success: they will avoid tasks of intermediate difficulty and prefer those that are either very easy or very difficult. They are apt to solve the easy problems, and they experience minimum pain if they fail at the very difficult ones.

Malcolm Weinstein reports that in eighteen studies using different types of groups and situations, the predicted relation between a strong motive to achieve and the preference for an intermediate risk—a task of intermediate difficulty—was confirmed with remarkable consistency.[20] These studies, however, used different measures of need achievement and different risk-taking situations. Weinstein's own study used eight measures of need achievement and twelve measures reflecting risk-taking preference in a variety of contexts such as problem solving, athletic tasks, choice of potential dates, betting preferences, and vocational preferences. Surprisingly, he found little correlation among the measures of achievement, and statistical analysis suggested that these measures belonged to different dimensions having little in common. A similar result was obtained for the measures of risk taking. His findings question whether need achievement represents a single dimension or a characteristic of an individual and further suggests that risk taking varies markedly depending on the situation in which it is studied. In other words, people do not have the same need for achievement in different tasks, and their needs vary further according to the situation.

The effects of achievement-oriented tendencies on *performance* in an achieve-

[20] Weinstein, 1969.

ment situation are also thought to vary with the strength of the motives to succeed and to fail. Where the motive to avoid failure is greater than the motive to succeed, an inhibiting, or dampening, effect on performance is predicted by the theory. Thus, better performance can be expected where the motive to succeed is the stronger. This prediction has received support from a number of studies.[21]

Finally, the theory predicts different reactions to the experiences of success and failure by those people with different achievement motives. Those persons whose motive to achieve success is greater than their motive to avoid failure will persist in the face of failure to a greater degree when their initial expectation of success is high than when it is low. They value success, and since they expect to succeed, they keep trying. On the other hand, those in whom the motive to avoid failure predominates will persist to a greater extent in the face of failure when they initially perceive the probability of success to be low than when they perceive it to be high. While they are afraid of failure, it is not psychologically costly to fail an improbable or difficult task, so they keep trying. These are nonobvious predictions and can be more fully understood by substituting values in the formulas and calculating the resulting motives.

Reactions to success or failure in terms of lowering or raising one's level of aspiration are also expected to be different for the two kinds of individuals. One would expect a person to raise his level of aspiration after success by choosing a more difficult task, and to lower his level following failure. But instead, the model predicts that those whose motive to avoid failure is greater than their motive to achieve success would choose an easier task after success and a more difficult task after failure.

This has been explained in the following way.[22] Success or failure on a task changes its attractiveness because the subjective probability of success is altered. For the person oriented toward avoidance of failure, success on an easy task increases the subjective probability of success, making the task seem still easier. But this also increases the strength of the motive to avoid failure, because the easier a task is, the more a person wants to avoid failing it. As a result, this stronger motive to avoid failure leads the person to choose a still easier task. On the other hand, if he or she fails a task, it lowers his or her estimate of the probability of success in subsequent trials. Since the cost of failing remains constant, but the task seems harder, this lowers the motive to avoid failure, and the person is able to choose a more difficult task. Similar deductions may be made for other cases, and predictions based on this reasoning were for the most part supported in several investigations.

Achievement theory has also been applied to more everyday situations, including vocational aspirations, occupational mobility, and differences in achievement motivation between class, ethnic, and national groups. Consistent

[21] Atkinson and Litwin, 1960; Atkinson and O'Connor, 1966; Karabenick and Youssef, 1968.
[22] Moulton, 1965.

Achievement motivation: chess champions in elementary school competition receiving their prizes. (Courtesy of United States Chess Federation, *Chess Life and Review*, June 1973, vol. 28, no. 6, p. 319)

with the theory, students who were unrealistic in their vocational aspirations, aspiring to occupations requiring abilities either greater or less than their own, were found to be low in achievement motivation and high in anxiety related to achievements.[23] The hypothesis that achievement motivation plays a part in explaining upward social mobility has also received some support. For the lower two levels of occupational status, but not in the top two, achievement motivation is associated with upward mobility.[24] Achievement motivation is also stronger among middle-class than working-class children, and stronger among Jewish than Italian children.[25]

In the case of the Jews, we again see important cultural factors operating, especially with regard to educational and intellectual achievement. The Jews have a long history, extending back thousands of years, of reverence for intellectual activity; moreover, it is part of their religion. Rabbis are not only men of

[23] Mahone, 1960.
[24] Crockett, 1962.
[25] Douvan, 1956; Milstein, 1956; Rosen, 1956, 1959.

God; they are also intellectuals and scholars. This emphasis on intelligence and education is reflected in Jewish family life; thus, it is no surprise that Jews have a strong need for intellectual achievement.

Sex Differences in Achievement Motivation

The Atkinson-Feather theory of achievement motivation has been worked out primarily on males, and there is some question about whether it applies to females. Almost no research has been done with females that uses their theory. A number of factors suggest that the results might be different for females, and the evidence has been reviewed by Aletha Stein and Margaret Bailey.[26]

Cultural training in sex roles leads to different orientations for men and women. Typically, social, verbal, and artistic skills are considered to be more appropriate for women, while mechanical, spatial, and athletic skills are thought to be more appropriate for men. Evidence supports the view that women are likely to have greater achievement orientation in those areas appropriate to their sex role.

A common belief has been that women achieve for a different reason than men: they achieve because of a need to gain social approval, while men achieve because of a direct need to succeed. Stein and Bailey review the evidence and suggest that this view is wrong, and that women do have a need to achieve social skills, which is one of the areas appropriate to their sex role. Females are not necessarily more sensitive to social approval.

Achievement striving in the male pattern on the part of women leads to mixed rewards and punishments for them. While achievement is honored and rewarded in our culture, some aspects of it may be at variance with the female role, and the achieving woman may be treated as masculine, unfeminine, and lacking in desirable womanly qualities. There are a number of adaptations women can make to avoid this outcome. Achieving women see achievement as more appropriate for women than do nonachieving women. Their self-image, therefore, does not suffer as much as it would otherwise. Some women may satisfy achievement needs vicariously through their husbands. Others may choose a career that is "feminine"—such as teaching or nursing. Still others may try to compensate for their professional success by emphasizing their feminine characteristics—they may be physically attractive, nonassertive, and generally feminine in social behavior.

Stein and Bailey conclude that females have a somewhat different achievement orientation than males have. They are apt to be more anxious about failure, more cautious about risking failure, and more likely to admit failure when it occurs. These characteristics increase in middle childhood and in adolescence—periods when pressures for adopting the female role are apt to be strong.

Fear of success. A particularly interesting hypothesis was suggested by Matina Horner in 1968, when she argued that many women do not do their best because they have a *fear of success.* No such component was included in the Atkinson-

[26] Stein and Bailey, 1973.

Feather theory which we reviewed. Horner suggested that women are apt to believe that success will be accompanied by rejection and alienation, that they will be less attractive to men. She based her conclusions on a study in which she asked men and women to write a story based on the following cue: "After first-term finals, John (Ann) finds himself (herself) at the top of his (her) medical school class." The men wrote about John, the women about Ann. She found that 65 percent of the women told stories that indicated a motive to avoid success while only 8 percent of the men did so.

One of the problems with this study is that the results could represent a response to the female sex role (of Ann) rather than to the respondent's own feelings about achievement. To control for this possibility, another study had men and women respond to both John and Ann, and used high school students as well as college students.[27] Both high school males and females gave more fear-of-success imagery to Ann than to John, but did not differ from each other in amount. This suggests that the difference obtained is simply sex stereotyping, and that it does not represent a difference in fear of success between the high school boys and girls. Consistent with this interpretation is the additional finding that college females gave much less fear-of-success imagery to Ann than men did, contrary to Horner's idea. Probably this is due to current awareness of women's liberated views on sex roles among college students. College males, like high school males, stereotyped Ann, but college women refused to do so. Certainly, awareness today is much greater than it was in the late 1960s when the Horner study was done. The lack of difference among the high school students could be explained by assuming that they are much less aware than college students of the women's movement. But further research is needed to verify this assumption. Finally, in another study, women performed *better* at male-oriented tasks than at female-oriented tasks, a result also inconsistent with Horner's hypothesis.[28]

The next section reviews evidence on the differences in the way boys and girls are socialized with respect to achievement orientation.

Childhood Antecedents of the Motivation to Achieve

Eight- to ten-year-old children with strong motivation to achieve were found to have parents who expected independent accomplishment at an earlier age, and who gave more frequent and stronger rewards for these independent accomplishments.[29] These findings were supported further in a study where interaction between parents and their child in a problem-solving situation was observed.[30] Parents of children with strong achievement motivation set high standards of excellence for the child, gave approval for progress toward those standards, and showed disappointment at poor performance. Moderate, rather than high or low warmth was also associated with achievement motivation.

[27] Brown, Jennings, and Vanick, 1974.
[28] Sorrentino and Short, 1974.
[29] Winterbottom, 1958.
[30] Rosen and D'Andrade, 1959.

A longitudinal investigation provides some suggestive evidence concerning the degree to which achievement motivation and parental practices are consistent over time, as well as the comparative importance of early and late childrearing practices.[31] There was moderate stability in achievement motivation over time—but the attitudes of mothers toward independent accomplishment during childhood and adolescence were opposite. The earlier a mother encouraged independence in her grade school child, the less she encouraged such behavior in adolescence. Independence and achievement training in early childhood and in later adolescence had little relation. Further, achievement motivation in adolescence and maternal practices at that time were not much related, in contrast to the relation during childhood found in an earlier study. The motivation to avoid failure at adolescence, however, *was* related to early childhood practices. And the later the maternal demands for independent accomplishment, the higher the adolescent anxiety in achievement situations.

Stein and Bailey point out that the parental practices that make for high achievement orientation are somewhat contradictory to those that emphasize the feminine role.[32] The feminine role would be emphasized by high rather than by moderate warmth, low rather than moderate or high permissiveness, and encouragement of dependence rather than of independence. Thus, if these are the prevailing parental practices, it is not surprising that women have, as a result, a weaker achievement orientation.

Situational Determinants

As in the case of aggression, recent research focusing on achievement motivation has shifted away from concern about childrearing antecedents to a consideration of situational determinants. How a person defines a situation affects the expression of achievement motivation in behavior. Important in this definition are the values and goals the person sees in the situation. For example, the relation between achievement motivation and grades in college holds only for those who see grades as instrumental for their future career success.[33] Further, strong achievement motivation leads to occupational choice only for those people who know about potential rewards and who see occupations as intrinsically satisfying.[34]

Features of the situation that affect a person's attribution of success or failure to his own efforts and abilities rather than to chance or luck also seem to be crucial in determining whether predictions from the theory will be borne out.[35] People differ in seeing the causation of events and their reinforcing consequences

[31] Feld, 1967.
[32] Stein and Bailey, 1973.
[33] Raynor, 1970.
[34] Leuptow, 1968.
[35] Feather, 1967; Weiner and Kukla, 1970; Crandall, Katkovsky and Crandall, 1965; Coleman, Campbell, Hobson, et al., 1966.

as either internal (under their own control) or external (beyond their own control). Strongly motivated individuals generally ascribe success to their own efforts, experience more reward, and therefore are more active in attempting to achieve. They also persist longer because they are more likely to ascribe failure to a lack of effort than to a lack of ability. Finally, they prefer tasks of intermediate difficulty, because these yield the most information about their own capabilities. This theme, of events as caused either by one's own actions or by external factors, will be expanded in the next chapter, dealing with knowing and evaluating persons, and will be brought up again in the final chapter, in connection with the achievement motivations of people whose behavior deviates from what is commonly accepted in our society.

Summary: Achievement Motivation

People and groups differ in the extent to which they try to achieve some standard of excellence in their work or other activities. The strength of an individual's efforts in a given activity can be calculated from: (1) the strength of motives to succeed (or avoid failure), (2) the probabilities that a given act will result in success (or failure), and (3) the incentive value attached to success (or failure) in that activity. Hope of success (or failure) varies as a function of these elements. When these elements are entered into a mathematical formula, it becomes clear that hope of success is greatest for tasks of intermediate difficulty, and the same is true of fear of failure. But when both hope of success and fear of failure are combined to predict what tasks will be attempted, it is clear that those strongly motivated to succeed will attempt tasks of intermediate difficulty, while those who strongly fear failure will try either easy or difficult tasks, but not intermediate ones. The theory also makes accurate predictions about how failure or success on a task will affect willingness to try the next task.

The common belief that women achieve for a different reason than men appears to be wrong. Moreover, the idea that women are afraid to succeed, because it might hurt their feminine image or otherwise disadvantage them, has not received support in more recent research. That this common belief is a stereotype held toward women appears to be true, especially for people not familiar with the women's liberation movement.

Parents of children with strong achievement motivation provide strong support for achievement behavior in a relatively consistent way over the development years. At different times, however, mothers do vary in whether or not they support independence on the part of their children. Whether individuals are achievement-oriented also depends upon the values and goals that they see in a situation, as well as upon whether they see events as under their own control or under the control of external agents or circumstances.

FIVE

DESCRIBING AND TYPING PEOPLE

O f the familiar objects around us, other people are the most interesting, and it is to other people that we direct most of our attention. In our ordinary contacts and actions, we share with other people common knowledge not only about meanings, places, and situations, but also about their expectations of us and how we should behave, and our expectations of them and how they should behave. Usually we take this common knowledge for granted, and our behavior is confident and smooth. But when we are unsure about others' reactions, our behavior is likely to be halting and confused. We share certain basic assumptions about our nature as human beings, and this knowledge is crucial in determining our actions. These assumptions become especially apparent when we read science fiction stories and notice how much like ourselves creatures from other planets behave. Those space creatures who are unlike Earthmen are often considered to be monsters and are frightening or evil.

THE DEVELOPMENT OF PERSON CONCEPTS

Differentiation of the Individual Person

It takes us a long time to learn how to know people and to anticipate their actions. The first thing we do, as infants, is to differentiate persons from the rest of the world. Within a few months of our birth, we can identify persons as physical beings separate from the inanimate world. Recent evidence, however, suggests that it takes many years to see another person as an independent *psychological being*.[1] When younger children look at other people they often confuse:

1 the person and his social setting or possessions
2 the person and themselves

Kindergarten children, for example, often describe their playmates by talking about their toys or their house. They also describe them in terms of their own feelings of like or dislike without any reference to the playmates' own characteristics.

Differentiating people from their possessions, their settings, and from oneself is only the first step. Simple descriptions of other people's physical behavior tell us little about them, because such behavior is usually in a social context and in relation to other persons. Actions are full of meanings, and infants gradually learn what other people's behavior means. Over the years, within their families and then out in the world of school and play, children learn how to anticipate other people's behavior. They learn first how to describe these different actions and then how to characterize individuals in terms of their actions. They learn, too, how people behave in different social contexts. They know, for example, that they are expected to display better table manners when they eat with guests than when they are having lunch alone in the kitchen.

An intensive study of the descriptions of peers provided by children and young persons yielded considerable information about the several ways in which descriptions differed at different ages.[2] Young children give us very little information about another person *as an individual;* college students and adults tell us much more. Descriptions by kindergarten children of their friends contain many items that say nothing about their playmates as persons. They refer to their possessions, such as toys or pet dogs, or their social settings, such as their rooms or the new baby sister. Or else they use items about the persons which are relatively noninformative and general, like "he's nice" or "I like her."

By the third grade, a few references to interests, activities, abilities, and beliefs and feelings begin to appear. These items carry much more information

[1] Peevers and Secord, 1973.
[2] Peevers and Secord, 1973.

about the person described. They greatly increase in frequency in later grades and among college students. They include such items as "she likes to play chess," "she's a good athlete," or "he's a conscientious objector."

The later grades and college students also use *dispositional* items in describing people. Dispositional words describe an enduring characteristic which holds across a variety of situations, such as "loyal," "sense of humor," "intelligent." Finally, only among high school seniors and college students do *depth* items appear *spontaneously*. These either identify the circumstances under which persons exhibit a characteristic, or they explain why the persons are the way they are. A recent study, however, revealed that younger children can produce such items if the interviewer probes for them with special questions.[3]

As children get older, they change the ways in which they enter into the description of another person. Young children are very *egocentric* and describe other people in terms of their own personal frame of reference: "she likes me," "I like his electric cars," or "she hits me too much." These descriptions suggest the inability of the children to distinguish between the outer world and their inner experience.

The *reciprocal* stance occurs infrequently at all age levels. It describes a mutual relationship ("we go to the movies together").

College students, in their descriptions of other persons, are *other-oriented*. They see other people as separate from themselves and their descriptions leave themselves out as observers ("John likes mountain climbing").

While these descriptions of the development of person concepts are useful to us in a general way, individuals of the same age differ a great deal in level of development. We see this ourselves when we ask different friends to describe a person we don't know. Some of them will give us "just the facts," others will explain motives and apparent contradictions within the person, and give a rounded picture of that person. We do not know why people's descriptive skills vary so much; future research on parent-child and peer group relations may help to explain it.

Summary: The Development of Person Concepts

Children take a long time to learn about people. Before school age, they do not see them clearly as individuals separate from their possessions or social setting. Their view of other persons is heavily egocentric: how they feel toward them or what they can do to them or for them is important. Gradually, school-age children move from using general, evaluative terms like "nice" or "bad" to more revealing attributes, concerning interests, abilities, beliefs, and feelings. Last to appear with any frequency are disposition, or trait, terms. These describe enduring characteristics which hold across situations. Also rare below the level of high

[3] Pratt, 1975.

school seniors are spontaneous mentions of situations under which a person possesses an attribute, or spontaneous explanations of why a person behaves as he or she does.

THE SOCIAL STEREOTYPE

In everyday life we often find that all we know about people is their category. That is, we know that one is a vegetarian, or a policeman, or a child. When we know little else about that person, the category affects our view very strongly. These categories are fundamental in our evaluation of other persons and in our relationships with them.

Typing people is enormously useful to us, because it would be too difficult to respond to other people in all their individuality all the time. We use, instead, a kind of "shorthand" to help us sort out the many people we meet in our lifetime. *Stereo*-typing, however, is an exaggerated sort of typing, which has often been attacked by social scientists. Stereotyping is done by people who share a common culture: the ideas in the stereotype are a part of the culture. When we stereotype other people we do three things: (1) we identify a category of people, like hippies or policemen, (2) we agree that the people in that category share certain traits, like unwashed hair, or cruel dispositions, and (3) we attribute these traits to *everyone* in the category (whether their hair is washed or not!).

Identification of a Person Category

People differ greatly in their visible characteristics. We select certain attributes to identify different categories, and ignore others. These attributes may be physical, that is, we may notice that someone is *black,* or *elderly,* or *female,* as our first definition of that person. They may involve membership in a group, as when we identify people as *delivery* people (by their uniforms) or *Sikhs* (by their turbans). We may also identify them by their behavior, such as *hippies* who panhandle for change. The greater the contrast between them and the observer, the more stereotyping there is.[4] That is why middle-aged bankers are often targets for stereotyping by young militants who in turn are often targets for the bankers.

Consensus on Attributed Traits

Most readily identifiable categories of persons are thought to have personal attributes in common as well. For example, we may group all long-haired, jeans-wearing, young people into a class, label them hippies, and assume that they are rebellious, antimaterialistic, pot-smoking, and promiscuous. Or we may describe all old people as conservative, grumpy, senile, and old-fashioned. People who

[4] Campbell, 1967.

hold a certain stereotype tend to agree with one another about the identifying characteristics of a group, and the attributes that members of the group possess.

An interesting series of studies shows us how this process works.[5] The research was conducted first in 1933, then repeated in 1951, 1967, and 1969. Each time, the participants were Princeton students. They were given a list of ten ethnic groups, together with eighty-four words describing personal traits. First they checked *all* the traits that seemed to be typical of an ethnic group, then they went over the checklist again to identify the *five* traits they thought most characteristic of each group.

The degree of agreement among the students was striking, but not unanimous. If the participants were to have selected traits entirely at random, each trait would have yielded a figure of 6 percent. But from Table 5-1 we can see that certain traits received percentages far greater than 6. Moreover, there are wide differences in the traits assigned to different ethnic groups. In some instances there is little overlap between the different groups in the five most popular traits.

At the same time, consensus on stereotypes is far from perfect. Data from a different study reveal that people may even disagree on the physical characteristics assumed to define a race.[6] While 94 percent of a group of eighty-four students claimed that dark skin is very characteristic of blacks, 6 percent said that it is only somewhat characteristic. "Wide nose" was believed very characteristic by only 71 percent. Agreement on personality characteristics was much less than that for physical characteristics. No more than 46 percent agreed on any one trait as being very characteristic.

Categorical Treatment of Persons

Two investigations demonstrated the way in which those people who hold a stereotype will attribute *all* the characteristics they believe typical of a certain group to any particular member of that group.[7] The studies used a series of photographs of persons varying in "Negroidness" from very Negroid to very Caucasoid. The question posed was whether stereotyping was reduced for the more Caucasoid photographs. The researchers discovered that as long as the subject was recognized as a black, stereotyping did not decrease, even though the picture became increasingly Caucasoid.

This response, however, may in part come from the methods of research used in studying stereotyping. If only a single piece of information is given— racial identification, for example—people are forced to ignore individual differences and respond to the person as a member of a class. One study proved this by inventing fictional national groups and adding them to a list of thirty-two other

[5] Katz and Braly, 1933; Gilbert, 1933; Karlins, Coffman, and Walters, 1969; Lewis, Darley, and Glucksberg, 1972.
[6] Secord and Backman, 1974.
[7] Secord, Bevan, and Katz, 1956; Secord, 1959.

TABLE 5-1 Percent of Princeton College Students Assigning Traits to Ethnic Groups

	YEAR				YEAR		
	1932*	1950†	1967‡		1932*	1950†	1967‡
AMERICANS				**GERMANS**			
Industrious	48	30	23	Scientifically minded	78	62	47
Intelligent	47	32	20	Industrious	65	50	59
Materialistic	33	37	67	Stolid	44	10	9
Ambitious	33	21	42	Intelligent	32	32	19
Progressive	27	5	17	Methodical	31	20	21
ENGLISH				**JAPANESE**			
Sportsmanlike	53	21	22	Intelligent	45	11	20
Intelligent	46	29	23	Industrious	43	12	57
Conventional	34	25	19	Progressive	24	2	17
Tradition-loving	31	42	21	Shrewd	22	13	7
Conservative	30	22	53	Sly	20	21	3
NEGROES				**CHINESE**			
Superstitious	84	41	13	Superstitious	34	18	8
Lazy	75	31	26	Sly	29	4	6
Happy-go-lucky	38	17	27	Conservative	29	14	15
Ignorant	38	24	11	Tradition-loving	26	26	32
Musical	26	33	47	Loyal to family ties	22	35	50
JEWS				**IRISH**			
Shrewd	79	47	30	Pugnacious	45	24	13
Mercenary	49	28	15	Quick-tempered	39	35	43
Industrious	48	29	33	Witty	38	16	7
Grasping	34	17	17	Honest	32	11	17
Intelligent	29	37	37	Very religious	29	30	27
ITALIANS				**TURKS**			
Artistic	53	28	30	Cruel	47	12	9
Impulsive	44	19	28	Very religious	26	6	7
Passionate	37	25	44	Treacherous	21	3	13
Quick-tempered	35	15	28	Sensual	20	4	9
Musical	32	22	9	Ignorant	15	7	13

* N = 100
† N = 333
‡ N = 150

SOURCE: Reprinted in abridged form by permission from Marvin Karlins, Thomas L. Coffman, and Gary Walters. On the fading of social stereotypes: Studies in three generations of college students. *Journal of Personality and Social Psychology*, 1969, **13**, 1, 1-16.

real ethnic groups.[8] Most of the students rating the fictional groups—"Danerians," "Pirenians," and "Wallonians"—showed no hesitation in assigning traits to the fictional groups and in rating those groups. And generally the traits they assigned were unfavorable. But sometimes in our everyday life we do have only one piece of identifying information. If, for example, we assign a person to the category of "hippie" on the basis of his hair and clothing alone, we will then often attribute to him all the other traits we associated with that class.

In most ordinary situations we see many differences among individuals. Also, interaction between us, as observers, and those we are observing, lessens our response to others as being simply members of categories. We can see how this worked when observers were permitted to compare subgroups within an ethnic group.[9] White participants were asked to characterize "upper-class blacks" and "lower-class blacks." They only stereotyped the lower-class blacks.

Even in the artificial situation of the research study, however, it would be oversimplifying to say that the request to judge on the basis of ethnic identification alone forces observers to *agree*. Consensus, in the research situation, suggests that social forces shape our perceptions of a class of persons. If there is a marked consensus, we can say that a stereotype exists.

Changes in Stereotypes

Since the studies of the Princeton students extended over many years, we can see changes in stereotypes, as well as some uniformities. For example, the stereotype of the American isn't as flattering and positive as it used to be, since *materialistic, ambitious,* and *pleasure-loving* took the three top places in 1967. The Japanese and Germans, in 1950, showed the influence of their position as our enemies in World War II, but their stereotypes had changed by 1967. Both the Jewish and the black stereotype have changed and become more positive in recent years.

It is interesting to see that stereotyping tends to change slowly. We can see this when we look at the black stereotype and see that it has not yet been affected by the "Black is Beautiful" slogan or by the rise of black militancy. We know from our personal experience that we often hold on to stereotypes that we have learned earlier.

Still another Princeton study which provides more information about stereotypes was carried out in 1969.[10] This investigation asked participants to provide *public* and *private* stereotypes. A public stereotype was defined as the manner in which students thought that the general American public would describe individuals. A private stereotype was the student's own description. Public stereotypes turned out to be very much like those in the 1967 study, while private stereotypes were much more favorable. This study suggests that people hold both

[8] Hartley, 1946.
[9] Bayton, McAlister, and Hamer, 1956.
[10] Lewis, Darley, and Glucksberg, 1972.

public stereotypes and private ones. We can see this kind of double vision operating in some male chauvinists who may publically agree, in a disparaging way, that "women are all alike!" while acting and responding with more respect and appreciation toward the very different sorts of women they work with or have for friends.

Princeton students are not alone in stereotyping. In fact, while college students in general stereotype people, they are somewhat less susceptible to it than noncollege adults. Moreover, stereotyping has been shown to be worldwide. UNESCO sponsored a study in nine countries: Holland, Italy, Australia, France, Germany, England, Russia, Mexico, and the United States.[11] Stereotypes about themselves and the people in the other countries were held by people of all the nationalities studied. Most agreement was found on Americans and Russians, but some agreement was found on all of the peoples.

Processes in Stereotyping

Stereotyping is not merely assigning a set of traits to a category of persons on the basis of a negative (or a positive) feeling toward them. That would be too simple a view. It is not true because most stereotypes combine favorable and unfavorable traits. In the UNESCO study, for example, even those who were negative about Russians viewed them as hardworking, brave, and progressive. In another study, where prejudiced and neutral judges were shown pictures of blacks, the prejudiced judges did not assign more unfavorable traits than the neutral ones did, provided the traits *were not part of the stereotype*. In fact, the prejudiced judges assigned *more* favorable traits when those traits were part of the stereotype.

We often use different language for the *same* traits so that they are seen to be favorable about our own group and unfavorable about another group.[12] We may praise *loyalty* in our own group and criticize *clannishness* in another group. Americans often describe the English as *cold* and *snobbish* and themselves as *open* and *friendly* while the English may refer to the same traits by saying that they are *reserved* and *respecting of privacy* while Americans are *forward* and *pushy*. We can see this in our own experience when we feel favorably or unfavorably toward another person. If the person has the trait of being openhanded with money and we feel favorable toward him we may describe him as "generous." If we have unfavorable feelings about him, we may describe him as a "spendthrift."

In much the same way as children fill out a "connect the dots" puzzle to make a picture from a seemingly unrelated series of dots, we fill out stereotypes when clues are presented to us. That is, if we are told that someone is reserved, we say he is quiet. If someone is described as warmhearted, we assume he is generous also. Stereotypes thus contain clusters of traits, which are associated with one another.

[11] Buchanan, 1951.
[12] Campbell, 1967.

Truth or Falsity of Stereotypes

Are stereotypes false, as social psychologists maintain? It appears that they are, because a stereotype requires us to believe that all persons in a certain group have certain traits *because* they belong to that group. We know from our own experience how much real individuals vary and we can understand that stereotypical traits don't apply equally to all members of a group. Still, if we are able to understand that some general traits apply to many members of a group, and if at the same time we can acknowledge individual differences, then stereotypes are not necessarily inaccurate. If, on the other hand, we assume that every member of a certain group has exactly the same characteristics as every other member, we are not describing reality.

In the artificial world of the laboratory we often assign traits to individuals much more readily than we actually do in ordinary experience. If we walk into a room containing an American, an Italian, a Frenchman, and a Chinese, all businessmen in dark suits, our ethnic stereotypes may very well affect how we perceive them. But the more respects in which they differ, the less likely we are to stereotype them.[13] If the American is a baseball player, the Italian an actor, the Frenchman a tuba player and the Chinese a computer programmer, their ethnicity will influence us much less.

Most stereotypes are either false or grossly distorted. But they may have a kernel of truth which has been twisted and exaggerated by language. We have seen how we can use flattering and unflattering terms for the same characteristic, depending on whether we are describing our own group or another. Some stereotypes, however, have truth in them because of sociological facts. That is, some members of an ethnic group may in fact have traits associated with a lower social class because society keeps them in that class. Sometimes prejudice against a group can in fact produce the very attributes that make it the object of prejudice. When, for example, Jews were excluded from Gentile groups, schools, and social organizations, and then formed their own organizations, they were then criticized and stereotyped as "clannish" and accused of "sticking only with their own people."

Summary: The Social Stereotype

Typing people makes our lives simpler, for we could not possibly grasp and react to the full complexity of each individual we meet. Stereotyping is an exaggeration of this process and has three characteristics: (1) people identify a category of persons according to certain attributes, (2) people agree in attributing sets of personality characteristics to that category, and (3) people attribute the complete set to any individual who belongs to that category.

Most stereotypes have a mixed set of favorable and unfavorable traits, indi-

[13] Bruner and Perlmutter, 1957.

cating that they are not simply a function of bias or prejudice. But two groups may have the *same* traits but use favorable language for describing their own group, and unfavorable language for the other group. While stereotyping obviously ignores individual differences, stereotypes do occasionally contain a kernel of truth, twisted and exaggerated though it may be. The attributes assigned may be present in some degree because society creates the very conditions that produce the stereotype traits.

ORGANIZATIONAL PROCESSES IN PERSON DESCRIPTIONS

The descriptions of persons we have talked about so far have been very organized. They were not simply strings of adjectives without a central theme or outstanding characteristic. Our discussion of stereotyping, too, was concerned with a set of related traits. Now we need to look at the organization of traits and how the structuring works. We need to ask some questions about the different elements in a description and how these elements relate to one another. We need to discover whether certain elements occur more often than others in describing people, and how the stimulus person (the one being described) affects this frequency. We need to look also at how elements occur together, that is, when we say that a person has one trait do we also tend to attribute a related trait? Is there some kind of basic scheme we can figure out by organizing the elements we use to describe people? Is this basic scheme different for different observers? Some of these questions have been convincingly answered by research studies; others have been answered tentatively.

Sometimes we receive verbal information about other people in everyday life, and that is all the information we have about them. The news media often provide just a few adjectives about a person. On the basis of that information we often make inferences about the whole personality. When they describe someone as a "tough-talking labor leader," we often make a whole picture of the person. Sometimes this is done in an even more economical way, as, for example, by printing pictures of public personalities picking their noses or scratching grossly, leading the readership to infer a whole set of less than desirable characteristics about these people.

In the laboratory, there are two similar procedures researchers use to understand how links or connections are made among various descriptive terms. In the first procedure, the observer is given verbal information about a hypothetical person and is then asked to write a sketch of the person or to fill out a checklist of traits. In the second, and more systematic, procedure, the observer is told that a person has a particular trait, *intelligence* for example, and is then asked to rate how probable it is that the person has some other trait, in this case, *education*.

Impression Formation Based on Inferences

Energetic. Assured. Talkative. Cold. Ironical. Inquisitive. Persuasive. Can you form an impression of the imaginary person to whom these *cue traits* apply? It is

A smile conveys warmth, a central trait which changes many other aspects of an impression.

rather like our experience when we lie on the grass and look up at the clouds to see forms which suggest elephants, or ships, or babies. The suggestion of the object we see may be there, and from that suggestion we have a whole impression of the image. Just as cloud watching produces differing impressions among different watchers, so do lists of trait-words produce differing impressions among different people who hear the lists. In a well-known research study, college students readily accepted the task of impression writing from the cue list.[14]

In this study, Solomon Asch also found that the list of traits was usually organized into a coherent picture of a person with one trait dominating the description and the others playing a minor role. The word *cold*, for example, from our list, was the central organizing trait in the impressions of the students. A similar experiment has been done with a live stranger described, before his appearance in different classes, as either *cold* or *warm*.[15] Even though some people do not elaborate upon the cue list, most people do indeed form impressions that go beyond the sparse information presented.

Even when the artificial nature of this experiment is changed from a list of traits describing an imaginary person to a more real-life situation, such as a

[14] Asch, 1946.
[15] Kelley, 1950.

realistic-appearing newspaper report about a tennis player, impression formation still works in the same way.[16] Another study described a police chief in identical terms except for one word—*humane,* or *ruthless*—which then colored to a striking degree the impression formed by the students, and confirmed the earlier, hypothetical findings.[17]

Several researchers have suggested that observers have an *implicit personality theory* which guides their inferences about other people. If we think about *cold* and *warm* and the inferences we draw from those terms we can see what kind of theory is implied. We make connections between bits of information about people, and we have ideas about what sorts of traits go with other traits. When we think about a "warm" person, we see someone who is friendly, kindly, open, and interested in other people. If we think about the image-making of politicians we can see how this idea works. A politician is usually described to us in a few simple words and we are then assumed to enlarge that description in our minds to a rounded and favorable idea of the person.

Most researchers have studied *groups* of observers to investigate implicit personality theory, and there has been little work on the single observer. We know from our own political discussions how persons differ in their ideas of descriptive terms for other people so that the same candidate can be seen in various ways. In the case of our police chief, the word *humane* might have very favorable associations for most people and be a positive description, while for some it would imply "soft on crime" and be a negative description.

Implicit personality theories held by individuals do not simply consist of connections between traits that hold for all categories of people. The connections may change for some categories. Research indicates that while they stay the same for such categories as *man* or *student,* they change for some roles, like *bank manager,* which overrides some of the cue traits.[18]

Multidimensional Analysis

Another way to analyze impressions of persons is to use *direct ratings* of them. One can use a scale, for example, to evaluate directly the boldness or timidity of a person without presenting any cue traits. One can also use *trait-sorting,* where a participant is asked to describe several persons by selecting from a list of traits a subset of traits suitable for each person.

When these procedures are used, there are three dimensions around which observers organize their judgments of other persons.[19] The first one is *evaluation,* where we organize judgments according to *good* and *bad.* The second dimension is *potency,* where we look at such characteristics as strong-weak, hard-soft, or stern-gentle. The third dimension is *activity,* where we become involved in judging such

---

[16] Warr and Knapper, 1968.
[17] Warr and Knapper, 1968.
[18] Warr and Knapper, 1968.
[19] Rosenberg and Sedlak, 1972.

traits as active-passive, and hardworking-lazy. In studies where the researcher provided the trait list, these three dimensions formed a relatively prominent and independent basis on which the judges could rate traits. When individuals used other methods to make their selection of traits, however, there were different results. The three dimensions were weaker, and were found to be dependent on or related to one another. Thus, a person high in evaluation would be high in potency and activity as well. An example of the independence of the three dimensions is Snoopy (an animal, but one imagined with person-attributes), who can combine a high level of goodness with submissiveness and energy, all at the same time. Charlie Brown, however, is rated by his associates—and by himself—as below average in all three dimensions.

It is difficult to summarize all the research that has been done on ratings of traits. There is one finding, however, that is particularly striking.[20] When we ask whether dimensions are characteristic of the person under observation, or whether they are representative of the way in which observers *use* the trait words, we find that the organization of traits has to do with the judgments, not with the observed person's actual characteristics. The *structure* of judgments remains the same whether judges are looking at friends or total strangers. The proverb, "Beauty is in the eye of the beholder," is true for most of our judgments of other people.

Summary: Organizational Processes in Person Evaluations

Some traits attributed to people, like "warm" or "cold," seem to be central; other characteristics are related to these. If we know about such central traits we quickly fill in the rest of the impression with related characteristics. These descriptions are altered further if the person is seen in a particular role. These connections among traits and roles constitute a kind of implicit personality theory that people have about other people. Prominent dimensions underlying such trait sets are (1) evaluation—judgments of good or bad, (2) potency—judgments of strength or weakness, and (3) activity—judgments of active or passive. Dimensions such as these appear to be properties of observers rather than of persons observed.

[20] Norman and Goldberg, 1966; Passini and Norman, 1966.

SIX

IMPRESSION FORMATION AND INTERACTION

In the previous chapter we saw how children gradually develop categories for knowing or understanding people. One of the most common ways of thinking about people on the part of both children and adults is to classify them into types. While stereotyping exaggerates the types, a certain amount of typing, which is perhaps more complex than stereotypes, seems inevitable. People are too complex for us to respond adequately to all of their qualities, especially in casual or temporary situations. We also discussed some of the more complex ways in which our knowledge of people may be organized.

The present chapter continues to expand our knowledge of how people are known and evaluated. Differences among observers in the judgments they make are considered. Bias and weighting of different attributes are common. Observers themselves vary in their characteristics and the way in which these attributes affect their knowledge of people. Also considered here is the role of nonverbal information in the impressions that we form of people. This includes not only facial features and body build, but also more active characteristics of the other person, such as gestures, postures, and the like. A final section of this chapter deals with the way in which interactions affect our evaluations of other people. The way in which the observer behaves in part determines what he sees in the other person, because he elicits from the other certain behavior and suppresses other behavior. We also "manage" the impressions that we allow others to form concerning ourselves. Finally, the chapter discusses the factors that affect whether we see the cause of our actions as lying within ourselves or in external sources, an issue that was raised earlier, in Chapter 4.

THE OBSERVER IN PERSON EVALUATION

We have been talking so far about the personality theories of observers in general without paying much attention to them as *individuals* or as *types* or observers. The questions we need to ask now are:

1 How do observers' judgments differ?
2 What are the characteristics of observers whose judgments differ?

Differences in Observer Judgments

We are all familiar with the commonest characteristic among observers—a consistent bias. We know the perpetual grouch who never has a good word for anyone or anything. And we know his opposite, the person who always sees the good in other people, and who trusts their good intentions and motives. The old definitions of a pessimist as one who wakes up to a sunny day for which a picnic is planned and says, "It will probably rain by afternoon," and of an optimist who wakes up to a rainy day and says, "It will certainly clear by afternoon," illustrate these common biases.

Essentially such biases can be interpreted as based upon "weighting" some traits more than others. This "weighting" is one major difference among observers' judgments of people. The other major difference is in the way *dimensions* or *traits* are used. Some observers use many traits and others use just a few. In one study, participants were asked to judge well-known politicians on the basis of similarity or dissimilarity to one another.[1] One type of observer used a simple *good-bad* dimension, while another type added a *Republican-Democratic* dimension to good-bad, and still a third type made many subtle distinctions which reflected a much more complex set of traits.

[1] Jackson and Messick, 1963.

We can see this even more vividly in a study in which participants were asked to rate intelligence based upon information about high school rank, social status, degree of self support, effectiveness in the use of English, and mothers' levels of education.[2] The investigators used statistical analysis to determine the weight each observer, or participant, put on each item of information. The participants fell into eight groups, each using a different weighting system. One group of forty-five observers, for example, judged intelligence almost exclusively on the high school performance and the number of credit hours taken. Another group saw English effectiveness as the principal criterion, with the high school performance secondary, and the other factors not relevant at all. A third group added responsibility and study habits to English use and high school performance.

Observers are not necessarily aware of the ways in which they weight information to form a judgment; researchers need to use statistical analysis to find these underlying bases of judgment. Perhaps the most powerful weighted information is the fact of belonging to a *master status*. This is a person category that leads to distortion of most other personal attributes. Examples include being labeled a criminal, a mental patient, or a genius. We will discuss this concept further in Chapter 16.

Differences in Observer Characteristics

Research attempts to identify the *observer* characteristics associated with different views of people have been less successful than research into the different views themselves. We can show the ways in which people differ in the descriptions they give, but it is difficult to find other common characteristics among observers who use similar descriptions. Earlier we looked at the ways in which young children differ from older children and adults in the way they describe people. We know that descriptions become more complex and varied as people get older. While popular wisdom claims that men and women show wide differences in the way they view others, most research in this area shows relatively few differences.

One possible place to look for observer characteristics in judging people is to investigate the way in which individuals *think* in general. That is, how persons see the world and things in the world should be related to how they view people. One way of describing how people interpret the world is in terms of *concreteness-abstractness*.[3] If people see the world in very concrete terms, they make more definite distinctions: good-bad, right-wrong, black-white; they depend a great deal on authority, "the way it's always been"; they don't like ambiguous or uncertain situations; and they find it hard to take the role of another person, to "put themselves in someone else's shoes." An *abstract* person behaves in opposite ways.

[2] Wiggins and Hoffman, 1969.
[3] Harvey, Hunt, and Schroder, 1961.

Abstract observers, clearly, should be better able to accept diverse information about another person and to integrate conflicting traits. One of the commonest cliches of the movies, the "prostitute with the heart of gold," suggests this combination of strikingly different traits which complicates an easy judgment of another person. In one study, judges were given two sets of adjectives having opposite meanings and were asked to form an impression of the persons represented by each set.[4] Then they were asked to combine these impressions into those of a single person. The more abstract judges were able to do this more easily than the more concrete ones.

In another study, participants were given behavioral information in successive pairs (up to a limit of six).[5] For example, an unfavorable item was "picked up tips for the waitress left by other patrons," and a favorable item was "frequently sent get well wishes to hospitalized friends." Participants were asked to infer the probability of the described person having other behavioral traits. When the information given was consistently favorable or unfavorable, concrete persons estimated higher probabilities than abstract observers did, no matter how many pairs they were given. But when the pairs were inconsistent (containing a favorable and unfavorable item), abstract observers were more willing than concrete observers to attribute other characteristics.

A study of the author Theodore Dreiser is perhaps the most successful attempt to relate the characteristics of a single observer to his descriptions of people.[6] In his *A Gallery of Women*, Dreiser was found to have three major dimensions underlying his ninety-nine descriptive traits. These three dimensions were *conforms-does not conform; male-female;* and *hard-soft*. The last two dimensions were closely related. Dreiser saw women in two ways: as sexual partners and as intellectual companions. The sexual aspect of his involvement with women is shown in the traits he associates with femaleness: attractive, beautiful, graceful, lovely, physically alluring, and sensual. But he also valued cleverness, and employed women as his literary agents. Here, in this aspect of his view of women, we see him assign the traits of defiant, intelligent, cold, and clever.

Throughout Dreiser's literary career he fought against social conventions and was contemptuous of the beliefs of ordinary people. In his descriptions of women we can see how important this theme was to him, as *conform-does not conform* is a major descriptive dimension.

Summary: The Observer in Person Evaluation

Individuals differ in their grasp of the complexities of other people. Some are more able than others to reconcile inconsistencies in the other person. People vary markedly in the "weights" they put on traits of persons. Some form their

[4] Harvey and Schroder, 1963.
[5] Ware and Harvey, 1967.
[6] Rosenberg and Jones, 1972.

impressions from just a few characteristics, while others use a greater number, with different weights. One of the most powerful weighting processes occurs when the person belongs to a "master status," as when he or she is labeled a criminal or a genius.

FORMING IMPRESSIONS FROM NONVERBAL INFORMATION

In many ordinary situations we form impressions of other people even if they don't speak. Or sometimes the speech is so conventional and ritualistic that we use other bases for our impressions. We also find ourselves in situations where we do have verbal information, but we want to check that information against more indirect observation. If we make another person angry, for example, and she insists she is not angry, we may want to check that out by observing her tone of voice, her facial expression, and her posture.

We use two categories of nonverbal information to form impressions of other persons—*structural* and *kinetic*. Structural information includes relatively unchangeable elements, such as the shape of the face and its various features, and body build. Kinetic information includes our gestures, movements, and the state of tension or relaxation we are in.

Nonverbal communication.

Structural Nonverbal Information

Facial features, body build, and general appearance are important in our interactions with other people. We form expectations about others from them, and treat others accordingly, especially when we have little other information. We know from our experience that when we want to make a good impression we try to dress well and pay attention to our posture and general manners and appearance. Our physical attractiveness in part determines how other people behave toward us. A group of nursery children were studied to find out their beliefs about attractive and unattractive children.[7] They saw aggressive, antisocial behavior as being more characteristic of the unattractive, and they saw attractive children as being more independent. The important feature of these beliefs is not whether they correspond to real differences, but that these beliefs advantageously affect the attractive children. Other studies indicate that physically attractive adults enjoy similar advantages.[8]

Specific impressions may also come from various structural features. The human face has fascinated artists and nonartists throughout history. Writers have often referred to the face as the "mirror" of character. The expressions, a "noble brow" or a "mean mouth" or an "aristocratic nose" suggest some of the readings we do of other people's faces. The features, the *physiognomy,* are unmodifiable structures, including the width and length of the face, the shape of the nose and mouth, the size and shape of the eyes, and the planes of the face taken as a whole. We often include also relatively permanent expressions, such as a perpetual frown or a pinched, tense mouth.

When observers have little other information, the facial features become important to impression formation. We may be quite wrong in our evaluations from physiognomy, but such judgments are nevertheless apt to shape our behavior.

Studies of physiognomy demonstrate that observers form impressions of persons from their photographs.[9] Furthermore, these observers use somewhat similar processes to arrive at essentially the same impressions. There is a high degree of agreement among judges working independently. This doesn't mean that their judgments are correct, or are the same judgments they would make if they had more information. But it does suggest that in a limited situation, where the only information available is a photograph of a face, individuals make judgments through processes that they share in common.

People seem to make judgments based on facial information according to various rules. Photos of dark-skinned faces, for example, evoke more unfavorable impressions among white judges; the persons are seen as more hostile, more conceited, less honest, and less friendly. Here the observer is using white-commu-

[7] Dion and Berscheid, 1974.
[8] Berscheid and Walster, 1972.
[9] Secord, 1958.

nity prejudices to make his judgment. Sometimes observers make judgments based upon conventionally agreed-upon ideas. If a photograph then shows a young woman using tastefully applied cosmetics and with well-arranged hair, she will be seen as sexually attractive. Cartoonists have used these ideas we have about faces to suggest to us in a kind of shorthand who are the "good guys" and who are the bad in their strips. While these are not pictures of real people, the sketches capture in the simplest ways some of our ideas about the character that ought to go with a certain facial appearance.

Sometimes the structural qualities of faces suggest expressions which have standard meanings. Persons with slight but permanent upward curves at the corners of their mouths which suggest the makings of a smile are rated as friendly and good tempered. Wrinkles in the brow which suggest tension or hostility are often seen as implying a quick temper, or hostility.

At other times we use metaphor or analogy to make inferences about other people. A person with a *coarse* skin may be seen as a coarse or insensitive person. We often make the analogy on the basis of the function of the *facial* feature. The mouth, for example, is used for talking. Thin, compressed lips, then, will suggest to us that the person should be rated low in talkativeness. We can see how this works in the disparaging description of an intellectual as an "egghead," where the high forehead, covering the brain, is seen as an analog for the brain itself. Eyes, which poets have told us are the "windows of the soul," can suggest dullness, by being closely set, "piggy" eyes.

We must be careful, however, not to overstress the features in isolation from one another. Many aspects of the impressions agreed upon by observers could not be related to specific features. Several studies suggest that the observer forms a total impression which is based upon some complex, patterned view of the face as a whole.[10]

Another cue to a person's identity is his appearance, or clothes. We usually check out instantly whether a person is male or female by his or her appearance and clothing. This is perhaps best expressed by the sure-fire scene in movies and television where someone addresses another, long-haired person from behind as "Miss . . ." and then the long-haired person turns around and is a man. The audience usually laughs at this, often in some discomfort because they find it unsettling to be misled by clues about gender.

The idea that personality and temperament are related to physique has a long history. We can see this illustrated in a famous passage from Shakespeare's "Julius Caesar" (Act I, Scene 2):

> Let me have men about me that are fat;
> Sleek-headed men and such as sleep o'nights:
> Yon Cassius has a lean and hungry look:
> He thinks too much: such men are dangerous.

[10] Secord, Dukes, and Bevan, 1954; Secord and Muthard, 1955; Stritch and Secord, 1956.

Effects of wearing apparel on impressions of personality.

Studies of the relation between physique and personality suggest that observers attempting to make personality judgments of people were influenced by their body build.[11] The close relation of body and personality here was similar to the way we reason by analogy when we make judgments from facial features. Heavy, fat persons, for example, were characterized as loving physical comfort, being slow to react, and being relaxed. Athletic looking people were described as energetic, assertive, enjoying physical exercise, and loving physical adventure. If we look at television commercials we can see how personality traits are conveyed to us through the use of models with specific body builds. The body builds of women in ads selling food items tend to be plump, rounded, and "motherly-looking," in contrast with the builds of women selling efficient household products whose builds are athletic, "modern," and streamlined. The body is used to

[11] Sheldon, Stevens, and Tucker, 1940; Sheldon and Stevens, 1942.

stand for a set of personality traits we are supposed to find admirable or desirable for very different reasons.

Kinetic Nonverbal Information

We can learn a lot about people from body posture and movement. One study used video tape to present verbal and nonverbal information in systematic ways to a group of observers.[12] The researchers found that nonverbal information shifted the observers' ratings $4\frac{1}{2}$ times as much as verbal information. This has sometimes been called "body language," and there seem to be three main kinds of communication.

The first kind of nonverbal communication helps to structure the interaction

[12] Argyle, Salter, Nicholson, Williams, and Burgess, 1970.

between people by giving us clues to *attitudes.* We can pick up information about attraction and about status. For example, in a relationship between a woman patient and a male psychotherapist, the woman may stroke her hair, adjust her skirt, and cross and recross her legs, while he may pull up his socks, touch his hair, adjust his tie. In these subtle ways they are conveying information to one another about their attraction for one another.[13] Another person may indicate a superior attitude toward someone by erect posture, a haughty, unsmiling face, a commanding tone of voice, and a manner of "looking down his nose" at others.

Nonverbal information also reveals emotional states. We often have much more difficulty controlling nonverbal signs of emotional turmoil than we do controlling verbal signs, or words, about our emotional state. It is easier to say "I'm not unhappy," than it is to control and restrain our facial expressions or our posture which can convey a picture of unhappiness to the observer. Finally, nonverbal information is important in self-presentation. By what we wear, how we speak, how we hold our bodies, we give a general impression of what sort of people we are. Some roles are also established nonverbally. When we enter a store, for example, we can spot a salesperson by the alertness of his attitude toward customers, and by the distinctive dress.

Recent research has made considerable progress in unraveling the difficult mystery of how information is conveyed nonverbally. A major research study by Paul Ekman and his colleagues describes how it works.[14] The first thing we must discover, in order to understand nonverbal communication, is how nonverbal behavior becomes a part of a person's repertoire, the circumstances under which he uses the behavior, and the rules which explain how the behavior conveys information. Ekman refers to these three categories as *origin, usage,* and *coding.*

This research found that observers who have had no special training can make accurate inferences about emotions, attitudes, interpersonal roles, and the depth of emotional illness. Different body areas convey different information. The face conveys information about the nature of an emotion. Bodily *actions* give information about both the intensity and the nature of the emotion. Body *positions* tell about the intensity of the emotion as well as the gross emotional state.

Certain actions have fairly specific meanings. Covering, or partly covering, the eyes is often associated with shame or embarrassment. Specific acts, however, must be judged in context because they often vary according to age, physical setting, social role, and different verbal behaviors.

Affect displays, where feelings are conveyed by facial expressions, are more revealing. The primary emotions distinguished by observers in our culture as well as other cultures are: happiness, surprise, fear, sadness, anger, disgust, and interest. The expression of these emotions is complicated by *display rules,* which we learn early in life. These display rules take different forms in different societies.

[13] Scheflen, 1965.
[14] Ekman and Friesen, 1969.

These rules are: *deintensification* (for example, a frightened person tries to look less afraid), *overintensification* (for example, a person expresses more pleasure or pain than he feels), *neutralization* (for example, an agitated person tries to look calm), and *masking* (for example, a person who feels sad tries to give the impression that he is happy).

Every society has rules for the display of affect. In our society a hostess masks her feelings of annoyance when a guest drops a cup of coffee on her new rug; a professor deintensifies his puzzlement when a student asks a difficult question; a person receiving an unattractive gift overintensifies his display of pleasure. These norms vary in different cultures; for example, in some societies it is appropriate to express wild grief and overintensified sorrow at funerals; in others it is expected that sadness be deintensified, and in still others grief is supposed to be masked. Our ability to judge emotions correctly depends heavily upon our familiarity with these display rules and the situations to which they appropriately apply.

Nonverbal Elements in the Communication Process

Recent years have seen an upsurge of interest in the process of nonverbal communication. *Body Language,* by Julius Fast, has enjoyed a considerable success among the general public. Its information is largely drawn from the investigations of Birdwhistell, who estimates that no more than a third of the social meaning of a conversation is carried by words, the rest being conveyed by paralinguistic means—tone of voice, inflection, rate of speaking, duration, pauses, and the like. Similarly, a variety of meanings are conveyed by body gestures, dress, and other aspects of a person's appearance.

Michael Argyle has distinguished several kinds of nonverbal symbols in the communications process, the use of which varies from situation to situation and from group to group.[15] Some of these, less obvious than gestures, head nods, or facial expressions, are:

1 Body contact. Body contact includes hitting, pushing, holding, striking, shaking hands, embracing, kissing, and so on. These activities vary with the relationship and the situation, depend upon whether the individuals are of the same or the opposite sex, are in public or private, and depend, too, upon culture. Contact seems to be somewhat less common in the United States and in Northwestern Europe than in Arabic or Latin cultures.

2 Proximity. The distance persons maintain from each other can signal the beginning or the end of an encounter, and can also reveal the degree to which persons are attracted to each other. Again, there are situational and cultural differences. Conversational distance in large public rooms appears to be

[15] Argyle, 1972.

Effects of posture on impressions of personality.

maintained at 5.5 feet, while in private homes the range is greater, chairs being placed eight to ten feet apart. Latins and Arabs stand much closer when conversing than do Northern Europeans.

3   Orientation. People may sit or stand face-to-face, side-by-side, or at some other angle. The angle of position seems to reflect the kind of relation between people. Cooperating persons are apt to sit at a table side-by-side. Competing persons face each other. Those conversing prefer a corner arrangement. Again, cross cultural influences operate—Arabs prefer the face-to-face position, while Swedes dislike the corner position.

4   Posture. Posture carries meaning. Conventions governing different situations require a different posture for sitting in church or in school than they do for sitting in a more informal setting. Posture is often used to convey superiority or inferiority in status, or to show emotional states as tension or hostility. Since posture is less well controlled than voice, it may serve as a clue to emotions which

might otherwise be successfully disguised. To some extent, posture is like facial expression and has some universality, but here again there are cross-cultural variations in meaning, particularly in the contexts of social situations.

5 Looking. Intermittent looks, changes in the angle of regard, and direct eye contact play an important part in communication. Not only may eye contact reflect attraction, suspicion, or other emotional states, but looking directly at a person or looking away appears to play a considerable role in regulating the flow of communication. There are differences between the sexes in their patterns of visual interaction. Women look more at a speaker than men do, and both look less when the content of a conversation is embarrassing. People look more when listening than when speaking. Proximity and mutual eye contact seem to be interchangeable cues to intimacy, for as persons come closer to one another, the frequency of their mutual eye contact decreases. And people seem to be quite sensitive to cues that indicate they are being observed.

6 Nonverbal aspects of speech. When we speak, there are, beyond the words, a variety of nonverbal, or paralinguistic, characteristics of our delivery, including voice tone, loudness, timing, pitch, speech errors, and pauses or hesitations, all of which have been studied in terms of how they convey meanings as well as control the exchange of communication. Finally, there are various features of the social context which both convey meanings by themselves and which modify and transform the meanings of other elements. Thus, verbal insults traded by people in a friendly situation may have quite different meanings than those exchanged by strangers or persons engaged in a serious conversation. Professional comedians will deliver a joke with a straight face, the seriousness of their facial expression making the joke funnier.

Summary: Impressions from Nonverbal Information

Nonverbal information is of two sorts: (1) "structural"—consisting of relatively unchangeable elements, such as the shape of the face and basic body build, and (2) "kinetic"—consisting of gestures, postures, movements, and so forth. The readiness with which observers use such information to form impressions suggests that they use it in those situations where it is the primary source of information. Kinetic or body language may be used to provide information about attitudes such as attraction or dislike, about emotional states such as anxiety or depression, and about status or role. Judgments depend heavily on "display rules," which specify the emotions that are appropriate for various situations, and which differ in different cultures.

PERSON EVALUATIONS IN ONGOING INTERACTION

The way other people behave toward us affects our evaluation of them. Less obvious than that fact, however, is that the ways in which we treat other persons are apt to bring out some of the other persons' qualities. In the studies we have looked at so far there was little opportunity for interaction. The studies were designed to weigh other factors in impression formation with the puzzling effects of interaction eliminated. To complete the picture of how we develop our ideas and feelings about other people we need now to look at the effects of interaction. There is more research in this field today than there has been previously, although there is not enough yet to yield conclusive results. Current studies do place *some* restrictions on interaction in order to assess its effects. Complete freedom would, in most cases, make it impossible to describe what influences persons to form the impressions that they do.

Effects of the Observer's Behavior

What persons are like and how they are evaluated depends in part on with whom they are interacting. Our view of other persons is based on the behavior that occurs in our presence, and that behavior is based in part on how we behave toward the other persons. If there are hostile observers, for example, they are apt to believe that other persons with whom they interact are more hostile than they are because their own hostile behavior draws responsive hostile behavior. The biblical injunction to "turn the other cheek" is clearly based on this awareness of behavior as responsive.

Impression Management

To some degree, we all try to manage the impression we want to present to other people. We act in certain ways to create a particular image of ourselves. This is not necessarily a calculating or devious way to behave, particularly in situations where the other person expects us to behave according to a certain image. When we go to a party we try to present ourselves as attractively as possible, and assume that everyone else there is trying to do the same thing. These images we create add to our enjoyment of the scene, and our perception that it is something special. When we go job-hunting we try very hard to create an image that will be favorable and help us get the job we want.

One motive for managing the impression we present is our desire for the support and approval of other people. A set of behaviors for accomplishing this has been termed *ingratiation tactics.*[16] These include giving compliments, behaving in a pleasing manner, and agreeing with, or conforming to, the expressed opinions of the other person. The word *tactics* suggests that these actions are performed to gain favor. Flattery succeeds only if we are able to conceal our intentions and show that we have nothing to gain from flattering. One study has also noted that flattery can show diminishing returns, that is, if it goes beyond a certain point it may produce an effect opposite to the one we intend.[17] At that point the person being flattered begins to suspect the motives of the flatterer and discounts entirely his "pleasing" words.

We are all familiar with the employee who is a "yes-man." In experiments involving mock job interviews, people often pretend to agree with the interviewer in order to gain his approval as well. A more subtle form of flattery occurs when we deliberately disagree with a third person present who is being obnoxious so that we can avoid being associated with this third person by our target person, or interviewer.

The social context in which ingratiation tactics are used is critical to their success or failure. The effectiveness of ingratiation varies with the status of the ingratiator. A high-status person appears to be praising another *legitimately* and his behavior is not suspect. When a low-status person praises a superior, however, his intentions *are* apt to be suspect. In one study, a confederate of the experimenter appearing to have high status was evaluated positively whether she gave valid or invalid praise or no praise at all.[18] But when she had low status the

[16] Jones, Jones, and Gergen, 1963.
[17] Jones, 1964.
[18] Iverson, 1968.

opposite was true, especially when she used flattery. In a different experiment, partners who *shared* winnings from a "game" in a *competitive* situation were not liked as well as those who kept their winnings.[19] Apparently behavior which is inappropriate to the situation leads to suspicion and discounting of the action.

Ingratiators act as if they accept certain expectations, but in fact they do not. They pretend to share with the target person a certain set of expectations, almost an implicit contract. If a sophisticated man attempts the seduction of a naive woman he is acting as an ingratiator. He acts the part of a man falling in love, is courtly, attentive, and appreciative. She accepts his actions as appropriate to a romantic lover. But his real purpose is her seduction, and, once that is accomplished, his ingratiating behavior is ended. If he were to attempt these tactics with a woman who was sophisticated and actually shared his goals, they would not be ingratiating tactics, because both parties would implicitly accept the nature of the relationship as transitory and exploitive. It is only when the tactics violate the expected norm that they are *ingratiation techniques.*

Responsibility and Locus of Cause

Fritz Heider has called attention to the fact that when we make inferences about other people based upon our interaction with them, we are concerned about whether the cause of the other persons' actions lies in themselves or in external circumstances.[20] We perceive the cause in one of two ways. First, we look at the extent to which individuals act of their own *volition*—do they try hard? Do they go out of their way to perform an act? Second, we look at their *situation*—do circumstances compel them to act in a certain way? Or do circumstances leave them free to act or not act as they choose? We hold people responsible for their acts when we see them in situations where they are free to choose. When we see them under external compulsion, however, we do not attach very much responsibility to their acts. Parents may be critical, for example, of their bright children who do poor schoolwork because they are considered responsible for their acts— or nonacts. The same parents would not hold responsible their slow children whose work was poor. In the Patty Hearst kidnapping case in 1974, much press speculation centered around this very point. Was she a bank robber by free choice, or was she under extreme duress? Her action, holding a gun during a bank robbery by a gang, could not be properly evaluated without knowledge about her responsibility.

Several experiments varied the actors' volition and put various constraints upon them. In one, a problem-solving situation was set up so that the evaluators were deprived of a reward as a result of the actions of the stimulus persons—who were confederates of the experimenters.[21] The situation was set up in two ways, so that the confederates were seen as either not trying, or as being confronted

[19] Kiesler, 1966.
[20] Heider, 1958.
[21] Jones and deCharms, 1958.

with an impossible situation. When they were seen as not trying hard enough, and therefore as being responsible for the evaluators' not getting a reward, they were less favorably evaluated than when they were seen as not being able to solve the problem, no matter how hard they tried.

Another experiment set up a situation where the participants tried to influence high-status persons (university instructors, or Harvard law students) and low-status persons (college freshmen with inferior backgrounds). [22] The hypothesis to be tested here was that high-status persons do not *have* to accept one's influence. If they do, you are likely to believe they have done so voluntarily, are "good guys," and your liking for them will increase. On the other hand, persons of inferior status are perceived as being more likely to accept influence because of pressure, and consequently their acceptance makes them less likeable than does that of high-status persons. This hypothesis was confirmed; those participants who influenced the more powerful persons liked them more than did those who influenced the lower-status persons.

In yet another experiment, persons listened to a tape recording where one particular man talked a great deal during a group discussion. [23] These persons evaluated the man as having good ideas, and as being the group's leader. Another group heard the same tape but was also told that the man was being rewarded for talking and for discouraging other group members from contributing to the discussion. This second group did not think his ideas were good, nor did they think he demonstrated leadership. They saw his behavior as *externally* caused, rather than springing from his *internal* qualities.

In addition to the notion of *responsibility*, we must also consider *justifiability*. If people are seen as the cause of an action they perform, they are assumed to be responsible for it. If their action is not within their control, they are not assumed to be responsible. An action performed without the actor's control, and under a powerful external pressure, is likely to be seen as justifiable. Whether or not people's actions toward you are justified strongly affects your feelings toward them. For example, if a friend broke a date with you for no apparent reason, you would be angry. But if he or she broke it because of illness, you might well feel sympathetic instead of angry. Society takes justifiability into account in more formal ways. All the degrees of homicide, for example, consider justifiability. A first-degree murder is one where the actor intended to kill someone, and planned to do it. A justifiable homicide is one where the actor kills someone in circumstances where outside pressures make it impossible not to do so.

The effect of justifiability on dislike for an experimenter was demonstrated by giving participants examination items of different kinds on a test where their performance was of great importance to them. [24] Among those participants who were led to believe that they had failed, those who were given items clearly

[22] Thibaut and Riecken, 1955.
[23] Hastorf, Kite, Gross, and Wolfe, 1965.
[24] Pepitone, 1958.

having more than one correct answer disliked the experimenter more than those given "fair or just" test items.

Intentionality is an additional aspect of cause. One child may break another's favorite toy by accident, or with malicious intent, producing very different reactions. As Albert Pepitone notes, intention and justifiability are separate concepts. A good-intentioned act may be unjustified because it is stupid or because it violates some moral value. The road to hell is paved with good intentions.

In one research study investigators worked with *intention*.[25] They presented recordings of supposedly authentic conversations among students with varying intentionality. The subjects were asked to put themselves in the place of one of the individuals in the conversation and to judge the other as if she had behaved toward them in that way. In the "overheard" conversations, O insulted S by disparaging her intelligence. One group of students was told that O had good intentions: she was trying to get S to study. Another group was told that she had bad intentions and was trying to impress her instructor. The researchers found that O was less disliked when she had good intentions than when she had bad ones.

Status is another factor in the attribution of responsibility and intentionality to other persons. The higher the persons' status, the more likely they are to be seen as being responsible for their actions, having good intentions, and engaging in justifiable actions. If we think of the status of United States President Richard Nixon at the beginning of his Watergate troubles, we can see that his extremely high status convinced many people that he had good reason for what he did, was powerful enough to be responsible for his actions, and acted justifiably. Many people simply refused to believe that a president of the United States would lie or would knowingly do anything that was illegal or criminal. Their respect for the office transferred itself to the man. Only after many months of intensive news reporting, with new incriminating facts repeatedly coming to light, did a majority of the public finally come to believe in his guilt. But, even then, many individuals with a special reverence for the office of president still refused to believe that President Nixon's actions were intentionally and deliberately dishonest or criminal.

Many factors may affect the way we attribute responsibility for acts to other persons. In a series of studies, individuals were asked to indicate the extent to which they felt persons were responsible for the accidents they had.[26] At first it seemed that the more severe the accident, the more the responsibility was attributed to the *victim*. One explanation for this refers to a process of *defensive attribution*. That is, the more severe the accident, the more threatening it was for the observers to consider that it might happen to them. They therefore blamed the victim for being careless or negligent rather than face the implications of blaming chance for the accident. Another view, with more evidence to support it, suggests

[25] Pepitone and Sherberg, 1957.
[26] Walster, 1966.

that the observers in this experiment were more interested in avoiding blame than anything else.[27] Here, the more similar the victims were to the observers, the less responsibility was attributed to them and the more they were seen as careful.

Summary: Person Evaluations in Ongoing Interaction

Each of us elicits certain behaviors from the people around us. Thus, our own nature biases how we see other people. Moreover, we actively create the impression that others have of us by presenting ourselves in a certain way. Ingratiation tactics are good examples of one form of self-presentation. A fundamental property of an action is whether its origin or cause is seen as lying in the person or in some external source. If individuals are seen as engaging in an act of their own volition, the cause is typically attributed to them. Perceived free choice also seems to be important for responsibility to be attributed.

---

[27] Shaver, 1970.

SEVEN

LIKING, FRIENDSHIP, AND LOVE

P eople interact with one another in many complex ways and it is often hard for us completely to understand any particular transaction between them. One of the ways that social psychologists try to understand interaction is to separate out the various parts of it. It is as if we bring a close-up camera shot to bear on relationships so that we can see them in sharper focus. Our "psychic" camera will focus in turn on affection, power, and status. All are different facets of interaction. In this chapter we will examine—and focus our attention on—liking, friendship, and love.

This particular kind of social behavior ranges from the "Hi, how are you?" "Fine, how are you?" interchange of two people on a street corner to the intimate involvement of romantic love. We need social intercourse for our well-being—a point most vividly imagined by all of us if we think of what it would be like to be exiled to a place where there was no one to see or talk to. When we do interact with other people, our attraction for them often increases, as does theirs for us. And sometimes it even leads to love.

Later on we will discuss attraction in groups larger than two persons, but here we will talk about *dyads*, or pairs of individuals in a relationship.

Drinking together: a form of friendly interaction.

EXCHANGE THEORY

One of the best ways of understanding dyads is in terms of *exchange theory,* introduced in psychology by John Thibaut and Harold Kelley, and in sociology by George Homans.[1] This theory refers to a set of ideas that are common to many concepts discussed in this book, but here we will examine how exchange theory helps to explain attraction between persons. In exchange theory there are four basic concepts:

1 Reward
2 Cost
3 Outcome
4 Comparison level

Reward is a familiar term. In social terms, any transaction that gratifies us can be considered rewarding. That is, in a friendly relationship, being liked or having fun with someone else are rewards. If other people are sympathetic to us, or if they share our interests, that is rewarding. Another kind of reward we often find in friendship is a validation of our own attitudes or opinions, including our own opinion of ourselves. When someone likes us, and chooses our company, it

[1] Thibaut and Kelley, 1959; Homans, 1961.

confirms our positive opinion of ourselves so that we find their choice very rewarding.

Cost, too, in some senses is familiar. In any exchange there are actual costs, such as effort, fatigue, or anxiety over possibly being rejected, as well as those costs that come from foregoing one activity to engage in another. That is, one cost of watching television all evening may be eyestrain, or sluggishness, and another may be the sacrifice of things we wanted to do but have not done, and now feel guilty about.

If we subtract the costs from the rewards we have the *outcome*. If the cost is more than the reward, we have a *negative* outcome. If, on the other hand, there is a "profit" left over after we have subtracted the cost, we have a *positive* outcome. If we go to a party that is very boring we can weigh the pleasure of the invitation and the satisfaction of fulfilling an obligation to the host against the time we spent being bored, and not doing something more amusing, and come out with a *negative* outcome. If we go on a hike, spend a lot of energy and get fatigued, but then suddenly come upon a spectacular view and a meadow of wild flowers we might, in weighing the costs and rewards, find a *positive* outcome.

The concepts of reward and cost should not be confused with the concepts of positive and negative reinforcement, discussed in Chapter 2. In exchange theory we go beyond these familiar ideas. We are concerned here with the *relationship between individuals*, rather than with the individuals themselves. We want to discover how the characteristics of a relationship emerge and how individuals exchange rewards as relationships change. When we talk about exchange theory, we must also pay attention to the individual's *feelings* about what is costly and what is rewarding. Rewards and punishments are effective only as they are interpreted in terms of the expectations of the people interacting. These expectations are influenced by commonly held ideas about justice and fairness in exchanges. When we are punished, if the punishment is strong but fair, we often feel it less than we do if it is mild but unfair.

Individuals can profit from relationships without necessarily liking the persons with whom they are interacting. For attraction to occur, there has to be an outcome above some minimum level of expectation, and that is called the *comparison level*. This is a standard by which individuals evaluate the current outcome in terms of what they feel they deserve. The height of the comparison level is influenced by all the outcomes known to the individuals: their past experiences in comparable relationships, their estimates of what outcomes other persons like themselves are receiving, and by their perceptions of what outcomes might be available in other relationships.

More recent outcomes are likely to influence the comparison level more heavily than less recent ones. Similarly, outcomes in readily accessible alternative relationships influence the comparison level more than outcomes in almost unattainable ones. The comparison level in a marriage, for example, is unlikely to be influenced by outcomes that might be imagined in a new relationship with some unattainable movie star. But it might be appreciably influenced by imagined or real outcomes in a new relationship with some available single person. This is why so many marriages end only when at least one of the parties has formed a new relationship with someone else. Under those circumstances, the comparison level in the marriage for that spouse is apt to rise considerably.

The comparison level also varies from one individual to another, depending on his or her personal characteristics and orientation. We all know people who expect very little from relationships and who are pleasantly surprised by outcomes that, for another, with higher expectations, would seem quite inadequate.

One study tested the effect of alternative relationships on attraction by using two groups of dyads.[2] One group, made of nine pairs, worked and lived in a small room for ten days with all outside contacts denied—that is, they had no alternative relationships possible. Thus, we would expect their comparison level to be lower than that of a control group of dyads which followed a similar schedule, but which was not cut off from outside relationships.

The interaction for the isolated dyads was strikingly different from that of the control pairs. There was much more self-disclosure, more intimacy, friendliness, and sociability. The relationships resembled those normally found between close friends. This finding is consistent with exchange theory. Because the comparison level of isolated dyads was lower, their outcomes exceeded the comparison level by a greater amount than would be the case for the control dyads. This produced greater satisfaction and attraction in the relationship, which in turn led to progressively satisfying interactions.

Exchange theory is also able to accommodate the idea that opposites attract. Persons who are opposites in such traits as the need for order would be likely to find interaction distressing. A messy and a neat roommate would irritate each other. But with some other traits, persons with different but complementary characteristics would probably provide each other with maximum reward at minimum cost. A nurturing person who likes to help others could be attracted to a dependent person who needs support and aid from others, and their attraction might well be mutual and viable.

SIMILARITY AND ATTRACTION

Do birds of a feather flock together? Or do opposites attract? These beliefs suggest two contradictory principles: First, that people who are similar like each other. And second, that people who are dissimilar like each other. Is one of these correct and the other not? Or could both possibly be correct? Sometimes a good theory can resolve what, on a superficial level, seem like contradictions.

We will briefly examine the evidence for the idea that similarity between people leads them to like each other. Then we will turn to reasons why similarity or dissimilarity might produce attraction, to see if we can make sense of the findings in terms of exchange theory.

[2] Altman and Haythorn, 1965.

Friendship and similarity—two college students.

The simplest test of whether similarity produces attraction is an experimental one. A paradigm developed by Donn Byrne is well known and has been used in dozens of studies.[3] Participants fill out an attitude scale before the experiment. Later they are told about a study designed to explore how individuals judge others under conditions of limited information, and they are asked to read attitude statements purportedly agreed to or disagreed with by another person. For different participants, the experimenters present a different proportion of statements that agree with their own previously made statements. In this way, likeness to or difference from the observer was manipulated with considerable precision.

Attraction was found to vary directly with the degree of similarity: the more similar in attitude the other person to oneself, the more he or she was liked. Attitude statements presented on tape recordings and in color-and-sound movies had the same effect on attraction as those presented in the written, questionnaire form. These findings have been obtained not only with college students but also with children and adolescents in the fourth through twelfth grades, with members of the job corps, and with hospitalized alcoholics and schizophrenics.

Dimensions of similarity other than attitude, including items from personality inventories and questions about personal finances, have been manipulated in

[3] Byrne, 1971.

the same way to produce positive and negative evaluations of attractiveness. Items that pertained to the way that observers thought that other persons had evaluated them—either positively or negatively—had particularly strong effects on the attraction of these participants to the other persons: approximately three times that of similarity in attitudes.

Not all evidence supports the idea that similarities produce attraction. Some recent studies using different procedures have found only very weak or inconsistent associations between attraction and similarity. A questionnaire study of the characteristics of male friends in an urban area found little if any support for the relation between attitude similarity and friendship.[4] More elaborate studies of same-sexed friends, using more complicated measures of attraction and of similarity, suggest that the effects of similarity depend on the things that are similar, and also on the sex of the individuals.[5] Perceived or actual agreement on specific issues may not always lead to attraction, but men who liked the same activities were mutually attracted, while women who agreed on abstract values were apt to like each other.

Quite possibly, experiments conducted with the Byrne paradigm are so positive because all other conditions that might affect attraction are ruled out. Observers are given only information about another person's attitudes, and nothing else. They are asked to make accurate judgments. Under these conditions, where no other information is available, the real relation between similarity and attraction is apt to be greatly exaggerated.

That the relation between attraction and similarity is in fact elusive is suggested by a number of field studies. Theodore Newcomb studied two groups of male college students in successive years.[6] Both groups were initially strangers who lived for a sixteen-week-period in a house provided by him. Various attitudes and values, as well as the students' feelings about themselves and toward each other, were measured before the experiment began and at later intervals.

The similarities with which they began led to distinctive patterns of attraction toward the end of the experiment, but there was no association between similarity and attraction in the earlier weeks. Attraction was greatest when two persons held similar attitudes toward both themselves and the other occupants of the house. As a pair became more closely acquainted, their opinions of the other house members also became more and more alike. Residents also liked those other residents whose feelings and thoughts were similar to their own. A close association was found between attraction and perceived agreement on self-descriptions. That is, students were attracted to others if those others saw them in the same way they saw themselves, including both their faults and virtues.

This dormitory study was repeated with nine smaller dormitory groups at another university, this time including both male and female students.[7] That

[4] Laumann, 1969.
[5] Wright and Crawford, 1971.
[6] Newcomb, 1961.
[7] Curry and Emerson, 1970.

Roommates and friendship.

residents like residents whom they perceive as liking them was again supported, but little association was found between *actual* similarity and attraction. The same study also supported the finding that two individuals who held similar attitudes toward a third person were apt to be attracted to each other. This finding varied considerably, however, among the nine groups studied, suggesting that certain conditions can wipe out the similarity effect.

An investigation of attraction among members of the American team who successfully completed the Mount Everest expedition suggested that the importance of similarity depends on both the *type* of group and the *stage* of group development.[8] Similarity is less important in such task-oriented groups, where people come together to perform a common task. Similarity is more important in groups whose main reason for being is to satisfy social or emotional needs. Such groups are oriented toward simply enjoying human company or toward gaining emotional support from one another for their feelings or beliefs. Just as the Everest team had an overriding goal to accomplish which made similarity less crucial for attraction, the people at a cocktail party, for example, have no other goal than sociability and therefore similarity becomes almost essential.

Similarity is also more important in the early phases of group development than in the later stages. The reason for this may be that later in a group's history

[8] Lester, 1965.

other sources of attraction become powerful enough to overcome any strain which comes from attitude dissimilarity.

One study of courting couples found little relation between attraction and actual similarity.[9] The same was true for several roommate studies.[10] Attraction was not associated with *actual* similarity between the roommates, but it was associated with *perceived* similarity. That is, roommates who liked each other thought they were similar.

Especially impressive is the investigation of roommates in Newcomb's groups, mentioned earlier. In his second-year group, one set of pairs that had great similarity was deliberately assigned as roommates, as was another set that had low similarity. Yet, at the end of the sixteen-week period there was no difference in attraction between the roommates belonging to these two groups.

Summary: Similarity and Attraction

Experimental studies creating a perception of similarity between the observer and another unseen person, and which do not allow factors other than similarity to operate, generally find an appreciable positive association between perceived similarity and attraction. Studies of flesh-and-blood persons in groups and other settings also demonstrate an association between *perceived* similarity and liking for one another. But these field studies find little support for the idea that attraction is associated with *actual* similarity between people. This finding, of course, must be considered in relative terms. Most participants in the studies were not really *dissimilar.* They were generally of the same age, social background, and educational level. Most often they were college students. So essentially the finding is that college students who are more similar to one another do not like each other more than students who are less similar to one another.

One kind of similarity that was most often found was the perception that another person viewed one in the same way that one viewed oneself. Two people who have similar attitudes to a third person also were often attracted to each other. Evidence suggests that, at least in part, these perceptions or feelings are generated by a state of attraction, although, under some conditions, attraction also may be generated by similar views. Similarity is less important in task-oriented groups than it is in social-emotional groups, and it may be more important in the earlier stages of group development. We conclude that similarity by itself is not a principle that can explain attraction. In the next section, we turn to exchange theory in a search for an explanation of the research findings.

EFFECTS OF SIMILARITY ON EXCHANGE TRANSACTIONS

Where do these various findings leave us? Apparently like attracts like—sometimes. But at other times, similarity has little effect on attraction. And the ques-

[9] Levinger, Senn, and Jorgensen, 1970.
[10] Newcomb, 1961; Broxton, 1963; Doherty and Secord, 1971.

tion of opposites has not yet been examined. Whenever we have contradictory results of this kind—and such results are the rule rather than the exception in social science—we must seek a theory which can specify the conditions under which the phenomena are expected to occur, and those under which they are not expected, or under which contrary results ought to be anticipated. So we turn now to theory.

The key is to examine the effects of similarity on the exchange—the way similarity or dissimilarity alters the rewards, costs, and outcomes. That direct reward can increase attraction has been amply demonstrated by Albert & Bernice Lott.[11] Our interest here is in identifying ways in which similarity (or dissimilarity) between members of a dyad can be rewarding. A successful demonstration would resolve inconsistencies in findings on similarity.

Similarities between friends who share the same social background and demographic characteristics—religion, rural-urban background, class in college, or age—may well be a product of two processes involving exchange: (1) opportunity to interact, and (2) the association between similarity of background and similarity of values.

Opportunity to interact is associated with attraction for several reasons. People who are located close to each other are more likely to be *able* to interact with high outcomes because of the low cost of initiating such interaction. This makes it more possible that they will discover behaviors that are rewarding to both. If you don't know a person, you can hardly come to like him or her. People who are roommates have the opportunity to interact whether or not they are similar, so, for them, initial similarity should make no difference in attraction. And that is exactly what Newcomb and other investigators found.

With frequent, continued interaction, each individual is better able to predict the behavior of the other, and predictability enhances attraction. Among other things, predictability reduces the costs of interaction and it increases the level of rewards that are exchanged. At the same time, people who are more similar in such background characteristics as socioeconomic class and ethnic identity are more apt to live or work in close proximity. Friendship among them, therefore, may develop directly from opportunity to interact, and background similarity may be important mainly in providing this opportunity.

There is another reason why similarity, alone, may not be a direct cause of friendship but only a condition, a contributing factor in a more complicated system. Similarities in background are often associated with similarities in values, and these values, being shared, tend to confirm the views of each of the parties. Aspects of the physical world are relatively easy to assess. We can agree that the wall is blue, or that the water is cold. Social facts, however, can only be validated by other persons, and the sharing of values and attitudes makes more likely this *consensual validation* of beliefs, attitudes, and, indeed, a whole version of social reality. People with values similar to our own are more apt to validate our views, and therefore we are attracted to them.

[11] Lott and Lott, 1974.

Further complicating this system are the expectations arising out of common knowledge. Folk wisdom holds that similar people are apt to be friendly, are apt to like us. And our expectation that these similar people will like us has an inevitable effect on the way we behave, makes us more friendly and less defensive, makes them feel that we like them, and in turn makes them like us. The expectation is a self-fulfilling prophecy, having an effect on the outcome, if only because we believe it to be true. One study asked individuals to predict whether or not a stranger would like them, and almost invariably if they thought the stranger would like them, they liked the stranger.[12] Liking for the stranger was related to the similarity of his or her attitudes to one's own, and this might have led participants to think they would be liked. This study shows that attraction could arise from the anticipation of being liked.

The likelihood of being liked is particularly important to individuals who are insecure, unsure of themselves, or especially concerned about being accepted. There are studies in which, compared to a control group, those people whose concern for being liked had been increased by experimental manipulation more frequently chose to associate with those they perceived to be similar.[13] Those persons, however, who expected to be introduced to a group of strangers in a manner that gave them confidence that they would be accepted and liked more frequently chose a dissimilar group.

If it can be assumed that adolescents are more insecure than college seniors, then a finding that similarity in personality traits was associated with friendship among high-school seniors and college freshmen but not among college seniors would be consistent with the explanation of liking in terms of expecting to be liked.[14] Birds of a feather, when nervous, may huddle together, but that is a particular kind of flocking. One recent, rather elaborate experiment, which used a number of groups receiving different treatment, demonstrated a causal chain having the following temporal sequence: (1) similarity in attitudes produced liking for another person, (2) liking for the other person generated the anticipation that one would be liked in return, and (3) the anticipated liking produced a further increment in liking on the part of the subject. A corollary is suggested by taking this experiment together with the data from another inquiry: that the anticipation of being liked also leads to *perceiving more similarity*.

Finally, there are similarities and there are similarities. Some similarities are more significant than others and work in complicated ways. Similarity in abilities and in personality traits is likely to produce an attraction between the similar persons because the trait or ability they have in common allows them to engage in an activity which is mutually rewarding. This is particularly clear in the case of abilities and skills—in a bridge game, the possession of similar skills allows partners to take pleasure in competitive teamwork and to avoid the annoyance and even anger one might feel if the partner were markedly inferior.

[12] McWhirter and Jecker, 1967.
[13] Walster and Walster, 1963.
[14] Izard, 1963.

Abilities and skills are, after all, like social reality in that they are not always physically evident but require validation and endorsement. Thus it may be that individuals have a need to compare their abilities with others who have similar abilities. In the bridge game, then, the players may not only be competing for points but also for consensual validation—which is why the arguments and criticisms over bridge tables are notorious.

Summary: Effects of Similarity on Exchange Transactions

Direct reward can increase attraction. And when the effect of similarity on rewards, costs, and outcomes is considered, it becomes clear that relations between similarity and attraction are brought about indirectly not by similarity, but by its consequences. These consequences differ with the situation, the social context, and the people involved. Similarity can sometimes increase the opportunity for people to interact, making it possible for them to discover mutually rewarding exchanges. And similarity in some attributes is often correlated with similarity in values, which may produce satisfying consensual validation. Where opportunity to interact exists anyhow, similarity would not be expected to be associated with attraction, and this has been found to be the case.

Perceived similarity is apt to increase the anticipation of being liked by those who are similar, as well as the anticipation of liking them in return. This is especially important in situations where one feels somewhat insecure about acceptance, or with persons who are chronically insecure or lacking in self-esteem. In the following section, exchange theory is extended further to identify additional important principles of attraction, principles that become apparent only when attraction is considered as a phenomenon that develops with time.

EXCHANGE THEORY, FRIENDSHIP, AND LOVE

A major advantage of exchange theory is that it reveals unifying principles underlying the various empirical generalizations about attraction between people. Even more important, however, is that such a unifying framework provides an explanation for the exceptions to these generalizations. And everyone has exceptions. You may not like the person next door or someone with whom you have had a lot of interaction. Your best friend may differ from you not only on some characteristic of social background but also on a number of attitudes or personality traits. He or she may on occasion criticize your faults or, even worse, your virtues. Exchange theory treats these apparent exceptions effectively by means of a *process analysis* of friendship formation.

Formative Stages

This analysis focuses upon the sequence of events and stages that leads to the development of a friendship. The sequence may be examined as we describe the

Romantic attraction.

process of an imaginary group, a group of students, say, from various universities, all strangers to each other, who are brought together for a weekend conference.

Exploratory stage   At the first meeting of the imaginary group, beneath the hum of polite conversation, the young men and women who are attending the conference look about them and engage in a process termed *sampling and estimation*. Each person explores, at varying degrees of cost to him- or herself, the rewards available in potential relations with other persons around the room. Consider, for example, Gary, who sees Sandra across the room. There are accidental factors operating at this phase, but there is also the important consideration of whether Gary thinks an approach to Sandra is worthwhile in terms of potential rewards and potential costs.

His estimate of costs will be affected by factors ranging from sheer distance—it takes less effort to talk to the girl standing two feet away than to Sandra, who is across the room—to his guess about the likelihood that he can strike up a conversation with Sandra. If she is already talking with several other people, he may be discouraged by the costs of breaking into the conversational circle, the competition, the waiting around until a suitable opening presents itself. And there is also the possibility that he would have to share with the others the rewards of her attention. These perceived costs and rewards are always weighed against the estimates of reward-cost outcomes in other relationships available at the same time. As for an estimation of rewards, a variety of cues might suggest to Gary that Sandra has possibilities in that direction. Her face, perhaps, suggests that she has certain personality characteristics that Gary finds rewarding in other people (see Chapter 6). She may, by her clothes or manner, suggest that she would have the same interests or outlook as Gary. Perhaps she looks intelligent, a characteristic which Gary values in women.

Assume that he makes the approach, that he strikes up a conversation with Sandra. The conversation, at least at first, may be governed by the dictates of conventional politeness, but a certain degree of exploration is also going on. For instance, one frequent feature in opening conversations is the attempt of one person to discover what he or she has in common with the other. Inquiries about where the other comes from, whether she knows a mutual acquaintance, what her college major is, and perhaps what she thinks about the purpose of the student conference, are all examples of such exploration. What each person encounters in the other depends in large part on what aspects of him- or herself each discloses. This is in part determined by the strength of the desire to continue interacting, which in turn depends on the costs and rewards being exchanged and the successive estimates that each makes about future costs and rewards relative to those anticipated in alternative relations. It also depends on the estimate each has of the effects of these various disclosures.

Bargaining: Negotiation and strategies   At this point, another process begins which, for lack of a better term, social psychologists have labeled *bargaining*. The trouble with the word is that it suggests a highly conscious, excessively rational process, and in this respect the word is inappropriate. The process is not conscious or even rational. And yet, actions occur that do have something of the character of the marketplace. Each person does make evaluations, and attempts to negotiate a definition of the situation and of the resultant relationship that will maximize the outcomes.

In part, such attempts take the form of strategies. Their common aim is to manage another person's perceptions of what one is giving and receiving and what one may expect in the future. One may exaggerate one's own value to others and the costs to oneself of what one is offering. Upon learning of Sandra's interest in skiing, for instance, Gary may exaggerate his own interest in this activity. Or both persons may indicate that alternative relations are open to them and that they are incurring some costs just by continuing the conversation with each other. One function of name-dropping is to indicate to another person the number and the high value of one's alternative relations.

In part, however, attempts to elicit rewards from the other person are likely to take the form of giving rewards that are progressively greater and that may prompt the other to return in kind. For Gary and Sandra, there may be especially warm smiles and a particular attentiveness to each other. At the same time, each person may attempt to lower the costs of the other so as to improve the other's profit position and ensure the continuation of the exchange. Both may discover a difference in views on some subject and tacitly agree to avoid the subject—which would be reducing costs for each other. For each recognizes that differences may be costly and that the rise in costs would reduce the profit of the other person. Where the bargaining process begins and then takes hold, it escalates in a kind of spiral so that, as each is rewarded, each is motivated to increase the profit of the other. This process would be expected to stabilize at the point where the costs of increasing the profit of the other person become so large that more can be gained from some alternative relation.

Although this discussion has focused only on the dyad, the interaction of Gary and Sandra goes on against a background of alternatives. In fact, during the course of the evening each person may sample alternatives and estimate possibilities in other relations. Gary and Sandra are less likely to do this as the evening progresses and their relationship develops. Other persons have also been forming subgroups, and such grouping progressively increases the costs of interaction with alternative persons. Gary might very well have reaped a higher rate of profit with Alma, but her involvement with Fred and Maurice discouraged the sampling and bargaining that might have resulted in attraction between them.

Commitment and legitimation Another process is called *commitment*. Members of a pair progressively reduce their sampling and bargaining with other persons. They stop looking around the room, stop thinking about other possibilities, and commit themselves to a particular other person. Gary and Sandra settle down to an evening together. Should their association endure beyond the evening, and should the couple continue to associate on an increasingly exclusive basis, a final stage, termed *institutionalization,* is achieved.

In institutionalization, shared expectations emerge, and the couple recognizes the rightness or *legitimacy* of the exclusiveness of their relationship and the patterns of exchange they have developed. These expectations will be clear not only to the two of them, but also to other members of the group as well.

Our exchange theory explanation is not intended to imply that the decisions and procedures engaged in by Gary and Sandra, or by anyone else, in the process of friendship formation are calculated and deliberate. It is not at all like shopping for a used car. Such conscious rational processes are perhaps implied by the terms *sampling, estimation,* and *bargaining,* but in a spontaneous, uncalculating way, through long experience in social situations, we all learn how to do these things, guided more by feeling than by any reasoning process. We learn to behave so that feelings guide us in maximizing our outcomes in social situations. Indeed, those who have not adequately learned how to manage their interchanges with others are often characterized as emotionally disturbed or neurotic. Their feelings are compulsive, contradictory, make no sense, are self-defeating, and interfere with the kinds of actions that are susceptible of rational explanation or, at least, this kind of rational analogy.

Romantic love   So far, we have made little reference to the more intense forms of attraction such as infatuation and romantic love. Falling in love is often a gripping, relatively rapid experience. Theories of attraction in terms of conditioning, similarity, or complementarity seem inadequate to explain it, almost absurdly so. To explain this intense form of attraction, we must emphasize physiological contributions to a state of excitement or emotional arousal, and then, along with physiology, the vital role of social definitions of love and romance that give meaning to this emotional state.

Romantic love is largely a product of Western society. Students from societies where romantic love is not a part of their culture and who come to study in British and American universities are puzzled when they read poetry and novels that are based upon love, that often use the love interest as the main plot line. They don't understand what all the fuss is about, and ask why the hero, if he wants the heroine so much, doesn't just offer her father a dowry and take her. The Western cult of love goes back to chivalric traditions of the middle ages, and has grown and been modified since then. Zick Rubin, and Elaine Walster and Ellen Berscheid have suggested that it still operates, and still gives a shape and form to the undifferentiated physiological and emotional pressures from which it takes its continually renewing force.[15] Through social learning, from books and films, from the lyrics of popular songs, from the experiences of our peers and our elders, we learn what the experience is supposed to be like, and we identify the physical and emotional arousal in social ways, defining the state as love. The definition comes with its own expectations—the thoughts and feelings, the attitudes toward the person who is the object of love, and the appropriate behavior toward that person, are all socially and culturally defined. We are coached by a vast crowd in which Petrarch and Shakespeare, Dore Previn and Carly Simon, all add their voices. Cultural norms also specify who shall be partners in love and set some of the conditions that facilitate or inhibit being in love. The dating situation in adolescence contributes to the likelihood of falling in love. The incest taboo prevents members of the same family from loving each other romantically. A widespread norm seems also to limit the age gap between partners, unidirectionally—females are expected to be of the same age as or younger than the male, or at least not much older than he is.

Some attention ought to be given to the nature of the interaction between love partners, particularly as this interaction extends over time. Among the factors that seem to be especially significant are the readiness to fall in love in the first place, mutuality of attraction, commitment and the exclusiveness of the relation, and self-disclosure. These conditions are all susceptible of illumination by exchange theory.

In a love relation, *mutual attraction* contributes in a special way to emotional arousal and gratification. As George Levinger has put it, love relations involve

---

[15] Rubin, 1973; Walster and Berscheid, 1974.

interaction at a relatively rare, deep level.[16] Mutual attraction produces a sense of personal worth, being liked produces liking, rewards in the presence of the other person are repeatedly obtained through shared experiences, and self-disclosure is followed by consensual validation. Especially important is the established principle that we are attracted to others who view us as we view ourselves. In addition, mutual attraction is a state where psychological costs of interaction are minimized. One-way attraction always runs the risk of rebuff. An individual initially attracted to another person without reciprocation is apt to make an effort to attract, an effort that is psychologically costly and becomes increasingly costly. Similarly, inadvertent self-disclosures in ordinary interactions are always a risk. When there is mutual attraction, however, this cost is reduced or removed entirely by an assurance that confidences will be accepted. Thus, a part of the explanation of a love relation lies in its mutuality. Loving and being loved provide special kinds of rewards and reduce costs in a unique way.

This delicate *balance* of mutuality is crucial for the growth or decline of the relationship. If one party becomes more deeply involved than the other, the relationship may curdle. The deeper involvement of one, say the man, can raise the psychological costs of the less involved party, and reduce the outcomes of the former. Unwilling to spend the time the other party demands, the woman, reluctant to commit herself to the same extent, may become cool and withdrawn, changing behavior in a way that is evident to the partner and, in turn, further upsetting the balance.

The mutual commitment in a love relation is important. Dissonance theory, to be discussed in Chapter 9, suggests that commitment to an exclusive source of satisfaction enhances the value of this source. The commitment provides each party with a strong, stable sense of security. Being loved produces a strong feeling of personal worth, and that in turn may generate previously latent aspects of self, bringing into play tastes, abilities, traits, that were formerly unsupported or negatively evaluated. The lover is thus uniquely valued in order to retain this special source of self-support. The sense of security and positive atmosphere created fosters further growth and change on the part of the lovers, and paves the way for realization of aspects of one's ideal self concept.

This commitment is associated with the growth of the idea that the other person is an exclusive source of rewards. The feeling that the other person is unique is commonplace among individuals in love. Possibly this results from the wide variety of activities the lovers have experienced together and can now dwell upon in memory or fantasy. Replaying these memories in fantasy can be rewarding and can generate positive anticipation of further gratifications. And, in fact, some of these activities may be unique because of the exceptional nature of the relationship. Because they have thoroughly explored each other, and disclosed much more of themselves, lovers have a much larger base upon which to build rewarding interchanges. And since the commitment usually excludes other per-

[16] Levinger, 1974.

Eye contact and romantic attraction.

sons as sexual partners, the intense rewards of sexual play and activities are exclusively associated with each other.

Memories and fantasy are apt to play a special part in the intensification of love. Coupled with the idea of romance, in fantasy and in the reconstruction of remembered experiences a lover can build an idealized image of the one he loves. All of us have engaged in such fantasizing, and such fantasy is there for all of us to see in the love poetry and love stories written throughout the ages. When we consider the importance of *perceived* mutual liking among strangers just getting acquainted, or among friends, it is not difficult to conclude that the much more intense constructions of what the loved one is like play a very important part in maintaining the love relationship.

In the early stages of a romance, exchanges are quite subtle. They may consist of a special attentiveness to the other person, a sensitivity to the other's actions and feelings, an effort to be close to him or her, and an unwillingness to leave his or her company. Several studies suggest that the desire for affiliation and the feelings of attraction are associated with greater frequency of eye contact.[17] And other researchers have discovered that the corollary is true: fre-

[17] Exline and Winters, 1965; Exline, Gray, and Schuette, 1965; Rubin, 1973.

quency of eye contact between opposite sex pairs, especially long glances, is associated with intimacy.[18]

These nonverbal behaviors are especially significant when we consider the delicate negotiations toward the mutuality which is so important in the relationship. These behaviors, because they are nonverbal, carry less risk, cost less in the sense that no overt, explicit commitment is made to the other person. Later on, exchanges of symbolic commitment may occur, such as hand-holding. Ultimately, the rewarding nature of the association may be greatly intensified through sexual behavior.

New romances The development of a romance between two persons requires a certain readiness, one that can be described in terms of exchange theory. According to exchange theory, experiences that lower persons' comparison level ought to make them particularly susceptible to becoming attracted to other persons. Readiness for new relationships should be produced by a low comparison level for rewards having to do with self-evaluation and emotional support. If people have not been receiving much support from their present companions, their expectations of support in their current circumstances would be low, and new sources of possible support would affect them more strongly than they would other individuals with higher comparison levels, or more strongly than it would affect them at another time when they, themselves, had a higher comparison level.

Exchange processes in well-known life situations operate to raise or lower the level of attraction or lead to leaving the relationship and forming a new attachment. These include adolescent crushes, broken love affairs, and divorce. The processes may be detailed as follows.

Adolescence is the period in which young people go through the complicated business of emancipating themselves from the emotional support of their parents. This involves a decrease in their reliance upon, and their support from, their parents. Less protected, less "mothered" than they once were, they find some substitute support from their peer group, but this is less intimate and less close than what they were accustomed to as children. Further, there can be pressure from the peer group as they look around and compare themselves with friends who have a boy friend or girl friend, or, sometimes in later adolescence, a husband or a wife. The comparison puts them at a disadvantage. Thus, their comparison level for emotional support is low. In addition, new aspects of self are emerging for which they need acceptance and emotional support. Most notable here is a view of self as a person who can be loved by an age-peer of the opposite sex. Meeting a boy or a girl who behaves as if he or she is strongly attracted to one may make their positive behavior intensely rewarding. If they, in turn, and for similar reasons, have a low comparison level, one's positive behavior toward

[18] Argyle and Dean, 1965; Rubin, 1973.

them will be intensely rewarding. These very high outcomes in relation to a low comparison level serve to heighten the attraction even further. Thus, what happens is a very rapid process of rising outcomes, and the couple comes to define itself as being in love. Mutual rewards are further intensified by engaging in rewarding sexual behavior.

Whether the relation lasts or not depends on its further progress. If types of rewards other than mutual attraction enter into the relationship and the couple finds that they have values, interests, and activities in common, rewards are likely to be maximized and costs minimized. If, on the other hand, they do not share the same values, interests, and activities, the costs are apt to rise, and, as time passes, the rewards of interaction will diminish.

After a broken love affair or after a divorce, there may be a brief period of disillusionment with the opposite sex and a certain wariness about interaction. But like the adolescents, the rejected lovers or the divorced persons' comparison level for emotional support is very low. Thus, it is easy for them to fall in love, and, should they encounter someone similar who behaves as if he or she is attracted, they will be particularly vulnerable and open. This phenomenon is so common that there is a phrase for it—love on the rebound. Or, as Theresa Brewer used to sing, "I don't want a ricochet romance. . . ."

The case of the middle-aged married man or woman who has an extramarital love affair may be explained in an analogous way. In many marriages, emotional outcomes undergo a slow decline from youth to middle age, probably for a variety of reasons. Each spouse may develop independent interests which lead them to give insufficient emotional support to one another. (A *New Yorker* cartoon caption, under a drawing of a man and wife at a dinner table: "I closed a three-hundred-thousand-dollar export deal. You had Mrs. Muncie polish the silver. I see we both had a productive day.")

The comparison level for emotional support gradually drops to keep pace with outcomes. Thus, a middle-aged wife often has a comparison level nearly as low as that of the adolescent or the divorced person. If she encounters someone who provides some outcomes considerably in excess of her depressed comparison level, her attraction toward this new source of emotional support will be very great. Moreover, increased outcomes from this new relation should have the effect of raising her comparison level to the point where it approaches or exceeds the level of outcomes that she experiences in her marriage, so that the marriage itself is threatened, even terminated.

The middle-aged husband's case may involve an additional exchange process. Not only may he be receiving a relatively low level of emotional support from his wife, but in some instances he will have advanced to a position of high status in his profession or work, his income, his possessions, and this may raise his comparison level for alternatives. He has his key to the executive washroom, his mountain cabin, his sports car, and his 30-foot sailboat, and he wants a woman to match.

Changes in Costs and Rewards

We have yet to consider some details of the longer, ongoing process of exchange in more enduring relationships, such as long-term friendships or marriages. We have touched upon some of the risks and perils, but there is more to be said about the rewards and costs and how these change in enduring dyads.

As we have pointed out, exchange theory views attraction as a function of reward-cost outcomes that persons experience in relation to some level of expectation of what these outcomes ought to be (the comparison level). From this standpoint, any change in affect in a positive or negative direction can be analyzed in terms of either a change in costs and rewards or a change in comparison levels. Thus, a person may be less attracted to someone if his cost rises rapidly relative to his reward while his comparison level remains constant, or if his outcomes are constant while his comparison level rises.

Changes in costs and rewards that people experience may stem from any of five sources. First, simply as a function of past exchanges, outcomes may either decline or increase. As each person continues to exchange rewards, the behavior rewarding the other may become increasingly costly to produce because of fatigue, embarrassment, or loss of alternative rewards. At the same time, the value of the reward may decrease as the needs of each person become satisfied and even satiated. Or changes in the direction of an increase in rewards and a reduction in costs might occur similarly as a function of past exchanges. Dependencies may be established, and the needs created may be satisfied by behavior that the partner, as a result of practice, is able to give both more effectively and at less cost.

To illustrate a decline in outcome, consider a hypothetical relation in which one partner makes continual demands for support of a precarious self-conception. Such demands may be met by the other partner at increasing costs in terms of feelings of loss of honesty and integrity, increasing distaste, loss of opportunities to engage in rewarding interaction with others, and so forth. On the other hand, an increase in outcome could be illustrated by a couple in which both partners share participation in some rewarding activity (a sport, making love) and become increasingly skilled at raising each other's outcomes. And as the partners learn to predict each other's behavior, the costs stemming from uncertainty diminish, and it becomes easier for each to elicit rewarding behavior from the other.

A second source of change in costs and rewards arises from shifts in the characteristics of the dyad members. We are not fixed, completed machines, but are continually growing and changing. Not only through the previous exchanges in the relationship, but as a result of experiences in other relations and with the nonsocial environment, new opinions, attitudes, and self-conceptions are developed that require consensual validation. New needs emerge; new goals may be embraced. These changes alter both the worth of rewards and the costs of a person's behavior to others, and theirs in return to him or to her. Such changes may lead to increasing attraction between two persons, as when one adopts a new attitude and finds that the other, whose views were unknown or of little account, is now a valuable ally because he or she holds a similar attitude. But a decline in attraction may also occur. Behavior of the other person that formerly had high reward value may now carry less value, or possibly the behavior demanded by the other, which at one time was expressed with little cost, now comes at a great sacrifice.

A third source of change is modification of the external situation so that the behavior of people in the relationship acquires different reward-cost values. The sudden increase in the attraction of the expert when the situation demands such skills or knowledge is a case in point. But there can be abilities and characteristics that are counterproductive, too. A man who climbs the executive ladder to reach success and opulence will find the behavior of his frugal wife, however helpful it once was, now inappropriate and actually costly in terms of exchange theory.

A fourth kind of change is that which occurs within the relationship itself. A person experiencing profitable interactions becomes increasingly motivated to ensure the continuation of such interaction by increasing the profit of the other. There is a spiral. But spirals go down as well as up. A person whose reward-cost outcome is adversely affected may be motivated to reduce the profits experienced by the other, who may retaliate and thereby continue and even accelerate the cycle.

A fifth form of change happens through the association of behaviors having certain reward-cost values with other behaviors having quite different values. An activity which is initially neutral may, through the association with other behaviors which are rewarding or costly, become rewarding or costly itself. A person may come to enjoy playing chess because such play has been associated with other rewards exchanged during the game—brandy, a fire in the fireplace, an hour of quiet affection and privacy, repeated over months and years. Or the activity may become rewarding to the actor because it elicits rewarding responses from the other—praise for good play, draws and victories, and expressions of affectionate admiration.

Changes in Comparison Level

Rewards and costs may remain the same and still the affect in a relationship can change through a lowering or raising of the comparison level of either of the partners or of both of them. The comparison level may be affected by a number of factors, including the reward-cost experiences in the dyad, the perception of the experiences of others in relations like one's own, and what each of the participants supposes he or she might legitimately expect in alternate relations. The women's rights movement, for example, has undoubtedly raised many women's comparison levels to a point where previous outcomes are no longer acceptable.

The comparison level rises as the outcomes of the dyad members become progressively better, or declines as the outcomes grow worse. The rise in comparison level relative to the profits received may underlie the generally experienced decline in noticeable satisfaction that follows the initial glow that characterizes many relations in their early stages—the first wild flashes of a romance, or the honeymoon in a marriage. Similarly, the decline in comparison level when outcomes are reduced may explain how people find satisfaction in situations they never thought would be satisfactory. The common emotion of envy when another person's outcomes are improved relative to one's own may produce a rise in one's comparison level. This is particularly true when the object of envy is one's partner in an exchange—a husband, say, having terrific expense account lunches, or going to Hawaii for a sales conference. This envy may contain a strong element of feelings of injustice.

We have been talking about the factors that can produce changes in relationships. On the other side, there are stabilizing factors that contribute to steadiness and permanence. Obviously, affect is important to permanence. In most relations, positive affect and permanence are closely associated, but in some pairings this is not the case. People may remain in a relationship even though the outcomes they receive are below their comparison level, and even though they are repelled by, rather than attracted to, the other person.

The loveless marriage, for instance, does exist and is a case in point. The couple may stay together even though their satisfactions from each other are below the level that would result in positive attraction. A couple may remain together because they perceive that in the available alternatives, the costs are even greater or the rewards even less. If it is the wife whose outcomes are below the comparison level, she may feel that she has no chance of getting a better husband, and that, without one, the prospects for adequate support for herself and her children are dim. There may also be guilt over the idea of depriving the children of a loved parent. Or one may fear the disapproval of persons outside of the dyad—the children, in-laws, and so forth. There may be religious sanctions. Or the fear of loneliness can be a powerful brake to the impulse to split. As long as a relation seems to provide outcomes above the *comparison level for alternatives,* the pairing may endure, even though the outcomes are below the comparison level in the relationship, and the members of the pair are not attracted to each other.

Summary: Exchange Theory, Friendship, and Love

The initial stages of attraction are characterized by sampling and estimation of the rewards and costs inherent in alternative relationships. Continued interaction with one person is accompanied by a similar exploration, searching for the more rewarding forms of interaction, and learning to avoid or reduce costly activities. "Bargaining" strategies are also used to enhance one's attractiveness and to obtain maximum outcomes from the partner. These exchange processes, however, are intuitive. They are not conscious, rational calculations, as in the marketplace. In a growing relationship, mutuality becomes important: rewards are given for rewards received. In a late stage, the relationship may be characterized by commitment—an agreement to a degree of exclusiveness. Ultimately, it may be considered institutionalized, a state where both the participants and other people consider the relationship legitimate.

Romantic love involves the arousal of powerful sexual feelings, coupled with an ideology of romance provided by Western culture. The ideology helps to define and structure the interpretation that an individual places upon sexual feelings. The mutual attraction inherent in a love relationship provides special kinds of rewards and reduces costs in a unique way. Mutual commitment provides emotional security and a feeling of personal worth; the partner is perceived as an exclusive source of satisfactions. Memories are reconstructed and fantasies are shaped in the direction of the romantic ideal. The lover builds an idealized image of the partner, which intensifies the love.

The early stages of a romance are characterized by subtle exchanges of a nonverbal character, which, in case of rejection, can be reinterpreted to protect the actor. These stages also require a certain readiness for romance. In terms of exchange theory, this is represented by a low comparison level in existing relationships. Thus, the positive outcomes of a new relationship seem especially attractive. Such life situations as adolescence, a broken love affair, or divorce contribute to low comparison levels and produce readiness for love.

Comparison levels in existing love relationships change for a variety of reasons. Some needs may become satiated. Interactions involving unavoidable conflict may become increasingly tiresome to maintain. The advent of children may, at times, increase the psychological costs of a love relationship; or, under other circumstances, may increase outcomes. Various other stages in the family cycle contribute to changes in comparison level. People change with age, with experience, with education, with psychotherapy, and with advancement in careers or jobs. Finally, whether or not a relationship endures rests heavily on maintaining outcomes above the comparison level for alternatives. If the latter is low enough, the relationship may continue even though its outcomes provide little real satisfaction.

EIGHT

SOCIAL POWER AND MANIPULATIVE STRATEGIES

A necessary condition for individuals to influence other persons to change their attitudes or beliefs is for those individuals to have some power over the other persons. The present chapter discusses the sources of such social power as well as the dynamics of changing power relations, either through the exercise of power or through the use of various strategies. Thus, we are concerned here primarily with the origins of social power and the ways in which its strength is determined. In the chapter after this one, we will look at social influence from a different perspective, considering what goes on in the individuals whom people are trying to influence.

Social power is a property of a relationship between two or more persons. Perhaps the best way of arriving at an understanding of the dynamics of social power is in terms of exchange theory (see Chapter 7). A tentative definition of social power is that the power of person P over person O is a joint function of (1) P's capacity for affecting the outcomes of O, and (2) the extent to which P's exercise of power over O affects P's own outcomes. Thus, the more control P has over O's outcomes, and the less adverse the effects of such control on his own outcomes, the more power he has over O. More simply, if P can give O a great deal at minimum cost to himself or herself, or can use strong coercion with little cost, he or she is apt to have considerable power over O. Parents, for instance, have considerable power over a small son or daughter because of their ability to provide material and psychic rewards or punishments at little cost to themselves.

Social power does not arise directly from the personal characteristics of the individual wielding power, but depends on the relation between individuals and the place of that relation in the context of the larger social structure. The power of corporation presidents, for example, does not come from the individuals themselves so much as it does from the authority vested in their position. As presidents, they can make decisions that radically affect the employees of the corporation and the manner in which the company functions. Even in a more informal relationship, say, between two friends, the social power of each stems from certain properties of their relationship as well as from their relations with other people.

Each exercise of power involves an exchange. Children who get their way with their parents by throwing tantrums get the rewards they want—but only at the cost of an emotional upheaval. The parents are relieved at resolving the emotional crisis, but they incur some cost in letting the children do something they oppose. Underlying this transaction is the mutual dependence of the children on the parents (who control rewards and punishments), and the parents on the children (who want the children to behave according to certain standards). This mutual dependency is at the base of the power that each has over the other. The more powerful persons may exact compliance from the less powerful, but in return they are expected to give their good will, their approval, or some other resource.

DETERMINANTS OF SOCIAL POWER

Most contemporary discussions of social power are based upon three interdependent properties of a relation that determine the type and amount of power that individuals can exert in a given situation: resources, dependencies, and alternatives. Each of these deserves some attention.

Resources

A *resource* is a property or condition of individuals—a possession, an attribute of appearance or personality, a position held, or a certain way of behaving—that

Hugging as a parental re-source.

enables them to modify the rewards and costs of other persons. The values of such resources are of two kinds. One kind consists of what the dependent individuals desire in or from other persons—things they find rewarding. An individual may be a source of love, reassurance, protection, knowledge, material rewards, and pleasures of various kinds. The latter may derive from wit, beauty, handsomeness, sexual passion, or other sources.

Even status may be a resource. People like to be associated with high status people and desire their acceptance. Some kinds of status seem to generalize beyond their base. For example, United States senators may find people acceding to their requests even in nonpolitical situations. Status may be deliberately used, leading to familiar abuses of power.

The other kinds of values consist of what individuals have that enable them to inflict costs on other persons. Possibilities include physical attacks or punishment, fines, insults, disapproval, withdrawal of love, and so on, as well as the *threat* of using these resources to increase the dependent individuals' costs.

Dependencies

The behavior or other characteristics of a person constitute a resource only if they satisfy another person. We can understand why P is able to influence O only if we know why O is dependent on P's resources. Such dependencies must have their source in O's characteristics or in the situation, or in some combination of both. Characteristics of a dependent person take the form of social needs or other attributes that make the resources of P especially valuable to him or her. A person with a strong need for approval and emotional support will be dependent on those persons who can provide it.

The more frequently situations encountered call for a particular resource, the more dependent on it an individual is apt to be. Leaders of juvenile gangs in part derive their social power from their physical strength and their agility and skill in fighting or in leading gang members in a fight. In other groups where friendship and social enjoyment are at a premium, ability to satisfy social-emotional needs is a much more important resource.

Alternatives

The potentialities for influence in a relation between two persons depend on more than just the characteristics of each person and the situation. They extend beyond the dyad itself and are a function of the availability of *alternative* sources of reward and alternative means of reducing costs outside the dyad. The power of a handsome man to attract women—at a party, say—depends in part upon the availability to the women of other desirable men, as well as the degree of cost involved in gaining their attention. Essentially, the power of individuals in a relation is in part a function of the difference between the dependent partners' outcomes in that relation and their outcomes in alternative relations. If they, themselves, have a resource in sufficient quantity, or if they can obtain the resource at low cost in alternative relations, then the power held over them will be weak. But if their outcomes in a dyad are strongly favorable, and alternative relations costly or unavailable, their partners in the dyad will have considerable power over them.

Types of Social Power

As we learned in the last chapter, rewards, costs, and alternatives are not static, but change with the situation. Similarly, resources, dependencies, and alternatives can only be fully understood when they are considered in the context of the exercise of power. The three elements combine in various ways to create different kinds of power. These powers vary in the range of behaviors they influence and in the degree to which their exercise changes the balance of power among people. These types of power are not entirely independent. In most cases they operate jointly. Still, identification of the pure forms is helpful in understanding the idea of power in social relations. We shall discuss five types of power that have been identified by John French and Bertram Raven: reward, coercive, referent, expert, and legitimate powers.[1]

Reward and coercive powers Person P can exercise reward power over another person, O, when O sees that P can provide rewards at minimal costs. A supervisor has reward power over an employee because the worker knows that the supervisor can recommend raises or promotions. A second kind of power is coercive power, which is based on O's perception that P can withhold rewards or increase costs, as when a supervisor denies raises or even gets one fired.

These two types of power, reward and coercive, are similar in a number of ways. In both, power is limited to that range of behaviors for which P can reward or punish O. The strength of both is a joint function of the magnitude of the rewards or punishments involved and the perception[2] that these will be incurred as one yields or does not yield to P's influence attempts. These perceived probabilities depend in turn on (1) the extent to which O thinks he or she is being observed by P, and (2) the past history of O's relation to P. If parents frequently threaten to reward or punish a child but seldom carry out these threats, their reward and coercive powers grow weaker. The effect of rewards and punishments also depends on the accuracy of P's judgments about what behaviors are costly to O.

One difference between reward and coercive powers is that surveillance is often more difficult when coercive power is being used. People will display behavior that is likely to be rewarded but hide behavior that may lead to punishment.[3] Thus, the use of coercion can be more costly to P than the use of reward. With coercion P must divert energies from other activities to watch O constantly.

Referent Power

Reward power has a property that coercive power lacks. It may gradually be transformed into referent power. Referent power is based on identification (discussed in Chapter 2). To the degree that O likes P, he or she will model himself or herself after P and in that way be influenced by P's behavior. Rewards from P tend to make P likeable, and he may become an object for identification.[4] Another determinant of identification, and, hence, referent power, is the *need for consensual validation*. In the absence of some physical basis for assessing the validity of their opinions and feelings, people compare their experiences with those of others, particularly persons similar to themselves. Thus, P may influence O by

[1] French and Raven, 1959.
[2] Collins and Raven, 1969.
[3] Thibaut and Kelley, 1959.
[4] Brigante, 1958.

acting as a model on which to pattern behavior and against which to interpret experiences. This form of power appears to be particularly effective to the degree that P is similar to O and the situation is ambiguous, requiring interpretation.

Expert Power

Expert power is based on O's perception that P has some special knowledge in a given situation, as in the case of a patient who is influenced by a doctor to follow a particular regimen. The rewards obtained in expert power involve feelings of confidence and assurance that the course of action is a correct one. Costs to be avoided by consulting an expert are feelings of uncertainty and fear of doing the wrong thing. The strength of this type of power varies with the degree of expertness attributed to P by O, as well as the perceived seriousness of the problem or emergency. The power of the expert is usually limited to behavior relevant to the area of expertise, but expertise in one area may give rise to expectations of proficiency in other areas as well.[5]

Legitimate Power

Legitimate power is based on the acceptance by O of standards and values which prescribe behaving in a particular fashion. This may include accepting the authority of P by virtue of such characteristics as P's age, social class, position in some recognized hierarchy, or designation by some authority as having a legitimate right to prescribe O's behavior in one or more areas. Because O accepts P's requests or commands as legitimate and right, he is apt to feel guilty if he does not comply. This increases the cost of resistance to legitimate power.

Examples of legitimate power abound. The power held by military officers, corporation executives, government officials, and parents rests, in part, on legitimate power. Somewhat surprising, however, is the extent of legitimate power in experimenter-subject relations. It has been known for some time that college students could be made to engage in extremely boring and seemingly irrelevant tasks at the request of experimenters. But the strength of the experimenters' power, stemming from their institutionalized positions, was not so well understood until, in a series of experiments, Stanley Milgram got a number of subjects to administer increasingly "dangerous" levels of electric shocks to a "victim."[6] The subjects complied with the requests of the experimenter even though the severely discomforting effects were convincingly portrayed by the confederate "victims." The legitimacy of this situation stemmed from the fact that the experimenter was a scientist from a high-prestige university, that both the individual and the "victim" volunteered, and from various comments the experimenter made whenever the participant giving the shocks objected to continuing—com-

[5] Allen and Crutchfield, 1963.
[6] Milgram, 1963; Mixon, 1972.

ments such as "Please go on," "The experiment must go on," and "It is absolutely essential that you continue"—and the participant continued.

The exercise of legitimate power may also include evoking social norms which require O to behave in a manner that favors P. A powerful norm governing the exchange process is the *norm of reciprocity*.[7] When a person does you a favor, you are obligated to return it in some fashion. Where P evokes this norm requiring O to repay some past social debt, he or she exerts influence on O.

The strength of legitimate power depends upon the degree of O's adherence to underlying norms and values. Although legitimate power may on occasion cover a broad area of behavior, more frequently it is narrow in scope. A mother may exert legitimate power over a wide range of her child's behavior, but a department head in a business firm must restrict his legitimate power to job-related behavior.

Continued exercise of power In continuing relationships, people use their resources to influence others only at some cost.[8] Thus, the strength of one's power over another person is a function not only of one's resources, but also of the cost of using them. Parents who spank their children to get them to behave incur the emotional cost of inflicting pain on the children. The more costly the resource is, the less the net strength of P's power over O. A person being blackmailed hesitates to tell the police because of the great cost of exposure.

The types of power differ in the extent to which they may be continually used and still remain effective. A change in the power relation resulting from such use of power may occur in two ways: (1) through the effects on rewards and costs, and (2) through creation of conditions that alter the bases of power.

The first of these changes occurs because continued use of power by P over O directly affects the rewards or costs experienced. Repeated use of the same rewards by P may make them less satisfying to O as O's needs become satiated. For example, repeated salary raises may eventually lose their incentive power, once one is earning a sufficient income.

One common change in the power base is the transformation of reward power into referent power, as noted earlier. At first, many behaviors of children are controlled by parental rewards and punishments, but later the children identify with their parents, performing these behaviors even in their absence. Similarly, the continued use of coercive power is likely to diminish O's feeling for and sense of identification with P, so that P's positive referent power is reduced or negative referent power is established. With negative referent power, O would be motivated to do the opposite of what P wants. Unlike reward and coercive power, expert power is not apt to be affected by continued use, except where its continuation increases or decreases P's stature as an expert, or results in O picking up the knowledge upon which P's expert power is based.

[7] Gouldner, 1960; Blau, 1964b.
[8] Harsanyi, 1962.

In contrast to reward and coercive power, the continued exercise of legitimate power is not apt to lead to an increase or decrease of power. Typically, the exercise of legitimate power by P does not use up his resources. The appeal is to a social norm which is accepted by O, who conforms to the norm because of belief in it. Thus, legitimate power is cheap and easy to use, and is less likely than coercive power to provoke retaliation. But this is true only when legitimate power is legitimately used. Legitimate power may be abused by exceeding the limits of authority. When abuses are flagrant, one's authority is challenged and weakened. Norms of justice discourage exploitation on the part of the more powerful person.[9] For example, for a psychotherapist to seduce a client would be a grave breach of ethics.

Summary: Determinants of Social Power

Social power is a property of a relationship between two or more persons and depends upon the past history of the relation and the larger social context in which it is imbedded. Both the relation and the social context help to determine the elements that enter into social power. These elements are resources, dependencies, and alternatives. A resource is a property or condition that enables an individual to modify the rewards and costs of another person. The value of such resources is determined primarily by the dependency of the second person on the first. This dependency is a function not only of our need for the resource, but also of the availability of alternative sources. If we can obtain it elsewhere at low cost, we are not dependent on a particular person.

The mix of resources, dependencies, and alternatives, as well as the nature of situations and relations, combine to produce a variety of different types of social power: reward, coercive, referent, expert, and legitimate powers. These different types vary in the extent to which they may safely be used without adversely affecting either the relation or the balance of power between the parties. How the elements of power may be manipulated to increase power or to resist increases in dependencies is discussed in the next section.

DYNAMICS OF SOCIAL POWER

Power, as we have seen, is not an attribute of a person. The exercise of power is a function of characteristics of both parties to the transaction, the one influencing and the one being influenced, as well as other people in the situation. But we must analyze further the ongoing process of the interaction.

In the light of exchange theory, an idea of power as a process whereby one person changes the behavior of another is inadequate because it ignores the symmetry implied by the notion of exchange. Not one but both persons are

[9] Blau, 1964a.

influencing and being influenced. They are exchanging behaviors that result in their experiencing certain costs and rewards. What is exchanged differs depending on the type of power used. When an employee complies with a supervisor's legitimate requests, the employee receives continued approval in exchange. Beyond this approval, there is the supervisor's power to facilitate or retard the employee's advancement. If power is based upon identification, the identifier gets psychic satisfaction in modeling his or her behavior after that of the model.

If it is true that each person is influencing the other, we can still understand how one person is understood to be more powerful than the other. The bargain may be such that one person receives valuable behavior from the other in exchange for behavior he can produce at low cost. A nod of approval for an arduous task completed illustrates the disparity between the higher-power person and the lower-power person. Another way of putting it is that the higher-power person can affect the outcomes of the lower-power person to a greater extent. In fairy tales, the king assigns Herculean tasks to the hero in exchange for winning the hand of his daughter, a beautiful princess. He is able to do this only because of her great beauty and royal status, resources which create a great disparity in power.

The power of P over O equals the dependency of O on P.[10] Similarly, the power O can exercise over P equals P's dependency on O. The dependency of one person on another is in part a function of the alternative relationships available to him or her. If the resources one person provides are readily available from other people, dependency on that one person is weakened.

Power relations vary in two independent ways. First, they vary in the amount of power each party has over the other. This depends on the strength of dependencies of each person on the other. Dependency may be weak, as in the case of two casual acquaintances, neither of whom has much influence over the other, or strong, as with two lovers, each of whom has the power strongly to affect the outcomes of the other. A second way in which power relations vary is in the degree of equality that exists between the two persons. A relation is balanced where, regardless of the degree of power and dependency, the parties hold equal power over each other. A relationship is unbalanced when one actor has greater power than the other.

Consequences of High but Equal Power: Balanced Relations

Where both members of a pair have high and equal power over each other, one might think that each person's power would be balanced by the counterpower of the other so that there would be a minimum of mutual influence. It would seem that each would be reluctant to make demands on the other if each were highly dependent on the other—because the other person could impose costly counterdemands or interfere with gratification by breaking off the relation. One might

[10] Emerson, 1962.

further suppose that the potential for conflict in such a situation would be great. But everyday observation as well as more systematic evidence suggests that people who are close friends exercise considerable influence on each other and at the same time maintain friendly relations.[11] This happens because certain arrangements emerge to facilitate influence without the struggles for power which are costly.

In one such arrangement, the two parties assign different values to different activities. A social norm, or rule, is established so that in one situation one party gives way, and in another situation the other gives way. For instance, a pair of friends whose preferences differ may agree to go ice skating one weekend and to go skiing the other. Or two children equally powerful and equally motivated to play with a particular toy may agree to take turns. Many of the rules of fairness or norms of justice have as their function the avoidance of the devastating costs that may arise from power struggles. Or, last, because two people are unlikely to be precisely equal in power, conflict may be avoided by the more frequent acquiescence of the slightly less powerful member. Of course, because the stronger of the two does not always get his way, the parties themselves may not be aware of this condition of slight inequality.

Resisting Influence of the More Powerful Party

An unbalanced relation—unequal power—is unstable because it encourages the use of power, which in turn sets in motion processes of cost reduction and balancing. Consider a man and woman who have been having a love affair, and suppose that in its current stage the interest of one person (P) has lessened somewhat, while the interest of the other party (O) remains high. P's power over O is then greater than O's over P, because of P's lessened dependency on O. If P uses this differential, P may be less punctual for appointments, have more conflicting engagements, more unaccounted-for weekends, and may occasionally see someone else.

These actions raise O's costs in the relationship, but O can reduce these costs to an extent by making excuses for P's behavior or attributing the causes to inadvertent failings in O's own actions. This resolution does not change O's power disadvantage. A second solution helps to restore balance: O may redefine the relation as less serious, more temporary, and casual, and occasionally date other people. This partial withdrawal from the relation reduces O's dependency on P, perhaps to the point where it is equal to that of P on O.

Complete withdrawal from the relation would occur when the costs incurred by the less powerful member result in a reward-cost outcome that is below any alternative, including the alternative of no relation at all. In a voluntary relation, this places a limit on the degree to which the more powerful member of

[11] Back, 1951.

a pair may exploit the less powerful. The alternative of no relation at all is poignantly expressed in Sara Teasdale's poem, "Effigy of a Nun":

> She must have told herself that love was great
> But that the lacking it might be as great a thing
> If she held fast to it, challenging fate.

In another balancing operation, *forming alternative relations,* O's dependency is also decreased so that it is equal to that of P. This happens if O develops an alternative source of satisfaction in a relation with another person. Other balancing processes can be seen operating in the following discussion.

Summary: Dynamics of Social Power

Each exercise of power is not a one-way influence, but is actually an exchange. What is exchanged depends upon the type of power exercised, and the difference in power between the two parties. Where one party is more powerful, the exchange is apt to be quite unequal, and yet be considered equitable. Power relations vary in two independent ways: in the amount of power each person can exercise, and in the degree of equality or balance of power between the parties. If each has high, but relatively equal power, this does not result in a stalemate where neither party has much influence. Both parties can still exert strong influence. This is achieved by adopting rules, or social norms, which typically control the different activities. The norm may call for the parties to take turns, so that each influences the other to engage in activities that each prefers. Rules of fairness help to avoid the considerable costs that are incurred in power struggles.

Several techniques are available for resisting the influence of the more powerful party. Weaker parties may reduce their costs by minimizing them in their own minds. They may participate more in alternative relations, thus weakening the power of their partner. A limit is placed on the power of the other person by the possibility of withdrawing altogether from the relation.

MANIPULATING POWER: STRATEGY AND TACTICS

Among the most interesting aspects of social power and influence are those maneuvers aimed at increasing one's power over another person. Most maneuvers involve manipulating the real or perceived outcomes that the other party experiences. They include actual withdrawal of one's approval or other resources; threats of withdrawal of resources; threats to increase costs of the other party; creation of a state of fear or anxiety that can be relieved by the communicator's resources; appeals to obligations, social norms, or moral considerations; or more complex, gamelike maneuvers in which the communicator induces the other party to act under the guise of some other acceptable behavior.

Most of these procedures will be discussed in the following pages. Two lines of research that explore two maneuvers will be discussed later in Chapter 9. One of these examines changes in attitude that one can create by inducing an individual to engage in a behavior contrary to his attitude. The other examines the conditions under which appeals to fear can be effective in changing attitudes and behavior.

One very direct, simple strategy is to offer some resource to the other party in exchange for a desired behavior. A salesperson may give away a little gift to gain entree into a house and thus gain the customer's attention. A car dealer may cut his commission to make a sale. In labor negotiations, the company's firm offer of a wage increase represents such a strategy. In everyday situations, doing a favor may be such a strategy.

Some less direct, sometimes subtle approaches have already been discussed in Chapter 6 under the heading of impression management. *Ingratiation tactics* are aimed at making one appear more attractive to the other person or at gaining approval and acceptance. These tactics included flattery, enhancement of the other person's self, conformity in opinion and behavior, and methods of self-presentation that either enhance the ingratiator or, by implication, enhance the strengths and virtues of the person who is the target of such tactics.

Invoking Norms

People may use legitimate power as a strategic base by invoking norms, or social rules. In presenting a particular identity, individuals often bring to the fore those norms that require other persons to behave toward them in an advantageous manner. Individuals who present themselves as martyrs make salient powerful norms of justice that constrain others to make amends to them.[12] Similarly, techniques of *altercasting* involve the use of both reward and legitimate power.[13] The term refers to the process by which another person *(alter)* is *cast* into an identity, or role, that would require behavior advantageous to the manipulator. For instance, students may ask a series of questions in a class in order to keep the teacher from presenting too much new material. The teacher may fall into the trap because of the need to enact the role of teacher. Some identities and roles (such as honest person or friend) have positively valued attributes, and being cast in them is rewarding. In this sense, altercasting would be a form of flattery or other-enhancement.

Generally, however, altercasting is used to evoke normative constraints over the other persons. Where altercasting is used to exert legitimate power in this fashion, one of several norms is likely to be invoked. First is the norm of *fairness or justice*. Here, the exchange process is governed by expectations as to what is a just or fair exchange. Sometimes justice calls for each person to receive equivalent

[12] Leventhal, 1967.
[13] Weinstein and Deutschberger, 1963.

The norm of reciprocity: exchanging gifts. (Michael Kahn)

outcomes. Two partners who put an equal amount of work into a task would expect an even split of the profits. In other situations, equity may prescribe that one person get more because he or she has contributed more. Second is the norm of *altruism.* If individuals present themselves as helpless or dependent, those with whom they interact will feel obligated to come to their aid. Finally, the norm of *reciprocity,* mentioned previously, is a pervasive expectation in the exchange process. People are expected to pay back benefits they get from others and thus to keep their social debts to a minimum. For example, those invited to a dinner party are expected to invite their hosts in return, or, if this is impossible, at least to bring a bottle of wine, some flowers, or another gift. Thus, presenting oneself as a creditor or casting the other as a debtor because of past favors is a way of exercising legitimate power.

Debt Management as a Counterstrategy

The norm of reciprocity pervades the exchange process. *Any* benefits we receive from others must be returned in some way. For this reason, the norm of reciprocity leads to problems where one party has much greater power or status than the other—or commands more resources. This creates a problem in repayment. The functioning of the norm of reciprocity is displayed in the popular cinema theme where a wealthy young woman loves a man who has no money and wants him to marry her, but he is reluctant. Sometimes she loses all her money; then his reluctance disappears. In another solution he performs some great feat which makes him famous or wealthy, and then marries her. Or sometimes he simply chooses another woman. In the first two instances the balance of power is restored; in the third, he leaves the relationship.

Whenever there is a large difference in power, various strategies are called into play to avoid the burdensome dependency incurred by the weaker party. First, the motives of the more powerful party may be carefully examined, and found wanting. The magnitude of social debt depends not only on the rewards and costs of both the donor and the recipient but also on the degree to which the donor's acts are perceived as voluntary and without ulterior, or sinister, motives.[14] If a recipient perceives that the donor's acts were required by his or her role, or were insincere, then the debt is reduced. A press agent who buys reporters drinks, or who throws a cocktail party for the benefit of a client, is understood by the press not to be spontaneously demonstrating friendship. Everyone knows that the agent is trying, for obvious reasons, to gain favor with the press. The experienced reporters eat the hors d'oeuvres and drink the drinks and forget about their debt. They don't perceive it as a debt in the first place. In instances where the burden of felt obligation is too strong, we may simply convince ourselves that the donor has some ulterior motive.

Several studies support the importance of the rewards and costs involved, and the intentions of the donor. In one, judgments of the amount of gratitude owing to a favor-doer in a series of hypothetical situations were directly related to judgments of whether the favor was intentional, what it cost the donor to do it, and the value of the favor to the recipient.[15] In another, the amount of help and the giver's intentions were directly related to the willingness of the recipient to reciprocate.[16]

The debt may be adjusted, also, by a consideration of the appropriateness of the favor. An unsolicited or an inappropriate favor is viewed as incurring less of an obligation. In one investigation, interviewers gave flowers to female interviewees both in formal and in informal sessions.[17] The formal setting was less appropriate for this act, and girls who got these flowers were less inclined to return the favor when given an opportunity to do so. Because favors can incur debts, we are careful about the ways in which we accept them, and deem some settings inappropriate.

Studies of how individuals react to having harmed another person reveal actions that reduce obligations in the same way.[18] Obligations can be incurred by harming someone, just as they can be when we accept a favor. Again, the norm

[14] Greenberg, 1968.
[15] Tesser, Gatewood, and River, 1968.
[16] Frisch and Greenberg, 1968.
[17] Schopler and Thompson, 1968.
[18] Walster, Berscheid, and Walster, 1973.

Creating a debt? (Michael Kahn)

of reciprocity operates. The common use of "Excuse me," or "Pardon me," for jostling someone is a means of denying intentionality and thus responsibility or obligation. Or we may reduce the worthiness or importance of the victim, or blame the victim for his or her own fate, cognitively restructuring the situation (see Chapter 11). Sometimes we make compensation, or we may even fall back on self-punishment.

There are times when reciprocation is necessary but impossible, or can only be made at high cost, such as loss of status or an overburdening obligation. In these cases, resentment is apt to accompany gratitude. This may explain the ambivalence many poor people feel about charity: they cannot reciprocate for the aid they have received. On the other hand, they may feel comfortable in accepting unemployment compensation because they have previously paid for it by paying taxes to the government.

Threats and Promises

The effectiveness of threats and promises deserves some attention. What is crucial, of course, is the credibility of the threat or the promise. To be effective, a threat must be convincing. Essentially, the model for this behavior is the game of "chicken," in which two crazy adolescents drive at high speed and head on toward each other, and the one who swerves first loses. Obviously, if neither one changes direction, they both lose, not only the game, but their automobiles, and possibly their lives.

In this situation there is not much incentive to carry out the threat because of the high cost of doing so, and power varies with the extent to which one party can make the other believe that the first one would be crazy enough, foolish enough, stubborn enough, or dogged enough to go ahead anyway. A driver in the game of chicken may speed up so that the only way the other driver can avoid the collision is to swerve. The ultimate ploy is to remove the steering wheel and throw it out the window.

The principle in this last ploy is to convince the opponent that you are powerless to modify your act or position. Negotiators frequently use this maneu-

Parental use of threat.

ver. Union officials on strike may argue that the rank and file will not accept a wage lower than the one they are demanding. Management may try to convince them that they cannot grant wage increases without going bankrupt. "Passing the buck" to one's superior or to one's constituency makes use of this theme so that the plaintiff cannot negotiate his plea with an adversary who has no power.

There is some controversy about the effectiveness of threats in situations where the goal is to arrive at some equitable exchange, as threats may interfere with achieving a cooperative solution in conflict situations. They may turn into a struggle for self-esteem, or into a game. On the other hand, threats as a form of communication may facilitate coordination and improved outcomes and deter competitive or exploitive responses. Probably they can have either kind of consequences, depending on the situation. One study suggests that where rewards are either very high or very low, threats are less likely to be used.[19] Where little is at stake, threats may be ineffective, but where a lot is at stake, they may be too costly. In middling situations, threat and counterthreat may be used, but their use turns into a competition to save face. People may engage in retaliatory behavior even where this reduces their own outcomes—and they will do so to an even greater extent if the other party to the negotiation is *unaware* of these costs of retaliation. So long as the other party is unaware of your costs, you have managed to save face.

Negotiation and Games of Strategy

The process of negotiation for advantage has been studied in laboratories with games of strategy and make-believe negotiations. These games and negotiation situations involve both cooperation and competition. People cooperate because the outcomes of each participant depend upon the behavior of the other participants. At the same time, they are motivated to compete because the interdependence of outcomes allows one person to gain at the expense of another. Because they involve both cooperation and competition, these situations are called *mixed motive* situations.[20]

The prisoner's dilemma is one make-believe situation which has been widely used in laboratory studies of negotiation. This situation has been described as follows:

Two suspects are taken into custody and separated. The district attorney is certain that they are guilty of a specific crime, but he does not have adequate evidence to convict them at a trial. He points out to each prisoner that each has two alternatives: to confess to the crime the police are sure they have done, or not to confess. If they both do not confess, then the district attorney states he will book them on some very minor trumped-up charge such as petty larceny and illegal possession of a weapon,

[19] Swingle, 1967.
[20] Schelling, 1960.

and they will both receive minor punishment; if they both confess they will be prosecuted, but he will recommend less than the most severe sentence; but if one confesses and the other does not, then the confessor will receive lenient treatment for turning state's evidence whereas the latter will get "the book" slapped at him.[21]

Each person is faced with a choice between two alternatives, in this case to confess or to remain silent. The outcome depends on each person's decision. This is represented in Figure 8-1 as a *payoff* or *decision matrix* with the outcomes for each party in terms of the length of prison sentences to be expected, and is read as follows. If X chooses not to confess, we look at the first row, and see that his outcome is a one-year sentence if Y also does not confess. But if Y confesses, X gets ten years! Other choices of X or Y are read in a similar way to identify the outcome. From Figure 8-1 it is clear that the best outcome for the pair where neither confesses is not so good as what might be experienced by either person if one confesses and the partner does not.

An important condition in bargaining and negotiation is trust. Individuals trust others if they behave in a way that would provide their partners with an opportunity to take advantage of them. In the prisoner's dilemma game, the choice of the first matrix alternative by each player can be considered a cooperative or trusting response because it is consistent with defining the situation as one in which the other partner will also choose the first alternative, despite the temptation to maximize his or her gains by choosing the second. In each trial of the game, each player is placed in a dilemma: one can make a trusting response by choosing the first alternative and exposing oneself to the possibility that the partner will exploit him or her, or one can choose the second alternative, hoping that the partner will make a cooperative response which will yield maximum outcomes. In the latter case, one takes the risk that the partner will also try the same tactic, choosing the second alternative, which would yield minimum outcomes to both.

If both players choose the first alternative, each gains five points. The scheme of payoffs (in points or dollars) is represented by Figure 8-2. By cooperating on such a choice, each player can maximize his or her net gain, since neither would have any losses. But this cooperative choice is not the most popular. Depending upon experimental conditions, the percentage of cooperative choices ranges from 10 to 90, with 45 percent being representative. A wide variety of task, situational, and personal variables have been related to the proportion of cooperative responses. In general, the relationships appear understandable in terms of how a given variable affects each player's definition of the situation, including perceptions of the objective of the game, the values and intentions of the partner, the purpose of the experiment, and so forth.

This is most obvious for variations in the experimenter's instructions to the players. Where instructions emphasize that players are partners and that both

---

[21] Reprinted with permission from R. D. Luce and H. Raiffa. *Games and decisions.* New York: John Wiley & Sons, Inc., 1957, p. 95.

Prisoner Y

	Not confess	Confess
Prisoner X Not confess	1 year each	X gets 10 years Y gets 3 months
Confess	Y gets 10 years X gets 3 months	8 years each

Figure 8-1 The prisoner's dilemma. (Reprinted with permission from L. Ofshe and R. Ofshe. *Utility and choice in social interaction.* Englewood Cliffs, N.J.: Prentice-Hall, Inc., 1970. P. 139.)

Player Y

	1	2
Player X 1	+ $5, + $5	− $5, + $10
2	+ $10, − $5	+ $1, + $1

Figure 8-2 Payoff matrix. (Reprinted with permission from L. Ofshe and R. Ofshe. *Utility and choice in social interaction.* Englewood Cliffs, N.J.: Prentice-Hall, Inc., 1970. P. 139.)

can win, they tend to choose the cooperative alternative. Where the instructions define their relationship as a competitive one, they make competitive choices.[22] Where communication is possible, and particularly where people can indicate their intentions and expectations concerning each other's behavior, a cooperative, mutually advantageous relation emerges.[23]

In one study, the responses of accomplices were prearranged by the experimenter in the game situation where players could behave in a cooperative or competitive manner.[24] Some accomplices adopted a "turn the other cheek" strategy, responding to attacks or threats with rewarding behavior and otherwise making cooperative responses. In a second experimental condition, the accomplices adopted a nonpunitive strategy, responding self-protectively to attack but otherwise reciprocating the partner's behavior. In a third study, the accomplices adopted a deterrent strategy, counterattacking in the case of attack and cooperating when partners made cooperative responses. Two additional strategies shifted behavior suddenly halfway through the game, with one group of accom-

[22] Deutsch and Krauss, 1960.
[23] Loomis, 1959; Scheff, 1967.
[24] Deutsch, Epstein, Canavan, and Gumpert, 1967.

plices adopting a nonpunitive strategy after having behaved aggressively and threateningly, and the other switching to a "turn the other cheek" strategy.

Both the responses of the players and their perceptions of the accomplices were clearly affected by the type of strategy used. Players cooperated more with nonpunitive partners, took advantage of those who turned the other cheek, and competed more with those who used a deterrent strategy. As the investigators suggest, the relative ineffectiveness of turning the other cheek may in part be attributed to a special feature of the experimental situation. People may think such behavior foolish and inappropriate in a competitive game situation. In other studies where experimental conditions made salient those competitive norms usually operating in social games, competition increased. For example, where a cumulative score allowed players to check their standing against that of their partners, competitive responses markedly increased. At the same time, features of the gaming situation that highlight the costs of competition through lowered outcomes reduce competitive responses. Thus, generally increasing the amount of rewards at stake increases cooperation.

There have also been considerations of the role of trust in nonlaboratory situations. It has been argued that making concessions creates trust, and on the other hand it has been suggested that making concessions encourages the other party to drive a harder bargain.[25] The model for the more hopeful view—that trust is engendered by making concessions—is that of international diplomacy, where mutual distrust and tension can prevent negotiators from making concessions. It is only when one party takes the initiative and makes a unilateral concession that negotiation can proceed, and a spiral of mutual concessions of increasing importance begins. But evidence for the making of concessions as a way of gaining trust is mixed. Several investigators find that the adoption of a firm bargaining position by a negotiator who makes only small concessions gains the most advantageous terms.[26] There is, of course, the risk of not obtaining any agreement at all. A moderately stiff position may be advantageous, but an extreme position may so drastically reduce chances of agreement that negotiations fail, with costly results for both sides. This would be especially true when the costs of not getting an agreement are high—as in a lengthy strike or a major conflict between nations. Unfortunately, the costs of nonagreement in most laboratory studies of negotiation have been insufficient to gauge the degree to which the second effect reduces the advantages of a firm bargaining position.

Another feature of the typical laboratory situation that makes it difficult to test adequately the relative merits of these two positions is that the attitudes of the participants in the lab must be quite different both in content and origin from the attitudes prevailing in conflicts in the everyday world. The international diplomacy model assumes a high state of tension and distrust between the parties, as in a cold war having a history of mutually escalated conflict. People in

[25] Osgood, 1959, 1962; Siegel and Fouraker, 1960.
[26] Bartos, 1965; Komorita and Brenner, 1968.

a laboratory game may simply be motivated to play the game well in order to maximize their advantage regardless of costs. Whereas unilateral concessions may have the result of engendering trust in a conference room, they may well be viewed as weakness, or at least as silly and inappropriate behavior, in a game. At any rate, more research is needed before any firm conclusions may be drawn.

Summary: Strategy and Tactics in Manipulating Power

Most maneuvers involve manipulating the real or perceived outcomes that the other party experiences. One's own resources may be directly offered or withheld. Or one may present oneself so as to enhance one's attractiveness. Another common maneuver is to call attention to a social norm, using legitimate power as a base. Altercasting places other persons in a role which requires them to adopt some normative behavior. This norm may concern fairness, altruism, or reciprocity—return of an obligation.

A large difference in power between parties calls into play strategies of debt management. The incurred obligation may be denied by questioning the other party's motives, or by redefining the favor which led to the obligation as inappropriate. Where an obligation results from harming another person, compensation may be offered. But sometimes the worth of the victims may be questioned; they may be blamed for their own fate.

Threats and promises are effective only to the extent that they can be made believable or credible. A negotiator may resist yielding by denying his authority—that is, by passing the buck. Or a threat may be made convincing by making it clear that it is beyond your power to stop it from being carried out.

Studies of games of strategy in the laboratory, like the prisoner's dilemma, involve mixed motives: the desire to cooperate and the desire to compete. Where the parties trust each other, they are more likely to cooperate. Distrust produces competition and the attempt to produce maximum gain for oneself. The strategy adopted by each party affects the strategy adopted by the other, and the moves made in these games also vary with the kind of situation that is set up.

NINE

SOCIAL INFLUENCE AND RESISTANCE TO CHANGE

he previous chapter focused on the conditions that give one person power over another and on how these conditions change when power is exercised. The present chapter approaches the problem of social influence from a different perspective and considers what goes on in the individual whom people try to influence. It also focuses in part on the kinds of influence exerted by the mass media. What happens when there is inconsistency between people's beliefs and what they do? If they behave contrary to their beliefs, what happens to the belief? In what way do people resist influence? Are they at the mercy of the mass media and propaganda agencies, or do they have resources for resisting that kind of influence? Under what conditions can fear be used to impel people to comply? What is the role of groups in creating or in resisting change?

BEHAVING CONTRARY TO ATTITUDE

One of the common experiences of everyday life is having to do things that one doesn't believe in. These include some acts that are fatiguing, require a lot of effort, or run contrary to our attitudes. Employees have to do work in a manner prescribed by their superiors, a manner sometimes different from what they would choose if left to their own devices. Often they must carry out a variety of tasks that run counter to their attitudes. In the family, each member cannot do as he or she pleases, but must show some regard for the wishes of the other members. This produces much behavior that is discrepant from attitudes. The housewife and mother, for example, often resents some aspects of her role, especially if she has a strong inclination to follow some occupational career.

These acts are of special interest to social psychologists because sometimes, as a consequence of behaving contrary to attitude, the individual changes attitude to conform to the new behavior. For instance, a newly married man may dislike cooking, but after a time, as he shares household tasks with his wife, he may come to enjoy it. A student may become interested in some "boring" subjects after he or she has studied them for awhile. A politician, urged by constituents to foster a piece of legislation, may actually come to believe in it. Social psychologists have attempted to develop theories that explain such changes of attitude and to discover the conditions under which they take place. These efforts have led to considerable controversy, but through continuing experimentation some insights into the effects of behaving contrary to attitudes have been gained.

The Induced-compliance Paradigm

Acts performed contrary to attitudes are things you do even though you don't want to do them. People have been induced to act contrary to attitude to see under what circumstances compliance may be most efficiently induced. These studies have used an *induced-compliance paradigm*. A *paradigm* is a model for an experiment. The term *induced compliance* is more accurate than *forced compliance*, which has come into common usage, because in these experiments the participants are *not* forced; they comply because they want to cooperate with the experimenters, or because they do not want to appear foolish. The technique in these experiments consists of using the experimenters' power over participants to induce them to behave contrary to their attitudes. As a participant, you reluctantly do something that runs contrary to your beliefs: under what conditions will you change your beliefs and wind up approving of what you've done?

The research divides into two lines, *dissonance theory* and *advocacy*, and the problem, as we shall see, is in reconciling these conflicting, almost contrary ideas.

Dissonance theory   Dissonance theory and its experimental investigation were developed by Leon Festinger.[1]

[1] Festinger, 1957.

Central to dissonance theory is the idea of the *cognitive element,* which is a single unit of knowledge, a blip, a single belief or evaluation held by people about some aspect of their environment, about their behavior, or about themselves. The following are examples of cognitive elements:

I smoke a pack of cigarettes every day.
I am engaged to marry Jane.
I believe that students should have a voice in governing colleges and universities.
I believe that smoking causes lung cancer.
I like John.

The term *dissonance* refers to an inconsistency between two or more elements. Elements are in a dissonant relation if, considering them alone, *the opposite of one element would follow from the other.* For example, the following elements are dissonant:

"I did not need a car."
"I have just bought a car."

In practical or experimental situations, more than two elements are always involved. The dissonance experienced is a joint function of two *sets* of elements. In the context of the present topic, one set is associated with the contrary, or induced, behavior, and the other with the attitude.

Dissonance theory presumes that a state of dissonance is uncomfortable, and that it therefore gives rise to pressures to reduce the dissonance. This may occur either through changing one's attitude or one's behavior, or by adding a new cognitive element. Thus, a smoker worried about lung cancer may stop smoking, change to filter cigarettes, get a physical examination, start a health routine, or simply decide that the evidence against smoking is insufficient.

The amount of dissonance created by behaving contrary to one's attitude may be expressed in the following formula:

$$\text{Dissonance} = \frac{\text{cognitive elements dissonant with engaging in the act}}{\text{cognitive elements consonant with engaging in the act}}$$

In the case of the smoker, the dissonance can be reduced either by adding cognitive elements to the denominator (which makes a smaller fraction) or by removing elements from the numerator (which also makes a smaller fraction). The former is illustrated by switching to filter cigarettes; the latter, by challenging medical findings concerning lung cancer.

There is, however, a curious and not entirely obvious result from the formulation as given above: the greater the pressure to engage in the contrary act, the *less* dissonance is aroused. Pressure to engage in the behavior is an element *consonant* with the behavior, and would enter the denominator, so that the fraction, say, of one-half might become one-third or one-fourth, thus *lowering the dissonance*. Suppose, for example, that several persons with a strong preference for Democratic candidates were paid $100 to go out and persuade other people to vote for Republican candidates, and that this amount was just barely sufficient to persuade them. This would represent much greater dissonance than if the payment were $5,000. In terms of our ratios, the magnitude of dissonance would look like this:

Greater dissonance	Lesser dissonance
Elements of Democratic attitude	Elements of Democratic attitude
Being paid $100 to urge people to vote Republican	Being paid $5,000 to urge people to vote Republican

If the only way of reducing dissonance in this example were for the Democrats to modify some elements of their political attitude in a Republican direction, we would predict that the Democrats being paid $100 would experience *greater* change than the Democrats being paid $5,000. This would happen simply because they would be more strongly motivated to reduce dissonance. (The maximum dissonance possible is reached when the ratio approaches 1.00, because, with a ratio higher than 1.00, the contrary act will not be performed.)

The paradox, then, is that the more we reward people for engaging in acts contrary to their attitudes, the less likely they are to change their attitudes. But if the amount of the reward is barely sufficient to get them to engage in the discrepant act, we should get maximum attitude change. In other words, dissonance theory predicts that there will be an inverse, or opposite, relation between the amount of reward and the degree of attitude change. This is illustrated in a well-known experiment, which has become a classic example of the induced-compliance paradigm. [2]

After completing a boring "experimental" task, participants were informed that a student helper usually brought in the next participant and told him or her how enjoyable the experiment was. It was implied that this helper had failed to show up, and the student who had just completed the task was asked to serve in this capacity. Two magnitudes of reward for serving in this role were used for different groups of students: $1 and $20.

Here, then, is an experimental situation in which the participant forms a strong attitude (that the task is boring) and is then asked to act contrary to that attitude—for a price and, presumably, for other considerations, such as the desire to cooperate with the experimenter. He or she agrees to tell the next student that the task was interesting and enjoyable. After the students had served as greeters, and had given their pep talks, they were interviewed and asked to rate their opinions concerning the experiment on an eleven-point scale from maximum

[2] Festinger and Carlsmith, 1959.

Psychological laboratory with one-way screen disguised as a mirror.

negative opinion to maximum positive opinion. As predicted by the theory, those who had received a reward of only $1 rated the experiment higher in terms of its enjoyability than those who had received $20. Our formula for this experiment would take the following form:

$$\text{Greater dissonance} \qquad\qquad \text{Lesser dissonance}$$

$$\frac{\text{Feeling the task is dull}}{\text{Pressure by E plus \$1}} \qquad\qquad \frac{\text{Feeling the task is dull}}{\text{Pressure by E plus \$20}}$$

In other words, if monetary reward is used as the pressure to win compliance from people, the more money they receive the less their attitude will change. The key to this is that dissonance is at its greatest when the opposing cognitive elements are equal in strength and importance, a condition that prevails when the numerator and denominator are approximately equal. Since the amount of attitude change is a function of the amount of dissonance, it is at the point where these opposing elements are equal that the greatest attitude change will occur. If the opposing elements are made unequal by strengthening the elements in the denominator, dissonance will be less and attitude change will be smaller. This is what happens when participants are paid too much for serving in the experiment.

The most common explanation for this dissonance effect is in terms of *justification*. After making their decision and engaging in the contrary behavior, the individuals experience uncomfortable dissonance. They can reduce this discomfort by *justifying* their behavior. If they can convince themselves that maybe the experiment wasn't so dull after all, then their welcoming speech to the new participants and their assurances that the task is enjoyable are not so disturbing—especially when they have been paid $1. If they are paid $20, then their behavior is easier to justify. The $20 is sufficient justification.

Advocating a Contrary Position

For the moment, we will leave the dissonance paradigm and take up another line of research, *advocating a contrary position*. In some studies, using dissonance theory, individuals were asked to advocate a position contrary to their own attitudes. In the famous $1 and $20 experiment, the participants did tell persons assumed to be the next participants that the experiment was interesting and enjoyable—when in fact it was dull and boring. In other studies, the participants wrote brief essays in favor of a position that the experimenter knew was objectionable to the writer.

Irving Janis has argued that change in attitude comes about not through dissonance, but through the very *advocating* of a position contrary to one's own attitude.[3] To advocate such a position, individuals must do two things. They must: (1) scan their memory for information that supports the advocated position, and (2) construct arguments supporting that position. In a sense, they must convince themselves that the position has at least some validity, and they must therefore change their attitude toward it. If this interpretation is correct, the amount of reward should be directly proportionate to the amount of change—and this would be the opposite of what we expect through dissonance theory predictions. What ought to happen, according to advocacy theory, is that the participants getting greater rewards should produce more and better arguments and reasons, and thus, change their attitudes more in the desired direction.

Various experiments have focused on the mechanism of advocacy as it relates to attitude change. In one, participants rotated as speakers and as members of the audience on different topics.[4] As speakers, they had to improvise a talk on a position with which they disagreed; as members of the audience they simply

[3] Janis and King, 1954.
[4] Janis and King, 1954.

listened. There was a much greater change of attitude when individuals served as speakers than when they served as members of the audience. A follow-up study set up three groups, one of which improvised an impromptu presentation after reading a magazine article, the second of which read the magazine article aloud, and the third of which merely read the article silently. The group that had to improvise a presentation showed a much greater attitude change than those who simply read, whether aloud or silently. Another experiment varied the arrangements by letting participants consider and reject arguments *before* advocating the position supported by the arguments.[5] When this was done, there was little attitude change after the contrary position had been advocated. This suggests that it may well be the generation of new arguments and *not* the rewarding of arguments after advocacy which brings about the change in attitude. In this study, an attitude change could not happen so readily because the participants had been given the arguments in advance and had rejected them.

But the central question is between dissonance theory (and its prediction that attitude change will be in inverse proportion to reward) and advocacy theory (which predicts that attitude change will be directly in proportion to the amount of reward). Several studies have tried to distinguish which theory holds and under what conditions, and the results are instructive, although inconclusive. Proponents of advocacy theory have attempted to explain the inconsistency of the results of their experiments by the idea of *interfering factors*. It has been suggested, for instance, that the usual operation of scanning one's memory and experience and inventing new arguments is disrupted if the reward is so large as to arouse suspicion.[6] While this may help to explain some of the results, it also makes clear that advocacy theory, in itself, cannot handle all the findings. Essentially this occurs because, like dissonance theory, advocacy theory focuses almost exclusively on nonsocial processes that occur within the individual participant, ignoring his relation with the experimenter (with large rewards, the participant is apt to be suspicious of the experimenter and his motives).

Confrontation and privacy   One experiment attempted to reconcile these conflicting results.[7] It focused particularly on the point that in previous studies participants advocating contrary positions had always had an audience (the experimenter, or sometimes a hypothetical audience) who *knew* that they were not expressing their own attitudes. Here, a situation was established similar to the $1 and $20 experiment where the participants were asked to tell another student (who was a confederate of the experimenter) that a dull experiment was interesting and exciting. The maximum reward, however, was only $5. Other participants were asked to write essays for the experimenter, who *knew* that the opinions expressed were not their own. The essays were to consist of a positive description of the experiment.

[5] Greenwald, 1970.
[6] Janis and Gilmore, 1965; Elms, 1967.
[7] Carlsmith, Collins, and Helmreich, 1966.

Under these conditions, the dissonance-predicted inverse relation was obtained between incentive and attitude for the face-to-face situation, while a positive relation was obtained for the essay situation.

The face-to-face and the essay situations differ in more ways than one. The former is public, with an audience whose opinion might be of some concern to participants. The latter is private and may be regarded as a mere intellectual exercise (although the experimenter may be thought of as an audience). So Barry Collins conducted a series of experiments to determine whether the public-private dimension was the critical factor—and discovered that it was unimportant.[8]

What seemed to make the critical difference in his experiments was the *personal commitment involved.* The face-to-face players make a strong commitment without any opportunity to explain to their audience, the other student, that they do not really believe what they're saying. The essay writers do not espouse views that appear to be their own, but are helping the experimenters in a writing exercise. Thus, these findings emphasize a social factor: commitment to an audience. This is a form of social commitment, extending beyond the commitment that occurs in a private, anonymous condition.

Reinterpretations of Dissonance Theory

At the present writing, it seems that some investigations have obtained results supporting each of the interpretations of attitude change, and that the reasons for inconsistencies among these studies are not entirely known. Collins and his colleagues have conducted over twenty experiments trying to find a dependable induced-compliance paradigm.[9] Not only has the original $1 and $20 experiment and its variants proven difficult to replicate, but even the essay design has not yielded consistent results.

If we look back over the research, certain patterns emerge. First, it is obvious that dissonance theory specifies too little. It does not even make clear exactly when two elements are dissonant. The elements of dissonance theory are more ambiguous than are those of certain other consistency theories.[10] For example, in several theories, the *object* is an element (such as John, lung cancer, and so forth), and the *evaluation* of the object is another separate element (such as *liking* John, or the *negative implications* of lung cancer). But in dissonance theory, a single element sometimes contains both an object and an evaluation of the object ("I *like John*"), and sometimes is simply a statement of fact or a statement about one's behavior. This imprecision is perhaps one reason that it is not always clear when two elements are dissonant.

The negation of "I smoke one pack of cigarettes per day" is not "I believe that smoking causes lung cancer," but, logically, "I do not smoke cigarettes." How one element is to *follow from* another, and what the logical sense of the

[8] Collins, 1969.
[9] Collins, Ashmore, Hornbeck, and Whitney, 1970.
[10] Heider, 1958.

connections should be, has never been made clear. There have been suggested answers to these kinds of problems. One idea is that "I should not smoke" and "I continue to smoke" are dissonant because they are two behavioral intentions rather than two evaluations. But is dissonance to be found in behavioral intentions only, and not in conflicting evaluation? The answer has never been specified.

Robert Abelson has suggested that we simply ask people when they think two items follow one from another, arguing that we are not dealing with logical puzzles but with psychological implications.[11] If people feel there is a contradiction, then there is a contradiction, and if there is dissonance, all we have to do is ask about what the dissonant elements are.

The trouble with this approach is that it does not solve all our problems. It does not provide us with a system for knowing in advance what will produce dissonance. Considered more broadly, then, dissonance theory does not provide a set of propositions that enable the experimenter to determine which situations will produce dissonance and which will not. Moreover, this approach is silent about the individual who experiences the dissonance and the effects that his psychological states might have on dissonance arousal and attitude change. This experiencing self, this reacting self, is the subject of some recent studies which have tried to consider the implications of serving in an experiment and the anticipation of future interaction, and how these must be included in any adequate theory.

Milton Rosenberg has also argued that active involvement is important. Participants paid $20 do not have to involve themselves; the $20 justifies acting contrary to their attitudes. But those paid only $1 do have to justify their actions; the actions have to be their responsibility. In Rosenberg's experiment, one group worked for six minutes actively promoting and elaborating a position counter to their attitude.[12] For this group, the greater the reward, the more the attitude change. Another group role played for only ninety seconds, without active advocacy, and their attitude changed inversely in proportion to the reward. Thus, Rosenberg sees the dissonance interpretation as applicable only in rather superficial situations where individuals are not actively involved.

Another emphasis on the individual comes from Daryl Bem's application of attribution theory. Instead of attributing the effects to cognitive dissonance, an internal state, his argument is that individuals observe how they have behaved. They analyze the stimulus conditions that were associated with their own behavior, and deduce *what their attitudes must have been.* This would explain an inverse incentive effect, because if participants are paid $20 for advocating an attitude contrary to their own, they can attribute their behavior to the high payment and not to a genuine attitude. But if they are paid only $1, then their behavior implies that they really hold the attitude advocated.

[11] Abelson, 1968.
[12] Rosenberg, 1970.

The experimental evidence is sketchy, despite the prodigious amount of work that has been done. But it does seem reasonable to assume that the different conditions of the many experiments on attitude change create different degrees of engagement of *self* on the part of the participants. The evidence suggests that this may be one of the conditions accounting for conflicting results.

The consequences of one's actions have also been shown to be important, and it is likely that this is related to engagement of self. In one study, participants learned either that they had succeeded in convincing their supposedly naïve colleague that a dull task was interesting and enjoyable, or that they had failed.[13] Only those who thought they had succeeded changed their attitude in inverse proportion to the amount of incentive. This suggests that resolving dissonance by justifying it through attitude change is necessary only when one's act has social consequences.

Elliot Aronson has also suggested that the crucial determinant in induced-compliance studies is whether or not the counterattitudinal behavior threatens to diminish the individual's self-concept by virtue of its consequences for the audience.[14] Dissonance, he argues, is between a cognition about the self and a cognition about a behavior which violates this *self* concept (such as, "I am a good and decent person"; "I have committed a bad and indecent act—misleading another person").

Actually, if we stop viewing participants in experiments as passive objects manipulated by the experimenter, and instead think of them as agents who are performing actions that have certain intentions, it is possible to use these ideas of self-involvement and the consequences of one's actions for other persons to form a theory that resolves some of the contradictory findings and helps to specify the conditions for various outcomes. One group of investigators has suggested a theory that accomplishes some of these objectives, proposing that it is not an internal state of "dissonance" that accounts for a person's change in attitude or behavior, but rather a desire to *behave consistently toward other persons*.[15]

First, this group calls attention to the point made in Chapter 6 that observers cannot infer the true intentions of actors as long as their behavior is controlled by external factors: for intentions to be attributed, they have to be seen as internal. They must be the locus of the cause. So, if pairs of *acts* are considered, rather than pairs of cognitive elements, the actors will feel a contradiction only if *both* acts are likely to be seen by other persons as internal to them. If one act is externally caused (by the payment of $20), the actors should not experience much contradiction. Such a contradiction *is* apt to be felt, however, when they accept only $1 for telling a lie to another participant about the nature of the experiment. Here they could much more easily have refused, and their acceptance can be seen as internally caused. And to resolve the contradiction, they change their attitudes toward the experiment to make their acts less deceptive.

[13] Cooper and Worchel, 1970.
[14] Aronson, 1968, 1969.
[15] Tedeschi, Schlenker, and Bonoma, 1971.

We may note further that the crucial point is not so much whether the actors *experience* a contradiction, but rather whether they think their audience *sees* one. Only in the latter case would they change their attitude to resolve the contradiction. So, if their behavior is anonymous, as in some of the essay writing experiments, they would not change their attitudes in inverse proportion to incentive. They are more likely to do so when their behavior is public and has significant consequences for the people affected by their actions. Moreover, this thinking stresses the participants' knowledge that they are performing under the critical eye of the experimenter, and how they think their performance is being viewed by him or her is critical in determining the direction that their actions take.

While this theory is too new to be evaluated with certainty, it does take into account more fully than other theories the social nature and setting of the influence process, and, with sufficient development, it may be able to encompass more of the empirical findings than the dissonance or advocacy theories are at present able to cover.

Summary: Behaving Contrary to Attitude

Being required to behave contrary to one's attitude is a common experience in everyday life. Psychologists have offered two theoretical explanations for the fact that these experiences are often accompanied by a change in the attitude to make it consistent with the new behavior. The first of these explanations is dissonance theory, and the other, advocacy theory. Dissonance is an uncomfortable state resulting from the contradiction between one's attitude and what one is doing. One way of relieving this state is to change one's attitude to conform to one's behavior. Although this sometimes happens in experiments, the results of many studies are quite inconsistent. This has led to the advocacy theory, which provides a different explanation for attitude change.

Advocacy interpretations have emphasized several explanatory mechanisms that are associated with the fact that, when individuals behave contrary to their attitudes, they are often advocating a position contrary to that attitude. Examples would be engaging in a debate while taking a position that has been assigned but which is not one's own, or writing an essay on some position in order to satisfy the request of an instructor or experimenter. The advocacy interpretation stresses that advocates are actively thinking up arguments and evidence for their assumed positions. Because the individuals are rewarded for these efforts, the arguments and evidence should be reinforced. As in the case of dissonance theory, research evidence supporting advocacy theory is inconclusive.

Our view is that the social nature of behaving contrary to one's attitude has not been sufficiently taken into account in the design of research studies and in the development of theory. More recent work on contrary behavior has examined the setting and the social context of the experimental work on this topic. For example, it has been shown that the consequences for other persons of behaving contrary to one's own attitude is important. The way in which one presents oneself while engaging in contrary behavior also appears to enter in. A final resolution of these lines of research will only be achieved by taking the role of the experimenter and the broader social context into account.

GROUPS AS AGENTS OF CHANGE

Groups may be powerful agents for change, or they may act to resist it. This section identifies some of the group processes that account for change in attitudes or behavior. At the end of the chapter we will discuss the role of groups in resistance to change.

Groups that engage in discussion as a preparation for action "loosen" or "weaken" some attitudes or behaviors, making them amenable to change. This is particularly the case where the discussion brings out the presence of disagreement that was unsuspected before. In such discussions, people *commit* themselves to certain beliefs or certain lines of action in a way that might differ from their earlier stands. Once having made a decision to act in a particular way, the act is more likely to be carried out, and, as we learned in the previous section, attitudes are likely to change to conform to the new behavior. Many group members may also have been undecided, and the high visibility that discussion gives to the group consensus is apt to influence them in particular directions. Finally, group leaders or other influential members influence the rank-and-file members by asserting their beliefs in discussion.

People-changing Groups

Powerful changes in attitudes and behavior can be wrought by groups organized specifically for that purpose. Let us consider a type of group where members are admitted only if they agree to change themselves radically. A group, moreover, where members eat together, work together, play together, live in the same building, and continue in this way for a long time. Not many groups meet these qualifications, because most groups quickly stabilize to enforce conformity rather than change, and accept new members who are like older members rather than different from them. One such set of groups, however, comprise the Synanon Foundation. Members of these groups are former drug addicts, and new members are individuals who, generally in desperation, come to Synanon to get rid of their addiction.

New members are questioned and their motivation to join is assessed; if they are unwilling to submit to the rules of the house, they can't join. Synanon houses constitute a kind of primary group. Members develop close attachments and experience intense emotions under house conditions. Once members have joined, they become totally dependent on Synanon—for a place to live, eat, sleep, work, and play. This powerful *dependency,* with Synanon controlling all *resources,* gives the house enormous power over its members. (See Chapter 8 for an analysis of the sources of power.)

While there has been no carefully designed, evaluative study of Synanon, it seems clear that it is often effective in rehabilitating people addicted to drugs. Central to the change process are group discussions, called *synanons* (the word comes from a mispronunciation of "seminars"). These sessions are held three times a week with ten to fifteen people participating. An older, experienced member of the house serves loosely as a leader. Emphasis is on extreme honesty, with expression of feeling not only allowed but encouraged. Typically, individuals with an addiction have built up certain delusions about themselves and their behavior and exhibit evasive and negative behavior both in house living and in the group. All such evasive behavior and pretenses are savagely attacked by members of the synanon who try to force individuals to adopt realistic views of themselves and to shape up their behavior. Yet in the background, underlying these attacks, is strong acceptance and emotional support of each individual member by the group. Members of the house are the only friends other members have; it is their only home, and they are one another's family. They have no *alternatives*. Synanon is their last chance, their last haven; the "outside" is hopeless. They must succeed in this setting or fail altogether. The following excerpt gives some of the flavor of a synanon session, in which the theme was antiprejudice. (Don is Jewish, Pete and Wilbur are black, the other members are white.)

NANCY: Don, you can do the right thing in here by spewing your prejudice garbage in a synanon, where more people can look at it with you. Get it out here and now. Then maybe you won't be spreading it all over the house.

PETE: You gutless mother-fucker, you won't call him [Wilbur] anything to his face. You'd rather go behind his back and call him something. Why don't you call it to his face?

DON: We've spoken about my prejudice already in synanons.

PETE: Tell it to him now.

DON: I'm not going to tell it to him again. I told him how I feel about him.

PETE: How do you feel about him, then?

DON: [in a ludicrous understatement of his feelings]: I can't see a colored guy doing executive work or in charge of me.

JACK: What did you tell Sherry [a black woman] the other night? You know, all colored broads ain't supposed to do nothing but clean up, you know?

DON: When did I tell her this?

JACK: In synanon the other—

DON: Oh, you say a lot of things to trigger the group.

JACK: That's how you feel. Man, why not admit it? Get it out. You might feel better!

GEORGE: This is how you feel. You know you've had this all your life. All colored women coming and cleaning your house and so forth, once a week or every other week, you know? And this is the condition you've had.

PETE: You fat, ignorant slob. That's exactly what you are. And you don't have any guts, man—not a gut in your whole fuckin' body. . . . You're the biggest asshole in the house and biggest coward.

DON: [Trying to act unprovoked] Right.

PETE:	I could probably get up and spit in your face right now and all you'd do is wipe it off.
DON:	Go ahead and try it.
PETE:	You fuckin' coward.
DON:	Go ahead and try it.

[A strict house rule against physical violence permits expression of real feelings without retaliation.]

PETE:	What do you think of me right now?
DON:	What am I suppose to do, get mad at you now?
PETE:	I'm mad at your crazy ass right now. You know what you are to me right now?
DON:	What?
PETE:	You're exactly like the suckers down in Birmingham last week that turned dogs loose on people to do what they couldn't do . . .
DON:	That's good; that means you respect me, you're afraid of me.
PETE:	[Sarcastically] Yeah, I respect you all right.
DON:	Definitely.
HERB:	Do you think anybody in here respects you, Don? . . . .
DON:	No.[16]

While Synanon living groups appear to be powerful agents for change their effect may be limited to in-house members. The leader and founder of Synanon, Charles Dederick, has stated that most of those who leave return to drugs.[17] Many other types of groups function *at times* to produce change. As we saw in Chapters 2 and 3, families socialize children by means of group processes. Groups that meet for psychotherapeutic purposes are common, and sometimes such groups bring about significant changes in the attitudes and behaviors of their members. This depends on the skill of the therapist involved, and on the motivation of the members as well as on their external situations.

Summary: Groups as Agents for Change

Any actions or processes that weaken a group open the way for change. For example, a discussion among group members may reveal group shortcomings, or may reveal dissenting opinions that were not clear earlier. This paves the way for departing from previous activities and attitudes. Commitment to a new line of action appears to be especially important in bringing about change. Living groups can be powerful agents for change because they provide members with deep gratification and create a strong dependency among them. The absence of alternative sources of satisfaction outside the group enhances the potential for change.

[16] Reprinted with permission from L. Yablonsky. *Synanon: The tunnel back.* New York: The Macmillan Company, 1965. Pp. 144–145.

[17] Brecher, 1973.

RESISTANCE TO CHANGE

Both classic and contemporary science fiction have pictured a future world in which communications systems are used to conduct surveillance and to control the citizenry. Undoubtedly, modern technology has made great gains both in distributing and monitoring information, and modern citizens are exposed to communications from every side. Yet the individual still has resources for resisting influence in all but the most rigid and totalitarian societies.

Selective Exposure

People can reduce the influence of the media communicators by withdrawal—selectively avoiding communications. We turn to another channel, or turn to another page. Even in the immediate presence of visual or audio information, as every professor knows, we can be nonattentive, fail to absorb the message, or learn it in a distorted form.

Considerable experimental work on selective exposure or selective avoidance, however, has *not* supported a simple proposition like: "We avoid exposure to information we don't want to hear or that we disagree with, and we expose ourselves to information consonant with our views and feelings." Instead, although we do this sometimes, often we do just the opposite. Under some circum-

Media communication.

stances, loyal party voters have been shown to pay considerable attention to the opposition.[18] Sometimes people avoid material that they agree with because it is familiar—it contains nothing new.[19] People also expose themselves to information that is useful, whether or not they agree with it.[20]

Finally, the sheer volume of information we are exposed to is heavily weighted in favor of material consonant with our beliefs. We talk much more with our friends than our enemies, and the attitudes of the former are more similar to our own. We belong to groups that share our values and our ideas— our families, clubs, churches, synagogues, teams, volunteer groups. If they didn't share our ideas, in most cases we wouldn't belong to them. Moreover, we are apt to check out information that is dissonant with our beliefs by talking to our friends and fellow group members. Usually they will help us to invalidate information or communications that are contrary to our beliefs.

Building Defensive Counterarguments

Another form of resistance consists of reducing dependency on a communicator by reducing anxiety about the topic and by developing counterarguments. Some early work suggested that when a communication is anxiety-arousing, it may produce defenses so that future exposure to similar communications results in less anxiety and little attitude change—as if we could produce intellectual antibodies.

One experiment was conducted in about 1950, before there was any widespread or public knowledge that the Soviet Union had produced an atomic bomb. An experimental group had been given a pessimistic communication— that Russia already had atomic bombs, atomic factories, and so forth. Control groups had not received this communication. Some months later, when President Truman announced that Russia did in fact have the atomic bomb, the reaction of the experimental group was compared with the reactions of the control groups.[21] The experimental group did not react to Truman's message with as much concern or worry as those whose first knowledge came from the President's message.

The investigators suggested that a form of "emotional inoculation" takes place when a fear-arousing communication is first presented and that later communications become less effective as a result. Apparently, the individual's defensive reactions come into play as a result of the arousal of fear. Studies of the intensive and persistent bombing raids in Britain, Germany, and Japan during World War II similarly suggest that, although at first the average citizen is greatly frightened, he or she later becomes relatively immune to subsequent raids.[22]

[18] Berelson, Lazarsfeld, and McPhee, 1954.
[19] Janis and Rausch, 1970.
[20] Canon, 1964; Freedman, 1965; Clarke and James, 1967.
[21] Janis, Lumsdaine, and Gladstone, 1951.
[22] Janis, 1951.

A number of laboratory studies worked out the details of the inoculation idea as it relates to propaganda.[23] Commonly held beliefs were attacked by *weak* propaganda arguments to stimulate the building of defenses for these beliefs, in much the same way as weakened viruses in the form of a vaccine stimulate the body to build up antibodies. Procedures designed to enhance immunization included active defenses, such as writing an essay, or passive defenses, such as reading an article. And the more active the participation, the longer lasting was the immunization—it lasted several weeks and was recalled easily. Resistance to counterpropaganda was tested immediately, after two days, and after a week, and time weakened the effect only slightly.

A qualification must be noted, however. While it is absolutely clear that the delivery of information contrary to attitude results in more resistance to contrary information presented later, the machinery of counterargument has not been identified with certainty. A review of all these studies and consideration of other possible mechanisms makes clear that some means of detecting the presence of counterarguing must be found if this explanation is to be convincing.[24] The difficulty arises from the fact that thinking of counterarguments is ordinarily a covert, unobservable process, and that certain types of attempts to measure it may well produce it—even though it was not present before the measurement was tried. Still, the idea of inoculation appears strongly supported, and the counterargument seems to be the best available explanation at the moment.

If we assume that these findings hold good, they have some very important implications. The most central values of our culture might be susceptible to change should forcible exposure to counterarguments occur, simply because no effort has been spent in developing defenses against attacks which never occur. Thus, belief in a democratic government, virtually universal among Americans, might be susceptible to a concerted attack in a situation where an American is isolated from his fellow believers and exposed to counterarguments—as in Korean prison camps where the Chinese Communists used intensive brainwashing procedures. The experimental work on inoculation suggests that the way to build resistance to such attacks is to challenge somewhat the concepts and principles of democracy, forcing the individual to develop defenses against such arguments.

Use of Fear Appeals

In recent years, the fear appeal has received intensive study in an attempt to pin down the means by which it succeeds or fails. Many mass communications use fear appeals. Government officials, for example, may try to gain support for national defense by stressing the dangers inherent in failure to prepare for emergencies. Health organizations, both public and private, may emphasize disease and pain in an attempt to promote better health. Advertisers sometimes use fear appeals—as in toothpaste and deodorant commercials that threaten unpopular-

[23] McGuire and Papageorgis, 1961; Papageorgis and McGuire, 1961; McGuire, 1961, 1962; Watts, 1967; Cook, 1969.
[24] Miller and Baron, 1973.

ity if one fails to practice oral or body hygiene by using their products. All these influencing attempts consist essentially of information describing a danger, and recommendations for action to avoid the danger. They "threaten" the individual with unfortunate consequences unless he or she follows the advice of the communicator. Thus, the terms *threat appeal* or *fear appeal*. Such appeals deserve study because of their widespread use and because of the theoretical problems they raise in connection with understanding persuasive communications.

Persuasion and the degree of fear aroused   One question asked in early research was whether strong fear appeals were more persuasive than weak fear appeals. If fear is a drive, a motivating force, then one might expect that the greater the fear, the stronger the influence. Several early studies suggested that the reverse was true: mild fear led to a change in attitudes and behavior, but strong fear produced little change.[25] In these studies, strong fears were aroused by vivid and realistic presentations—color photographs of cancerous lungs, for example. Milder effects were produced with x-rays or more impersonal and schematic illustrations of the effect of smoking on the lungs. The explanation was that when fear was too strong, other processes entered in. For instance, strong fear appeals may be seen as offensive and exaggerated, as deliberate attempts to scare, thus producing a discounting of the communication and a resistance to change. Or, when people actually become afraid, they may generate defenses against the fear, such as arguments counter to the communicator's.

But these neatly plausible explanations had to be abandoned. The early model proved to be too simple. More recent studies found that mild fear is associated with *less* persuasion, and that, contrary to the early findings, intense fear is associated with *greater* persuasion.[26] That, too, makes a kind of logical sense. To resolve these contradictions it has become necessary to develop a more adequate theory explaining the means by which fear facilitates or inhibits persuasion, and to specify the conditions under which it does so. In the process of designing experiments to discover this information, investigators have been led to elaborate an ever more complex model of the fear-persuasion process. The work of Howard Leventhal is a major contribution to this topic, and our discussion leans heavily on it.[27]

The parallel model explanation   Leventhal has proposed that a fear-arousing communication produces two *parallel* and *independent* reactions. One reaction is to *control the fear;* the other is to *cope with the danger.* While many actions that do the one also do the other, some actions that control fear are irrelevant when it comes to coping with the danger—or even interfere with that coping. Defenses against fear might include closing one's eyes, literally or figuratively. Thinking up counterarguments, not thinking about the danger, getting reassurance, developing fatalistic rationalizations for not worrying—all these may help to control the fear

---

[25] Janis and Feshbach, 1953; Hovland, Janis, and Kelley, 1953; Nunnally and Bobren, 1959.
[26] Higbee, 1969.
[27] Leventhal, 1970.

but do little about the actual danger. If the danger is that you might develop lung cancer, not thinking about lung cancer may leave you less frightened but it leaves you no less susceptible to the disease.

To cope with the danger, you must face and acknowledge it, accept the recommendation of the communicator, or adopt other adequate means of avoiding the danger.

Leventhal notes that, typically, there is some correlation between the fear and the coping reactions. More serious threats elicit stronger coping responses *and* stronger emotional reactions. But this occurs because of the nature of the communication. There is no *necessary* connection between fear arousal and coping behavior—one does not cause the other. This model of independent but interacting reactions suggests explanations for some familiar phenomena. One is the paradox that fear is often strongest *after* one has successfully coped with a dangerous situation. Leventhal gives the example of controlling a car that has started to skid dangerously. Only after the car has been brought to a stop does the driver experience fear. In this instance, coping with the danger also controls or inhibits fear, but when the coping behavior ceases, the fear reaction occurs.

In other instances, however, a fear response may interfere with coping, as when the danger has to be faced and one refuses to go to the hospital or have an x-ray taken. Obviously, fear often generates avoidance responses that interfere with coping. Thus, because these reactions are independent and interact in different ways, a wide variety of ways of handling fear-arousing communications becomes possible.

We can, for instance, consider situations involving *delayed responses.* When persuasive fear communications are presented under conditions where it is *not* possible to act immediately, the normal dissipation of fear over time permits coping with the danger later. In contrast, where the recommendation may be acted upon immediately, and strong fear is aroused, defenses against the fear may be dominant.

Leventhal compares his explanation of delayed response with the quite commonly accepted alternative explanation that treats fear as a drive, or motive. The fear-drive model works when an immediate response *is* possible, fear is aroused, and subsequent behavior is motivated by efforts to deal with the fear. This fear-drive model predicts that messages arousing high fear will produce greater persuasion than those arousing low fear, provided that the recommendations presented are fear-reducing. This is an application of the reinforcement idea from learning theory. The fear-drive model assumes that mentally rehearsing the communicator's recommendations reduces the fear, which in turn reinforces the recommendations. The model also recognizes situations where, instead, fear is reduced by denying or ignoring the danger: this reinforces resistance against the communication so that, later, those who have felt high fear will be even less accepting of the recommendation.

But now consider the delayed-response situation. The fear-drive model makes opposite predictions from the parallel-response model. Under the fear-drive model, messages arousing high fear are more effective than those arousing low fear when action is taken *immediately* after the message. If fear is strongest immediately after, it is most reinforcing then. The reverse is true if action is *delayed*. The communication is then less effective because the fear is weaker and is thus less reinforcing.

The experiments actually support the parallel-model prediction that communications arousing high fear will be more effective if the response is delayed (as opposed to the fear-drive model). In one experiment, different films on lung cancer were presented to three groups of individuals.[28] The films were designed to arouse low, medium, and high degrees of fear. The film arousing high fear showed an actual lung cancer operation, in color, including the initial incision, the forcing apart of the ribs, the removal of the black and diseased lung, and the open cavity with the beating heart. This film was very effective in arousing fear. All the films included advice to stop smoking and to get an x-ray at a mobile unit nearby.

The outcome was that fewer smokers went for x-rays immediately after the high-fear film than after the low- or medium-fear messages. Nonsmokers were equally willing to have x-rays taken, regardless of the level of threat. This reduced persuadability for smokers immediately after a communication arousing high fear is inconsistent with the fear-drive model, which predicts that such a message *will* be effective immediately, but not later. The alternative explanation based on the parallel model is that when fear is intense immediately after the communication, it disrupts the attempts to cope with the danger. After the fear subsides, the danger can be coped with. And this is consistent with a follow-up five months later, which found that smoking reduction was *greatest* among those smokers who had been exposed to the *high-fear* condition.

While the fear-drive model cannot explain why communications arousing high fear are more effective later, it does allow for less effectiveness of communications arousing high fear than those arousing low fear. Under certain conditions, high-fear communications are presumed to produce defenses against the fear, or denial and avoidance of the threat. Some of the older studies were consistent with this view, including a classic study of the effects of fear appeals on dental hygiene, where the minimum fear appeal was most effective. But the parallel-response model suggests an alternative explanation that is consistent with more recent investigations—that the high fear prevents one from coping with the actual danger.

Factors affecting coping with danger Several factors might affect coping with the threat presented in a persuasive communication: (1) personality traits that interfere with or facilitate coping actions, (2) other characteristics unrelated to personality but associated with coping actions, and (3) situational conditions that affect coping. In one study, participants were classified by means of a word association test as *avoiders* or *copers*.[29] The avoiders were less accepting of the

[28] Leventhal and Watts, 1966
[29] Goldstein, 1959.

recommendation in a communication arousing strong fear than in one arousing low fear. The copers, on the other hand, reacted equally to high- and low-fear communications. Several additional studies indicated that low-esteem participants, in contrast to those with high esteem, are less likely to accept the recommendations of high-fear messages.[30]

Another condition that might affect a person's reaction to a threatening communication is his or her feeling of vulnerability or invulnerability to illness. A person may feel immune, or may feel especially vulnerable. When a person in one of these states hears a fear communication, we would expect the feeling of vulnerability or invulnerability to affect the reaction, including his or her coping response. We would expect that the participant who feels vulnerable will be less likely to act on the recommendations in a strong fear communication for several possible reasons: (1) the feeling of vulnerability may lead him or her to grapple with the fear rather than cope with the danger, and (2) the feeling of vulnerability might make him or her think that the threat is uncontrollable.

There is some clarification of the issue in one experimental manipulation of the feeling of vulnerability.[31] Four conditions were used: (1) a control group not exposed to a communication, (2) a group exposed to a communication that created feelings of vulnerability to cancer, (3) a group exposed to a communication that created a strong fear of cancer, and (4) a group exposed to a communication that created feelings of both fear of, and vulnerability to, cancer. One week, and then one month later, the two groups exposed to either the fear or the vulnerability communications were smoking less than the control group. But participants made to feel both fearful *and* vulnerable continued to smoke as much as the controls. Thus, these participants rejected the recommended action, presumably because feeling both vulnerable and fearful interfered with realistic coping and caused the respondents to deal only with their fears—even after a month had passed.

Coping and action instructions   Leventhal has stressed the individual's manner of coping with the actual danger. He points out that motivation is not enough, but that the individual also needs to perform a series of actions in order to cope with the danger. These actions need to bridge the gap all the way from the receipt of the communication to the final act (such as finding out where to go for a tetanus shot, making the appointment, and keeping it). This provides the possibility of experimenting with action instructions to discover the most effective form in which they can be given.

In one experiment, all participants were asked to read a booklet recommending tetanus inoculations. Different amounts of fear were aroused in participants, and selected students were given specific instructions on where to get a tetanus shot, and were encouraged to schedule it so that it would fit into their daily routine.[32] Other students were not given these instructions for carrying out

[30] Dabbs, 1964; Dabbs and Leventhal, 1966; Kornzweig, 1967; Leventhal and Trembly, 1968.
[31] Watts, 1967.
[32] Leventhal, Singer, and Jones, 1965.

the action. The instructed students were provided with a map of the local campus, with the health service building circled. Several routes were suggested for reaching the health building while the students changed classes, and the students were asked to review their daily schedules and pick an appropriate time for a shot. Five types of subgroups were used: (1) high fear was aroused, and action instructions were provided, (2) mild fear was aroused, and action instructions were provided, (3) high fear was aroused, but no action instructions were provided, (4) mild fear was aroused, but no action instructions were provided, and (5) no fear was aroused, but action instructions were provided.

High fear by itself produced favorable attitudes toward getting the tetanus shot, but action instructions by themselves had no effect on attitudes. But favorable attitudes were not enough to obtain compliance. Only 3 percent of those not receiving action instructions took the tetanus shots, while 29 percent of those in the high- and low-fear groups *and* receiving action instructions took the shots. But action instructions alone were insufficient—no one in that group took shots. Thus, while some degree of fear is necessary for action instructions to be effective, compliance does not increase with an increase in fear.

This experiment has important implications for planned change in behavior. Students who did not receive action instructions still knew where the health center was and how to get there. Moreover, according to their expressions of intention, they were motivated to get their tetanus shots. But few of them did so. However, more students who were given a *specific plan* that fitted the action into the larger pattern of the day's activities did get tetanus shots.

The previous experiment introduced a *new* action into the students' normal activities. Another study was done to determine the effect of action instructions on an *established* habit—smoking—and there, too, the practical action instructions, about avoiding occasions to smoke, and believing that one could control the habit, were related to a reduction in smoking—and much more so than merely seeing cigarettes as a threat or as relevant to a vulnerable self.[33]

Groups as Agents for Resistance to Change

Groups may reinforce or interfere with the effect of a communication in three general ways: (1) through the effects of group structure on exposure, (2) through determining the credibility of various communicators, and (3) through providing social support for attitudes.

Effects of group structure on exposure The group structure may affect the manner in which a communication is filtered as it passes from one person to another. This filtering process determines the degree to which group members are exposed to the various elements of the communication. Of particular relevance here is the fact that some members are more active in relaying messages

[33] Leventhal, Watts, and Pagano, 1967.

to other members, and usually these members reflect the value structure of the group. Thus, they may block or distort messages that are dissonant with group values, and facilitate messages that are consonant.

To illustrate, studies of voting have shown that people talk politics primarily with members of their family and with friends. Since these other persons usually have similar political attitudes, the chances of encountering dissonant views through interpersonal channels are reduced. The degree to which family members have similar political attitudes is emphasized by a study of a panel of voters in one county where it was found that only 4 percent of the voters had relatives who voted differently from themselves.[34]

Credibility of communicators   The members of a group are likely to have not only similar opinions on a variety of issues, but also similar opinions regarding the credibility of various communicators. For a highly religious group, a minister of their faith has high credibility, and an atheist has low credibility. For a group of physicians, a cardiologist has high credibility, and an athletic coach talking about health has much lower credibility. In general, communicators likely to transmit messages consonant with group attitudes and values have high credibility, and those with dissonant communications have low credibility. A factor multiplying the effectiveness of highly credible communications directed toward groups is that key positions in the group's communication structure are usually held by members who personify group values. These members are apt to relay communications consonant with their values and filter out dissonant ones.

Group support for attitudes   Groups are not so homogeneous, nor are the communication channels so uniform, that people are never exposed to contrary communications. Indeed, people are continually bombarded with a great variety of messages, many of them contrary to their attitudes. Perhaps the most dramatic source of resistance to this continual pressure is found in the social support provided by the group. This support is one of the most important reasons that attitudes do not constantly shift with each new barrage of communications. In a general sense, people's reward-cost outcomes are lowered if they adopt attitudes or behaviors that deviate from the social norms of the group, while their outcomes are maintained if they conform. Essentially, the support of the group may be characterized in the following terms.

People are attracted to others who have attitudes similar to their own. When confronted with a person whose attitudes are at variance from theirs, they exert pressure on him or her to change. It has been suggested that these tendencies arise from a need to validate one's attitudes, to find support for them in social reality. This concept of *social reality* and its validation was discussed earlier, in Chapter 7.

These pressures toward uniformity arising from the need to validate atti-

---

[34] Lazarsfeld, Berelson, and Gaudet, 1948.

tudes are particularly effective in small, intimate groups, because people in such groups are normally highly dependent on one another for the satisfaction of their emotional needs—such as the needs for affection, companionship, and encouragement. Such groups have been traditionally called *primary groups.*

An excellent example of how membership in a primary group may produce strong resistance to persuasive communications may be found in an analysis of the Wehrmacht in World War II.[35] The most important factor accounting for the strong resistance of the German troops to Allied propaganda, in spite of the hopelessness of their situation toward the end of the war, was the loyalty of the individual soldiers to their own units—which met their physical needs, providing them with food, clothing, shelter, protection, and also affection, esteem, and support. Allied propaganda disseminated among German troops—dropped from planes, for the most part—urged surrender, but the leaflets had little effect. Asking the soldiers to surrender had small chance of success if it meant that they had to desert their comrades. Even less effective were Allied communications attempting to cast doubt on the Nazi ideology—most soldiers did not concern themselves with politics, and devotion to nazism was not a basis for their resistance to Allied propaganda.

On the other hand, once the primary group was broken up through physical separation during a hasty retreat, or once its functions were disrupted by the lack of food or ammunition, the need for physical survival often became so strong that persuasive communications urging surrender and offering safe-conduct were frequently effective. Thus, either the virtual dissolution of the primary group, or group agreement on surrender, was a necessary condition for the effectiveness of Allied persuasive communications. Similar feelings of loyalty to the primary group existed among American soldiers who, when asked what factors enabled them to keep going when things were tough, stressed that they couldn't let their outfit down, that "buddies" depended upon them, and so forth.

According to several authorities, attempts of the Chinese Communists to brainwash American prisoners captured in the Korean War were successful in destroying resistance and obtaining minor cooperation in part because primary groups were deliberately broken up.[36] The Chinese captors segregated leaders or resistors, instituted an informer system, gave special privileges to those who cooperated, and removed all recognition of military rank. As a result, the average American stood alone against his captors, although he was physically in the midst of his fellow prisoners. He could no longer trust them, since he could not tell who had become informers. And those officers who could best maintain the group had been removed. Group cohesion was lost.

On the other hand, virtually all the Turkish prisoners successfully resisted attempts by their captors to obtain cooperation. Although the lack of success of the Chinese Communists in manipulating Turkish prisoners may have been due

[35] Shils and Janowitz, 1948.
[36] Committee on Government Operations, 1956; Schein, 1958.

in part to the fact that only one Chinese interrogator spoke fluent Turkish, it also appeared to be due to certain group factors among the Turks. They maintained a high level of discipline and organization. Deprived of their officers, the Turks acknowledged leaders according to the next highest military ranks, and provided full support for these leaders. In this way, the Turks managed to maintain group morale, trust, and mutual support. This kind of group strength and cohesiveness is beautifully illustrated in the movie, *The Bridge on the River Kwai.*

Summary: Resistance to Change

One way of resisting communications in the mass media would be to avoid receiving them—by changing the television channel, reading news media selectively, and so on. One could also avoid talking at length with people with whom one disagrees. While some of this selective avoidance undoubtedly occurs, it is not a consistent or invariable principle. Sometimes people do listen to communications that disagree with their views. They especially do so if the communications have some use.

A rather subtle, undercover process occurs in some instances where people hear communications that they don't want to believe. Apparently this is a kind of mental defense process. If people are exposed to weak propaganda, they may be stimulated to build counterarguments against it. Later, they are better able to withstand stronger propaganda. The more active they are in building counterarguments, the more effective is their resistance.

A communication that arouses anxiety or fear gives rise to two parallel and independent reactions in the recipient. One is to cope with the fear or anxiety, and the other is to cope with the danger identified in the communication. Doing the former tends to make the communication ineffective, since coping with the fear seems to get in the way of taking effective action. But if it is not possible to act immediately, the fear dissipates somewhat, and the recipient is more likely to cope with the danger. This varies, however, with certain personality characteristics. People who are already insecure or lacking in self-esteem are apt to cope only with the fear if they are exposed to a really frightening message. A mildly fear-arousing message would be more effective with them. Finally, specific action instructions on precisely how to cope with the danger increase the probability of the effectiveness of the message.

Groups help to resist communication in several ways. One is by filtering out objectionable messages as they are passed by the leader or from one member to another. A second is by labeling some communicators or sources as not believeable. Finally, primary groups—intimate face-to-face groups—provide powerful satisfactions for those members who adhere to group values and attitudes, and deter members from accepting messages contrary to group views by threatening deprivation, punishment, or ejection from the group.

TEN

HUMAN GROUPS

Any group of people observed over a period of time will show distinctive patterns of association or structured arrangements. Some members are together more often than others. A few members are relatively isolated. Many aspects of group structure are illustrated in Figure 10-1. This represents a youth gang, the Erls, on Chicago's Near West Side, studied by sociologist Gerald Suttles.[1]

Looking at the figure, we see immediately that when the gang members are not at their hangout—the vicinity of a certain street corner—they divide into two "traveling groups." The inner circle includes boys whom others expect to show up daily at the hangout; the middle circle includes those expected to show up somewhat less frequently; and the outer circle includes those who show up quite irregularly. Note that the higher the boy is placed on the figure, the more respect or *status* he has. Other features include three pairs of brothers, who spend a lot of time in each other's company. Leaders are identified by a box around their names. Antagonisms between members are represented by a dashed line.

Despite the fact that Figure 10-1 represents a youth gang, it illustrates the main structural features that characterize almost any human group. One feature

[1] Suttles, 1968.

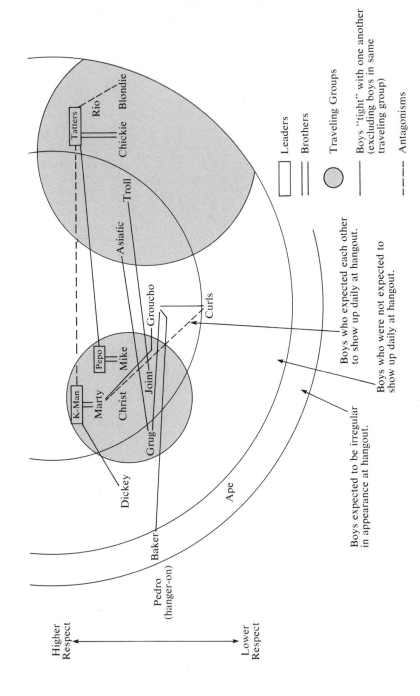

Figure 10-1 Sociometric relations among the members of the Erls gang. (Reprinted by permission from G. D. Suttles. *The social order of the slum.* Chicago: University of Chicago Press, 1968. P. 189.)

Higher Respect

Lower Respect

Pedro (hanger-on)

Baker

Dickey

Ape

K-Man

Marty

Pepo

Christ

Mike

Grug

Joint

Groucho

Curls

Asiatic

Troll

Tatters

Rio

Chickie

Blondie

Leaders

Brothers

Traveling Groups

Boys "tight" with one another (excluding boys in same traveling group)

Antagonisms

Boys who expected each other to show up daily at hangout.

Boys who were not expected to show up daily at hangout.

Boys expected to be irregular in appearance at hangout.

Behavior in small groups.

is hierarchical—representing higher or lower status, which will be discussed in the last part of this chapter. Typically, group leaders have the highest status of all. Another feature, frequency of association, reflects several structural features. First, it reflects the preferences or positive feelings that each member has for certain other members. Often this is characterized by reciprocal feelings—each member feels the same way toward the other. Second, it also reflects the communication structure of the group: members who associate more frequently usually exchange more communications. And in some groups it may also reflect an activity or work structure.

SOCIOMETRY AND GROUP STRUCTURE

Structural features of groups have long been measured by *sociometry*.[2] Essentially, a sociometric test is a means for obtaining information on the preferences of group members for associating with other members. In a sociometric test, persons choose other group members for association in some specified activity or context. By asking the right questions, we can obtain information on patterns of liking, association, status, and communication.

[2] Moreno, 1953.

Individuals may be asked to indicate whom they prefer as friends, or simply whom they like or dislike. More often, some more specific criterion is used, such as the choice of a roommate by college students, of a flying partner by Air Force pilots, of a group leader in a fraternity, or of a work partner by employees. Through such choices, it is possible to identify by objective means the persons in the group who are generally liked or disliked, associated with or ignored, respected or derogated. It is also possible to identify cliques, as well as the kind of feeling that exists between the clique and other subgroups or between the clique and the group as a whole.

Exchange Theory and Sociometric Choice

Our previous discussion of attraction, in Chapter 7, as well as many studies of the sociometric structure of groups, suggest a variety of factors which determine the sociometric choices of group members based on liking. These can be summarized as follows. People are likely to select: (1) those with whom they have a greater opportunity to interact, (2) those who have characteristics most desirable in terms of the norms and values of the group, (3) those who are most similar to themselves in attitudes, values, and social background, (4) those whom they perceive as also choosing them or as assigning favorable characteristics to them, (5) those who see them as they see themselves, and (6) those in whose company they have achieved gratification of their needs.

We can gain some insights into the reasons for these sociometric choices by applying exchange theory (see Chapter 7). Those who are chosen must have characteristics that have considerable reward value to an appreciable number of group members. In the Erls gang, for example, the leaders, K-man and Tatters, were good at *initiating* activities in their traveling groups. It must also be possible to interact with preferred group members at low cost. This is reflected in the members' views of K-man and Tatters as being absolutely *trustworthy*.

A classic analysis of leaders in a girls' home provides more systematic evidence.[3] First, preferred members facilitated rewarding interaction for other girls. They helped other members, protected them, and increased the rewards and reduced the costs that other girls—particularly the less-popular ones—experienced in interaction, not only with them but also with other group members. Second, the ability of the preferred member to handle her own emotional problems minimized the cost to the other girls of interaction with her. Finally, a look at people who were rejected sociometrically also supports this exchange theory interpretation. These people displayed domineering, belligerent, inconsiderate behaviors which raised the costs to other persons of interaction with them.[4]

Some characteristics of an individual facilitate high outcomes for members in one kind of group but not in others. A leader who could bring high outcomes

[3] Jennings, 1950.
[4] Kidd, 1951.

to members of the Erls gang would be unlikely to be able to do the same thing at a dinner party with his relatives. Choices of a leader made by a member depend upon: (1) the leader's characteristics, (2) the member's characteristics, (3) other group members' characteristics, (4) properties of the group, and (5) the general situation in which the interaction occurs.

For instance, in the girls' institution mentioned above, independence and self-confidence to the point of rebelliousness were highly valued. These traits enabled the popular girls to stand up to the housemothers when the occasion demanded. Other traits help in the achievement of some shared goal—intelligence, knowledge, experience, and aggressiveness can be popular when they help to attain an important objective of the group. On the way up the mountain, an experienced climber is very popular. Back down in the village, when you are safe and sound, that climber may be ignored.

When members have attitudes that correspond to group norms, they are likely to be frequently chosen. As mentioned earlier, one of the rewards people achieve in interaction is consensual validation. The person whose attitudes and behavior correspond to the norms of the group provides rewards to members at low costs to himself or herself by validating their attitudes and feelings. He or she does so because norms are, by definition, widely shared by group members.

Properties of Sociometric Structures

Choice criteria and structure   By using different criteria for choice, different group structures can be readily identified. For instance, when the girls in the institution chose others with whom they wanted to spend their leisure time, they preferred a girl who could satisfy their social-emotional needs. These needs include that for consensual validation, support for one's self-conception, sympathy and understanding, someone to confide in, and so on. A somewhat different structure appeared when a living or working companion was chosen. This choice appeared to be based on the person's group role, her contribution to the smooth functioning of the group, and her conformity to group norms.

By varying the choice criterion in this manner, we gain a thorough understanding of the group structure. Another major difference that is shown up by comparing the work and the leisure-time criteria is the following. When the partner is chosen for work or daily functioning, choices of all the members are concentrated on a few persons whose group role is crucial. When the partners are selected for leisure-time activities, choices are more widely distributed, since needs or dependencies differ from one member to another.

Member characteristics and group structure   No analysis based upon the characteristics of the members of a group will provide a complete explanation of choice. One reason is that people do not accurately assess the attributes of others. In a group, it isn't only what you are that counts, it's also what people think you are. We saw in Chapter 7 that perceived patterns of liking always differ from the actual patterns.

Another reason is that the final structure that emerges is always a compromise between the outcomes members *would like* to get in interaction with their fellow members and what they *are able* to get. *The group structure moves toward an equilibrium in which each person's position is the best he or she can get in terms of the reward-cost outcomes.* This *compromise process* produces two distinctive structural features: (1) choices that are mutual, or reciprocal, and (2) choices of persons who are roughly equal to oneself in status. These features come about in the following way.

In a newly formed group, all members may at first like those few persons who have the most attractive characteristics—attributes likely to produce high rewards. But these popular members cannot interact frequently with every member, returning their affection or other rewards. They interact selectively. Being attracted to someone who doesn't return the affection becomes costly and, gradually, the neglected members shift their attention to others who do reciprocate. Thus, mutual choices become common in every human group. In the Erls gang, this was especially true among the three pairs of brothers, as well as among several other pairs.

The process also results in the choice of others who are equal to oneself in popularity.[5] Mutuality and the choice of persons who are similar in status occur because through such a choice members eventually obtain their best available reward-cost outcomes.

We make two assumptions in explaining this process. One is that persons are chosen according to the value attached to their behavior and to their other characteristics. The higher the status people have, the more valuable their behavior is to others. The second, true by definition, is that popularity reflects the quantity of alternative relations available to each member. The more popular people are, the greater the variety of alternative relations they can form with others. These two principles operate to maximize the mutual satisfactions experienced through interactions with others of equal status, and to minimize the outcomes experienced through interaction with others having a widely different status from one's own. Thus, the equal status relationships are fostered and maintained, while different status relationships are discouraged.

Consider first the case where Zachary, a person of low status, is attracted to Alfred, a person of high status. The chance for the development of a mutually satisfactory relationship is low because Zachary's behavior is of a much lower value than Alfred can obtain in his many alternative relationships. Alfred is not motivated to provide Zachary with valuable outcomes because Zachary is unable to reciprocate. In this case, we would expect Alfred to withdraw from the relationship. Under certain circumstances, however, Alfred might be able to exact behavior from Zachary that was of high value to him. But since Zachary

[5] Newcomb, 1961; Backman and Secord, 1964.

has low choice status, such valuable behavior would not be typical of him and he would normally produce it only at high cost to himself. In that event, the outcomes to Zachary would be low and he would be the one to withdraw.

Such a relationship would be maintained only when the initial assumptions stated above did not hold. If, for example, Zachary was a good chessplayer and Alfred liked to play chess, this behavior could be produced by Zachary at low cost, and Alfred would have a positive outcome. Finally, the relationship might be maintained if Alfred were prevented, either through inaccurate assessment of his alternatives or by some force of circumstances, from establishing more valuable alternative relations (for example, if they were cellmates in prison).

The fact that movements toward mutuality and equality of choice status between members are observable fairly early in the formation of a group, particularly at high levels of attraction, suggests that persons become relatively adept at gauging their chances of satisfactory outcomes in a relation. Skill at estimation undoubtedly comes from previous experiences in relations with people of markedly different status that have led to poor outcomes. Probably "crushes" in early dating—characterized as they are by a lack of mutuality and equality—provide useful training and lead persons in courtship to select and fall in love with those whose value in the marriage market is roughly the same as their own. The average man does not try to attract a woman who is a glamorous celebrity. And a similar process of self-appraisal functions in groups larger than dyads.

Experimental evidence provides positive but not wholly consistent support for these speculations. Participants' choices of work partners in a laboratory experiment, and of roommates, appeared to reflect a compromise between the desirability of the other person and an estimate of his or her availability.[6] Presumably, individuals had learned that to aim too high can lead to rejection or an unsatisfactory relationship. One study did *not* provide evidence to support the compromise process, however.[7] College students who attended an arranged "mixer" where they were randomly paired did not display any tendency to compromise but desired and liked those persons who were more physically attractive, without regard to their own attractiveness or their perceptions of their own attractiveness. Probably in this transient situation there was no serious commitment to anyone nor was any high cost attached to "rejection." These considerations would lift the constraints that, in an enduring group, normally keep choice of another person within bounds of one's own status. In two other studies, individuals were asked to rate photographs of persons of various degrees of attractiveness in a number of respects—including choice as a date.[8] Compared to individuals who rated themselves as attractive, those who rated themselves as unattractive were more likely to consider unattractive people and less likely to

[6] Rosenfeld, 1964; Bechtel and Rosenfeld, 1966.
[7] Walster, et al., 1966.
[8] Stroebe, et al., 1971; Berscheid, et al., 1971.

consider attractive people as possible dates. The large number of unknowns in choosing a date from a photograph introduces an appreciable risk; thus, cost enters into the choice. The second of these photograph studies also used a personality test to measure an individual's chronic fear of rejection. Although such a fear should presumably increase the tendency to choose a partner of equal attractiveness, this was not the case.

The compromise process, then, consists of adjustments in relationships among group members in the direction of a state of equilibrium in which each person's reward-cost outcomes are maximized. This state of balance is characterized by many mutual choices, especially among persons equal in choice status.

Cohesiveness of groups   Two people in a relationship, as we have noted, are attracted to each other to the extent that their reward-cost outcomes exceed their comparison levels. People may remain in a relationship, however, even where the outcomes drop below their comparison levels and they are no longer attracted. They remain as long as the outcomes are above the comparison level for alternatives—the outcomes they might expect to get in other relationships. If these are even worse than the outcomes presently experienced in the existing

Black is beautiful: a sign of group cohesiveness. (Photograph from Ebony Magazine, Johnson Publishing Co.)

relationship, including the alternative of no relationship at all, they are apt to maintain the relationship. The binding force, in such instances, is not attraction but the awareness that the outcomes in the relation are better than the outcomes that could be obtained in other relationships. With groups larger than a dyad, the term *cohesiveness* is used to refer to the combined forces acting on group members to remain in the group. While cohesiveness is generally equated with attraction to the group, our analysis suggests that in some instances this interpretation may be incomplete, in that the comparison level for alternatives has not been considered by some theorists.

Bases of attraction to a group can be sorted into three categories.

1   Members may be attracted to a group because of the interaction itself. Interaction results in high reward-cost outcomes to participants because the needs of various members are complementary, their interests and attitudes are similar, or the organization of the group and the situation in which interaction takes place are conducive to a cooperative, friendly atmosphere. Members of a political action group, for example, may enjoy exchanging ideas with each other because of their similar values.

2   Members may be attracted to a group because they find the activities *inherently* rewarding. Groups formed to pursue a particular recreation or hobby such as basketball or tennis are examples. Here, each individual enjoys the activity itself.

3   Members may be attracted to a group because membership is a means of achieving other ends. They may perceive that only through group action can they achieve a goal. There may be a political group formed not for the pleasures of interaction, but to get a particular piece of legislation enacted. Or perhaps membership is a source of favorable reward-cost outcomes in terms of the status one can achieve among persons outside the group.

These bases of cohesion have been incorporated into a theory[9] designed to explain people's attraction to a group as a function of four interacting sets of variables: (1) their motive base for attraction, their needs and values that can be satisfied by group membership, (2) their perception of the incentive properties of the group, including goals, programs, activities, and group member characteristics, (3) their expectancy that actual membership will have favorable or unfavorable consequences, and (4) their comparison level. While much research has been devoted to the first two sets of variables, less attention has been paid to the last two. Our discussion of exchange theory should underscore the importance of the comparison level of group members. A consideration of a related concept, the comparison level for alternatives, suggests that the total force operating on group members is a function not only of attraction to the group but also of the *outcomes available in alternative relations outside the group.*

[9] Cartwright, 1968.

Some groups are highly cohesive even though their members are experiencing low reward-cost outcomes. This could occur because outcome has to be considered in relation to comparison level, which might be unusually low. For example, a baseball team which has recently moved from eighth (last) place to fifth place may have a good team spirit. The level of attraction among members may be higher than one might expect from their fifth place standing alone. If the team had been in last place for years, the low level of outcomes previously experienced and the perceptions of what other players like oneself have been obtaining in the past all would establish low expectations for satisfaction—a low comparison level. Since attraction to the group is a function of the degree to which outcomes are above the comparison level, attraction among members of the team in fifth place may well be higher than that which would be expected from their standing alone.

For similar reasons, people may remain in a relationship even when attraction is absent and their outcomes fall below their comparison level. This happens only if their outcomes remain above their comparison level for alternatives. They are held in the group by the realization that leaving it would result in even lower outcomes. The inclusion in the above theory of *expected* outcome levels also helps to explain changes in group cohesion that might otherwise be puzzling. Thus, group cohesion may change not because the group's ability to satisfy the needs of its members has changed, but because the members' expectations have changed. In the early phases of a group's existence, members may have unrealistically high expectations and thus may maintain a higher level of cohesion than they do when, through experience, comparison levels become more realistic.

Summary: Sociometry and Group Structure

We have described a number of distinctive features of group structure: patterns of association based on liking or on group activities, status hierarchies, mutual or reciprocal choices, and other features. Sociometry is a method of depicting structure based upon members' choices of other members as partners for various activities. Findings obtained by sociometric methods have been explained in terms of exchange theory.

Group members who are most frequently chosen are those who can provide other members with satisfying interaction at minimum cost to those members and to themselves. The traits that such popular group members have vary with the type of group, and even with the presenting situation. Members' choices are based upon a balance between what they would *like* to get in interaction and what they *can* get. This is called the compromise process, which produces two distinctive features: mutual or reciprocal choices, and choice of persons roughly equal to oneself in status. Both of these features emerge because they maximize reward-cost outcomes of members.

Cohesiveness of a group consists of the forces of attraction acting on group members to remain in the group. Attraction has three bases: (1) high reward-cost outcomes stemming directly from interaction among members, (2) group activities that are rewarding for their own sake, and (3) membership in the group as a means of attaining other ends. Attraction also depends on the comparison level of each member, and the outcomes available in alternative relations outside the group.

THE STATUS STRUCTURE

The previous section emphasized attraction among group members and its relation to the structuring of interaction among members. Sociometric choice was a

Status based on height and age.

means of identifying such structures, particularly choices of leisure-time companions. Choice of work partners, however, is not based solely on attraction, but also on another element—*status*. In small groups, the *worth* of each member is evaluated in an agreed-upon way by the other members. The pattern that these evaluations form is called the *status structure* of the group.

Status is accorded on the basis of values and needs that are jointly held by group members. In the Erls gang, trustworthiness was the single most-important status attribute. On a science research team, creativity and productivity would be important status attributes. While *status* is based upon shared needs or values, *liking* is based upon needs and values that differ considerably from member to member. There is a subtle but real difference between liking and status, between affection and admiration. Anyone who has been told, "I admire you immensely but I don't love you," knows the difference. Affect and status are different sentiments and produce different group structures.

Status is also a property that extends beyond the small group to the larger society. Star athletes are admired not only by teammates, but by the sports fans in the stands; successful business executives make the covers of news magazines; scientists, professors, physicians, and lawyers are respected by most people; statesmen and -women and heroes and heroines are honored by all. Status in the larger society is necessarily based on even more widely shared values. Often these values are inherent in, or regularly associated with, the social category or position that a person occupies—personal attributes are almost irrelevant. An excellent example of this is found in the following quotation, describing the moment just after John F. Kennedy, watching the television broadcast with his friends and colleagues, was nominated to run for office as President of the United States. His new status was immediately acknowledged by the public distance that these friends and colleagues suddenly felt obligated to maintain between themselves and him.

> Kennedy loped into the cottage with his light, dancing step, as young and lithe as springtime, and called a greeting to those who stood in his way. Then he seemed to slip from them as he descended the steps of the split-level cottage to a corner where his brother Bobby and brother-in-law Sargent Shriver were chatting, waiting for him. The others in the room surged forward on impulse to join him. Then they halted. A distance of perhaps 30 feet separated them from him, but it was impassable. They stood apart, these older men of long-established power, and watched him. He turned after a few minutes, saw them watching him, and whispered to his brother-in-law. Shriver now crossed the separating space to invite them over. First Averell Harriman; then Dick Daley; then Mike DiSalle, then, one by one, let them all congratulate him. Yet no one could pass the little open distance between him and them uninvited, because there was this thin separation about him, and the knowledge they were there not as his patrons but as his clients. They could come by invitation only, for this might be a President of the United States.[10]

[10] Reprinted with permission from T. H. White, *The Making of the President 1960*. New York: Atheneum, 1961.

But status extending beyond the small group need not be associated with a special position. There may be some almost universally shared values in those personal attributes which account for status. Women, in some situations and at certain times, have achieved distinctive status simply by being beautiful. Such a status might, of course, be recognized by conferring a title, such as Miss America or Miss Universe. We should note that current views of many men and women object to the use of female beauty alone as a sign of status because of its possible implication that the woman is a "thing" of beauty, an *object* only, and therefore subordinate to males.

Which characteristics contribute to status depends upon the persons making the evaluation. Among adolescents, having a car can confer status; among lawyers, doing corporate work often carries more status than does handling negligence cases; among physicians, holding board certification as a surgeon or an internist goes with status; with teachers, having high rank, tenure, and being the author of publications of significant research all bring status.

Attributes can be broad or narrow, depending upon the group and the criteria of judgment, but they must be generally shared and similarly valued by the group members. If a person has some unique characteristic which is of value to only one or two members of a large group, it will not contribute to status. Suppose, for instance, that two members of a professional football team know how to play chess. This skill may be valued by the two members, and each of them may value the other's skill, but it will not confer status upon them with the other members of the team. On the other hand, the ability to run a hundred yards in nine seconds would carry very high status.

Determinants of Status

As with attraction, status attributes may be understood in terms of exchange theory. Among the bases for status are the capacity of persons to reward others, the extent to which they are seen as receiving rewards, the types of costs they incur, and their investments.

Reward value of high-status persons People are accorded high status to the degree that their attributes and behavior are rewarding to an appreciable proportion of group members. The attribute that provides—in Jeremy Bentham's famous phrase—"the greatest good for the greatest number" is accorded the greatest social approval and enjoys the maximum status. An additional element is that these rewarding attributes must be relatively rare. Certain activities contributing to highly important values of the group are engaged in by all members, and thus no one member gains an advantage in terms of status. It is only in the land of the blind that the one-eyed man is king. Among sighted people, vision is highly important but generally available; when vision is rare it acquires status.

It has been inferred from exchange theory that the high-status evaluations arise from the inability of group members to reciprocate in kind the valuable contributions of those persons with rare but important resources.[11] Receiving the benefit of such resources leaves members indebted to these persons. They pay off the debt with deference, which motivates the valuable group member to continue in the group.

Rewards received and costs absorbed   People are also given status according to the extent to which they are seen as receiving rewards. A person who is skilled in business and makes a lot of money is likely to be accorded status because there is a tendency to consistent, holistic evaluation. We tend to associate one good attribute with others. Not only do we reward values, but we value rewards—and reward *them*. Esteem, after all, is another kind of reward.

Persons may also be ranked in terms of the costs they experience. Disabled persons, or others who, despite great obstacles, go on to make a life for themselves and contribute to society, win admiration. So do winners of the Congressional Medal of Honor, because of the disregard for personal safety they have shown, and because that award is so often posthumous. But unlike rewards, only certain costs contribute to status: those that help the group to realize its values, and that are not incurred by almost everyone. The work of ditch diggers and garbage collectors is strenuous, demanding, unpleasant—personally costly—and certainly necessary, but does not carry high status. The soldier who exposes himself needlessly to the enemy without achieving an objective is not likely to get a medal, but more probably a reprimand.

Investments   As George Homans has pointed out, another basis for status is a person's *investments*.[12] While the attributes previously discussed have reward value, investments may or may not have intrinsic value. They are, nevertheless, accorded value through consensus of opinion, and confer upon a person the right to a certain status. Such an investment might be ethnic background, family, or distinguished achievements in science, literature, or sports. A Boston Brahmin, a member of one of the First Families of Virginia—such a person has status through consensus. An investment that is apt to have some intrinsic value is seniority, since experience often gives rise to competence and knowledge. But whatever the intrinsic value of the investment, it is the value that people attribute to it that counts. A factory worker who has been on the job a longer time expects certain privileges and enjoys certain rights not available to newer employees—higher salary, vacation at choice times, longer vacations, and, in the event of layoffs, the right to be retained while newer employees are let go. Faculty members who have achieved the rank of full professor enjoy the benefits of the investment—they have the right to specify their teaching hours, to get the larger offices, to be paid higher salaries, and to have tenure.

[11] Blau, 1964a.
[12] Homans, 1961.

Comparison Processes and Status

Basic to the phenomenon of status is the process of comparison. Persons compare themselves and others with reference to rewards that are received, costs incurred, and investments accumulated, and each is satisfied or dissatisfied with the comparisons. George Homans has suggested that these reactions can be understood in terms of two principles: distributive justice and status congruence.[13]

Distributive justice   When the outcomes, or profit, of persons—their rewards minus their costs—are directly proportional to their investments, the result is *distributive justice,* a concept discussed at length by sociologist George Homans. While most people do not quantify and calculate in a deliberate way, there is, as with affection and exchange theory, an intuitive formulation by which we compare our standing with that of another person and estimate where we stand— higher, lower, or more or less equal. The equation works out this way:

$$\frac{\text{Own investments}}{\text{Other's investments}} = \frac{\text{Own rewards minus costs}}{\text{Other's rewards minus costs}}$$

When there is an equality, distributive justice prevails. Marked inequalities are perceived as unjust. Where investments are not proportional to outcomes, feelings of injustice arise—as in the instance of two groups of female employees in a utility company, the ledger clerks and the cash posters.[14] These groups were equal in pay and independence, but the ledger clerks were superior in such investments as knowledge and seniority, and their costs in terms of responsibility were also greater. Their work had more variety and more intrinsic interest, but it was not in proportion to their superior investments and their costs of responsibility. Therefore, in accordance with the principle of distributive justice, they complained about being underpaid and not having greater independence than the cash posters.

Another investigation, of workers in an oil refinery, supports the principle of distributive justice.[15] If one worker earned more than another, only 14 percent of the respondents in the investigation were dissatisfied or thought it was unfair— providing that the worker was superior in such investments and costs as seniority and education. But if that worker was equal or inferior to the other, then 75 percent were dissatisfied.

Status congruence   *Status congruence* is a condition where *all* of one's status attributes are at the *same* level. People have a strong drive to achieve this condition, and they tend to present themselves so as to create an impression of status con-

[13] Homans, 1961.
[14] Homans, 1954.
[15] Patchen, 1961.

gruence. If they are high in one status characteristic, they expect to be high in all others. If a professor is a brilliant Sanskrit scholar, he or she expects to be a wise committee member and a gifted teacher. Status congruence is what that professor feels, as he or she strives to maintain a position of leadership as a committee member and as a teacher in a way that is compatible with his or her acknowledged excellence as a scholar.

Status congruence explains status symbols. Characteristics which initially have no status value but which are regularly associated with certain status levels eventually come to be perceived as symbols of that status. In an American business corporation, the status of executives is often associated with such features as the privacy and size of their offices, the cost of their office furnishings, the number of secretaries assigned to them—even such things as water caraffes on their desks, so that they don't have to go to the water cooler for a drink of water. The importance of status symbols may be illustrated by the report that in one corporation, when an executive of lesser rank was moved into an office previously occupied by an assistant vice-president, a maintenance man was sent to the office to remove a foot of carpet from the borders of the room. This was done so that the office would no longer have wall-to-wall carpeting, a status symbol reserved for higher-ranking people.

As with distributive justice, status congruence follows from exchange theory. Individuals learn that when the various statuses they present to other people are not consistent, others will behave toward them in an unpredictable manner— sometimes in a rewarding fashion and sometimes not. For example, business executives without college degrees may hide or try to fudge on their educational background for fear that others will treat them in accordance with their educational level rather than their level of competence and income. Thus, persons strive toward a state where they are ranked uniformly in all respects because such a state is associated with the rewarding certainty that others will behave consistently toward them.

Interpersonal comparison It is through periodic comparison with others—interpersonal comparison—that individuals develop a clear idea of their own status. People frequently compare themselves with others in respect to income, possessions, skills, or other attributes. But they don't do this with just anyone. They may feel angry or embarrassed if certain persons make more money than they do, but the incomes of some others will be of no interest to them. The principle of distributive justice, people's perception of their own power to obtain rewards, and the availability of comparative information, will determine with whom they compare themselves. John Thibaut and Harold Kelley have suggested that the conditions for status comparison include the following.[16] First, it must be possible for persons to observe the rewards, costs, and investments of

[16] Thibaut and Kelley, 1959.

others, and to be able to compare them with their own. Second, when a more powerful authority is the source of rewards or costs, observers and those they are comparing themselves with must have approximately the same power to obtain rewards, or to avoid incurring costs, from that person. This creates the rivalry which is associated with comparison (such as sibling rivalry with respect to parental rewards). Third, people are more likely to compare themselves with someone whose rewards and costs are not too different from their own. And the principle of distributive justice suggests a fourth condition—that comparisons are likely to be made with persons having similar investments, because those persons should have similar costs and rewards.

Many small face-to-face groups meet these conditions. Prisoners, medical students, graduate students in an academic department, work groups in industry, are all such groups, and their members make such comparisons continually. Brothers and sisters make the same sorts of comparisons, concerning allowances, bedtimes, punishments, and privileges—particularly if they are close in age. Sibling rivalry is most apt to be avoided only if there is some sort of noncomparability, such as a great difference in age.

People compare costs as well as rewards. This is what happens when a child becomes indignant if her sister is *not* punished for something for which she, herself, has been punished. The same kind of reaction may be observed in adults, although it is often clothed with pious declarations. Assuming that people incur costs in resisting temptations to commit crimes, a similar comparison of costs may underlie the public reaction over "easy" treatment of a criminal.

Stability in the Status Structure

Most status structures are quite stable. Each member of a group remains at approximately the same level over an appreciable length of time. Stability is a result of a number of processes, including, first, the tendency toward status congruence and distributive justice. Forces toward incongruence or injustice are likely to be resisted, and this resistance lends stability to the system. A second set of processes is the increase of the value consensus in a group. Through continued association, people arrive at greater agreement on what they value. Since status attributes depend on group values, the greater the consensus with respect to group values, the greater the stability of the system. Third, members' positions in the status structure allow and encourage them to behave in a manner that validates their status.

Finally, through a process called *status conversion,* one status attribute may be used to create or raise (or lower) others.[17] Wealth may translate to power. Good looks may translate to popularity. Knowledge and education may translate to wealth. High status tends to produce high confidence, which may affect perform-

---

[17] Benoit-Smullyan, 1944; Blau, 1955; Homans, 1961.

ance in various areas of endeavor. The reverse effect may also occur. A low-status attribute may convert other attributes to a lower level. Observations of status and performance in a street corner gang found that the bowling scores of the members consistently reflected the member's status in the gang, especially at the lower end.[18] When a low-status member started to bowl better than high-status members, he was mercilessly heckled until he fell back to his "proper" place.

Certain external processes that contribute to value consensus among group members also contribute to stability of the status structure. Obviously, persons high on the various dimensions of status are going to support values related to these dimensions. But low-status persons also support these values. This is partly because they see some prospect of achieving these values and earning higher status. The values are also functionally important to the achievement of group goals, bringing rewards and reducing costs. A subtle factor is that, by acknowledging the superior attributes of high-status persons, the low-status persons secure their own positions and in some measure reduce the power of the high-status persons. This occurs because the high-status persons become dependent on the deference of the low-status individuals, which is given in exchange for whatever rewards their status attributes provide.

Change in the Status Structure

We have been considering the forces that tend toward stability in status structures. But there are also possibilities for change, and we can analyze these changes by considering the already discussed variables of status congruence, distributive justice, value consensus, and a fourth variable—the need for self-enhancement (see Chapter 15). This need for self-enhancement is expressed in the efforts of people to maximize their own status. They may present themselves in a way that will increase their status on a particular dimension. They may also misperceive their own characteristics and those of other persons to convince themselves that they occupy a higher status. For example, people may consider themselves more talented and intelligent than they really are, and more deserving of a coveted position than the person who actually holds it. He or she is seen as getting it through political pull or lucky breaks. But even a real change in status does not necessarily threaten the stability of the system as a whole unless competition for position becomes excessively disruptive.

Stability can be upset, however, by another kind of status-seeking. When there is an attempt to disrupt the value consensus, the system is weakened. For example, if workers in a labor union divide sharply into two groups—those who favor striking for higher wages and those who do not—union leaders will have

[18] Whyte, 1943.

difficulty in maintaining the status they would enjoy if all workers were in complete agreement. If they favor a strike, those workers opposed to a strike will criticize and devalue them. If they oppose a strike, those favoring a strike will become angry with them. Perhaps this is one reason why so many politicians do not take strong positions on controversial issues and concentrate instead on universal values like morality, motherhood, patriotism, and the protection and care of children. In this way they hope to maintain their status through having a strong constituency to support them.

One way in which people can increase their estimate of their own status relative to that of others is to place a high value on attributes they have and to devalue those they don't have. The older workers in a firm are more likely to emphasize seniority than education. The younger employees are more likely to emphasize education. Upper-middle-class persons emphasize wealth in overall class position and deprecate the importance of coming from an old family. Upper-class persons emphasize the importance of coming from an old family. When group members emphasize different values in this manner, the status structure becomes less stable. This is particularly apt to happen when a long-established group or organization expands rapidly, adding a large number of relatively young members with better training and less conservative values than those previously holding status in the group. This happened at some of the lesser colleges and universities undergoing rapid expansion of graduate programs in the 1950s and 1960s, because the young faculty emphasized scholarship and research to a greater extent than older faculty members, whose status was based upon administrative skills or committee work.

Value consensus can also be weakened if objective conditions are changing the value structure of a group. Attributes that were once important determinants of status lose their importance and become less relevant as the values, goals, requirements, and condition of the group change. For example, in primitive societies the hunters and warriors may have the highest status. As technology advances and the group becomes agricultural, it may be the farmers and the priests—who pray for rain for the crops—who become most important and have the highest status. In the early period of a group's existence, a "promoter" may be needed and may have high status; after the group becomes established, administrative abilities may become more important.

Status congruence has been emphasized as a source of stability in the group structure in that departures from it are likely to encounter resistance. But in a period of change, the same tendency toward status congruence may spread the effects of change from one dimension to others, and exert a dynamic influence. As a new dimension emerges and becomes important—administrative ability, for example—the ranking of this dimension will spill over and exert pressure toward realignment of other dimensions to reestablish status congruence at the new level. The perceived need for distributive justice will produce similar effects.

Distinctions between Status and Affect Structures

Those people we like and those we respect may not always be the same. Or, even when they are, the ranking may be different. The distinction between affect and status structures is one of the bases of evaluation for making these sometimes separate judgments. People accord status to others on the basis of values and needs that are *jointly held* by group members; they like each other on the basis of *personal* values and needs. This is not to say that affection is based on completely unique values. Certain persons are widely liked—and likable—because their behavior meets common needs and coincides with widely held values. But liking includes a unique component and status does not.

Because of this difference, the status structure is more hierarchical than the affect structure, and this in turn helps to explain why persons are so concerned about their status. Whatever people's needs and values, they are apt to find someone who likes them. But if their needs and values are not important to the group, no one will accord them high status. This is true because status is based on agreed-upon criteria, while liking is not. The moral element peculiar to status, as well as its importance to the individual, follows from this. Status comparisons always involve relative worth—people are evaluated on how well they measure up to widely shared, important values. That these values are widely shared means that other people will react uniformly to individuals in terms of the degree to which those individuals' behavior is consistent with the group values. As far as liking goes, people may find one person but not others whose unique needs and values match well, and they will like that person, as that person probably will like them. But the person will be accorded higher or lower status uniformly, by all persons. Status, therefore, becomes strongly associated with rewards that individuals experience in interaction, and people become crucially concerned about their status.

Summary: The Status Structure

Status arises out of the consequences of interaction. People are accorded high status to the degree that their attributes are rewarding to group members. To contribute to status, however, such attributes must be relatively rare: only these confer status. The more that persons are perceived as receiving rewards, the higher their status is likely to be. Similarly, high status is associated with absorbing relatively rare costs that contribute to the realization of the values of the group.

Comparisons of people's outcomes and investments through the principles of distributive justice and status congruence determine status levels. Distributive justice is obtained when the outcomes of each person are directly proportional to his or her investments. If one individual's investments are greater than another's, his or her outcomes should be higher. Status congruence is a condition in which all of one's status attributes are at the same level. Movement toward congruence occurs because, if these statuses are out of line, and the *total* status is therefore not clear, people behave unpredictably toward an individual. Status comparisons are most often made when there is not too much difference between individuals in outcomes or in the capacity to obtain rewards or avoid costs.

Forces toward incongruence or injustice in a status structure are actively resisted, helping to maintain stability of the structure. Consensus on group values also helps to maintain stability. Insofar as possible, people behave so as to confirm their status. And they sometimes convert one form of status into another, thus achieving status congruence. Several factors drive toward changing the status structure. These include successful attacks on value consensus, changes in the value structure through factors external to the group, and shifts from status incongruence to a congruent state.

A number of distinctions can be made between the status and affect structures. Status is accorded on the basis of needs and values that are jointly held, or shared, by members. Liking is determined more by personal values and needs. This makes the status structure more hierarchical than the affect structure. While almost everyone can find someone to like and to be liked by, a member of a group will be ranked in status by the group as a whole. Thus, status becomes a matter of concern—especially to those members who are ranked low.

ELEVEN

SOCIAL NORMS AND CONFORMITY

M embers of all groups show certain regularities in their patterns of behavior. These regularities don't just happen, but are the result of pressures the members exert on one another to conform to some recognized standard, to fulfill some shared expectation. These shared expectations about what one does or says, or even what one thinks or feels, are *social norms*. The social norms of a fraternity, for instance, might include making moderately good grades, dating girls from certain sororities, helping on fraternity projects, being loyal to the fraternity, being congenial with fraternity brothers, and believing that one's own fraternity is the best on campus. Conversely, being placed on probation for poor grades, dating girls from the "wrong" sorority, refusing to cooperate on fraternity projects, disliking or being disloyal to the fraternity, or fighting with fraternity brothers, would be regarded as inappropriate behaviors, departures from and violations of the social norms of the group.

Closely associated with social norms are the mechanisms through which they are enforced, the ways in which group members communicate to each other the nature of appropriate and inappropriate behaviors, and the ways in which pressure is brought to bear on members to conform. We shall consider all of these aspects of normative behavior, as well as those conditions that maximize or minimize the norm-defining and norm-enforcing processes. This chapter will focus

Conformity to a peer-group norm of dress.

primarily on the processes and conditions of social norms, while Chapter 13 will deal with norms as rules of conduct, in connection with the topic of social roles.

NORMS AND NORM FORMATION

The formation of a norm as a standard against which one evaluates one's perceptions has been illustrated by a well-known experiment in which three people were brought into a dark laboratory room and told that a light would appear, would move a short distance, and would then go out.[1] The instructions were to call out the number of inches each person thought the light had moved. The light was turned on repeatedly, and each time the subjects made a judgment—in no particular order, but whenever they were ready. There was a catch, of

[1] Sherif, 1948.

course, which depends on a commonly known perceptual effect: a stationary point of light shown briefly in a dark room appears to move. The phenomenon is known as the *autokinetic* effect (after *auto = self; kinetic = movement*). Thus, the light was not moving at all, but only appeared to do so, and there was no real basis at all for judging the amount of movement.

What happened was that the three individuals started out with somewhat different judgments, and then, after a number of experimental runs, narrowed their differences until the estimates were within an inch or two of each other. For example, on the first appearance of the light, one individual might have guessed 2 inches, another 8 inches, and a third, 12 inches. But with repeated appearances, the individuals gradually shifted their guesses more or less together. Eventually all three judgments stabilized around a mean of 7 inches, with a range of 6 to 8 inches. In the absence of clear perceptual cues, the participants turned to one another for guidance. Many groups have been studied in this type of basic situation and in related ones, and the result is nearly always consensus on some very narrow range of judgments. This agreed-upon range is an example of a social norm.

If individuals have formed a norm in a group situation and are then tested alone, they will still respond in terms of the group. But if they have formed their norms in individual situations and then are put into a group, they will gradually change their individual norms to arrive at a common group norm. Yet curiously, most individuals in this laboratory situation state that they have *not* been influenced by the judgments of others. What this experiment and its related variants suggest is that a small group of persons faced with a novel, ambiguous situation will, in a short time, arrive at a normative interpretation which they share; that this process happens without the participants being aware of it; and that this norm will persist in later situations.

Another set of variations on the basic experiment demonstrated sources of pressures toward consensus. New participants were paired with a high-status person who, by arrangement with the experimenter, established a norm at one point—and then shifted to another. Participants were observed to follow the high-status person's judgments. If the norms were shifted too often and too radically, they became very uncomfortable—presumably because of conflict about whether to conform to their subjective experience or to the judgments of the high-status person. Finally, the amount of change in this situation, as well as in other situations where a person is exposed to the opinions of others, appears to be related to the size of the discrepancy between opinions. A small discrepancy between two or more participants seems to have little or no effect on subsequent judgments; moderate discrepancies have significantly greater effects; large discrepancies have, again, little or no effect. Extremely large discrepancies have large negative, or "boomerang," effects—instead of following, participants maintain an even larger discrepancy wherever possible.[2]

[2] Whittaker, 1964.

Forces Toward Norm Formation

The tendency toward consensus operates not only in the laboratory but outside, in everyday life, as well. Pressures toward conformity in the behavior of group members arise whenever reward-cost outcomes are adversely affected by non-conformity. Such pressures are likely to arise for behavior that relates to the achievement of group goals. For instance, rules against all members of a committee talking at once are obviously useful. In a squadron of military planes, strict conformity to carefully defined patterns of maneuver is essential in order to avoid accidents. But there is also a pressure to conformity that works on thoughts and feelings as well as on behavior. It is interesting to consider why one's opinions or beliefs tend toward conformity.

Physical versus social reality Human beings need to evaluate their opinions, as Leon Festinger has emphasized.[3] Incorrect opinions can be punishing or even fatal. The false belief that the girl you are dating is in love with you can be embarrassing, painful, and punishing. The mistaken opinion that the gun wasn't loaded can lead—as reported frequently in newspaper stories—to fatal consequences.

There are two sources we rely on to determine the validity of our opinions: physical and social reality. We use our senses to obtain a great deal of information about the physical world, and, to some extent, our opinions are validated by such information. But we also receive information about the world from other persons who, to a large extent, interpret the world for us. Our parents warn us about the dangers in the environment or explain away our unfounded fears. They also direct us toward rewarding aspects of the external world. Ultimately we learn to lean on the opinions of others to validate our own. An important difference between physical and social sources of information is that social reality is often less certain—people often do not agree on their opinions.

The relative weight of these sources of information varies with differing circumstances. In general, where clear information is provided leading to an obviously correct answer, we are less influenced by the judgments of others. Where the information is ambiguous, so that the correct answer is not clear, as in the autokinetic situation, we are more likely to rely on the judgment of others. Also, social pressure may vary in different circumstances.

A minority of one Unanimous opinion is especially powerful and may shape our responses even where our senses tell us that we are making a mistake. Solomon Asch demonstrated this in a classic study in which a college student entered a laboratory along with seven other students and was seated at the end of the row.[4] The experimenter explained that the investigation concerned perceptual discriminations, or judgments, and presented sets of lines to be compared with a

[3] Festinger, 1950, 1954.
[4] Asch, 1956.

"standard" line. In each set, the particular line that equaled the standard line had to be picked out, and individuals were to call out their judgments by identifying the correct line. A series of eighteen sets was shown and judged.

During the first few trials, the student found the judgments were simple and obvious—any fool could see which line was equal to the standard. To his great dismay, however, he discovered that on the next trials, the line he saw as the obviously correct answer was not chosen by the other participants. In fact, as the experiment went along, he found that the rest of the group agreed with his perceptions on only one-third of the trials.

Most people put into these circumstances felt great pressure to disregard their own perceptions and to conform to the rest of the group by going along with answers that seemed obviously wrong. About two-thirds of them yielded somewhat to this pressure, conforming to the group on two or more of the trials. A quarter conformed on four or more of the trials. Another quarter did not conform at all, but experienced considerable discomfort in resisting the pressure. What the student did not know was that the other seven participants were in the confidence of the experimenter who had previously arranged with them to make unanimous wrong judgments on two-thirds of the trials.

The importance of unanimity was demonstrated quite simply. When the experimenter put *two* unrehearsed students into the situation instead of one, conformity was greatly weakened. The two students usually made correct judgments, instead of following the staged (faked or simulated) performance of the participants. Presumably each provided support for the other. So, while a minority of one with a unanimous majority opposed to him is quite weak, a minority of two is considerably stronger.

In the above experiment, the correct lines were clear and unambiguous, on the basis of the visual information. A variant of this experiment tested whether more ambiguous information, whose basis was in social reality only, would be even more susceptible to group pressure.[5] A related question was whether difficult judgments would show more conformity than easy judgments. The experiment used several situations. In one, participants were asked to guess how many clicks were sounded by an instrument—simply a matter of counting them. In another, they were asked the answers to easy arithmetic problems. In both of these clear and unambiguous situations, more than half of the participants gave the right answers, even though they heard wrong answers given by three other persons (experimenter confederates). Ambiguous situations involved more difficult arithmetic items, and also multiple choice answers to questions about war and peace. Here, the participants conformed much more frequently to the answers given by the rehearsed group, even though it was arranged that the latter would choose the most unpopular answers on war and peace.

Similar results have been obtained in other research. One important excep-

[5] Blake, Helson, and Mouton, 1956.

tion concerns items that are clearly matters of taste or preference (such as degree of liking for a painting). On these items, conformity is much lower.

We can conclude that with a minority of one, the clearer and more definite the situation, the more resistance there is to conformity. But where the situation is unclear or ambiguous, there is considerable conformity. Judgmental situations that depend on social reality alone show more conformity. Finally, a minority of two or more successfully resists a good part of the pressure from a majority.

Mechanisms underlying conformity Morton Deutsch and Harold Gerard have suggested that two processes operate in these experiments and in conformity behavior in general.[6] One is *normative influence,* which occurs when an individual conforms to an expectation of another person or group because he or she thereby maintains a satisfying relationship with that person or group. But in some of these experiments, the participants did not really form a group, weren't faced with a common task requiring cooperative effort, but were merely individuals in the presence of other individuals, each making judgments "independently." In these cases, another form of influence may well have been at work—*informational influence*—which occurs when information from a source is accepted as evidence about reality.

These two kinds of influence are separate, for individuals may conform to another person's judgment because they want to avoid embarrassment, or they may conform because they think the other chose the correct answer. Informational influence is likely to be strongest when the judgment depends on social reality—where there are no objective facts to contradict the information provided. This is what happened in the experiment using the autokinetic effect, but not in the experiment judging the length of lines.

An experiment that tried to distinguish between normative and informational influences contrasted a public making of judgments with anonymous ones, thus reducing the degree of normative influence. If no one knows what judgments you are making, you should feel less pressure to conform—the principle of the secret ballot. The finding was that there was more conformity to the judgments of other group members under public conditions—partly because of the participant's unwillingness to disagree in public, and partly because the others' judgments were used as a guide to the correct answers.

But another interesting result of this experiment was the discovery of what we may call the *counternorm* effect. One process producing resistance to conformity was *self-commitment. Before* being exposed to the judgments of others, participants either wrote their judgments on a paper which was to be handed to the experimenter, or on a magic slate which they erased after each judgment. Both forms of commitment reduced conformity to the judgments of other participants.

There is a form of self-commitment which takes place in the presence of the

[6] Deutsch and Gerard, 1955.

group: once having made a decision, participants feel constrained to persist in choices consistent with it.[7] To reconsider would be to revive the original conflict with its doubts and misgivings. Having decided to differ from the group, the individuals support their stand by generating appropriate evaluations of themselves, of the other persons, and of other persons' evaluation of them. If they have chosen to be independent, they tend in time to view their own performance favorably, that of others who disagree with them unfavorably, and to perceive that the others evaluate them unfavorably.

While it may have been assumed in many of these studies that normative influence stemmed from the group, one investigator showed that individuals appear also to be subject to unintentional influence from the experimenter.[8] Such an effect decreases conformity to the group since the individuals expect that the experimenter will judge them favorably or unfavorably on whether they are making a correct or incorrect response. After years of taking tests and exams, student participants have learned to try to do well and to perform not only for classmates but for the teacher, in whose role the experimenter must, in some ways, appear to stand. It is also possible that individuals who behave independently are not necessarily following their own evaluation of information but, instead, may be deliberately taking an anticonformist stand.

Norm-sending processes The operations by which norms are communicated and enforced have been termed *norm-sending* processes,[9] and norm-sending has three essential components: (1) defining the attitudes or behavior in question, (2) monitoring the extent to which the person conforms to the norm, and (3) applying the sanctions—rewards or punishments—for conformity or nonconformity. Sanctions take many forms. Positive ones may consist of money, praise, gifts; awarding respect or admiration, promoting, conferring honors or special titles; giving a nod of approval or a hug. Negative ones include physical punishments, like spanking; fines, imprisonment or other penalties; firing, censuring, removing title or rank; disapproving or ostracizing.

Clearly, there is no need for group controls where people spontaneously behave appropriately. But where the environment provides little structure or few cues, or where individuals resist performing particular actions that are necessary to group function, the processes of norm-sending come into play. These processes may be direct and explicit, as when an instructor tells a class what reading is expected, what the examination questions will be, and what the attendance rules are, or they may be indirect.

The same instructor who spells out for first- and second-year college students what is required, may believe that for graduate students it is no longer appropriate to lay down such explicit rules. But the rules are there, more subtly

[7] Gerard, 1965.
[8] Schulman, 1967.
[9] Rommetveit, 1955.

implied, but no less strong in their operation. Professors have considerable social power over graduate students, who need good grades and strong recommendations to get financial support through fellowships or assistantships and, later, full-time positions. Professors who are enthusiastic and demanding in their own research set an example for graduate students and use their social power to obtain similar commitments from them. By giving heavy assignments, they make clear what they expect and what the profession expects. They react decisively to signs of resistance to onerous tasks, and ridicule the typical objections or excuses used by undergraduates. The graduate student who asks how many pages an assigned paper should be is likely to get a raised eyebrow from the professor. The raised eyebrow not only communicates information, but can be an implied threat. Additional pressures arise from other graduate students who are also sending norms by setting examples and by according respect and sometimes envy to the most brilliant and competent students.

Summary: Norms and Norm Formation

A social norm is an expectation shared by group members about what one does or says or even what one thinks or feels. Pressures toward conforming to the norm arise whenever reward-cost outcomes are likely to be adversely affected by deviant behavior. Often these pressures shape behavior toward achieving the group goals. Norms also control opinions and beliefs, especially those relevant to maintaining the group or achieving its goals. Information about the environment often takes a normative form which enables individuals to check their opinions and beliefs against those shared by others—so-called social reality. Two forms of influence operating in small groups are: (1) normative, and (2) informational. The former involves conformity to group expectations, and the latter, to social reality. Norm-sending has three essential components: (1) defining attitudes or behavior, (2) monitoring the extent to which persons conform to the norm, and (3) applying sanctions—rewards or punishments—for conformity or nonconformity.

A THEORY OF NORMATIVE BEHAVIOR

Any theory that attempts to account for the normative character of social interaction must answer three questions. These concern the focus, extent, and distribution of conformity in a group:

1 What determines the kinds of behavior or attitudes that become the targets of norm-sending? Behaviors subjected to conformity pressures vary greatly from society to society and from group to group within a single society. In some occupations you can wear what you please, but in others conservative business dress is required. An adequate theory must explain why some behaviors and attitudes are subjected to normative control and others are not.

2 Why is much greater conformity found in some groups than in others? Some religious groups, for instance, conform much more strictly to the tenets and requirements of their faith than others. Or, similarly, the amount of discipline and obedience is greater in some military outfits than in others. An adequate theory must account for these differences in group control.

3 What determines the distribution of conformity *within* a group? Some college students carry out assignments and attend class more regularly than others in the same class. How can we account for this?

These three questions deal respectively with the focus, extent, and distribution of conformity to norms. Relying extensively on concepts from exchange theory, we can answer them in terms of the effects of four conditions: (1) the degree to which group members find the behaviors or attitudes of other persons rewarding or costly, (2) the power structure of the group as determined by the distribution of resources, dependencies, and alternatives, (3) the degree to which

Observing a society-wide norm of politeness: covering a yawn.

behavior in accordance with the norm is intrinsically rewarding or costly, and (4) the degree to which behavior is open to surveillance and to imposition of sanctions.

The following three sections discuss the focus, extent, and distribution of conformity in terms of the four conditions outlined above.

Behavior and Attitudes for which Norms Emerge

Social norms have a variety of *indirect* reward-cost outcomes. A norm may make unnecessary the exercise of interpersonal power, so that a person's costs are reduced. A norm may affirm group membership, so that rewards are raised. But norms also have more *direct* outcomes which are related to needs arising in the process of group formation and development, and our emphasis will be on these direct outcomes.

Rewards and costs: group goals   People form groups to satisfy a variety of needs. Normative controls arise for behaviors where members have become dependent upon the group for satisfying their needs. Consequently, norms encourage behavior that increases members' satisfaction and discourage behavior that interferes with satisfaction. The prevalence and strength of the norms depends at least partly upon the extent to which the members rely on the group for satisfaction of particular needs, and partly on the strength of those needs.

Groups generally fill task-related needs or social-emotional needs or both. Behaviors that contribute to accomplishment of a group task are likely to be subject to normative control because they lead to achievement and satisfaction and help to avoid failure. Norms develop to ensure cooperation and to establish consensus on attitudes relevant to group goals. For example, members of a group may be required to attend meetings regularly; leaders and officials are expected to serve. Without such norms, nobody would show up, nobody would work, and nothing would get done. In one study of professional thieves, it was found that normative pressures apply with great force.[10] Behaviors that would result in failure and arrest have strong negative sanctions. For example, failure to appear at the appointed time and place, or revealing plans to outsiders, endangers the project and can lead to arrest. So punctuality, dependability, and being close-mouthed are greatly valued by professional thieves, and behavior contrary to these values is apt to be met with scorn, ostracism, or being "taken for a ride."

Groups formed to satisfy social-emotional needs strongly emphasize individual satisfaction. Fraternities and sororities, for instance, emphasize friendship, emotional support, acceptance, and belonging. Norms arise to encourage fair treatment and to prohibit competition and aggression. Similarly, families apply strong sanctions for aggressive actions of children toward each other or toward their parents.

[10] Sutherland, 1937.

The distinction between task-related and social-emotional needs is not absolute. Most groups in part satisfy both needs. In spite of their task orientation, industrial work groups provide some emotional support to workers to counteract various anxiety-producing aspects of the work environment. And the Boy Scouts and Girl Scouts, while fulfilling social-emotional needs, direct a lot of attention to the acquisition of skills and the earning of awards that recognize these skills.

Power structure of the group   The attitudes and behaviors that are necessary to the satisfactions of the most powerful persons in the group are most likely to be subject to normative control. In a family with small children, for instance, norms develop in directions desired by the parents rather than by the children, because of the great discrepancy in power. This is vividly illustrated by a selection from Oscar Lewis's *Children of Sanchez:*

> Living in one room one must go at the same rhythm as the others, willingly or unwillingly—there is no way except to follow the wishes of the strongest ones. After my father, Antonia had her way, then La Chata, then my brothers. The weaker ones could approve or disapprove, get angry or disgusted but could never express their opinion. For example, we all had to go to bed at the same time, when my father told us to. Even when we were grown up, he would say, "To bed! Tomorrow is a work day."[11]

As children reach adolescence and young adulthood, however, the norms change as a result of the shift in the balance of power toward more equality. This happens because of the increase in the alternative satisfactions that become available to the young people, in their peer groups and in their reduced economic dependence on their parents. These norm shifts are revealed by the adolescents' criticism of some of the parents' behaviors and by the greater freedom they have in the hours they keep and the activities in which they participate without parental supervision.

Intrinsic costs and rewards   Some behaviors are less susceptible to controls than others because of their intrinsic rewards or costs. Smoking, for example, becomes a persistent habit and is difficult to break because of the physiological contributions to satisfaction. Any behavior associated with powerful biological or social motives may fall into the high-reward class, and negative sanctions are unlikely to be effective in reducing such behavior.

Costly behaviors, too, are often exempt from normative control, because nobody can be required to perform them. For example, dangerous commando missions behind enemy lines are not assigned, are not normative requirements, but depend on volunteers. When behavior is very costly, norms are likely to arise to reduce cost. Medical students, burdened with far more than they can possibly

---

[11] Reprinted with permission from O. Lewis. *Children of Sanchez.* New York: Random House, 1961.

Intrinsically satisfying behavior. (Michael Kahn)

accomplish, have to make decisions about priorities. But this is a common problem for all medical students. In this situation, to avoid excessive competition from brilliant or strongly motivated students, the group is likely to develop norms about how much work is to be done and what aspects of it will have priority, as well as norms to ensure cooperation in sharing the work burden.[12]

Surveillance and sanctions Obviously, attitudes and behaviors that are difficult to monitor are less likely to be subject to normative control. Sanctions cannot be applied unless transgressions can be observed. Thus one's public behavior is controlled to a greater extent than one's private behavior. People may pick their noses or scratch their genitalia in private but not in public. The importance of surveillance may be illustrated by comparing open hostility with the indirect expression of aggression—which occurs much more frequently. Open hostility and physical violence can be observed and sanctions can be readily applied; but subtle forms of aggression, such as criticism in a context of pretended well-meaning (as in a classroom), are more difficult to detect, define, and punish.

[12] Becker, Geer, Hughes, and Strauss, 1961.

Conformity in Different Groups

The second question which any theory of normative behavior must answer is why greater conformity is found in some groups than in others. Why are discipline and obedience to orders greater in a military unit than in a classroom group? The answers to this question are again found in the four conditions previously listed. The first is the degree to which members find the behavior of the other persons in the group rewarding or costly.

Conditions intensifying rewards and costs   A group can exert pressure on its members to conform to some norm only to the degree that the group is cohesive, cohesiveness being the forces acting on members to remain in the group.[13] In Chapter 10, we noted several bases of attraction to the group, including high reward-cost outcomes stemming from interaction among members, group activities that are rewarding for their own sake, and membership in the group as a means to attaining other ends. Cohesion is also relative to the comparison levels of group members. The total force operating on group members to remain in the group depends not only on these outcomes internal to the group but also on outcomes available in alternative relations outside the group.

A group cannot impose negative sanctions that are any stronger than the cohesive forces that hold the group together. If it does, members will leave the group rather than bear the sanctions. Casual observation of groups that are able to impose severe negative sanctions on their members supports this formulation. In such groups, members either have high outcomes, or they have very low comparison levels and comparison levels for alternatives. The latter might be low for two reasons: (1) the members can command little in alternative relations, or (2) their alternatives are blocked. Some illustrations follow.

Most adolescent groups have high outcomes for individual members, provide satisfaction for powerful needs, and are highly cohesive. Military units, religious sects, and prisoner groups have members with low comparison levels or comparison levels for alternatives. The alternative to conformity in the military is often a court martial and imprisonment, or a dishonorable discharge. Members of religious sects often have low alternative sources of satisfaction.[14] This may be true because their distinctive values and behavior patterns make interaction with outsiders more costly or because they are rejected by other groups. Consequently the sect may very effectively control its members through such techniques as ostracism should they attempt to deviate from the norms of the sect. In prisoner groups, there are high walls and guards. There are no choices even about which cellblock a prisoner lives in, and therefore no alternative associations.

Various studies have presented evidence that pressures toward conformity are stronger in more cohesive groups. One investigation of the uniformity of

---

[13] Festinger, Schachter, and Back, 1950.
[14] Pope, 1942.

attitudes and behaviors in campus housing groups found that the more cohesive the group, the more uniform the attitudes and behavior of the members.[15] In the more cohesive groups, moreover, those who deviated from the norms were less likely to be accepted as friends. Exchange theory suggests why this should be so. In more cohesive groups conformity is more rewarding and deviation more costly. Where cohesiveness is high, members place more value on being liked, and if conformity is required for being liked, members of a highly cohesive group are more likely to conform.

Power structure of the group   The degree to which persons in a group are able to influence one another depends on the basis of power that exists between members, and it follows from this that group conformity will also vary with such bases. To the extent that the power structure of the group is based on forms of power that increase over time, the conformity level of group members ought to be high. Where the prevailing modes of control have bases that lose effectiveness over time, the level of conformity may be expected to be low. Studies support this theoretical conclusion and we discuss them below.

Coercive power initially increases the likelihood of conformity—particularly public conformity. Used repeatedly, however, it arouses resistance to conformity, and, at the same time, reduces the level of attraction. A laboratory experiment focused on coercive and legitimate power and their relation to conformity.[16] Participants were informed what fines would be levied for working too slowly. When the supervisor levied fines outside this legitimate range, resistance to conforming to the norm increased. An important condition for minimizing resistance, it would seem, is that sanctions perceived as illegitimate must be avoided. Another study suggests that reward is more effective than punishment in bringing about conformity, because of the resistance aroused by punishment.[17]

Coercion in laboratories is rather mild. An exception to our generalization about the ineffectiveness of coercive power for normative control may occur under extreme conditions of coercion. The basis of power may be converted to referent power. Some of those imprisoned for a long time in Nazi concentration camps in World War II strongly *identified* with their captors, adopting their attitudes and behaviors and even incorporating pieces of Gestapo uniforms into their dress.[18] In large part this probably happened because the tremendous coercive power of the guards could be used as reward power. In the terminology of reinforcement theory, *avoidance of a punishing contingency* is, itself, rewarding. Thus, by easing various constraints, sometimes in exchange for informing on other prisoners or other cooperative behavior, captors exercised powerful reinforcements. With this condition continuing over a period of years, it is not surprising that the coercive power was converted into referent power.

[15] Festinger, Schachter, and Back, 1950.
[16] French, Morrison, and Levinger, 1960.
[17] Zipf, 1960.
[18] Bettelheim, 1943.

In those instances where normative controls are based primarily on referent power from the start, groups are likely to exercise strong conformity pressures over a long period. This explains the durability of parental control in most families and the relative permanence of an individual's religion.

Intrinsic costs and rewards   In groups where behavior that happens to be in conformity with group norms is rewarding for its own sake, conformity is likely to be high. This is often the case in groups where satisfaction of social-emotional needs is dominant or in task groups where the tasks themselves are enjoyable. Examples of the former might be fraternities and sororities; of the latter, sports clubs. Where conformity involves behavior that is costly, however, as where the tasks are boring, fatiguing, or dangerous, conformity is likely to be lower unless the costs of nonconformity are correspondingly increased. In work situations where sanctions for nonconformity are weak, the level of conformity to official norms concerning production may be low. This line of reasoning is often used as an argument against seniority, tenure, and civil service systems, which protect the worker against severe sanctions.

Surveillance and sanctions   Where conforming behavior is not intrinsically satisfying or is costly in terms of time or tedium, surveillance becomes necessary. Unless behavior is monitored and sanctions are imposed for failure to conform, conforming behavior is likely not to occur. An obvious example is the military group in peacetime, where risks are low and many activities are not satisfying for their own sake. Many places of work have organized systems of surveillance— time clocks, whistles, foremen, and supervisors mark the start and stop of work and ensure a minimum of interruptions. As the work becomes more intrinsically satisfying, surveillance and sanctions become much less evident. Skilled crafts and professional work situations illustrate the point, for the skilled craftsman works with a minimum of supervision and control, and the physician or lawyer is rarely monitored. If these people are not intrinsically motivated, they are not likely to do a good job.

There is another condition which may make surveillance unnecessary. In a study where individuals felt they were moderately accepted by other members of a group and they had a possibility of becoming completely accepted, a high degree of conformity to the group norms in *both* public and private behavior was found.[19] On the other hand, people with a low degree of acceptance and who thought they might be rejected conformed closely to the norm in public behavior but deviated markedly in private. Thus, certain types of motivating conditions can be created that will lead a person to conform both publicly and privately, without the need for surveillance. Where the major motive of conformity is insecurity over status, public conformity is likely to be high, but private conformity is unlikely to occur.

[19] Dittes and Kelley, 1956.

Two other conditions require careful surveillance if conformity is desired. These are the use of coercive and nonlegitimate power. Under surveillance, these processes create public compliance accompanied by marked resistance which expresses itself in sharp dissension in private.

Distribution of Conformity in the Group

The third question to be answered by a theory of normative behavior is why individuals differ in the extent to which they conform to norms. While answers to the first two questions were found largely in group processes, the question of individual differences in conformity within groups requires attention both to group processes and to personality factors. Certain group conditions, such as the power structure, may increase or decrease variation among members, but personality factors also play an important part in variation through their relation to structures or processes that characterize the group.

Individual differences in rewards and costs   We have already seen that where outcomes in a group are high and those available in alternative relations are low, there is a uniformity in behavior and attitudes among group members with all conforming to approximately the same degree. Where cohesiveness is low, there is a much wider variation in conformity. Those members who have important satisfactions elsewhere will frequently deviate from the norm, as will those who do not find much satisfaction in the group. Illustrating this situation is a study of books on psychology written by the clergy and books on religion written by psychiatrists.[20] Ministers writing on psychology shifted their religious norms toward those of psychology. Psychiatrists writing on religion shifted their psychiatric norms toward those of religion. Allegiance to outside groups, both here and in the previously cited study of conformity in housing groups, is likely to produce deviation.

Another factor determining individual differences in conformity is the varying pressure exerted upon different persons in a group. When a member begins to deviate from normative behavior, other members place increasing pressure on him or her to conform.[21] In terms of exchange theory, we might say that this happens because the deviant behavior has reduced the rewards and increased the costs of other members. But if he or she behaves in an increasingly deviant fashion, there is a point of diminishing return where pressures toward conformity are reduced and the member is rejected.[22] There is only fragmentary evidence, but one can discern the glimmer of a principle here—that pressures on someone toward conformity are associated with the perception of the likelihood that he or she will conform. If a person is thought of as a "hopeless" deviant, pressures to conform are light—too costly to exert, in time, energy, and frustration, for the

[20] Klausner, 1961.
[21] Festinger, 1950.
[22] Schachter, 1951.

reward received. The "weirdo" may remain in the group, but with low status, and with little pressure to conform.

Individuals vary in their susceptibility to conformity pressures. Those people are most susceptible who are more submissive, less self-confident, less inclined to nervous tension, more authoritarian, less intelligent, less original, low in need achievement, high in need for social approval, conventional in values, and, finally, high in need for conformity.[23] A group with members who vary in these characteristics will have variation in conformity.

But personality differences do not always have the same effect. Under different conditions, the effect of individual differences will grow or diminish. A study of conformity that dealt with three different tasks (of perceptual judgment, of self-reports of agreement with peer group norms, and of self-estimates of acceptance of pressures from authority) found only a small, although consistent, trend for persons who conform in one situation to conform in the other two.[24] Another investigation suggested that while there may be extreme conformists and extreme nonconformists, most people who lie somewhere in between vary in their susceptibility to pressures according to the situation in which they find themselves. The more important the norm, the less deviance will be permitted . . . or exhibited.

Power, status, and conformity   The higher one's status, the more likely one is to conform to group norms. High school students who are best liked are seen as having the greatest number of conforming traits;[25] high-status workers in an industrial group conform most closely to the output norms of the group;[26] successful politicians reflect the values of the voters.[27] It has been suggested that such leaders and spokespersons, playing these central roles, must represent group opinion and not their own desires.[28] But one of the curious aspects of leadership is the need, from time to time, to break away from norms. There are circumstances when the group must change if it is to function well or fairly or efficiently, and the role of the leader is to introduce changes in norms, which may involve deviation from current and established norms. Congressional representatives voting according to conscience rather than following the pressure of the mail from constituents are departing from norms. At the same time they are conforming to the expectations of their constituency toward the role of leader.[29]

Paradoxically, leaders must be both conformists and deviants. In early phases of interaction, leaders are likely to conform in order to build up status, power, and a credit of favorable attitudes among followers. In later stages, they can engage in deviant behavior, using some of their favorable credit in the balance. Or, more generally, conformity and deviation will vary according to the

[23] Blake and Mouton, 1961.
[24] Back and Davis, 1965.
[25] Riley and Cohn, 1958.
[26] Roethlisberger and Dickson, 1939; Homans, 1954.
[27] Fromm, 1941.
[28] Verba, 1961.
[29] Hollander, 1958.

leaders' perception of their security at the time. The more threatened and insecure they feel, the more they conform to group norms; the more secure they feel, the more they can afford to deviate from those norms. Security, in turn, is a function of the basis and amount of power the leaders have, so that when they have expert knowledge and legitimate power, they feel secure enough to deviate.

The degree to which high-status people are pressured to conform also depends on the behavior in question. High-status people are punished less than others for minor infractions, but more than others for behavior that prevents achievement of important group goals.

The greatest conformity is exhibited by those members with intermediate status. A study of the relation between conformity and sociometric status in cliques of delinquent boys found that, in cliques of four or five boys, the conformity was least for the highest-status boy, next least for the lowest-status boy, and most for the one with second-highest status.[30] George Homans has observed that high-status persons have credit to draw on when they are wrong. When they are right, in their leadership and decision-making, they validate their high status so that the balance of potential outcomes favors nonconformity.[31] Similarly, for low-status persons, there is little to lose, since they are already at the bottom of the hierarchy. Wrong behavior is merely ignored. If they conform to the group and are right, little is gained, for they have only behaved like other members. If they act independently and are also right, they have the satisfaction of showing up the rest of the group, so that for them, too, the balance of outcomes favors nonconformity. For persons of intermediate status aspiring to move upward, the rewards and costs are otherwise and favor conformity. If they go along with the group and are right, they add a slight increment to their status. If they are wrong, they lose little, being in company with other members. But if they act independently and are proved wrong, they suffer an appreciable loss of status, having neither the credit of the high-status members nor the rock-bottom security of the low-status members. Middle-status persons have room to move downward, and this risk outweighs any benefits they might achieve through independent, correct decisions.

Intrinsic costs and rewards   For some people, there is intrinsic satisfaction in conforming. In a social-emotional group which has norms of friendly, cooperative behavior, persons with high needs for affiliation enjoy conforming to these norms. For others—persons with marked hostility feelings, for example—conforming is difficult and unrewarding. In task groups, people with strong needs for achievement or who are skilled in the group activities may experience pleasure in carrying out the tasks, while others, unskilled and less achievement-oriented, may experience difficulty and frustration. There is, in the interaction between group processes and personality characteristics, a range of different reward-cost outcomes for the various members. One investigation, supporting this exchange

[30] Harvey and Consalvi, 1960.
[31] Homans, 1961.

theory interpretation of conformity in terms of intrinsic motivation, showed that people made to feel accepted by a group are more attracted to the group if they have low self-esteem.[32] They conform to a greater extent. Presumably, they have a greater need for acceptance, and possibly they perceive fewer alternatives.

Another study has identified two patterns of reaction leading to conformity: social accommodation and self-correction.[33] These are essentially the normative and informational tendencies toward conformity we have discussed before, but they open the way to a further suggestion: that conformity may be either a reaction to the source of a communication (a person) or to the communication itself.[34] People who react to the source of a communication are thought to be motivated by a need for acceptance, while those who react to the communication are assumed to be motivated by a need for success.

Surveillance and sanctions The extent to which the position of group members exposes them to public view appears to be important in determining conformity. Certain kinds of high-status positions are highly visible and are therefore subject to monitoring and punitive action. School principals, or civic and governmental officials, feel strong pressures to conform and can deviate only where the position itself calls for deviant behavior. Other types of leadership positions are less public, and the incumbent is less constrained by surveillance.

Whether or not people of low group status are likely to be affected by surveillance and sanctions depends upon certain conditions. Low-status people receive less attention and are therefore less likely to be punished for norm violation. On the other hand, either their characteristics or those of the group may expose them to public view. If they really want to move up, or are anxious about slipping down, or if the group conditions create feelings of insecurity, they may take pains to make their behavior public in the hope that conformity may help them move up, or at least keep them from sliding down. This is what we see in relatively low-status executives who go out of their way to agree with senior executives.

Summary: A Theory of Normative Behavior

The focus, extent, and distribution of conformity to norms depends upon four conditions: (1) the degree to which group members find the behaviors or attitudes of other persons rewarding or costly, (2) the power structure of the group, as determined by the distribution of resources, dependencies, and alternatives, (3) the degree to which behavior in accordance with the norm is intrinsically rewarding or costly, and (4) the degree to which behavior is open to surveillance or to imposition of sanctions.

People form groups to satisfy a variety of needs. Normative controls arise in the areas of behavior in which members have become dependent upon the group

[32] Dittes, 1959.
[33] Wilson, 1960.
[34] McDavid, 1959.

for need satisfaction. Where accomplishing certain tasks is important, group norms develop to shape behavior toward that end. If the group is oriented toward social-emotional behavior, behaviors that provide emotional support, friendship, or love become subject to norms. Behaviors that are supported by strong inner needs, that are costly, or that are hard to monitor are difficult to control. If group goals can be achieved only through costly behavior, norms that help to reduce costs or to distribute the costs equitably among the members often arise.

Groups vary in the conformity pressures that they can exert, for several reasons. To the extent that conformity is costly, the forces exerted toward it cannot exceed the forces to remain in the group. These forces are a function of cohesiveness, based on satisfactions attainable through membership in the group and the outcomes available in alternative relations outside the group. The extent to which a group may exert negative sanctions for nonconformity depends upon its cohesiveness. In addition, the degree of conformity which a group can extract from its members depends upon the nature of the power structure. Finally, where group behavior is intrinsically satisfying, group conformity is apt to be high.

Conformity within different groups may be relatively uniform, as in a highly cohesive group, or may vary widely from member to member, as in a group with low cohesiveness. Different members experience different conformity pressures depending upon their status. Leaders may be more conforming in some respects, and less conforming in others, because their role as leaders may demand that they lead the group in new directions, as well as conform to the main values of the group. Conformity varies with the status of members, with those of moderate status exhibiting the greatest conformity. Differences in personalities and needs of members may also be associated with different reward-cost outcomes for conformity, thus creating differences among members in the extent to which they conform.

CONFORMITY TO NORMS OF SOCIAL RESPONSIBILITY

In the 1960s, a young girl named Kitty Genovese was attacked in a residential section of New York City by a man with a knife.[35] Stabbed repeatedly, she screamed for help and tried to fight him off until she died of the numerous wounds inflicted on her. All this time, thirty-eight people remained in the safety of their apartments, many of them listening and even watching from their windows, but none of them came to her aid or even called the police. The crime received great publicity in the press and on television, along with much speculation about why people do not aid victims in such situations. A similar incident again occurred in the same area in 1974.

A number of social psychologists have tried to identify the conditions under which people will or will not aid others in distress. Underlying the idea that such situations require all of us to aid people in distress is a *norm of social responsibility.*

[35] Rosenthal, 1964.

Altruistic or helping behavior. (Michael Kahn)

We are expected to help those who are helpless, dependent upon us, defenseless in a dangerous situation, or in any way in need of assistance. As we will see, situational factors play an important role in conformity to this norm of social responsibility. These factors seem to operate through their effect on the rewards and costs for conformity or through the individual's definition of the norm as relevant or irrelevant in the situation.

We are also expected to feel empathy or sympathy for a person who is hurt or being hurt, which should also arouse us to help. But this expectation has its origin in social norms as well. These feelings are modeled for us at an early age by our parents, and we are taught to define our feelings in this way when someone in the family gets hurt. Eventually the feelings become our own, and there is little sense of controlling them through norm-sending.

Defining the Situation

Heroic or altruistic behavior typically involves costs to the hero/heroine or altruist that are not adequately compensated by the rewards in the situation. People conform to such norms because nonconformity results in the costs of lowered self-esteem and of guilt. Such costs, however, can be avoided if one can define the situation so that the norm does not apply. There are two conditions that must be satisfied before one feels compelled to behave in accordance with a moral norm.[36] First, the situation must be defined as one in which one's acts will have consequences for the welfare of others, and, second, it must be defined as one in which one must take responsibility for those acts and their consequences. Insofar as either one or the other of these conditions is absent or minimized, people's behavior will be unaffected by the appropriate norm, no matter how strongly they may believe in it. Conversely, maximizing these two conditions produces altruistic behavior and minimizes doing harm to others.

Studies of bystander intervention in contrived emergencies are consistent with this formulation. In one experiment, participants heard, over an intercom, what appeared to be an epileptic seizure of a fellow participant.[37] More than eight out of ten of those who thought that they alone were aware of the seizure reported the emergency before the intercom was cut off. Less than one in three, however, did so when they believed that four other participants were also aware of the incident. The investigators concluded from their observation that the possibility of *diffusing responsibility* to other persons altered the perception of the costs in the situation.

The investigators suggested that the seizure created a conflict of the *avoidance-avoidance* type. This is a standard concept in learning theory and is depicted by a spatially arranged situation in which individuals are placed between two objects they wish to avoid. This is a dilemma, for as they move away from one, they get closer to the other.

Individuals could avoid guilt over not helping the victim by making a move to help. On the other hand, only by not helping could they avoid the risk of making fools of themselves (by overreacting, ruining the experiment, destroying the anonymous nature of the situation). Where an individual was alone, the obvious distress of the victim and the need for help was important enough to resolve the conflict in favor of action. For the participants who knew that other bystanders were present, the cost of *not* helping was lessened, and the conflict was more acute. Trapped between two negative alternatives (allowing the victim to suffer, or disrupting the experiment to help), the participants vacillated between the two and were unable to make a decision.

In other situations, the failure of bystanders to act seemed to be related to their definition of the situation as one that did not require action. Inaction was not thought to have adverse consequences for the welfare of another person. Here again, the presence of other people was associated with a failure to act. In one experiment, individuals found themselves in a room where smoke began to billow up from the ventilator.[38] The experiment was done in one of three settings: the individuals were alone, were with two experimenter accomplices who ignored

[36] Schwartz, 1968.
[37] Darley and Latané, 1968.
[38] Latané and Darley, 1968.

the smoke, or were with two other naïve participants. Three-quarters of the individuals who were alone reported the smoke, but one-third or less of the participants in either of the three-person groups reported the smoke.

Similar results were obtained in another experiment. In this instance, persons heard what seemed to be a woman's scream and cry of pain from the next room.[39] This experiment was done in one of four settings: the individuals were waiting alone, were waiting with an experimenter accomplice who remained as passive as possible, were paired with naïve strangers, or were paired with naïve friends. Here again, the presence of another person who did not react to the emergency markedly inhibited reaction. Three-quarters of the people who were alone responded with aid to the victim. Only one in fourteen of those who were with experimenter confederates responded. In fewer than half of the groups of two strangers did at least one person respond. Although more persons responded in the presence of friends, response was still inhibited.

In addition to the idea that the presence of other persons leads to a diffusion of responsibility and less pressure to conform to the normative demands of the situation, a second process may lead persons to *misperceive the situation* as one that does not require them to act.[40] Many emergency situations are ambiguous. It is not totally clear that something is dangerously wrong, and, even when it is, an appropriate path of action is not always clear. Moreover, bystanders partly interpret a situation in terms of the behavior of other bystanders. To appear cool and in control is a norm for public behavior. Thus, each individual may look at the others, and be influenced not to act by their inaction and apparent "cool."

These observations cast some doubt on the old adage that there is safety in numbers in emergency situations, but a related study in a field setting suggests that it may be true.[41] Four teams of investigators, each made up of a victim, a model helper, and two observers, staged collapses on express trains of New York's Eighth Avenue subway. In these incidents, which involved over 4,000 subway riders unknowingly, as participants, they used victims "who appeared to be either drunk or ill, and who were Negro or white." In some situations, there was no model helper; in others a model intervened either early or late in the incident. Unlike the behavior of participants in the laboratory, in a much higher proportion of incidents bystanders responded with aid. In sixty-two of sixty-five instances the victim who appeared ill received spontaneous help before the model intervened; even the drunk received spontaneous help half the time.

These investigators suggest two possible explanations for the difference between their results and the laboratory work described earlier. First, the emergency situations were markedly different. Bystanders could actually see the victim, and this made it hard to conclude that an emergency did not exist. It may also have prevented the spread of responsibility. Second, even if there was a

[39] Latané and Rodin, 1969.
[40] Latané and Rodin, 1969.
[41] Piliavin, Rodin, and Piliavin, 1969.

tendency to diffuse responsibility, it was outweighed by the probability that *someone* in a subway car with forty-five passengers would eventually intervene. One could say that one good apple will save the whole barrel. Drunken victims were presumably helped less because the costs of helping were perceived as greater, the victims more responsible for their own plight, and drunkenness less serious than illness. Of further possible importance is that subjects who know they are in an experiment (as in lab studies) assume a passive attitude, leaving responsibility for anything that happens to the experimenter. Thus the contrast between lab studies and subway experiments.

Other experiments demonstrate conditions that contribute to the assumption of responsibility and the awareness of consequences, both of which, in turn, affect the degree to which people conform to moral norms. One study varied the degree to which participants were psychologically close to the victim.[42] The participants were instructed to administer electric shocks to victims, some of whom were in the next room so that the participants could only hear their pounding on the wall in protest, and some of whom were in the same room, in fact were in physical contact—because the participants had to force their hands onto a plate for the shocks. Where the victims were in the next room, only one in three defied the experimenter and conformed to the norm against inflicting pain on other people. Where the victims were in close contact, more than two out of three refused to shock the victims. Obviously, where people can observe their own involvement and the victims' responses, it is more difficult to deny responsibility or to fail to see the consequences of actions.

A further factor concerns the experimenter's role. The stronger the norms governing the relation of the experimenter to the participant, and the greater the transfer of responsibility from the participant to the experimenter, the more willing the participant will be to deliver a painful shock to the victim. When the experimenter was physically close and able to exercise surveillance, obedience to his demand was strongest.

Other studies are consistent with the finding that helping another person is related both to awareness of consequences and the feeling of responsibility. Experimental manipulations that make people realize the consequences of their behavior increase their conformity to the norm of social responsibility. To the degree that people feel less responsible, such conformity is reduced. Conformity is also affected according to how prominently the norm of social responsibility presents itself. Seeing another person engage in helping behavior increases the likelihood that one will aid somebody who needs help. One study put a woman whose auto had a flat tire on a freeway with a confederate already helping her. Seeing that the woman was being helped increased the frequency with which motorists stopped to offer aid to another car placed further down the road. Similarly, observing a model contribute to a Salvation Army kettle increased the frequency of donations on the part of bystanders.[43]

[42] Milgram, 1965.
[43] Bryan and Test, 1967.

Finally, a group of experimenters in Manhattan "lost" a number of open envelopes, each of which had a wallet protruding from it.[44] With each wallet there was a letter addressed to the owner, so that it seemed that a previous finder had been in the process of mailing the wallet back but had lost it again. The letter also described the previous finder's feelings about returning the wallet. Finders of the envelopes and wallets most often mailed them back when they perceived themselves as similar to the previous finders and when the feelings about returning the wallets were positively expressed in the letters. When the previous finders were seen as dissimilar, their feelings (positive or negative) had no effect on the number of intact wallets returned. This is consistent with modeling theory discussed earlier, in Chapter 2.

The Norm of Reciprocity

Other conditions also increase the likelihood of helping behavior, often because they make the norms of either social responsibility or reciprocity stand out. The norm of reciprocity suggests that receiving prior help from another person, whether or not that person is later in need, would increase helping behavior. Blocking or hindering someone instead of helping also follows a reciprocity norm—a kind of tarnished golden rule. Prior blocking from another person will lead to hindering a victim who is similar to the person who originally blocked the individual, and to helping one who is dissimilar. The *heightened* tendency to help the dissimilar other person in response to having been hindered is due to the heightened awareness of the norm of responsibility. Perhaps a heightened sense of justice also operates in some of these situations. In one experiment it was demonstrated that individuals who had been betrayed by earlier partners exerted greater efforts on behalf of later partners who had been similarly betrayed than they did on behalf of partners who had been rewarded last time around.[45] Here it seems that altruistic behavior arises to establish social justice.

Norms and Harming Another Person

It isn't just a matter of helping others in distress. The norm of social responsibility also requires that people under most circumstances refrain from hurting others. The fact that hurting can appear justified under certain circumstances (self-defense or justified retaliation) suggests that the norms against harming are related to general norms of equity or fairness in human exchanges. Elaine Walster and Ellen Berscheid have suggested that when individuals hurt other persons, they experience discomfort from two sources.[46] One is anxiety over possible retaliation, and the other is distress over having behaved in a way that violates ethical principles and self-expectations. People may relieve such distress by re-

[44] Hornstein, Fisch, and Holmes, 1968.
[45] Simmons and Lerner, 1968.
[46] Walster, Berscheid, and Walster, 1973.

storing equity through an actual exchange—compensating the victims or punishing themselves—or through certain psychological processes.

To illustrate, the harm-doers may derogate the victims, making them responsible for their own fate. Or the harm-doers may minimize the harm done by their acts or deny responsibility for them. Whether there is an actual exchange or a psychological exercise of manipulation depends on a number of conditions. First, increasing the outcomes of the victims through compensation is more common than reducing the outcomes of the harm-doers through self-punishment—because, generally, people select the technique that is the least costly. Compensation appears favored when it can be done without excessive cost and without creating further inequities. Several experiments have shown that where persons are limited to either *under*compensating or *over*compensating a victim, or using some other means of restoring equity, they are less apt to use the *exaggerated* compensation than they are to use compensation when it is fair and adequate.[47]

When available modes of compensation are inappropriate or too costly, individuals often resort to cognitive distortions to restore psychological equity by justifying their behavior in a manner that seems plausible to themselves as well as to others. The type of justification and its success depend on the credibility of available justifications, which, in turn, depend on the degree to which reality must be distorted. Where people have had considerable contact with each other, or anticipate considerable contact in the future, maintaining distortions is difficult. Thus, people are more apt to derogate a stranger than a friend who has been victimized by their acts. People who are literally out of sight can simply be kept out of mind. Members of a dominant group can believe that members of a disadvantaged minority are shiftless, lazy, or happy with the little they have—so long as there is enough social distance maintained through segregation. To the extent that such justifications are effective, people can persist in behavior that runs counter to norms specifying that one should help—or at least not harm—other people.

Summary: Norms of Social Responsibility

People agree that they should aid other persons in distress. This is the norm of social responsibility. A corollary norm is that one should not intentionally harm other persons. The way in which people define the situation appears to determine whether or not they help another person in trouble. If they feel responsible for giving aid, and if they think that the aid would be effective, they are more likely to help. This fits with the fact that individuals who are by themselves more often give aid. But when they are with others, responsibility is less clear—it is spread among all those present. Conditions that make them question whether their aid would have positive consequences reduce the chances that they will offer it.

[47] Walster, Berscheid, and Walster, 1973.

Harming other persons seems related not only to the norm of social responsibility, but also to norms of equity or fairness. Discomfort at harming another person arises from two sources: (1) anxiety over possible retaliation, and (2) distress over having behaved in a manner which violates one's ethical principles. People relieve such distress by compensating the victim, punishing themselves, arguing self-defense, derogating the victim, blaming the victim, or denying harm or responsibility.

NORMS AND DEVIANCE IN SOCIETY

Our discussion has been mostly concerned with norms and conformity in small groups, but a great deal of work has been done on conformity in the larger society. Generally the emphasis in this research has been on the other side of the coin—on deviation rather than on conformity—but many of the principles outlined for small groups apply in the larger context.

Contemporary theories of deviant behavior show two general themes. The first is that pressures toward deviance and the resulting breakdown in conformity arise when ways of behaving are normatively approved but do not result in achieving the goals that are valued in a society. The second theme emphasizes the reaction of society in labeling acts and persons as deviant. We will discuss both themes here, but elaborate upon the second theme in the last chapter of the book.

Deviant Behavior and Lack of Fit between Means and Values

In our discussion of the forces leading to the emergence of new group norms, we touched on this first theme when we talked about how people can fail to achieve satisfactory reward-cost outcomes through conformity to the norms that specify how these outcomes are to be achieved. In these cases, pressures emerge to devise new means of achieving societal goals—means that involve behavior deviating from widely accepted norms. Widespread adoption of these deviant behaviors are normatively approved, but only by those who engage in the deviant behavior—not by society at large. The end result is a state of normlessness, a state that Robert Merton has called *anomie*, and which involves indifference toward, or a rejection of, the norms of the larger society.[48]

It has been argued that the widely accepted values of material success in a democratic society, coupled with the barriers to achieving success through legitimate channels, explains the high rates of deviance in some groups (low-income groups, racial and ethnic minorities). In addition, deviant behavior is not only high in these groups because they lack the access to legitimate means to achieving material success, but also because they have more immediate access to illegit-

[48] Merton, 1957.

imate means than many groups with lower rates of deviance.[49] Thus, the poor, living in the inner city, have more immediate access to prostitution, drug peddling, and other forms of criminal activities than do those who live in the suburbs.

A state of anomie at the societal level may be accompanied by a widespread feeling of alienation among individuals in a society. The dimensions of this state of feeling include powerlessness, meaninglessness, normlessness, isolation, and self-estrangement.[50] Powerlessness involves the conviction that one's behavior cannot determine one's outcomes, but that one is controlled by fate, or luck. Meaninglessness is the inability to make favorable predictions about the future. Normlessness is the feeling that socially disapproved behaviors are necessary to achieve one's goals. Isolation refers not to a lack of warmth in social relations, but to a kind of detachment in which the person views unfavorably the goals and beliefs that are generally highly valued in a society. Finally, self-estrangement is when one's activities are not satisfying in themselves. One's work, for example, is perceived as a means to an end rather than as a satisfying end in itself.

The idea that anomie at the subcultural level is accompanied by alienation at the individual level, and the theory that both are related to deviant behavior, were given careful examination in a community study.[51] An attempt was made to account for both the differential rates of deviancy among three ethnic groups and the individual differences in deviancy within each group. There were sharp differences in deviancy rates. American Indians had the most deviance, Spanish Americans next, and Anglo Americans least. These differences were found to be related to three conditions. First, each group differed with respect to the degree to which it had access to goals through legitimate or socially approved means. Anglo Americans had greater access than Spanish Americans or American Indians, and the American Indians were a little better off than the Spanish Americans. Second, each group differed in the degree to which its members agreed on norms, with much less anomie for the Anglo Americans than for the American Indians and the Spanish Americans. Third, each group differed in the degree to which its situation made available illegitimate means of goal achievement. These situational factors were exposure to deviant role models, opportunities for deviant behavior, and protection against possible punishment. Again, the Anglo American group was favored, in that it had less access, and the Spanish Americans had less access than the American Indians.

The people in this study were also classified on an individual measure that paralleled the group measures, and the relation of each of these to individual differences in deviant behavior was investigated. Included were a measure of the degree to which individuals expected to achieve valued goals, a measure of alienation based on the dimensions outlined above, and measures of internal controls including attitudes against deviancy, the tendency to think and plan ahead, and the tendency to defer gratification.

[49] Cloward, 1959.
[50] Seeman, 1959.
[51] Jessor, Graves, Hanson, and Jessor, 1968.

With the exception of the last two measures of internal control, these individual characteristics were found to be related to deviance both in terms of excessive use of alcohol and a variety of other forms of deviancy ranging from speeding to stealing. This study supports the idea that deviancy may occur as a result of pressures toward deviance that come from a lack of fit among culturally approved goals, means of achieving them, and weak social and personal controls. Additional support comes from another study that showed that, the greater the pressure toward success exerted by parents, the higher the rate of cheating by their children on an experimental task.[52] Too great a pressure raises the standard so high that it cannot be reached in the normal way, and cheating results.

That a condition of anomie at the sociocultural level may produce alienation at the personal level was supported in part by the finding of a much higher rate of alienation among American Indians and Spanish Americans than among Anglo Americans who, as a group, were found to be lowest in anomie. Also consistent with the theory that groups experience alienation when their access to culturally valued goals is limited is the finding that, in a Southern community, a higher rate of alienation prevails among blacks and among the poorly educated than among well-educated whites.[53] Without education, legitimate channels of achievement are blocked. Alienation has also been related to the breakdown of normative restraints that characterize riots. A study of riot-torn Watts found that those blacks high in measures of isolation, powerlessness, and racial dissatisfaction were more prone to participate in violence than were blacks scoring lower on these measures.[54]

Summary: Norms and Deviance in Society

The theme discussed here is that pressures toward deviant behavior arise when many people cannot achieve satisfactory reward-cost outcomes by conforming to existing norms. This situation creates a lack of fit between the normatively approved ways of getting ahead in the world and the values, or goals, that people want to achieve—which leads, in turn, to a breakdown in social norms. It so happens that these are also the people who have access to and develop illegitimate or nonnormative ways of achieving their goals. Often associated with this state of anomie in society is an individual state termed *alienation*, which includes feelings of powerlessness, meaninglessness, normlessness, isolation, and self-estrangement.

[52] Pearlin, Yarrow, and Scarr, 1967.
[53] Middleton, 1963.
[54] Ransford, 1969.

TWELVE

LEADERSHIP, GROUP PRODUCTIVITY, AND SATISFACTION

T ake me," says the Martian, "to your leader." We have all seen the variations on the line, the cartoons and bits of business in films and on television. And we find it reasonable that the Martian just emerging from a gaudy spaceship would want to see someone in authority. Leaders are important and have played a vital role in human affairs since earliest recorded history. Leaders are highly rewarded in government, business, and all kinds of human association. Some of them ride in the big black cars, have aides and secretaries, and make important decisions as they sit behind opulent desks. But who are the leaders and how did they get to be where they are?

Both the popular view of leadership and the early research of behavioral scientists put too much emphasis on the importance of the contribution of the individual leader. Their choices are less wide, and their possibilities for effecting change are considerably smaller than historians used to believe. Current formulations of the problem focus more on the nature of leadership behavior and its relation to individual personality, to the composition and function of the group, to the situation, and to the group structure in which the leader operates.

The history of research on leadership reflects in capsule form the gradual evolution of social psychology into an increasingly sophisticated discipline. Like much early research in the behavioral sciences, the initial approach to leadership was to compare individuals—in this case to explore how leaders differ from nonleaders. But few stable differences were found. It may be interesting that Napoleon was short, but there are many short men who are not leaders. A later approach focused on leadership *behavior,* emphasizing those acts leading either to goal achievement or to the maintenance and strengthening of the group. In this approach, all members of the group were seen as performing leadership acts in varying degrees. Subsequently, the identification of different *kinds* of leader behaviors made it possible to identify some individual characteristics associated with these behaviors.

The focus on leadership behavior was accompanied by an interest in the situation and its effects, and in the composition of the group and how that related to leadership behavior. There was also a concern about the effects of various kinds, or styles, of leadership behavior and how they affected productivity and the satisfaction of group members. From this line of investigation, there developed an interest in structural determinants of leadership: it was believed that relatively permanent patternings of group interaction developed and provided a context within which leadership was exercised. An evolving view of leadership stresses the leader-follower relationship, recognizing that the behavior of the leader depends upon the complementary behavior of the followers. It has also become increasingly apparent that a type, or style, of leader behavior that may be effective in one situation may not be effective in another. Finally, many present students of the topic regard leadership as the assignment of leadership roles to certain members of a group in a way that may be explained by exchange theory, which considers the leadership process in terms of the reward-cost outcomes of leaders and followers.

The attributes of leadership are any or all of those personality characteristics that, in any particular situation, make it possible for a person to contribute to achievement of a group goal, to hold the group together, or to be *seen as doing so* by other members. The last qualification, concerning the perceptions of group members, should be emphasized. Certain characteristics of an individual may not directly contribute to goal achievement or to the maintenance and strengthening of the group. But if they are perceived as being related, other members will accord leadership status to the individual who has these characteristics. Our focus, then, is on those actions that actually are, or are perceived to be, related either to goal achievement or to maintaining and strengthening the group. Such behavior is engaged in by most group members. At the same time, some individual personality characteristics or abilities are associated with these actions, but vary according to the type of group and the task situation.

ROLE DIFFERENTIATION

The behavioral approach to leadership emphasizes that leadership behavior may be performed by any group member. Still, as a group develops from its earliest formation, certain members increasingly assume various leadership activities— they come to specialize in them. This specialization has been called *role differentiation*.[1] The concept recognizes that other members come to expect these specific behaviors from their "specialists."

Since this role differentiation is most readily observed in newly formed groups whose members differ little in status or in other attributes related to leadership, most of the relevant research has been on laboratory groups of strangers. While many of the findings have implications for leadership behavior in well-established groups, their application to such groups requires careful consideration of the social context and prevailing conditions.

In groups that are initially leaderless, the frequency, direction, and content of communication become established quite early at different levels for different members. The individuals who talk the most also receive the most communication from others. They direct a larger proportion of their comments to the group as a whole rather than to the individual members, and these comments are more often in the positive task-oriented categories—giving suggestions, information, and opinions. Other group members are likely to consider the persons who most frequently initiate actions as having the best ideas and as doing the most to guide discussion effectively. Such specialization of behavior and the development of consensus in recognition of that specialization is the substance of role differentiation.[2]

Task and Social-emotional Specialization

The distinction between the leader and the nonleader is one kind of differentiation but not the only kind that occurs. Under certain circumstances, both a *task leader* and a *social-emotional* leader may emerge.[3] The task leader is a person who supplies ideas and guides the group toward a solution. The social-emotional leader helps to boost group morale and to release tension when things are difficult. The task leader is ranked high on initiation, attention, and guidance, but not on liking. The social-emotional leader is ranked high on liking and is indeed the one most liked by the group. This division does not always occur. Sometimes

[1] Bales and Slater, 1955.
[2] Heinicke and Bales, 1953.
[3] Bales and Slater, 1955.

both qualities, or sets of qualities, are found in a single leader, but at other times conditions arise which make the performance of the two roles incompatible.

Descriptions of family life from earlier periods illustrate differentiation of this kind in the roles assumed by the father and mother. When the family acted as a group much of the time, the father was the task leader, and the mother was the social-emotional leader. Father presided at the dinner table every evening. He led group activities, such as reading the Bible, working on the farm or around the house, perhaps leading excursions to museums, or camping trips. Mother saw to the emotional needs of the children, ministering to them when they were hurt or ill, singing and reading to them, and providing sympathy and support. In modern families, these two leadership roles are more often shared or exchanged. And the feminist movement appears to be striving to eliminate these distinctive features entirely.

Studies of newly formed groups have followed the development of role specialization from the initial formation to the later stages. In the initial stage, the person whom members ranked first on ideas for task action was also best liked in over half of the groups studied, but by a late stage this held true for only 9 percent of the groups. Differentiation of the task and social-emotional roles had occurred: they were assigned to different group members.

Role differentiation and equilibrium   Such role differentiation has been related theoretically and empirically to certain basic tendencies toward a state of equilibrium in groups. While this equilibrium problem will be treated in the next section, which is on group productivity and satisfaction, we might briefly note here that focusing exclusively on group work frustrates individual needs and incurs other costs. Thus, forces arise to direct group activities away from the task and toward dealing with these needs and reducing or compensating for costs. These social activities, because they interfere with task accomplishment, eventually in turn give rise to forces directing the group back to the task.

The effect of these two sets of forces is one of balance between the task and the social-emotional activities. One sign of the forces toward equilibrium is the development of hostility toward the task leaders. At first, the task leaders are liked because they satisfy the needs of members for completing the task. But in time they arouse hostility because of their prestige, because they talk a lot and give orders, and because they make the other members focus on the task. The more they talk and give orders, the more ambivalent the other members become toward them. Eventually, they transfer some liking to another person who is less active and who contributes to the release of tensions by joking or by diverting the group momentarily. This social-emotional leader reasserts the desirable values and attitudes that have been disturbed, deemphasized, threatened, or repressed by the requirements of the task.

To the same degree that hostility toward the task leader manifests itself, so do the two leadership roles separate. There are two reasons for this. First, the hostility toward the task leader makes performance of both roles incompatible, and, second, the personalities of the members attracted to and capable of playing the two roles are likely to be different. The social-emotional specialists must like others and be liked by them if they are to meet their social-emotional demands. In contrast, the task specialists must be emotionally detached. If they are to lead the group toward its goals, they cannot become so emotionally dependent upon other members that they are unable to exercise power over them. Best-liked persons like other group members strongly, but about equally. The idea specialists are more choosy: they like some members of the group much more than others. For task leaders to use the members of the group most effectively, they must make distinctions among followers. The social-emotional leader likes to be liked; the task leader must be able to accept negative reactions from others.

Conditions favoring role differentiation   From what we have discussed up to this point, it follows that the degree of role differentiation is likely to vary directly with the extent to which task functions are unrewarding or costly. The less satisfaction experienced in working toward a goal, the more costs incurred, and the more likely task and social-emotional functions are to be found in different persons. Rewards would be low where task success is unrelated to member needs. Costs would be high where members disagree both on the importance of the task and on how it is to be done. Similarly, costs are apt to be high when influence among group members must be largely personal. As we noted in the previous chapter, when members strongly agree on group values, goals, and ways of behaving, following social norms allows activities to be performed with maximum rewards and minimum costs, and makes the costly exercise of personal power unnecessary.

Where accomplishment of the task is uppermost in the minds of all the members, and where skilled, highly coordinated teamwork is required, the task and social-emotional functions are apt to reside in the same person. Examples would include sports teams, where every member wants to win, and where the leader is usually one of the most capable players. The team leader must not only play well, but must also coordinate the efforts of the other players and give them strong emotional support for their efforts. Thus there is much encouragement during the course of a game.

But in business and industry, productivity is more important to management than it is to the worker, for the former bears most of the responsibility. The company and factory are structured so as to sharply focus task responsibility in specific persons. Workers receive wages so long as they do not goof off totally. Under these circumstances, social-emotional leaders emerge among the workers themselves or among semisupervisory personnel. They help to relieve boredom, monotony, or tensions that might arise from unrelenting attention to one's work.

In experimental groups, the conditions are especially conducive to role differentiation, because the participants rarely get really interested in the task itself. For this reason, efforts of the task leader are not appreciated. Moreover, these initially leaderless groups are often composed of college undergraduates who, with few exceptions, have been strangers and who do not differ in ways which might be the basis for status differences (age, sex, social background). Attempts among people equal in status to assume leadership without any basis provided by an established group structure may be viewed by group members as overly aggressive or pushy. A comparison of leaders emerging in newly formed groups with leaders in groups with established structures suggests that established leaders are less directive and evoke less resistance on the part of followers than do emergent leaders. This leads us to the question of legitimacy of leadership, to which we now turn.

Legitimacy   We have seen that where costs incurred by group members are perceived to be due to the personal acts of the task leaders, hostility is likely to be directed toward them. But where group members perceive the directive attempts of the leaders as legitimate, hostile reactions are not apt to occur. For example, children might recognize the right of their father to direct them, but might be less willing to accord the same right to a stepfather. One way in which the actions of leaders acquire legitimacy is through formal recognition of their leadership role. This was demonstrated in an experiment where one supervisor was elected and the other was assigned by the experimenter. Under these circumstances, the elected supervisor—who is likely to be perceived as having more legitimate power—was shown to exert a greater influence over the work group than the nonelected supervisor.

There is another mechanism which serves to protect the task leader from the damaging psychological effects of withdrawal of positive affect. In time, norms develop to encourage a degree of social distance between leaders and most of their followers, thus preventing the development of emotional dependency by leaders on all but a few followers. This allows them to carry out their functions without experiencing too painfully the emotional attacks or rejections they may encounter. Social distance also allows them to avoid playing favorites.

The distinction must be made, after all, between liking and esteem. Leaders are often respected—particularly if they have earned respect through skillful leadership; but they are less often liked. To the degree that task leaders are successful in providing the group with many rewards, they may be liked. In the long run, however, their control over the rewards and costs received by the members of the group, and their superior status, are likely to produce some feelings of resentment. In most groups outside the laboratory, a full-blown distinction between the two roles does not occur. And so, when the two activities are performed by the same leader, he or she finds leadership behavior somewhat costly because of the mixed feelings that members will have toward any leader who carries out the functions of both roles.

Summary: Role Differentiation

Under certain circumstances, a task leader and a social-emotional leader emerge to lead the group. The task specialist organizes and directs the activities of members so that they are focused on achieving group goals with maximum efficiency. The social-emotional specialist boosts morale and releases tensions arising from the group's work activities. These two types of leaders help to maintain equilibrium between these two sets of functions necessary to all groups. Task specialists are seldom the best-liked group members. Their focus on achievement occasionally generates hostility toward them. Also, to function adequately, they cannot become overly friendly with the group members. The social-emotional leader is better liked, and is more friendly with the members.

Separation into these two leadership roles depends on the extent to which task functions are unrewarding or costly. The lower the outcomes for task performance, the greater the role differentiation. Differentiation is also greater where the group lacks structure, lacks consensus on values and activities, or on how their situation is to be defined. In established groups, leaders' positions are supported by norms and have a legitimate basis, which reduces hostility toward them. In most natural groups, leaders perform both functions, at least to some degree. This is the main reason that members so often have mixed feelings toward leaders.

GROUP STRUCTURE AND LEADERSHIP

It follows from social exchange theory that: (1) Persons exercise leadership behavior to the extent that such behavior provides favorable reward-cost outcomes to both leaders and followers. (2) Rewards and costs are in part a function of the requirements of the situation. Those whose interests, abilities, and needs maximize their own outcomes and those of their followers become leaders. (3) Where leadership is stable, it is owing to the leader's possession of characteristics that work effectively in a wide variety of situations. These characteristics maximize reward-cost outcomes. Were we to concern ourselves exclusively with laboratory groups, which have a short existence, these characteristics might explain why some persons manage to retain leadership over a long period. But in groups that have functioned long enough to develop stable structures and a certain routine, much of the stability in leadership personnel can be explained in other terms. What we must ask ourselves is why the leader-follower relation that emerges in one situation continues into a new situation.

The answer lies, at least in part, in the fact that the mutually rewarding pattern in the initial situation has created stabilities in the affect, power, and status structures that reinforce the initially established leadership patterns. These structural stabilities are established and become habitual so that patterns of activity persist from one situation to another. The affect structure continues to support liking of the social-emotional leader. And leaders who partially perform this function continue to benefit from the stabilized affect which group members feel toward them.

The status structure, having been established, is likely to be perpetuated. The high status derived from leadership in the first instance provides a cue for

Leadership based on age, status, and expertise.

leadership in other instances. This is particularly true in the absence of other information. A new team, organized to play a new sport—frisbee-throwing or bladderball—is likely to start out with the stars of the conventional sports, like baseball, basketball, tennis, or swimming, as the leaders of the new team.

The power and status structures reinforce each other. Status, itself, is a resource which adds to the power of high-status persons, but at the same time it may serve as a brake on power because people who have it don't want to lose it, and they risk losing it if they use their power too freely, too nakedly, or too often. Established leaders also gain an advantage through greater access to the information that is widely distributed among group members. Since many others in the group must exert their influence through them, they are in the best position to put all the information together. Moreover, they can often control the flow of information to their own advantage. Their central position thus makes the group dependent upon them for the performance of its leadership functions. Both they themselves and others are apt to define them as leaders. This idea is supported by experiments which varied the extent to which communications either flowed through a single member who was advantageously placed, or flowed equally through all members.[4] When the participants were asked to indicate who was the leader in their groups, the person with the most advantageous position was most frequently named.

[4] Leavitt, 1951.

Finally, the experience of being a leader produces the skills that are necessary for the exercise of leadership—an opportunity denied to nonleaders. At the same time, the greater investment of time and energy by leaders, as well as the tendency for the role of leader to become a part of their self-concept, results in a strong motivation on their part to maintain their position. The lesser investment of the followers, which may be accompanied by a sense of obligation to the leaders, further maintains all in their respective roles.

Leadership, Authority, and the Normative Structure

Stability in leadership is also a product of the normative structure. After awhile, the expectations that group members share concerning one another's conduct are such that leaders are expected to lead and the followers to comply. In informal groups, the initial influence of the leader over a follower rests on an exchange of outcomes in which the follower, in return for compliance, obtains task-related rewards at low cost as a result of the task competence provided by the leader. In time, the followers come to respect the leaders' guidance and competence, their fairness, and their concern for group achievement. Members exchange views concerning their leaders and arrive at consensus. At that point, social pressures arise to provide continued support and recognition to the leaders: their position is *legitimized.* The consensus and the attending social pressures discourage individuals, who might otherwise oppose the leaders, from expressing their resistance. Once they have been recognized as legitimate leaders of their groups, leaders get willing compliance at little cost to themselves or to other group members.

There is, however, a basic dilemma of leadership.[5] This lies in the necessity of the leader remaining both independent of and dependent on his or her followers. To become a leader, one must have power, and the group must approve the use of that power. But the business of attaining power and of attaining social approval are somewhat incompatible. One gets power by providing other people with resources that raise their outcomes and make them dependent, but, in order to retain a power advantage, one must also remain independent of any resources the followers might offer in return. Still, for leaders to earn social approval from the group members, they must not maintain complete independence; they must accept some support from members. The refusal of leaders to accept member support may be resented. Thus, both independence or the lack of it may at times antagonize some of the group members.

The solution to the dilemma involves changing one's role over time. In the early phase of a group's existence, leaders mobilize their powers in ways that do not lead to follower approval beyond what is necessary to gain leadership; in later phases, they use their power in a way that leads to approval and legitimation. Thus, in the earlier phases, they do not hesitate to compete with group members for power. They attempt to demonstrate their competence as the best

[5] Blau, 1964a.

persons for the job of leading the group. For instance, the potential leaders of street gangs use physical strength first against the other members in order to assert their dominance. Only then can they organize their activities and lead the gangs in street activities. Similarly, persons who use their intelligence, skill, and experience in problem-solving groups first demonstrate their competence to lead. Once established, the leaders may then use their augmented resources to keep group members happy, to gain their approval, and to maintain recognition of themselves as the group's legitimate leaders. As Blau notes, established leaders can exercise their power so as to appear generous and benevolent, thus enhancing their legitimacy.

When leaders have formal authority from the start—a crown princess who becomes queen or a vice-president who inherits a presidency—this first phase of power mobilization is bypassed. The initial power of formal leaders rests on the conditions of their contract in which actions contrary to their orders allow them to punish obstinate followers. In time, however, they exercise their authority to augment their power. They are in a position to furnish important services to subordinates in exchange for their support. They can raise the pay of followers, or promote them, or give them valuable advice or training. They can grant special privileges and assign tasks in desired ways.

Summary: Group Structure and Leadership

Leaders more often remain in power when the group has stable structures. When the group operates effectively, the mutual rewards experienced by the members create stabilities in the affect, power, and status structures so as to reinforce the initial patterns of leadership. Leaders also have an advantage over other members in their access to information and in their role as a focus of communication within the group. Occupying a position of leadership gives them an opportunity to acquire leadership skills, and increases their motivation to maintain their status. Followers have less opportunity to develop these skills, and also develop a sense of obligation to support the leader. Finally, normative expectations emerge that give the right to the leaders to lead, and the obligation to the followers to comply—the position becomes legitimate. Deviations from these expectations are enforced by group sanctions.

GROUP PRODUCTIVITY

One important group process remains to be discussed—the ongoing work aimed at achieving a particular task or solving a problem. Various names have been applied to this process, including group decision, group problem solving, and group productivity. This aspect of group behavior pervades every part of our daily lives. Probably, most important decisions in most human societies are made in group settings, whether they be tribal councils, legislatures, cabinets, juries, parole boards, corporate boards, school boards, commissions, or more informal, specialized groups such as committees, work groups, families, and friendship groups. Departments or sections of factories, offices, and institutions consist of small groups of workers who influence one another with respect to the quality and quantity of the services or products with which they are involved—and almost all goods and services come out of group situations.

We must be interested, then, in the process by which such groups arrive at decisions. Two kinds of problems face all task groups. One kind arises from the task and its setting, and typically the focus here is on using available group resources in a way that will maximize productivity. A second kind revolves around the maintenance of internal relations that promote satisfaction, keep members in the group, and contribute to group efforts. Especially important in this regard is the distribution of rewards among members so as to maintain optimal levels of motivation and satisfaction.

Early laboratory studies usually assigned to a group some problem that had a single correct solution. In everyday situations, however, groups often arrive at consensus on issues that have no single answer. Many recent studies have assigned this kind of task to laboratory groups—mock committee decisions, jury decisions, case conferences, and the like. Further, many types of groups have been studied in actual field situations. Productivity in problem-solving laboratory groups has usually been defined in terms of the quality and speed of solutions to problems set by the experimenter. In field situations, productivity is usually defined in terms of the quality and quantity of the daily work output.

Groupthink

A phenomenon that Irving Janis has called *groupthink* nicely illustrates some of the problems in arriving at a high-quality solution through group activity.[6] Janis calls attention to some of the major failures in decisions at high policy levels: the Pearl Harbor disaster, the aborted Bay of Pigs invasion of Cuba, and the decisions to escalate the Korean war and the Vietnam war. These decisions, all of which led to disastrous consequences, were made by groups of highly intelligent and capable people sitting at the highest levels of government. How was it possible for them to be so wrong? Was it just human error? Or was there some phenomenon common to group decisions that accounted for the blind spots?

Three top-level groups—the command of the Pacific Fleet in Hawaii, the Army command (which included the Air Force) in Hawaii, and the President's War Council of policy-makers in Washington, all believed that the Japanese would not attack Pearl Harbor. Yet, before the attack, cryptographers had succeeded in breaking the Japanese secret code, and voluminous information was collected, all of which pointed to the conclusion that Japan was preparing a massive attack destined for some unknown location. On November 27, 1941,

[6] Janis, 1969.

Washington notified the naval command in Hawaii that an aggressive move was expected from Japan in the next few days (location not specified). On December 3, it was learned that Tokyo had ordered diplomatic missions all over the world to destroy their secret codes. Finally, it was also learned that Japanese carriers were "blacked out"—their radios silent, and locations unknown. Yet, in spite of all this information, all three responsible groups remained unconcerned about a possible attack on Hawaii.

Janis makes clear that this was in part a result of groupthink. Groupthink can be described as the way in which members of a group tend to think alike, without considering alternatives to their established opinions. The remainder of our chapter will bring out many group factors that contribute to groupthink, but several can be illustrated here. Admiral Kimmel in Hawaii had a devoted, highly cohesive group of advisors. Because of their loyalty and support, he felt free to reassure them about their anxieties, and also to express his own doubts. But they, too, saw their function *as one of supporting him.* The day before the attack, Kimmel expressed concern about the safety of the U.S. Pacific Fleet. One of his staff promptly reassured him that "the Japanese could not possibly be able to proceed in force against Pearl Harbor when they had so much strength concentrated in their Asiatic operations," and another told him that nothing more need be done. Such cohesiveness creates powerfully shared norms that are difficult to deviate from. This is dramatically illustrated by the deviant position on the Vietnam war eventually taken by Robert McNamara, Secretary of Defense under President Johnson.

The case differs from that of Admiral Kimmel in that President Johnson placed a tremendous emphasis on loyalty and conformity on the part of his chief advisors. In the spring of 1967, Johnson's inner group of advisors were nearly unanimous in supporting the Vietnam war policy—the one dissenter was McNamara. After McNamara presented some impressive facts to the Senate about the ineffectiveness of bombing raids, Johnson made the bitter comment to one senator: "That military genius, McNamara, has gone dovish on me." To a member of his White House staff, Johnson expressed heated anger and declared that the Secretary of Defense was playing into the hands of the enemy. Apparently Johnson felt that any advisor who disagreed with the official line was virtually a traitor. Here the need of a powerful leader to stifle dissent sets the stage for an all but unanimous, highly cohesive group to engage in groupthink. Shortly thereafter, McNamara was eased out of the government.

Our subsequent discussion will at many points bring out a variety of group factors which encourage conformity and discourage independence, and which consequently contribute to poor-quality group solutions.

Group Structure and the Task Situation

The outcome of a task situation is affected by group factors if the group structure causes changes in any of the following: (1) the resources available to the group,

(2) the application of these resources to the task, and (3) the likelihood that the task will be carried out—or at least the likelihood that there will be agreement as to the proper approach.

If task groups are observed in action, the process is seen to follow a fairly uniform sequence. Group members exchange information relevant to the problem, one or more solutions based on this information are then proposed, and, finally, agreement is reached. In everyday situations, the agreed-upon solution usually carries implications for change in the behavior of group members, as they subsequently carry out the task in some manner. Decisions of a work group, for instance, concerning new production methods, would be implemented by a change in the group's work activities. In laboratory studies, this phase of the task process is sometimes ignored or is considered to follow from the agreement achieved. All four phases should be kept in mind, however, in discussing the relation between a particular factor and the quality of the group product. This is necessary because the effects of a condition may contribute to high quality in one phase but to low quality in another phase. A particular factor affects the quality of the group's work product through its effects on group structures, group viewpoints, and group cohesiveness.

In a given problem-solving phase, certain group structures or conditions are more important than others. In large part, ease and effectiveness of communication determine how well a group marshals its resources; the power structure determines the combination of elements that becomes the group solution; and group cohesiveness determines how quickly a group reaches agreement and the extent to which it is motivated to carry out the solution.

Structural effects on early phases Since the importance of various features of the affect, status, and power structures vary depending on the phase of the problem-solving sequence, early and late phases will be discussed separately. The early phases, discussed here, include the amassing of such resources as information about the problem and the environment, and the later phases, discussed in the next section, refer to combining these resources into some proposed course of action and then implementing it. Since, in the research literature, the effects of leadership have been dealt with somewhat independently of the other structural features, these will be discussed later in the chapter.

Throughout the problem-solving process, groups often accept solutions too soon (groupthink), thus excluding the consideration of better ones. Before the dimensions of the problem are adequately explored, solutions may be offered, and before many possible solutions are advanced, they may be evaluated and a decision made which ignores many potentially good alternatives. The technique of *brainstorming* has been suggested as a way of preventing evaluation from short-circuiting the earlier phase of idea generation.[7] Brainstorming instructions encourage group members to list all ideas that come to mind—even the most

[7] Osborn, 1957.

harebrained—and not to evaluate their quality. While some investigators have found this technique useful, others make the point that brainstorming groups do not generate as many ideas as the same number of persons working alone. Another approach has shown that better solutions are produced by instructions which direct group members to focus on clarifying the problem before even considering possible solutions.

The affect structure has important consequences for the performance of task groups, particularly as it affects communication. Unless special restrictive conditions prevail, communication is likely to follow friendship links. Liking may facilitate communication, but, on the other hand, when members talk about social matters instead of the task, it often interferes with performance. And when cohesiveness is strong, members find it more difficult to disagree. This may lead members with good, but deviant, ideas to remain quiet.

Status and power structures can interfere with communication in a similar way. Ideas perceived as contrary to the opinions of high-status or high-power individuals are unlikely to be communicated (groupthink). Moreover, low-status persons often engage in communications irrelevant to the task to compensate for their low position, or expend energy in a struggle for power and status that might otherwise be spent on the task itself. Status congruency leads to more friendly interaction among group members, which has two undesirable effects. First, friendly interaction is socially rather than task-oriented. Second, by contributing to cohesiveness, conformity to norms is increased. When group norms specify low productivity, this increased conformity lowers production. Among undergraduates this can produce what has sometimes been called "the gentleman's C."

Factors affecting later phases   Just as premature closure sometimes occurs in the information-gathering phase of problem solving, a similar tendency occurs in the later phase. Even a unanimous decision is no guarantee of the best solution to a problem. To counter this tendency, techniques which slow the group down as it moves toward problem solution, which protect minority opinions, or which require the group to retrace its steps and arrive at a second solution, have all been shown to improve the quality of group problem solving.

There are a number of ways in which a group can close discussion too soon or arrive at the wrong solution. A group's acceptance of a solution is not necessarily associated with its quality. Personal characteristics of the members and structural features of the group often determine acceptance. For instance, the sheer talkativeness of a member influences group decision, but this is beneficial only if the talkative member also happens to be capable. Similarly, persons who have been successful in past group activities may, by virtue of their reputations, exert undue influence. While this can be helpful when past successes are relevant, it can be indifferent or harmful when they are unrelated to the new task. The influence of these formerly successful members may therefore thwart the possibly valuable contributions of other members.

Although a high degree of cohesiveness among group members may facilitate communication, it can also reduce the quality of the solution by equalizing the weight given to the contribution of each member. If a group is mixed in ability, giving equal attention to poor-quality solutions weakens performance. Where the group is similar in ability, cohesiveness increases the amount of discussion but not necessarily the quality of the solution. Cohesiveness may, however, contribute to the effective implementation of the solution.

Contributions from individuals of high power and status are weighted more heavily because of their greater control over the reward-cost outcomes of members and their greater opportunity to communicate their ideas. If these individuals are competent, the group is effective. If they are less competent than the average member, the power and status structure will inhibit effective performance.

Individual versus Group Risk-taking

A study made over a decade ago showed that decisions made by a group after discussion are likely to be more risky than decisions made by individuals before discussion.[8] This finding is interesting in that it appears contrary to widely held expectations—that groups are more cautious than individuals. And it is important, considering how many decisions, such as in government, business, and education, are made by groups.

A dramatic example of group risk-taking is again provided by Irving Janis:

> Consider what happened a few days before disaster struck the small mining town of Pitcher, Oklahoma, in 1950. The local mining engineer had warned the inhabitants to leave at once because the town had been accidentally undermined and might cave in at any moment. At a Lion's Club meeting of leading citizens, the day after the warning was issued, the members joked about the warning and laughed uproariously when someone arrived wearing a parachute. What the club members were communicating to each other by their collective laughter was that "sensible people like us know better than to take seriously these disaster warnings; we know it can't happen here, to our fine little town." Within a few days, this collective complacency cost some of these men and their families their lives.[9]

What this example shows is the support that group members find in each other for established opinions, which enables them to take a considerable risk. The phenomenon of the *risky shift*, however, is considerably more complex, as will be brought out in our discussion.

Many studies have been conducted to test the generality of the early research on risky shift and to explore the validity of the explanations that have been offered to account for them. A consideration of some of these studies and of the ideas developed to explain the findings is quite instructive in demonstrating

---

[8] Stoner, 1961.
[9] Reprinted by permission from I. L. Janis, *Victims of groupthink: A psychological study of foreign-policy decisions and fiascoes.* Boston: Houghton Mifflin, 1972. P. 3.

the complexity of group process and in showing the limits of simple conceptualizations of them.

A typical experiment asks individuals what decisions they would advise a person to make in various risk-taking situations. For example, would they advise a male engineer to remain in his present secure but moderately salaried job, or to take a less secure job which might eventually enable him to share ownership? Then an experimental treatment is introduced, usually consisting of a group discussion in which members arrive at a consensus as to what should be done. The difference in the degree of risk-taking between the average position of group members before the discussion and their position after making a group decision defines the amount of change. This change is known as the *risky shift*—the shift toward greater risk after discussion.

There are a number of variations in the kinds of decisions the experimenters ask for. These can be hypothetical "real life" situations, such as the employment question that was mentioned above. They can be risk-taking situations which require individuals to select a level of difficulty they wish to attempt on examination items. If they choose too high a level, they run the risk of failing the items. They can be gambling situations in which the participants must choose between bets with lower payoffs and better odds, and riskier long-shot bets that pay more. Sometimes the procedure requires group consensus, and sometimes, not. There may or may not be face-to-face communication. The experiment has also been tried without group discussion but with participants being made aware of the risk preferences of other members or groups. The risky shift persists most of the time, although, in some instances, it is a cautious shift instead.

There are various explanations for the risky shift. One of the first was that discussion and a group decision spread responsibility among members, weakening individual responsibility.[10] Consequently, an individual can take a greater risk—a mistake would be the group's fault, not his or hers alone. But then experimenters found that the risky shift persisted even when there was no group decision. So one current view is that there is a four-part causal chain, not requiring a group decision. The links in the chain are the following: (1) group discussion creates affective bonds; (2) affective bonds encourage diffusion of responsibility; (3) diffusion of responsibility reduces fear of failure; and (4) reduced fear of failure results in the risky shift.[11]

Research relevant to these conceptual links has produced generally conflicting results. As we noted, some of the experiments involved group discussion, and others had no discussion but members were informed of the decisions of other members of the group. In some experiments, subjects were allowed to observe the discussion of another group. The affective bonds that arose from watching and listening to the discussion of another group were, at best, minimal, and how fear of failure would be reduced by such indirect contact is not at all clear. Neither is it clear how a decrease in fear of failure would increase willingness to take risks.

[10] Kogan and Wallach, 1967.
[11] Dion, 1970.

Our discussion in Chapter 4 of the role of fear of failure in motivation does not suggest that this would occur. Still, it is possible that some of the increased risk-taking results directly from a diffusion of responsibility.

Another explanation argues that persons who are more persuasive take a more risky position—either because they are more self-confident or because they have available to them a more powerful rhetoric with which to argue their case.[12] It has been suggested that our language, itself, provides advocates of risk with a more dramatic, more appealing array of linguistic strategies. So that when people talk about the decision, they make riskier decisions than when they silently make an individual decision. Further, the doubts and uncertainties which advocates of risk may feel within themselves can lead to more intense, active discussion as they try to assure not only other members of the group but their own questioning selves. This notion connects leadership with risky positions.

A third explanation is that the risky shift is due simply to increased familiarity.[13] Initial strangeness of a choice situation might reasonably mean initial caution, which is replaced by confidence after the participants become more acquainted with the problem. Research pertaining to this idea has yielded mixed results. Further, this explanation fails to account for the cautious shifts typically observed with two of the choice dilemma items.

A fourth explanation, offered by Roger Brown, appears to handle most adequately the facts concerning the risky shift.[14] It involves two ideas: *value* and *relevance*. In any risk situation, one of two values has to be engaged—risk or caution. In some situations (in fact, in most of those used by experimenters on this topic), taking a risk is valued in our society. For example, people are encouraged to risk current assets for the sake of future profits. In a few other situations, such as those involving the welfare of innocent people, caution is valued. As these values emerge in the group discussion, the weight of certain arguments increases and makes itself felt in the group decision.

The second part of this explanation is that group members adjust their own positions to the value that is relevant to the situation. Before discussion, individuals imagine that they are about, or above, average concerning the relevant value. Thus, where risk is the approved value, individuals see themselves as willing to take as much risk as, or slightly more than, the average group member, but, in the absence of knowledge about the risk preferences of other people, they must guess what this is. Some guess wrong. When, during the discussion, they hear the actual risk preferences of other persons expressed, or when they learn of this in other ways (through an experimenter's telling them, or through observing another group's discussion), those who are below or close to the average change their choice in the risky direction, thus shifting the mean of the group and accounting for the risky-shift effect.

There are certain clear advantages in this last explanation. Perhaps most

[12] Kelley and Thibaut, 1969.
[13] Bateson, 1966; Flanders and Thistlethwaite, 1967.
[14] Brown, 1965.

important is that it can account for the cautious shift as well as for the risky shift. But it also offers a plausible explanation of how the shift can occur in the various situations substituted for group discussion. But this theory, even though it seems to handle many of the observed facts better, does not absolutely preclude the possibility that the mechanisms suggested in some of the other theories have their effects in some situations. Furthermore, the situations generally used in these experiments involved hypothetical or relatively inconsequential losses, and we must be careful in generalizing to real life situations where there is risk of real loss. Finally, the theory is still incomplete and it is difficult to predict whether a cautious or a risky shift will occur in a given situation. This depends on the unknown characteristics that evoke either caution or risk as a value.

Summary: Group Productivity

Early phases in task activities include the exchange of information and the presentation of many solutions or plans of action. The affect structure has important consequences for the performance of task groups, particularly through its effect on communication. Without special restrictions, communication is apt to follow friendship patterns, and such social-emotional communication may limit performance. Status and power structures may interfere with problem solving in a similar way. Ideas contrary to those of high-status or high-power individuals may not be communicated, and low-status members may talk about irrelevant topics if they hold such ideas. Power and status struggles also interfere with group achievement. Sometimes group norms specify low productivity, and if the group is cohesive, they will be effective in limiting production. Groupthink tends to occur in highly cohesive groups which emphasize loyalty and conformity. The process places severe limits on independent thinking and cuts off ideas proposed by a minority before they have an opportunity to be fully developed. Cohesiveness can, however, lead to effective implementation of whatever group solution is arrived at.

Group decisions are often more risk-taking than individual decisions. This may be in part because of the spread of responsibility among many, which reduces the fear of failure—the group would be responsible, not the individual. Apparently this risky shift depends on the type of action, however. Risk is valued for some kinds of action, but not for others.

LEADERSHIP AND TASK PERFORMANCE

The style of leadership may also have great effects on group satisfaction and productivity. Three styles of leadership distinguished in a classic study of boys' "clubs" were: *authoritarian, laissez-faire,* and *democratic.*[15] The leaders adopted these styles according to instructions from the experimenter. The authoritarian leader

[15] Lewin, Lippitt, and White, 1939.

gave orders and assignments, and directed the recreational activities of the boys according to prescribed routines. The laissez-faire leader left the structuring of activities mostly up to the boys themselves, and refrained from giving directions. The democratic leader encouraged participation from the boys and encouraged them to develop their own directions.

This study indicated that, in most situations, authoritarian leadership produced great dependency on the leader, as well as irritability and aggressiveness among the group members, low frequencies of suggestions from the members about action and policy, and a high quantity of low-quality production. Laissez-faire leadership produced less dependency on the leader, great irritability and aggressiveness among members, high frequencies of suggestions for action and policy, great discontent about progress and achievement, and intermediate productivity. Democratic leadership produced low dependency on the leader, low incidence of irritability and aggressiveness, high frequencies of suggestions for action and policy, and an intermediate quantity of high-quality production.

Further investigations have, in the main, confirmed these findings in club activities, classroom settings, and a variety of work situations. But some qualification is necessary. In a study of decision-making groups in government and industry, a high level of member participation was associated with *low* satisfaction—presumably because, in such groups, members expected and wanted strong leadership and these expectations were not met.[16] The history of a person's experiences with groups affects how he or she reacts to leadership style. Moreover, age, marital status, educational status, personality characteristics, and the job situation all relate to expectations about leadership and influence the degree of satisfaction group members experience, as well as their productivity.

Leadership and Satisfaction

Satisfaction comes from need gratification. In the course of problem solving, individual needs may be satisfied through task accomplishment, through the work itself, or through interaction with other persons on the job. In some situations, supervisors who do not supervise closely, but who allow their subordinates a degree of self-determination, have groups that are more satisfied with their jobs.[17] Presumably this style allows the needs for self-determination and self-realization to be met. In other situations, however, the reverse may hold true. One study of white-collar workers found that freedom from close supervision produced dissatisfaction.[18] However, rewards must be assessed against expectations, and it was believed that these employees were less satisfied because the lack of close supervision led them to expect greater rewards than they were getting; they were carrying greater responsibility, in that to a degree they were supervising themselves, and therefore they felt that they should be paid more.

[16] Berkowitz, 1953.
[17] Katz and Kahn, 1952.
[18] Homans, 1961.

Leadership and Productivity

We have already noted that the quality of solutions can be improved if group solutions are thoroughly considered before they are evaluated. Leaders who encourage this activity are apt to achieve better performance. None of the three styles we have discussed would meet this criterion. Authoritarian leaders would cut off discussion too soon, while laissez-faire leaders and democratic leaders would allow the majority to impose its solution on the minority. The correct style would require that leaders be directive in encouraging consideration of a maximum number of solutions and in making sure that unpopular solutions received due consideration. At the same time it would require that they be permissive in refraining from evaluating the various solutions and in encouraging contributions from every member.

In one investigation, a number of groups were provided with a problem, as well as with a discussion leader to help them solve it. The leader was permissive and yet in some ways directive, asking questions to stimulate thinking and encouraging participation of all members, even though refraining from expressing his own opinions.[19] Another set of discussion groups was set up as a control, with no discussion leaders. The performance of the two sets of groups was compared through a series of questions asked both before and after discussions. The groups did not differ significantly in the proportion of correct answers before discussion, but after discussion the proportion of correct answers was significantly higher for groups that had discussion leaders. A further analysis revealed that this improvement was particularly marked in groups where a minority initially had the correct solution. In such instances, the discussion leader served to encourage the expression and consideration of the ideas of the minority (sometimes a single individual) which otherwise might have been suppressed by the majority.

We have already seen that one consequence of the group-decision process is the increased likelihood that the decision will be carried out by group members—not only because there is an increased understanding of the solution, but also because of the emergence of a normative structure favoring actions that accord with the solution. Through the sharing of information and exertion of social pressures (the giving or withholding of social approval), gradual consensus is achieved.

Such consensus not only helps cooperative action but it also reinforces individual motivation. Thus, in an industrial setting, investigators studied changes in work procedures and the way in which they were introduced and found that productivity of the workers varied directly with the amount of participation in discussion.[20]

In most work situations, rules regarding quality and quantity of production are set up by management, an agent *external* to the work group. It has long been known that norms very rapidly arise *within* a group to govern quality and quan-

[19] Maier and Solem, 1952.
[20] Coch and French, 1958.

tity of production. The degree to which these norms are affected by the standards of management depends in large part on the attitudes that group members have toward the management. To the extent that supervisors, by their style of supervision, create favorable attitudes toward themselves and management, the production rules they represent are apt to be more in line with group norms. This may well be one of the reasons that democratic supervisors often have groups with higher productivity.

Our discussion has for the most part emphasized the advantages of democratic as opposed to authoritarian leadership, but these advantages depend upon the demands of the situation, the distribution of skills within the group, and the group's expectations, as well as other variables. There are some situations in which authoritarian leadership is more effective.[21] These include situations that emphasize speed and efficiency, situations in which members are not sensitive about their skills and abilities, and emergency situations that call for decisive action. A platoon of soldiers under attack, for example, is not likely to want to sit down and discuss, in a democratic manner, all the possible responses to the onslaught.

Fred Fiedler has done considerable research identifying the situational factors controlling the degree to which leaders may influence the performance of a group.[22] Situations vary in the extent to which they enable the leader to influence the group. Major situational elements include: (1) the leaders' personal relations with members of the group, that is, the degree to which they are liked and respected, (2) the degree of structure in the task, ranging from the highly routine, clearly spelled-out to the vague and indefinite, and (3) the legitimate power and authority associated with the leaders' position.

Leaders who are liked and respected by their groups, who are faced with a highly structured task, and who wield considerable power by virtue of the authority vested in their position, are in a favorable position to influence the group. On the other hand, leaders who are disliked by a group that is faced with a vague, unstructured task, and who have little formal power, may find great difficulty in exercising influence. In very favorable or very unfavorable situations a style of leadership involving active intervention and control is apt to be effective. In moderately unfavorable situations, however, a more democratic, permissive style focusing on human relations is more effective.

Summary: Leadership and Task Performance

Although there are some exceptions, a democratic style of leadership appears to generate more satisfaction and more effective group functioning than an autocratic or a laissez-faire style. Exceptions occur when members want strong leadership. Groupthink is avoided and quality of productivity is improved if the

[21] Gibb, 1969.
[22] Fiedler, 1964.

leader protects minority opinion and sees to it that all suggestions receive a thorough hearing. Certain situations require relatively authoritative leadership for effective functioning, and sometimes active intervention is important. The effectiveness of leadership varies with the leader's personal relations with members of the group, and with the extent to which the position is vested with legitimate authority and power. Different leader attributes are required depending upon whether the group and its activities are highly structured or whether these structures are ambiguous and vague.

THE PROBLEM-SOLVING PROCESS

So far, group problem solving has been considered primarily from the standpoint of factors affecting the quality of the group product with only occasional attention to member satisfaction. Let us now look at certain features of the ongoing process of problem solving and its relation to satisfaction.

Actions are different at different phases of problem solving. In the early phase, orientation to the problem and tentative evaluation of initial steps are important. In the final phase, controlling and focusing group action to reach the final solution is critical. An overall tendency is for the number of *both* positive and negative responses to increase from phase to phase. The relative predominance of various forms of action in different phases is in part related to the demands imposed by the need to solve a problem, but it is also related to several other factors. One of these is the need of the group to obtain conformity from its members. As the group shifts from initial orientation to evaluation of the first tentative steps, it reacts negatively toward those who do not conform and positively toward those who do. In the initial part of the final phase, the high frequency of negative reactions occurs because of persisting disagreements. The later part of the final phase is marked by many positive reactions—which restore positive feeling in the group, feeling that has been depleted by the many influence attempts aimed at achieving agreement.

Member Satisfaction

Every human organization, after all, must solve two problems. The first is how to achieve group purposes. The second is how to provide satisfaction to members. In short-lived laboratory groups typically studied in experimental work, satisfaction is of little concern. Presumably, participants in these studies either receive enough satisfaction to remain in them, or, if they don't, they find it too costly to refuse to cooperate and to leave. But quite the opposite is true in everyday situations. Here the group must solve the problem of satisfaction or it will cease to exist.

Satisfaction is a function of need gratification, but to understand satisfaction in task groups it is useful to distinguish among needs according to the source of the rewards that lead to their satisfaction. One such source is obvious—the individual rewards offered in exchange for tasks done, which include money, heightened status, social approval, and other "psychic" rewards. A second source of reward lies in the features of the task itself, features that allow for the satisfaction of such individual needs as those for self-expression, self-development, and self-determination. A third class of needs and rewards is related less to the task performance than to features of the group. These arise from interaction above and beyond task activity: group-controlled rewards rather than external or management-controlled rewards. A tournament golfer may receive monetary rewards and self-fulfillment, but a professional football player may also find this third category of reward in team spirit and morale.

The satisfactions individuals receive are more than simply a function of the *amount* of reward obtained in a group. Whether the reward is in terms of dollars, intrinsic job satisfaction, or approval, an amount that satisfies one person may not satisfy another. Individuals vary in their needs. They also vary in the number of possible alternatives for need gratification. Persons who are receiving considerable gratification from other groups depend less on a particular group for gratification and may be able to exact more rewards than persons who depend more on the group. Because of their alternatives, the comparison levels of the first-mentioned people are higher, and they expect more from the group.

Whether a reward is adequate will depend on what persons expect in the situation—their comparison level—and what they regard as an equitable, or just, reward. We have emphasized (Chapter 10) that the exchange process is greatly influenced by conceptions of justice, or equity. Rewards as well as costs are more complicated, therefore, than a simple arithmetic of need gratification or deprivation. The experience of inequity is, itself, a cost. The achieving of justice and equity is a reward.

Basic to equity theory is *social comparison.* J. S. Adams has worked out the details of equity theory as applied to work situations.[23] Individuals compare their "inputs" and "outcomes" with those of other persons. "Inputs" are a person's "investments" in a job, and "outcomes" parallels our use of the same term (see Chapter 10). Inputs can be any set of attributes that both parties in an exchange recognize and that the possessor uses as a basis of comparison. If an attribute is relevant to a work situation, then a just return is expected by the person possessing the attribute. In a work situation, the most obvious input is effort toward doing the work. Outcome is a similarly broad category, including anything both parties recognize as being useful to, or desired by, the recipient. Outcomes may have either positive or negative weight: costs may exceed rewards, or vice versa. Comparisons occur either between two parties in a reciprocal exchange, or in an exchange relation with a third person (two workmen, say, employed by a third person).

A state of equity exists when the ratio of inputs and outcomes of an individ-

[23] Adams, 1965.

ual is equal to that of the person with whom he compares himself. Thus, the *principle of equity* is that the more an individual puts into an activity, compared to another person, the more he or she should get in return. This principle parallels the concept of distributive justice, discussed earlier (Chapter 10). Obviously, two states of inequity can occur. If my outcomes are proportionately lower than yours, I will feel that this is unfair or unjust. On the other hand, if my outcomes are proportionately greater than yours, I may feel guilt or embarrassment because I perceive this situation also to be unjust. Either kind of inequity can be uncomfortable, although the discomfort for me is less when the inequity is to my advantage.

Inasmuch as both departures from equity are uncomfortable, there is motivation to reduce inequity. While it is not surprising that people try to change situations which are *disadvantageous,* it would be surprising and interesting to find that people tried to alter situations which are *advantageous.* If it were shown that the impulse toward equity works in both cases, it would throw considerable light on some troublesome situations in which productivity and satisfaction are not related directly to the amount of reward.

Attempts to restore equity may take many forms. Individuals may actually attempt to alter their inputs or outcomes or to change those of other persons in a manner that will restore equities between ratios, or they may cognitively distort them so that they appear to be more nearly equal. They may stop comparing outcomes with a particular other person, choosing someone else, or they may finally quit the job. Cognitive distortion of inputs or outcomes of others can be managed by exaggerating or minimizing a given input or outcome or by alteration of the weight of a given attribute in determining inputs or outcomes. Thus, the older worker who is paid a lot more than a younger one doing the same job may decide that this is only right and that seniority should be heavily emphasized in fixing rates of pay. Or outcomes or inputs that were previously considered irrelevant may be invested with new importance so that an executive in a branch office in San Francisco can decide that living in that city is of sufficient value to equalize his or her ratio of inputs and outcomes in comparison with a better-paid colleague in New York City.

In choosing among the ways of reducing inequity, people are likely to try to maximize positive outcomes and to avoid increasing inputs that are effortful and costly to change. In particular, people resist real and cognitive change in inputs as well as outcomes that are central to their self-esteem. Since they are more aware of their own outcomes and inputs, they find it more difficult to alter these cognitively than to alter those of other people. Leaving the field, quitting the job, except perhaps temporarily through absenteeism, is apt to happen only when inequity is high and other means of reducing it are unavailable.

Much of the research on this theory as it applies to work has focused on the effects of inequitable wage payments, and especially on the somewhat unexpected prediction that overpayment may result in *lower* productivity and satisfaction. The reason for focusing on inequitable *over*payment rather than *under*payment is that this is a more severe test of the theory. Moreover, inequitable underpayment would have more competing explanations as alternatives to equity theory—hence the test of overpayment, if successful, would provide more conclusive support.

In one study, university students were hired as interviewers and led to believe that they were being overpaid (because they were earning the same as qualified interviewers).[24] The students were paid on an hourly basis, and the prediction was that the overpaid students would reduce inequity by increasing their inputs and doing more interviews—which was what happened. In the second experiment, which in part replicated the first, there were new groups either equitably or inequitably paid on a piecework basis. For the inequitably paid group, the prediction was more complex. Participants in the experiment could not increase their inputs by increasing the number of interviews because their outcomes would correspondingly increase—they were paid according to the number of interviews completed. Thus, the investigators predicted that on a piecework basis, overpaid participants would complete fewer interviews. In that way they would receive less money, and be paid more equitably to match their low level of skill as interviewers. And this prediction was also confirmed.

A field study of supermarket cashiers and baggers illustrates the dissatisfaction arising from underpayment.[25] Cashiers have higher status in supermarkets than baggers, because the cashiers are full-time employees and are paid more than the part-time baggers. Furthermore, the baggers are perceived to be working for the cashiers, so there is a psychological superiority. Yet in other ways— age, education, and so on—the baggers might feel they had more valued inputs, as when college students find themselves paired with younger cashiers who have only high-school educations. In these instances, the baggers with higher inputs would be receiving inequitable pay and status for their educational level. Interviews revealed that when such pairings occurred, those baggers with superior inputs of age and education worked at a slower pace, thus bringing their inputs down and into line with lower outcomes. An analysis of the financial operation of the whole supermarket chain found that when stores were ranked on labor efficiency and on an index reflecting discrepancies in inputs and outcomes between cashiers and baggers, there was a nearly perfect correlation of inefficiency to discrepancy.

In general, the studies of the effects of underpayment have supported prediction from equity theory.[26] Results concerning overpayment have been called into question, however, on several grounds. First, in the laboratory experiments, the manipulation used to create the condition of overpayment for some students may unintentionally have threatened the participants' self-esteem as well as their feelings of security regarding further work or the continuation of a high piece

[24] Adams and Rosenbaum, 1962.
[25] Clark, 1958.
[26] Pritchard, 1969.

rate. Reaction to these effects might be to improve the quality of performance and reduce quantity. Further, at least one study suggested that the effects of overpayment dissipate rapidly, either because individuals gain security and prove themselves capable fairly quickly, or because they are able to convince themselves that their performance does merit the high pay. Also, it has been suggested that in everyday work situations, pay inequities are created by an impersonal firm so that advantaged workers are less apt to feel that their being overpaid constitutes any unfairness on their part. While it may be true that, under some conditions, overpayment is not considered inequitable, by and large equity theory seems to have appreciable support and to provide explanations for otherwise puzzling phenomena.

Satisfaction and Productivity

A remaining problem that is perplexing is the relation between group productivity and satisfaction. Personnel policies in many organizations are formulated on the assumption that satisfied workers are productive workers. Research, however, does not support this assumption.[27]

While not closely related to productivity, satisfaction or morale *is* related to employee absences and employment stability. Less-satisfied workers have higher absenteeism and are more likely to quit their jobs. But the failure to find a direct relation between satisfaction and productivity has prompted a reexamination of the reasoning that led early investigators to expect a positive correlation. One line of reasoning assumed that satisfaction and productivity were both a function of rewards and therefore should be tied together. But the relation between productivity and rewards bears another look, because there are some very good reasons that rewards, satisfaction, and productivity do not necessarily vary together in the typical work situation. Not only are such rewards often removed in time and space from production, but also, instead of being administered according to a worker's productivity, they are frequently given out according to broad classifications, such as length of service, type of work, or similar characteristics.[28] Such rewards, furthermore, are obtained only if a worker remains in the system. They may, therefore, motivate a sufficient level of productivity to ensure continued employment, but a level that does not result in differences among workers or departures from the group norms.

Arguments about the direct relation between productivity and rewards assume that the rewards which management thinks are important are in fact important to the workers. It has been suggested that, on the contrary, differential monetary rewards and their importance to employees have been overestimated.[29] While wages are not unimportant, there are other sources of rewards

[27] Brayfield and Crockett, 1955.
[28] Katz and Kahn, 1952.
[29] Brayfield and Crockett, 1955.

which affect productivity and satisfaction—the style of supervision, the intrinsic activity of the job, and so forth. Many studies have emphasized the rewards deriving from interaction. Some investigations which found no relation at all among satisfaction, productivity, and monetary rewards, have demonstrated that the group norms, the idea of what constitutes a fair day's work, play an important part in productivity, especially with those workers who are dependent upon and rewarded by the group for conforming to those norms.

These findings suggest another reason why productivity may not be simply a function of rewards provided by an *external* agent. *Internal* rewards may *counteract* the effects of external rewards so that, for example, workers who are given a raise for high productivity may be deprived of the social-emotional rewards of the group because their performance exceeds that of the group. For most workers, the social-emotional rewards are more important. We find, therefore, small differences in productivity among workers even though the system of payment may be designed to encourage larger differences. Where differences do exist, they can be explained mostly in terms of the workers' position in the group and the way it affects and is affected by their adherence to group norms.

In some situations, monetary rewards are probably more directly important. For instance, where the work setting isolates workers, or where the task is dull and routine, money would be the main reward, uncomplicated by other kinds of rewards. Finally, one way of relating productivity, satisfaction, and rewards is in terms of workers' expectancies.[30] If they perceive that increased performance will produce increased rewards, they are apt to increase their effort. And satisfaction is apt to depend upon what workers expect, what they believe to be equitable.

Summary: The Problem-solving Process

What action takes place in various stages of problem solving depends upon the demands imposed by the problem and also by the need of the group to reach agreement. The general trend is from orientation toward the problem to evaluation of potential solutions. Satisfaction in groups has several sources. One lies in the task itself, which may be rewarding. Another lies in the enjoyment of social interaction. The relation of reward-cost outcomes to both productivity and satisfaction can only be understood in terms of equity. Whether an outcome is adequate depends upon what people expect from the situation—their comparison levels—and on what they regard as equitable, or just, rewards. The more one puts into an activity, the more one expects to get out of it. And one compares one's inputs and outcomes with those of other workers to see whether one is getting a fair deal. A nonobvious point is that, under some circumstances, workers may be disturbed if they are getting *more* than they deserve, in relation to their input.

[30] Vroom, 1964; Porter and Lawler, 1968.

THIRTEEN

HUMANS AS ROLE PLAYERS

An understanding of social interaction in terms of roles requires an emphasis on the subjective side of interaction—how people see it and feel it. We have already discussed some of these aspects of interaction in our exposition of group structure and process. First, we saw that shared perceptions develop about the position occupied by each member in a group structure. Members agree on the status of other members and on their positions as leaders or followers. We have also noted a second feature of interaction in our discussion of how members agree in their expectations concerning the behavior of those who occupy particular positions. A person in a position of high power is expected to influence others readily and effectively; a leader is expected to suggest constructive actions resulting in achievement of group goals; and a follower is expected to refrain from offering suggestions and to agree with the leader's ideas.

A third idea we have developed is that of the social norm—shared expectations about what one says or does or even what one thinks or feels. For the most part, norms were considered as they applied to all group members, but considerable emphasis was given to the fact that different expectations are held for leaders and followers. We devoted great attention to the mechanisms through which norms are enforced and to conditions that minimize or maximize norm-defining and norm-enforcing processes.

The present chapter pertains to virtually all forms of human interaction, focusing upon the idea of norm as a rule of conduct and applying it to any individual who occupies a definite position in the social structure. When it pertains to a position in a social system the norm is associated with a social role. What we do in this chapter is to develop further these ideas of social role and social system. In Chapter 14, following, we use these concepts to describe certain types of conflicts that occur in groups, organizations, and institutions, and to describe the various means by which the conflicts are reduced or resolved.

NATURE OF SOCIAL ROLES

The first concepts to be considered are: position or role category, role expectation, role behavior, and the inclusive term, *social role.*

Position or Role Category; Role Player or Actor

The term *role category* or *position* refers to a category of persons whose behavior is subject to similar expectations. The person in the role category is called the *role player,* or *actor.* Role categories may be perceived in the same way by all members of society, or by only a few individuals. In Chapter 5, we discussed the typing of people under the heading of stereotyping. We saw there that children and adults type people around them, sometimes in the form of a stereotype. Some of these types are role categories.

There are three bases for grouping people into a role category: (1) they occupy the same position in a social relation or system, (2) they occupy a special position in a small group, and (3) they have qualities that constitute a type. The first of these is most common, and is illustrated by actors in the role category of *mother* in the system of social relations called the family. People agree on how a mother should behave—they share expectations. Only those categories of actors defined in the same way by two or more persons meet the criteria for defining a position. Widely perceived roles would include age-sex positions (small boy, small girl, young man, young woman, old man, old woman) or persons whose occupations bring them in contact with a wide range of clients, customers, and patrons (lawyer, taxi driver, teacher, barber, doctor).

In the second type of role category, a member of a small group is assigned to a particular category based on his or her function. Most small groups have such positions peculiar to themselves, but we have all seen such small-group roles as the water boy, storyteller, clown, expert, and director.

The third basis for classification focuses on qualities of the actor occupying the role. These types are more generally recognized in the larger society—social types like the good Joe, the worrier, the eternal optimist or pessimist, the grouch, or the yes man. The skill of a stage actress or movie actor in part consists of their ability to portray the special style and mannerisms of these universally known

Social roles in the nuclear family: wife and mother, son, husband and father.

"characters." For the most part, our analysis will be concerned with the first of these role categories—those roles in the larger social structures.

Role Expectations; Social Role

Role expectations are expectations associated with a role category which may be shared by as few as two persons or by nearly everyone in a society of millions. Expectations associated with age-sex positions illustrate culturewide expectations. In American society, for example, the role category "little girl" includes the expectations that the actor likes dolls and clothes, that she cries more readily and shows more open affection than her brothers, and that she talks earlier and matures earlier socially than little boys. There are also beliefs about what she should not do—outbox all the boys in the neighborhood, play football with them, or be interested in playing cowboys and Indians or cops and robbers. Currently, such differences in normative expectations for boys and girls—and for men and women—are under vigorous attack. In essence, the argument is for the elimination of sex roles as such so that each individual can develop according to his or her own potentialities, regardless of gender.

We may also illustrate subgroup expectations. People in lower socioeconomic classes have distinctive expectations about the role category "child," and expect more obedience and respect toward adults than persons in the middle and upper socioeconomic classes do. But some expectations associated with a position may be unique—as when a particular mother and child share the expectation that the mother should sing a certain lullaby at bedtime.

Role expectations associated with a category may vary with respect to consensus. Some expectations are widely held; others are unique to particular individuals. Most people in our society expect an actor in the role of husband to provide the major part of his family's income. That a twenty-one-year-old unmarried son or daughter should also earn income for the family would, in contrast, be a topic of considerable disagreement among different families or individuals.

The more general term *social role* (or, simply, *role*) is used to refer both to the position and to its associated expectations. When the role of mother is referred to, both the position in a family system and its attached expectations are designated.

Two features of *expectations* are especially important for understanding the idea of social role. These are: (1) the anticipatory nature of expectations, and (2) the normative quality of expectations. Both are discussed below.

1. *Anticipatory nature of expectations.* We regularly expect to behave in a certain manner, and we usually have definite expectations concerning the behavior of people with whom we interact. The importance of this aspect of interaction becomes clear if we consider unfamiliar situations where expectations are at a minimum—a child away at summer camp for the first time, feeling homesick; a teenager, tense and nervous on a first date; a young person, apprehensive about a new and unfamiliar job. Similar feelings of uncertainty and a resulting tentative and shifting quality of interaction occur in any newly formed group. There is, at any party, the ice that needs breaking as people who don't know each other are introduced, get to know each other, get to feel comfortable. All these situations in which expectations are minimal may be compared with others where expectations are well developed. For example, compare these situations with the smoothly functioning, comfortable interaction between two old friends.

The anticipatory quality of interaction is important because it guides people's behavior. They anticipate how someone else might react to their actions and shape their behavior accordingly. Often these anticipations take the form of rehearsing social interactions before they actually happen. The attitude of strangers is inferred from the cues provided by their appearance, expression, posture; by their previously known (if any) and current behavior; and by the situational context of the interaction. From such information, individuals may infer what other persons feel and think about them and how they are likely to behave toward them. In everyday interaction, the process of anticipating attitudes and behaviors of other people is greatly simplified. Through long experience, we learn to classify the behavior of others in various situations into categories that represent the distinctive attitudes of each class of persons-in-situations. This allows us to anticipate the attitude of the other people in each new encounter simply by placing them and the situation in the appropriate category.

Some of the anticipatory quality of interaction has been strikingly illustrated in a demonstration in which a teacher asked his students to behave contrary to expectations in everyday situations.[1] In one of these demonstrations, students were asked to behave for a time as if they were boarders in their own homes instead of members of the family. In most cases, the family members were utterly stupefied and struggled to make the strange behaviors intelligible and to restore normal relations. One student embarrassed his mother in the company of friends by asking her if she minded if he had a snack from the refrigerator. "Mind if you have a little snack?" she asked, astonished. "You've been eating little snacks around here for years without asking me. What's gotten into you?" Another mother, enraged because her daughter spoke to her only when spoken to, began to shriek in angry denunciation of her daughter's disrespect, and refused to be calmed by the student's sister.

2. *Normative quality of expectations.* People anticipate the behavior of others, and therefore interaction has a contingent quality. People's behavior is contingent upon their anticipation of how others will react toward them. When they tell a joke, they anticipate that others will laugh; otherwise they are unlikely to tell it. If they confide a personal problem, they expect some sympathy; if they don't want sympathy, they keep the problem to themselves. Since many powerful social-emotional needs are satisfied only through interaction, individuals must be able to anticipate correctly the reactions of others to their own behavior. Otherwise, they will be unable to satisfy their own needs.

Usually our anticipations are reliable only in situations we have been in before, where we and others involved have certain shared experiences in common. The parties to the interaction share expectations concerning their own and the others' behavior. Such shared, established expectations usually have an obligatory quality. The others are not only expected to behave in a certain way, but they *should* behave in that way. Their failure to do so is likely to provoke surprise, disgust, anger, or indignation. This normative quality of expectation arises from the fact that only by anticipating consistently and accurately the behavior of others can we maximize our reward-cost outcomes. The more important the rewards and costs involved, the more normative the expectations become. Norms involve important rewards and costs to the extent that they lead to achieving or maintaining cherished group values—like protection of children, honor of the nation, freedom of speech, and the like.

Role Behaviors

Role behaviors are the behaviors of an actor in a role category that are relevant to expectations for that role. These behaviors may or may not conform to expectations. For example, a professor may explain some ideas very poorly. Explanation of ideas is relevant to the role and consequently would be role behavior—

---

[1] Garfinkel, 1967.

even though it does not conform to the expectation that the explanation will be clear. While performing the professorial role, he or she also engages in behavior irrelevant to it. Smoking, for instance, would be an action that has nothing to do with the role.

Role expectation and role behaviors should be clearly distinguished from each other. Expectations represent how actors should behave; particular individuals, however, may deviate markedly from these expectations in their actual behavior. The behaviors that make up a particular role enactment are generally the result of role bargaining, or negotiation, between partners. The initial expectations of role partners often have considerable leeway in them, and the partners are rarely in perfect agreement. Often this looseness is tightened up through negotiation between partners who ultimately arrive at greater agreement and more precise expectations as a result of this process.

Summary: Nature of Social Roles

Social roles are described by several concepts: position or role category, role player or actor, role expectations, and role behaviors. The term *role category* or *position* refers to a grouping of persons whose behavior is subject to similar expectations. The person in the role category is called the *role player*, or *actor*. People may be placed in role categories on three bases: (1) they occupy the same position in a social relation or system, (2) they occupy a special position in a small group, and (3) they have qualities that constitute a type. *Role behaviors* are the ways in which an actor in a role category actually behaves—ways that are relevant to the role, but that do not necessarily conform to its expectations.

Role expectations are the ways in which an actor in a category is expected to act. They have an anticipatory quality: normally when we direct some action toward other persons, we have a clear idea of how those persons will react—we expect them to respond in a particular way. Because these are norms, these expectations have the force of a *should,* an appropriateness. Not to behave in the fashion expected would be considered a violation of what is proper and right.

THE SOCIAL SYSTEM

Particular social roles cannot be considered apart from their relation to other social roles. Every social role has others to which it is related. And taken all together, these related roles make up a system within which people interact. Such interlocking social roles are commonly called *social systems,* and would include the structure of a family—not a particular family but the systematic relations between the positions of husband and wife, father and child, mother and child, brother and sister, and so forth—or the structure of a prison, a monastery, a hospital, or a school.

Relations among Social Roles

Role partners   The expectations associated with a role category specify particular behaviors toward actors in other related categories. Actors occupying these other categories are called *role partners*. You can't play the role of a mother without the role partner of the child. Or, if you're a doctor, you need patients, and if you're a teacher, you need students. An actor may have many role partners. The mother would have not only her children but also her children's father, teachers, playmates, neighbors, pediatrician, dentist. These people, when acting as her role partners, relate to her as a mother of the children with whom they have to deal.

Role obligations and rights   The intimate connections among related role categories may be better understood by considering role relations in terms of *obligations* and *rights*. These emphasize the normative character of expectations in terms of both the actor and the partner. Take the role categories of husband and wife. Associated with the position of husband are expectations about how he is supposed to behave toward his role partner, the wife, and how she is expected to behave toward him. These relations can be described from the standpoint of the husband or from that of the wife.

From the standpoint of the husband, the expectations about *his* behavior are his obligations, and the expectations about *his wife's* behavior are his rights or privileges—in relation to the role of husband. From the standpoint of the wife, these same expectations become privileges and obligations, respectively. For example, according to the traditional division of labor in the American family, an obligation of the husband is to provide money for food, clothing, shelter, and the amenities of living for his wife. From the wife's point of view, this is a right or privilege she enjoys. Conversely, a husband expects his wife to take care of the house and the children, and to do the shopping and laundry. From his point of view, this is a right; it is an obligation associated with the role of wife. The obligations of an actor are the rights of his role partner; his own rights are the obligations of his role partner. These traditional views of rights and obligations of husbands and wives are currently under severe attack, an attack which might well result in extensive changes in these roles.

Social Roles in Ongoing Interaction

Sometimes actors simultaneously occupy a number of positions in which both they and their role partners define the actors in terms of several different categories. Physicians treating members of their own families, or teachers having their own children as pupils in the classroom, illustrate situations in which behavior is influenced by the role expectations attached to different categories. As will be discussed in the next chapter, the simultaneous occupation of more than one role category can lead to role strain—when the expectations of the two or more simultaneous roles are contradictory.

Many other roles assigned to the same individual are not enacted at the same time. People never enact at one time all the roles that they might occupy. At any given moment, some of their positions are active and are used by them and by others to anticipate behavior and to judge its appropriateness. Later, other positions become active while the former positions become dormant. The people are no longer placed in the same categories. During the day, they may enact a particular occupational role. But they may shift to a friendship role during a coffee break, or into the spouse or parent role if a member of the family telephones. When they go home, they are back into the family role, but in the evening may adopt a leadership role at the PTA meeting.

Interactional context At any given time, the interactional context is an important determinant of the role categories a person occupies, of the expectations applied to the role category, and of the range of permissible behavior defined by the expectations. The two features of the interactional context that determine these factors are the *characteristics of the situation* and the *characteristics of the actors*.

Persons are put in a role category appropriate to their characteristics and behavior. How they are categorized will determine what expectations emerge. If a person enters a bank and, with a passbook in hand, approaches a woman who

Teacher-student roles are easily inferred from the interactional context.

is standing behind a partition with a window grill, each will use certain information to categorize the other; the passbook carrier defines the woman as a teller and she defines the passbook carrier as a customer. As soon as such categorization is made and as long as it is maintained, certain expectations and interactions occur. There is probably a polite exchange of greetings, the passbook changes hands, and so on. Should the customer suddenly produce a gun, however, he or she would be categorized differently by the teller and new expectations and behavior on her part would undoubtedly occur. Similarly, if the woman behind the teller's window behaved in a way that indicated she was not a teller, the customer would change his or her expectations and behavior. The point is that expectations are always tied to categories of persons as well as to categories of situations. Before expectations can emerge, categorization must take place, and should categories shift, expectations will shift also.

A number of features of the situation may alter expectations or make them relatively ineffective in influencing behavior. The expectation that a bystander should come to the aid of a distressed person appears to be nullified where features of the situation (such as the presence of many other persons who might help) allow the bystander to perceive that action on his or her part is neither necessary nor morally required.

Summary: The Social System

A social system is a group of related social roles. Each role category in a social system relates to one or more other role categories. Persons occupying these other categories are known as role partners. The obligations of actors in role categories are the rights of their role partners; their own rights are the obligations of their partners. Individuals assume various roles at different times and on different occasions. Sometimes they simultaneously perform more than one role. When expectations associated with these multiple role categories are incompatible, role strain results. The role categories an actor occupies, the expectations applied to the role category, and the range of permissible behavior defined by the expectations depend upon the interactional context. The interactional context is defined by the characteristics of the situation and the attributes of the actors.

SOCIAL NORMS AND ROLES

We have already stressed two important properties of expectations: their anticipatory and their obligatory nature. Actors are not neutral concerning whether or not their expectations are confirmed by the behavior of others. They not only anticipate another person's behavior, but they feel the other person is obliged to behave in accordance with their anticipations. This is because the other is assumed to share with them these common role expectations. Role expectations, then, are normative, and actors are disturbed if the other person does not conform to expectations. When we discussed group norms in Chapter 11, we confined ourselves mostly to pressures toward conformity and the conditions that produce varying degrees of conformity. This section will deal with normative expectations within the larger perspective of social roles.

Properties of Normative Expectations

Social norms have a variety of properties, each of which we shall consider in turn:

1 They shape behavior in the direction of shared values or desirable states of affairs.

2 They vary in the degree to which they help to realize important values.

3 They are enforced by the behavior of other persons.

4 They vary as to how widely they are shared—societywide or belonging to groups as small as dyads.

5 They vary in the range of permissible behavior, some being more stringent than others.

Norms and the value structure   Behavior that is contrary to expectation may arouse surprise, disgust, anger, or indignation. Psychologically, these reactions can be explained in terms of social learning. A well-reared Muslim has learned to react with revulsion to the eating of pork, somewhat as we, in our society, would react to a serving of chocolate-covered ants. Some American males would react with feelings of embarrassment or even indignation to a host's suggestion that, as a guest, they should sleep with the host's wife, while in societies where wife-lending is expected under certain circumstances, the guest *and* the wife might react with similar feelings if such an offer were *not* made.

On the sociological level of analysis, these reactions relate to the value structure of the group. Actors in a group share expectations about one another's conduct, just as they share notions concerning desirable conditions or states of affairs—which are called values. Values can be ranked in terms of their importance to the members of a group. Among conservationists, for instance, prominent values might include the aesthetic qualities of land, the protection against ecological ruin by man and his machines, the preservation of wildlife species, and the spending of time out of doors—all of which would be desirable conditions or states of affairs. The ranking of these values would constitute the value hierarchy of that group. The conservationists would have very different priorities from a group of lumbermen or miners. Norms are functionally related to values because conformity to certain rules of conduct fosters achievement of certain desired states. Health, for example, is a value in our society, and the various hygienic rules are norms that direct behavior toward that state of affairs.

Some norms are functionally more important than others. A social norm about covering one's mouth while sneezing has a causal connection with preservation of the health of others, but is less important than the norms of cleanliness in an operating room in a hospital.

Enforcement of norms Norms are enforced by means of sanctions, which can be rewards (positive sanctions) or can be punishments or deprivations (negative sanctions). Some of these sanctions are external—the source of the reward or of the punishment is the behavior of others. Others are internal—the source of reward or punishment is from within the actor. External sanctions would include raises or bonuses for hard work, or cuts in pay for lateness. Internal sanctions would include the employee's feeling of pride for having done a good job, or feelings of guilt and inadequacy for having done a poor one. The strength of the sanction varies with the importance of the value and the extent to which the norm is instrumental in the achievement of the value. While external sanctions enforce norms that are of relatively little importance, norms that relate to the important values and that are highly instrumental in achieving those values are rarely enforced by external sanctions alone. Groups socialize their members so that they develop strong internal sanctions for these norms.

Variations in sharing normative expectations Expectations may be shared by any number of persons, from all the members of a society down to small groups, even dyads. The kiss, the handshake, the bowed head for prayer, are all regulated by norms that are societywide. Many behaviors are specific to smaller groups so that in particular church denominations, for example, there may be behaviors which are required of members, but not of nonmembers who do not—and are not expected to—participate. Work groups set standards about how much or how little work is to be done and punish members who violate these standards. On college campuses there are often subgroups of students who maintain norms about how much time ought to be spent studying, with those who study too much getting called such derogatory names as "grinds" or "eggheads." The smallest group, a dyad, may engage in behavior that is normative but peculiar to them. A husband may walk the dog in the mornings, and the wife may be the one to drive the children to school.

Variations in limits of behavior Some rules may be honored by a rather wide range of conduct, while others are more exacting and require a specific line of behavior. Norms, then, should be viewed as specifying the limits of permissible or required behavior in a given interactional context. The invitation time for a cocktail party, for example, has a wide range, and guests may come at the appointed hour or considerably later (but not earlier). For a dinner party, the range is narrower, and while all the guests are unlikely to arrive at the same moment, few will arrive very much later than the specified hour, because there is a dinner involved and food has been prepared with a serving time in mind.

In sum, normative role expectations have a variety of properties: (1) They shape behavior in the direction of shared values or desirable states of affairs. (2)

They vary in the degree to which they help to realize important values. (3) They are enforced by the behavior of other persons. (4) They vary as to how widely they are shared—societywide or limited to a dyad. (5) They vary in the range of permissible behavior, some being more stringent than others.

SOCIAL ROLES AND SOCIAL INTERACTION

In the remainder of this chapter, we will analyze social interaction in terms of role concepts. Our previous emphasis on the normative aspects of expectations was not intended to imply that role behavior is simple conformity to role expectations. Role expectations provide a broad script for the drama of role enactment and leave much leeway for ad-libbing. From our experience we know that the performances of different actors enacting the same role can vary considerably. There is a role for professors, but not all professors behave in exactly the same way in the classroom. Some are very informal, cracking jokes, wearing informal clothes, and perching on the edge of a desk, while others are more formal and businesslike, serving primarily as task leaders but not as social-emotional leaders.

We are interested in identifying the guidelines for portrayal of a role in certain directions. There are at least four: *situational demands, personality and role skills, intruding roles,* and then, in addition, the process of *role negotiation* with role partners. These four sources operate to give direction to role enactment within the wider range of expectations associated with the role category. We shall discuss each in turn.

Situational Demands

Many situations call for a specific kind of role performance, and the elements that call out this performance are called *role demands.*[2] Even though the role may be the same, each situation has demands that vary slightly or greatly. A teacher meeting with a single student in his or her office may behave quite differently from the way he or she acts in the classroom. And if a faculty team plays a game of volleyball against a graduate student team, their actions vary considerably from their behavior in the classroom because of different role demands. Although there is no systematic analysis of various roles, it seems probable that some roles vary widely from situation to situation, while others are more similar across situations.

Personality and Role Skills

A second source directing role enactment stems from personality characteristics and the skills of the actor. People's aptitudes, attitudes, self-concepts, needs, and *role identities* all affect how they enact a role. In the next chapter, we will discuss

[2] Sarbin and Allen, 1968.

how a difference between aptitude or personality and role expectations can create considerable *strain* in role enactment. For example, a pacifistic, peace-loving young man may be either unable, or able only with great difficulty, to perform the role of wartime soldier. But here, we are more concerned with the *special direction* that personality and role skills may give to role enactment. Two nurses with very different personalities and aptitudes might both experience little role strain and be successful nurses, but might enact this role in quite different ways.

Role identity is the way individuals present themselves in enacting a role— the way they like to think of themselves as being. A role identity is a somewhat idealized conception of one's performance. There are thoughts or anticipations, imagined performances, or rehearsals portraying one's identity. Thus, a young girl might anticipate in advance, plan, and rehearse the identity that she will present in a ten-minute speech at school.

The identity presented in imagination may be evaluated or modified by imagining the reactions of other people to one's role performance and further modified or reconstructed in the light of these imaginings. These idealized conceptions can also be used to evaluate how one enacted one's role, to identify mistakes and over- and underplays. Role identities are the expression of relevant aspects of an actor's self-concept. We may think of the self-concept as an interlocking set of views that individuals hold about themselves as persons. This serves as a core from which role identities are formulated in connection with particular situations, particular role categories.

Intruding Roles

A third source of direction lies within the system of roles itself. An actor's behavior is rarely influenced by one role alone. He or she simultaneously occupies a number of role categories. One role will usually be dominant in a given situation, but other roles may, to a certain extent, influence behavior in that role. Thus, the portrayal of the role of doctor, for instance, may be somewhat different when acted out by men and by women because of the intrusion of their sex roles. At a party, a teacher might enact the role of a guest and genial participant, but the role of teacher may intrude to some degree. In the next chapter, we will discuss in greater detail the effects of system features which facilitate and which interfere with a particular role performance.

Role Negotiation

Actors and their role partners can be seen as working out through negotiation, either direct or indirect, how each will behave in particular encounters, as well as the more general forms that their relationship is to assume in the future.[3] The use of the term *negotiation* should not be construed to mean that this process is as deliberate as the negotiation of a sale price between a salesperson and a cus-

[3] Goode, 1960.

tomer. Role negotiation may be subtle and indirect, and one or both parties may even be unaware that they are striving for a particular role bargain. The nature of the bargain depends upon several factors including (1) the role identities of both parties, (2) situational demands, (3) the social power of each person in terms of resources, dependencies, and alternatives, (4) interpersonal skills, and (5) the effectiveness of third parties in influencing the outcome of the negotiation. Many of the principles of interpersonal strategy discussed in Chapter 8 can be applied to role negotiation.

Role negotiation is especially apt to occur where: (1) the limits of the roles are so broad as to leave unspecified the particular nature of role performances, (2) the role expectations held by actor and role partner are not in agreement, (3) the actor's characteristics preclude performance of the role in the usual way, (4) the situational demands interfere with role enactment, (5) other roles intrude upon performance, and (6) the difference in social power between actor and role partner is not so great as to rule out negotiation.

We can illustrate role negotiation by considering the marriage relation where, at least at times, *all* of the above circumstances prevail. The roles of husband and wife are culturally prescribed only in broad terms; partners rarely agree on all aspects of the relation; personality, aptitudes, skills, or role identities of one or both partners are frequently unsuited to the role of wife or husband; situational demands often interfere with role performance; other roles (such as careers) often intrude; and the relative disparity in social power—in Western societies anyway—is not great.

The need for negotiating marriage roles has been especially clear lately, as society has changed, and the advent of the women's liberation movement has raised additional questions about some of the traditional assumptions upon which marriages have been based. Such negotiation has been apparent for centuries, but it has been generally true that the tasks of raising children, maintaining the home, providing meals, and doing the cleaning and the laundry have fallen primarily upon the wife. Husbands often share in these activities, but not equally, and not with the primary responsibility for them. And to the extent that these obligations fall primarily upon the wife, they interfere with other roles she might wish to enact, such as that of a career. Traditionally, the husband's career has taken precedence over that of the wife, so that family moves to a new location have been made with his career in mind but not hers. Traditional roles of husbands and wives with respect to sexual behavior have also been unequal. Greater emphasis has been placed on the sexual satisfaction of the husband than that of the wife. The male has been the aggressor and the initiator of sexual behavior, and the traditional female role has called for relative passivity. The husband has also had more freedom to engage in extramarital affairs than the wife has.

The advent of the pill, the concern about attaining orgasm, the growing economic opportunities for women in employment, and the women's liberation movement have all combined to weaken these traditional assumptions about marriage and to stress equality in negotiation and, ideally, in the results of these negotiations. In some new marriages, the terms of negotiation are explicit, and actual contracts have been worked out specifying what the behavior of each party should be, what the rights and obligations are for each, and what the limits are for each role.

William Goode has identified many elements that enter into negotiation, and we classify them as follows:[4] (1) the role identities of the parties, (2) the opportunity structure of the situation, (3) the social power of each party in terms of resources, dependencies, and interpersonal skills, and (4) the presence and relevance of third parties. Each of these can be illustrated for the marriage situation.

A man who defines the role of husband in traditionally male-dominant terms and a woman who defines the role of wife in the new liberal tradition would have great difficulty negotiating these role identities—they would clash on many points. Role identities are easier to negotiate if they can be made to fit each other in some way.

The opportunity structure is being modified in modern times to improve the position of the wife in negotiation—she no longer needs to be economically dependent on the husband, since she can more readily find employment or even have a career.

The social power of each party is understood in terms discussed earlier in Chapter 8: the greater the resources, the fewer the dependencies, and the greater the alternatives, the more power a party has. Interpersonal skills include the ability to persuade, manipulate, use various tactics, and so on. One spouse may attempt to be especially nice to the other, buying a gift or performing special favors to invoke the norm of reciprocity and make the partner feel obligated to return the treatment. (It may also make the partner feel guilty and raise a whole new set of problems.) Threats or deprivations may be used. Partners may sulk and refuse to speak to each other. They may stop doing little things for each other that had been routine. More powerful moves involve threats to leave home, to have an affair, to get a divorce, or sometimes even to engage in physical violence. Another tactic involves the use of cognitive distortions. One party may be able to convince the other that the present arrangement is equitable, even when it is not. But most negotiation, at least in new marriages, takes the form of discovering differences in expectations, and working them out through discussion and argument to arrive at normative agreement on performances.

Third parties may enter into the negotiation. Where other members of the primary or extended family live with the husband and wife, this is particularly true. The continued dependence, either psychological or financial, of the marital partners on their parents can bring about third-party influence. Many of the old mother-in-law jokes are based upon an intrusion by the mother-in-law into the negotiating process—which can happen only when it is permitted by the marital partners.

While there has not been much research on the determinants of role por-

---

[4] Goode, 1960.

trayal, findings are consistent with the above formulation. One role-playing experiment showed that if a particular role portrayal was inconsistent with the self-concept, an actor would resist the attempt of a partner to get him to play that role.[5] As will be explained in some detail in the next chapter, such inconsistencies (or incongruencies) are costly. Males who regarded themselves as dominant, for instance, resisted the attempts of a female confederate of the experimenter to get them to play a submissive role as a price for her agreement to go out with them. The degree of resistance varied with the attractiveness of the female confederate. Male participants were more willing to assume an identity contrary to their self-conception where the female confederate was attractive than where she was unattractive. Her attractiveness added to the rewards of complying and thus raised the outcomes.

Finally, in the same study, those who scored high on a test of *Machiavellianism* (designed to measure both the motivation and ability to manipulate others) were more apt to adopt a role opposite to their self-concept when such behavior would lead to a date. The fact that the behavior of the male participants in the study was influenced by whether the role-playing episode was held in private or thought to be observed by others supports our previous suggestion that the final role bargain that emerges is often influenced by other persons as well as the two actors involved in negotiation.

Summary: Social Roles and Social Interaction

Many kinds of role enactments are usually possible for a given social role. The direction that these performances take is guided by several forces other than the role expectations themselves: situational demands, individual personality and role skills, intruding roles, and role negotiation between partners. Elements of the current situation that call for a specific kind of role performance constitute situational demands. Personality and role skills include an individual's traits and other characteristics, aptitudes, needs, and role identity, which is an extension of one's self-concept. Intruding roles are imposed by the social system in instances where expectations from more than one category are relevant to a given role performance.

Negotiation arises from lack of agreement between role partners on the appropriate role performances. Situational demands and third parties to the interaction may also create the necessity for negotiation between partners. Negotiation is not necessarily deliberate; one or both parties may be unaware that they are vying for a particular role bargain. The progress and outcomes of negotiations depend upon the social power of each party and their role identities. The actual process of negotiation ranges from intelligent discussion and argument to the use of many other forms of interpersonal influence.

[5] Blumstein, 1970.

SOCIAL ROLE AS AN INTEGRATING CONCEPT

The idea of the social role is one of the most central in the behavioral sciences. It links together the varied actions of an individual, shows how the diverse actions of members of a group form a unity in group action, and serves as a link between the individual, the group, and the society. If we were to follow persons around, we would find that their actions at different times are strikingly varied. They have a variety of role identities that are extensions of their self concept. By taking these together we are able to view them as persons and thus see unity in the diversity of their actions.

Sociologists who focus on an analysis of social systems, and anthropologists who study comparative social structure, have found it useful to conceptualize the systems of recurring interactions in a group in terms of social role concepts. The behavior of any group can be analyzed in these terms. In a university, for example, one may note interactions that recur from day to day. In room after room of a classroom building, certain patterned interactions take place: one person stands before a group of others: that person speaks and the others write in their notebooks. The pattern can be analyzed in terms of the role categories of teacher and student. In other buildings on campus, patterned interactions occur between actors in other role categories—deans and secretaries, professors and laboratory assistants, members of the board of trustees and administrative officials. All these patterns can be conceptualized in terms of position and role expectation and can be studied as a system, a unity of interdependent parts. Certain large problems—such as what happens to the other parts of the social system when a particular position drops out of it or when the role expectations associated with a role category change—may be treated profitably on this level of analysis.

In the past, social psychologists were chiefly interested in those roles which are recognized in the whole society, because their main concern was with societywide regularities in behavior rather than with regularities common to the members of smaller subgroups. In more recent years, as social psychologists have become interested in smaller groups, they have become concerned with less general roles and even with those unique to particular groups.

At a different level, social psychologists are also interested in features of social systems that relate to personality formation. Such features as clarity of role expectation, consensus (or lack of it) among actors about these expectations, and the integration of these expectations so that actors do not encounter conflicting expectations, all have implications for problems in the area of personality formation and social interaction.

In the next chapter, we shall be concerned with the ideas reviewed here about the concept of role and what they can add to our understanding of human interaction. We shall focus on situations where contrary forces make role enactment difficult, first, because most of the research has concentrated on role conflict, and second, because it is easier to detect factors underlying human interaction when its normally smooth-flowing character is disrupted.

FOURTEEN

ROLE STRAIN AND ITS RESOLUTION

R ole strain occurs whenever an actor is confronted with having to enact expectations that, for a variety of reasons, cannot be carried out. The sources of the strain may lie in the social system, the individual, or the culture. Where such strains are common, forms of resolving them become familiar. These means of resolution, also, may lie in the social system, the individual, or the culture. Thus our discussion of role strains and their resolution will be organized under these three sources.

SOCIAL SYSTEM AND ROLE STRAIN

Throughout this discussion, we have emphasized the importance of expectations in the interaction process. Such expectations make interaction possible to the extent that they are held in common and fulfilled by the members of a group. When group members do not share expectations, or when they behave contrary to them, interaction becomes difficult or impossible. Where there are conflicting expectations, strain results, role bargaining is difficult, and the resulting bargain is rarely satisfactory to all concerned.

On the individual level, the strain from conflicting tendencies to action produces feelings of inadequacy, guilt, embarrassment, and frustration. On the social system level, the strain is associated with interpersonal conflict and the failure of the system to maximize achievement of its goals. On the cultural level, the strain produces inconsistencies and ambiguities in the shared perceptions and understandings that people have of the world and their relationships with each other.

An illustration of strain resulting from different conceptions of role held by actors and their role partners may be found in the early sessions of psychotherapy. New patients frequently come to the sessions expecting that the therapist, like other kinds of doctors, will provide some prescription for their problems. They expect the therapist to be active, to ask questions, and to tell them how to solve their problems. The therapist, on the other hand, usually expects patients to solve their own problems through a process in which they report their feelings and thoughts, and in which they arrive at a new view of themselves and their place in the world. In short, the therapist expects the patients to talk a great deal and sees his or her own role as facilitating the patients' verbalizations, while the patients expect the therapist to do most of the talking and perceive their role as passive and dependent.

Clarity and Consensus in Role Expectation

When role expectations are unclear, strain comes from individual uncertainty about what is expected and from the conflicting interpretations of what role behavior is appropriate. Newly developed roles or changing roles often lack clarity. For example, one study of psychiatric nurses found considerable strain when the nurses were required to change from responding in established nurse-patient ways to freer, more individual interactions.[1] The new directives called for nurses to recognize each patient's needs and try to satisfy them, and permitted extreme freedom to the patients (all of whom were chronic schizophrenics), limited only by considerations for their health and safety and for the nurses' own physical and psychological comfort.

These expectations for the roles of patient and nurse conflicted with the nurses' personal norms, preferences, and capabilities, with the traditional role of nurse, and with the institutional requirements of the hospital. They also failed to offer a sufficient guide to action, or to allow for consistent treatment of the patients by different nurses. Other studies of emerging roles similarly document the point that lack of clarity in new roles leads to role strain. And strain, in turn, leads to periodic attempts by the actors occupying positions in the system to clarify their roles. In large systems, such as business organizations, one such attempt takes the form of developing and elaborating manuals of operation and procedure that make explicit what is expected of each person in each position in the system. The same process shows up in a more informal way in small systems,

[1] Schwartz, 1957.

such as a family or even a two-person relation like that between lovers. One function of lovers' quarrels is to redefine their relations to each other, or, in our terminology, to clarify their respective roles.[2]

Not only may expectations be incorrect or unclear, but it is also possible that the role categories themselves may lack clarity, and produce strain. In categorizing others, we use a variety of cues, such as dress, voice, and behavior, as well as more explicit identifying information such as titles or uniforms. Where such categorization cannot be made with confidence and accuracy, uncertainty and inappropriate behavior with attendant role strain occurs. A study of over 1,000 embarrassing incidents reported by students and others shows that vagueness of role category was a frequent cause of embarrassment.[3] Incidents included a man entering a ladies' room, a boy with long hair being mistaken for a girl, and a customer being mistaken for a sales clerk.

One kind of disagreement is between an actor and a role partner. Another is between two or more role partners with respect to a given actor. Moreover, the way in which the parties disagree may take many forms. They may disagree on what expectations are to be included in a role, how narrowly or widely these expectations limit behavior, what situations they apply to, the normative force behind the expectation, and the priorities to be assigned to the expectations. For example, should a wife be allowed to work? Must this be just part-time work, or may she have a full career? Is this only in the case of economic necessity? Does the husband insist, or does he merely have a preference? Which comes first, her career or the family? We will give further examples of these forms of disagreement later.

Many conditions are related to consensus or the lack of it. Studies of consensus on various roles have shown that it is far from perfect; some disagreement is more usual than unusual. One important source of disagreement arises from the places of the actor and the role partners in the social system, and the relation of their places to related social systems. For example, teachers usually want a good salary, partly because of the needs of their family. One of their role partners, however, school superintendents, may be interested in keeping the budget low, partly because of pressures from the school board. Or, in a hospital, doctors have certain expectations for themselves and for hospital orderlies which arise from their professional training and affiliations, while hospital orderlies may entertain certain constraints on their roles that arise from their union affiliations.

Individual needs and reward-cost outcomes associated with accepting certain role expectations also relate in important ways to create agreement or disagreement on role expectations. If actors and their partners benefit to a relatively equal extent from supporting a set of expectations, they are apt to be in considerable agreement. But where holding an expectation would be beneficial to the role partner but not to the actor, there may be considerable disagreement. For

[2] Waller and Hill, 1951.
[3] Gross and Stone, 1964.

example, considerable strain would arise if a husband supports the traditional role for his wife and expects her to perform household services, to care for the children, and not to devote large portions of her time to activities outside the home, while she expects him to share equally these activities and wishes to have her own career.

In life situations, there are usually more than two parties involved in a role strain. For example, expectations that husbands and wives have concerning each other may be in conflict with expectations held by other role partners, such as parents-in-law, grandparents, or children. In most instances of conflict in expectations, especially in relatively new relationships or circumstances, the parties try to negotiate new expectations on which they can reach a higher degree of agreement.

Mechanisms for Increasing Consensus

Role strain often builds to a crisis so that participants have to clarify their rights and obligations. Such attempts range from informal rap sessions in small systems to elaborate negotiating committees in large systems. As problems of clarity and consensus increase, either because of the growing size and complexity of a system or because of rapid changes, social machinery evolves to deal with the lack of consensus and related problems.

Such machinery takes a number of forms. First, special positions and subsystems emerge to cope with the lack of consensus—coordinating and liaison committees. Second, more active efforts are made to formalize relations with manuals of operations that specify how each actor is to behave toward his role partners in the system. Along with this effort, there are other techniques to ensure standard socialization—elaborate selection procedures, orientation and training programs, refresher courses, and the like. Finally, rituals and ceremonies develop which increase identification with the group and serve to reinforce agreement on the rights and obligations of each person.

Frequently, such mechanisms fail. Continued crisis produces confrontations between role partners that result in a change in the terms of previous role bargains. This happens most often where the expectations governing a relation have sharply different implications for the outcomes of the participants and where the disadvantaged role partner has recently gained greater power. Thus, the increased power of blacks in American society and of students on campuses have forced, through a series of crises and confrontations, a new consensus in altered relations between whites and blacks, and between students and college administrators and faculty.

Conflicting and Competing Expectations

Another source of role strain lies in conflicting or competing expectations that make up a role. Such conflict or competition may relate to expectations regarding the same role partner—a mother who knows that she should not hurt her child but who also knows she must discipline him. Or it may involve different role partners—a woman with a new baby who finds that its demands interfere with her obligations to other family members.

Conflict arises when one expectation requires behavior that is incompatible with that required by another expectation. The actions may be physically incompatible (one action is the opposite of the other), socially incompatible (they are not expected of the same person), or psychologically incompatible (they require the actor to adopt opposite psychological sets). Nurses are expected to be sympathetic and warmly involved with their patients but this may interfere with the clinical detachment necessary to carry out some form of therapy, such as requiring a patient to engage in some painful but necessary exercise.

Competition between expectations occurs when actors cannot adequately honor both expectations because of the limitations on their time or energy.

Conflict and competition in relation to the same partner Several examples of conflict and competition within a role involve the relation of professionals toward their clients. For example, three facets of doctors' roles have been distinguished: (1) they are scientists-warriors on the frontiers of knowledge, (2) they are technicians-saviors of the sick, and (3) they are small-business retailers of the knowledge they have acquired at considerable cost to themselves.[4] Aggressive bill collecting is consistent with the small-business retailer aspect of the role but is inconsistent with the altruistic scientist or gentle healer aspects.

Other such treatment roles—nurse, clinical psychologist, social worker—have been studied, and have the same configuration of conflicting elements. A study of stockbrokers similarly revealed a number of facets of the role that were in conflict.[5] As investment advisers, they are expected to give customers impartial and sound advice. As brokers, however, they are expected to close sales. Brokers who buy and sell excessively for their customers are said to be "churning" the account. The behavior is disapproved by the ethics of Wall Street, but is rewarded by the fat commissions.

Conflict and competition in relation to different partners Think, again, of the superintendent of schools who must interact with teachers, board members, PTA members, civic leaders, and the public at large.[6] Often, the demands of each relation raises problems of time allocation as well as difficulties in meeting diametrically opposed expectations. The city council, the taxpayers' associations, and the elected school board, all want to hold the line on salaries and be reasonable in budget recommendations; the teachers and the active PTA parents want to fight for maximum salary increases.

[4] Lee, 1944.
[5] Evan and Levin, 1966.
[6] Gross, Mason, and McEachern, 1958.

Actors in Several Roles

Competition between roles   Normally an actor occupies a number of positions at any one time. The role expectations associated with these categories compete for the actor's time. School superintendents suffer strain in allocating time to their roles as spouses and parents and their roles as heads of school systems. Should they spend their evenings at home, or go to meetings and devote their evenings to school and community business? Most students do not have to go beyond their own experience to observe competing role demands. In addition to the demands associated with the position of student, there are also those associated with the positions of husband or wife, son or daughter, employee, and so on. Not only does this result in strain within the individual, it also interferes with the effective functioning of the educational system.

Conflict between roles   Role expectations may not only compete for time, but they also may conflict with each other. They may be incompatible, so that the actor cannot do both. A military chaplain is a religious leader and also a military officer, and in some ways these roles are incompatible and their expectations are in conflict.[7] If the chaplain is to retain his status as an officer, he must keep his distance from enlisted men—which makes it difficult for them to share personal problems and confidences with him. If he gives up his officer status in order to be a more effective chaplain, he has a problem of identity, loses his authority, and cannot function. Similar incompatibilities have been observed in the roles performed by elected officials.[8] Partisan behavior is expected of the party leader, but it may conflict with the impartial behavior expected of an administrator or judge. Teachers in school settings, lawyers working for large corporations, scientists in government bureaucracies, feel strains from the conflict between expectations for autonomy associated with their role as professionals and expectations that they will submit to organizational controls.

The severity of conflict arising from enacting several roles at once varies with (1) the relative incompatibility of the expectations involved, and (2) the rigor with which these expectations are defined in a given situation.

For example, if we look at the three roles of wife, mother, and employee, we find that the roles of wife and mother contain more common expectations than either would have with the role of employee. A woman who occupies only the roles of wife and mother would experience, therefore, less conflict between roles than a woman who occupies the roles of wife and employee, where she would be under greater strain because of the greater incompatibility of these roles. The conflict would be further accentuated if her husband and her employer held traditional expectations for each role. Finally, research on role strain in industry suggests that strain varies with the number of roles in a worker's role set.[9] The more the roles a worker must perform, the greater the chance of conflict.

[7] Burchard, 1954.
[8] Mitchell, 1958.
[9] Snoek, 1966.

A woman in two roles: mother and psychologist.

Reduction of Conflicting Role Expectations

Social systems have features that reduce the strain resulting from conflicting role expectations. These include certain structural features, the establishment of priorities for different role obligations, special rules that protect actors in certain positions from sanctions, and the merging of conflicting roles.

Hierarchy of obligations　A hierarchy of role obligations is recognized by participants in the system. Where obligations have equal priorities, strain arises. But if obligations of one category take precedence, little strain results. Think of someone in role conflict and the excuses he or she is likely to make. One of the most commonly heard excuses is, "I'd like to but I can't because . . ." followed by an assertion of a higher priority. "I'd like to go to the party, but I have to study for an exam," or "I can't be present for the exam, because I have to report for an Army physical." The excuse resolves the conflict because both persons in these instances—speaker and listener—accept a given order of priorities. Such excuses for failure to conform to expectations are therefore accepted, and, at the same time, avoid disapproval.

Such a hierarchy of role expectations reflects the value structure of the group, and the difficulty of avoiding a role obligation. Obligations are higher in the hierarchy if their enactment helps to achieve the group's values, and if changing these obligations would disrupt the system.

Structural features that reduce strain　Some of the structural features of systems that reduce role strain are differences in the power of various role partners to exert sanctions, restrictions on allowing actors to take more than one role, and spatial and temporal separation of situations involving conflicting role expectations. If one partner in interaction is able to apply only very weak sanctions, his or her expectations may be disregarded. The pervasiveness of power differences in most systems prevents much strain that would otherwise arise from role conflict.

Preventing actors from occupying more than one role category is another feature of systems that reduces role conflict. Doctors who do not want to act like bill-collecting retailers turn over all such functions to their accountants or office help. Sometimes there are norms prohibiting a person from occupying two conflicting positions simultaneously. The nepotism rules of many organizations, specifying that no more than one person from a family may be employed within the organization, are designed to prevent conflict between an actor's occupational and family obligations.

Temporal and spatial separation of situations involving conflicting role expectations is another feature that reduces role conflict. On the job during a working day a person is exposed to the expectations associated with the occupational role. For the most part, these expectations do not operate at home during the evening hours where they might conflict with family expectations. Those who work at home—writers, for instance—can be caught up in conflicts arising from incompatible expectations from several roles. Disaster workers, who are more spatially separated from their homes, feel less strain over potential conflict between family and work obligations than do workers who are closer to home.[10] Conflicting loyalties, ordinarily latent, can swell to bursting intensity as incompatible demands of different roles come together. Should the police officer keep order in a riot and allow his or her own family to survive as best it can? Should the fire fighter fight the raging fire or dash home—a block away—to be sure his or her own family is safe?

Protection from sanctions Actors who are especially subject to sanctions because their positions expose them to conflicting roles are likely to be protected by the system.[11] They may be insulated from observation, or a special tolerance may be established for their actions, or they may be protected from reprisals by those whose expectations they violate. Or they may join with other actors in the same difficult position and develop patterns of concerted action.

Where role partners have conflicting expectations concerning actors, the actors may be protected by norms which insulate them from observation. Lawyers, doctors, the clergy, are often accorded the privilege of withholding from police or other authorities information given to them by clients, patients, or parishioners. Some role positions call for behavior that is highly visible and public, and yet require difficult choices which are subject to challenge. Often, in such instances, special provisions are built into the role to protect the actor. For example, umpires or referees in sporting events are given absolute authority of decision as well as punitive power over the competing participants if they challenge their authority.

When the actors in a system are all aware that another actor is subject to incompatible role expectations, they may tolerate his or her failure to meet either set of expectations, or even both. Or patterns may emerge to protect the actor from reprisals. The union steward who behaves contrary to management's expectations is normally protected from reprisals by contract rules that specify job security. Another illustration is the pattern of social distance that develops to protect the superior in an organization from emotional dependence on subordinates. Officers' clubs are for military officers only, with no subordinates allowed. This prevents socializing that could lead to friendships between leader and follower, friendships that might create strain when the officers must act in ways that are not to the subordinates' liking.

Finally, actors subject to conflicting expectations may develop various patterns of concerted action to protect themselves. Lawyers and doctors are reluctant to testify against a colleague in malpractice suits. They form bar associations and medical associations, and work together to protect their members from conflicting role obligations. These group solutions often become normative and sometimes are formalized into written codes.

[10] Killian,
[11] Merton, 1957b.

Merging of roles   Whenever many individuals are required to enact two roles that have conflicting expectations, systematic changes slowly reduce the strain, often resulting in the emergence of a single role replacing the previous two.[12] For instance, the parent and spouse roles often merge into one, so that the husband calls his wife "mother," and she addresses him as "father," especially in the presence of the children. Or the politician role permits one to perform simultaneously as a party representative and a government official. The therapist-researcher in a hospital devoted entirely to clinical research frequently experiences strain from conflict between expectations attached to the role of therapist as well as to the role of researcher.[13] In some instances, this conflict is resolved by role segregation. Patients are treated in terms of one or the other role, but not both. They get therapy from one staff member, and participate in a research program of other staff members. A second way of reducing strain is redefinition of the role, creating a unique combination of obligations and rights drawn from each set of role expectations.

Discontinuities in Status Passage

We have seen that role strain arises when an actor simultaneously occupies two or more positions that subject him to conflicting expectations. Strain also arises where a system is so organized that the positions an actor *successively* occupies involve conflicting expectations. There are both long-term and short-term position shifts or *status passages*.

Ruth Benedict, in a now classic discussion, has illustrated the problematic aspects of the long-term shift in our society by demonstrating that the role expectations for children are often diametrically opposed to those associated with the role of adult.[14] She notes that the child is expected to be sexless, nonresponsible, and submissive, while the adult role requires just the opposite traits. A person growing to maturity, then, must not only learn new role behavior, but must also unlearn the opposite kinds of behavior. A great deal of the strain in the passage from childhood to adulthood is associated with the discontinuities between the two roles. A similar analysis could be made of the transition from the middle-adult role to that of the aged, from the worker to the supervisor, or from the enlisted person to the commissioned officer. The degree of strain seems to depend on more than the difference between expectations. It is also a function of the certainty, clarity, and abruptness of the transition, as well as of the relative desirability of the positions involved.

There are also short-term shifts which lead to conflict. The ten-year-old's masculine aggressiveness on the ball field must give way suddenly to the dutiful obedience expected at home. The busy career activities of the hustling businessperson must suddenly be replaced by warmth and tolerance toward family members in the evening.

[12] Turner, 1962.
[13] Perry and Wynne, 1959.
[14] Benedict, 1938.

Factors reducing transition strain One expects less strain in systems where status passage depends on the possession of certain attributes rather than on the actor's performance. Chronological age, seniority, years in grade, and so on, are gained automatically and there is high certainty that one will pass on to the next position in the system. But where positions are achieved on the basis of performance, as where competitive examinations are used, one can expect greater strain from the uncertainty of the outcome. Where this kind of strain becomes acute, informal patterns frequently emerge that guarantee the position change. In many organizations, a given position may technically be filled by anyone, but the informal practice is to choose the person who already occupies some other specific position. For example, presidents of such organizations can expect to be elected to the board of directors at the expiration of their terms of office.

Anthropologists have long emphasized the importance of ceremonies in connection with the degree of clarity of the transition. In all societies, important transitions are given ceremonial recognition called *rites of passage*. These mark initiation into life (birth), adulthood, marriage, and death, as well as entrance into various special groups. They often involve renaming the actor. As a result, neither the actor nor the role partners can be in doubt as to how to behave toward one another.

Rites of passage: a birthday celebration dramatizes role transition.

Learning the role of mother while still a child reduces role strain when role transition occurs.

The exotic character of such ceremonies should not blind us to the presence of rites of passage in our own societies. Confirmations, bar-mitzvahs, debutante parties, graduations, weddings, parties celebrating promotions in business . . . these are just a few. Many features of adolescent behavior in our society are a consequence of adolescents' attempts to clarify their position in the absence of such forms of ceremonial recognition.[15]

The change in status is often less abrupt than it might appear. There are often stages of passage within each position, with the final stages serving to prepare the individual for the next position.[16] Many graduate students, for instance, in the later stages of their training may teach a course or two, and this eases the transition into the faculty status they may soon occupy. The early stage

[15] Bloch and Niederhoffer, 1958.
[16] Strauss, 1959.

of role enactment frequently involves tolerance for the behavior of the actor. Other people realize that a person needs time to get used to the new position. Such "honeymoons" are recognized not only for newlyweds but also for United States presidents.

In many systems, there is a kind of *coaching* that eases status passage.[17] People who have gone through a series of transitions guide and advise others who follow. In this process, the coach interprets the beginners' present experience and instructs them about what lies ahead, what they should be learning, and what they should guard against. Upper-class students in college often coach entering students in such ways about various phases of college life. Sometimes coaches conspire with others to set the stage for experiences they feel will help their protegés to develop. Thus, executives may give particularly challenging assignments to junior executives being groomed for advancement.

Finally, if a system is organized so that movement is normally from a position of lower desirability to one of higher, the strain is apt to be less. In some societies, age-sex positions are organized this way, so that the roles of infant, youth, mature adult, and elder adult are increasingly desirable categories. In our society, this is the case for several stages of the sequence, but not the last. Movement from the position of mature adult to that of the elder is considered undesirable. A number of devices on both the individual and the system-wide level are intended to reduce the damaging effects on self-esteem of this movement. It is common practice, for instance, to create new positions of equal or higher status for a person who is about to be "demoted."[18] Or retirement may be formally recognized by attaining of a new title—such as professor emeritus. In industry, employees may be given a gift and a party. As elders increasingly come to regard retirement as unfair, they are more frequently viewing these societal ceremonies as sham actions, intended to "cool them out," lessening the effectiveness of the rituals.

System Organization and Role Strain

One further characteristic of social systems associated with role strain is the way they are organized to reward actors for their conformity to the expectations of their partners. This tendency is inherent in the previously discussed reciprocal nature of role expectations: obligations of actors in one position are the rights of their role partners. From the standpoint of a particular position, a system may be so organized that the rights associated with the position are not rewarding enough to motivate actors to carry out their obligations. For example, enlightened housewives may feel that their right to be supported in exchange for their obligation to do household duties is insufficiently rewarding. Actors in such circumstances feel that they are being taken advantage of, being treated unfairly.

---

[17] Strauss, 1959.
[18] Goffman, 1952.

This, in turn, generates ambivalence toward meeting the expectations of the role partner. What usually happens is an attempt at restructuring the relation to equalize the rights and obligations associated with the two positions. A wife might take a job and negotiate an agreement with her husband to share equally duties associated with the home.

Fulfillment of role obligations is often insufficiently rewarded where these obligations are unique to the relationship (for example, preparing a special diet for a spouse who requires it). This is so because, in this type of expectation, the reward stems only from the partner. In the case of more widely shared expectations, the general approval of others for conforming to cultural and subcultural expectations provides some reward, even when the partner doesn't. A wife who isn't meeting some of the traditional expectations associated with her role and who is an inadequate homemaker is not meeting her husband's expectations if he defines her role traditionally. Yet he is not likely to react to this by developing ambivalence about his obligation to support her because so many other people strongly sanction his obligation. Strain may arise, however, in connection with the violation of complementary expectations unique to a particular married couple—for example, the expectation that a visit to the wife's parents will be followed by a visit to the husband's. Each partner must reciprocate or be prepared for vigorous protests.

Strain in connection with cultural and subcultural role expectations is particularly likely at a time when role expectations are going through a process of great reexamination and change. Studies of the changing roles of husband and wife that were conducted in 1955 showed that college men and women overemphasized the rights associated with the marital role of their own sex and underemphasized its obligations.[19] Now, twenty years later, the change is more accelerated, especially in view of the strong pressures toward equality for women.

It is not always the person who receives fewer rewards in a relation who experiences role strain. Because of the operation of equity norms, including the norm of reciprocity, there are situations where obligations do not match rights and where actors receiving superior outcomes feel guilt that contributes to role strain.[20]

We have been talking about strain that arises from inequalities in role rights and obligations. Another kind of strain can occur in systems where the content of roles leads to continuous interference on the part of the actors in one position with the goal achievement of actors in one or more other positions.[21] The structures of competitive games are set up this way, and in bridge or football players are supposed to frustrate their opponents. But such conflicts can develop in nongame systems. Few systems are so perfectly developed that they entirely avoid strain from this source.

[19] Kirkpatrick, 1955.
[20] Evan, 1962.
[21] Foskett, 1960.

There is one final source of strain—where an actor relates to two different role partners. There the stage is set for the development of coalitions of two versus one in the triads thus formed. In a psychiatric hospital, for example, the patient is a role partner of both the nurse and the psychiatrist.[22] Under such circumstances, two of the three parties may combine to control or block the goal achievement of the third party. Or one may play the other two off to his or her own advantage. This is what a small child does in asking father's permission to attend a movie, prefacing the request by saying, "It's okay with mom if it's all right with you."

Many problems in interpersonal relations, then, are a function of the social system and of features of the system that lead to role strain rather than unique aspects of the "personalities" of the participants. Similarly, reduction of such strain is more than a matter of individual dynamics or processes—a point we shall get back to shortly.

Where strain comes from inequality in the rights and obligations of reciprocal roles, there are tendencies within the system toward development of a more equitable balance. Such pressures toward fairness occur either when the actors are inadequately motivated to fulfill their obligations, or when, because of frustration, they engage in behaviors that interfere with need gratifications of their partners. The conflict between management and labor over the past fifty years arose out of inequalities in rights and obligations and has produced a new equilibrium between roles of leaders representing these two interests.

Summary: Social System and Role Strain

Expectations associated with roles in a social system vary in clarity and in the degree of consensus among actors and their role partners. One kind of disagreement is between an actor and a role partner. Another is between two or more role partners with respect to an actor. Moreover, the way in which the parties disagree may take many forms. Various conditions are related to consensus or the lack of it. One important source of disagreement arises from the places of the actors and their role partners in the social system, and the way in which these places relate to other social systems. These related systems pressure the actors or role partners to adopt certain expectations which may be in conflict in the system focused upon. Individual needs and reward-cost outcomes associated with accepting certain role expectations may, under certain circumstances, also create disagreement.

Role conflict, or strain, arises when one expectation requires behavior that is in some degree incompatible with another. Competition arises when an actor cannot honor two or more expectations because of limitations of time. Role strain within a system is greatly relieved by the emergence of a system of priorities specifying which expectations take precedence. These priorities arise out of the

[22] Martin, 1961.

value structure of the group. Actors especially subject to sanctions may be insulated from observation, or a special tolerance may be established, or they may join with other actors in similar positions to develop joint action that relieves the strain or changes the expectations.

Another source of role strain occurs through successive occupation of role categories that are somewhat incompatible, such as the passage from childhood to adulthood, or from active employment to retirement. Social system mechanisms which mark the passage with ceremonies or other means of legitimation help to relieve this strain. Sometimes strain is relieved by anticipatory preparation for the new role, and sometimes a transition period is recognized during which expectations are not forcefully applied.

PERSONALITY AND ROLE STRAIN

So far, we have been examining the characteristics of a social system that lead to role strain and interfere with the smooth, almost automatic quality of interaction between persons. Similar disturbances may stem from characteristics of individual actors that interfere with role enactment or performance, or from the fact that a role to which an individual is assigned may be readily performed but is not suited to his or her needs.

Individual characteristics that lead to difficulty in meeting role expectations fall into three classes. First, actors may lack certain abilities and attributes necessary for successful enactment of the roles involved. Second, they may have a self-concept contrary to the role expectations they are supposed to enact. Finally, they may have certain attitudes and needs that interfere with the enactment of a particular role.

Individual Attributes

Individual attributes that facilitate or interfere with successful role enactment may be either personal qualities, such as physical characteristics, abilities, skills, or personality traits, or socially conferred attributes, such as an academic degree, a license, or certification. These may be related to role enactment in two ways. The attributes may directly facilitate or interfere with the expected behavior, or may merely be traditionally associated with a role. The latter is important because expectations that others have concerning actors refer not only to behavior but to attributes of the individual as well. For instance, those who look the part often function more effectively in a given situation than those who don't. A young doctor could be, by virtue of youth, vigor, and up-to-date training in medical school and in residence, a better and more able physician than an older, white-haired colleague. But the fact that people often think of a male doctor as a fatherly person may well diminish the confidence the young physician inspires in his patients and therefore reduce his effectiveness. A study of the academic profession also indicates that those who are judged to look like professors are judged to be more successful as performers in this role.[23]

More often, a given attribute interferes directly with the role behavior itself. The dullard in the graduate course, the shy, retiring person in the role of salesperson or public relations representative are cases in point.

There is considerable evidence that particular positions attract individuals whose personalities allow them to perform the role more readily and, presumably, with less strain.[24] Students high in authoritarianism are found in greater proportions in military academies and Southern colleges where there is more respect for authority.[25] Hard-core Nazis have been found to be more given to projection, to extreme antisocial sadism, and to contempt for tenderness.[26] These traits presumably enable them to perform the Nazi role more adequately.

Attitudes and Needs

An actor's attitudes may hinder or facilitate role enactment. A person who accepts the dictates of authority figures would be able to play a subordinate role without strain; another who rejects authority might well suffer considerable strain in the same role.

There is also role strain that arises not because people are unable to live up to the expectations of a role, but because the role does not allow for the expression of their needs, does not require them to make use of their skills and abilities, or is not suited to their personality and temperament. This is not individual inadequacy, but dissatisfaction with a role. People with strong needs for achievement may be frustrated by an occupational role in a government bureaucracy that offers no risk, no challenge, and no opportunity for advancement. People in roles that allow them little contact with other people may be dissatisfied if they are naturally gregarious and are deprived of the social interaction they enjoy and are good at.

Individual Processes

When actors are exposed to role strain, in addition to the resources available to them through participation in the social system they have certain individual processes at their command that can reduce the strain. They may adjust to conflicting expectations by restructuring the situation. A study of conflict between the roles of college man and "hasher" revealed a variety of defenses that male student waiters and kitchen help in sorority houses use to resolve conflict.[27] These included rationalizing the job as being just temporary; using verbal ag-

[23] Ellis and Keedy, 1960.
[24] Inkeles and Levenson, 1963.
[25] Stern, Stein, and Bloom, 1956.
[26] Dicks, 1950.
[27] Zurcher, 1966.

gression against the girls; and withdrawing into various kinds of horseplay. Horseplay has also been observed in seven- and eight-year-olds on a merry-go-round, who seem to be establishing role distance by clowning, because to take the role of a merry-go-round rider seriously would imply attributes associated with the role of young child—which they are attempting to abandon.[28]

Another mode of individual resolution takes the form of reducing dependence on the group or the role partner supporting one of the expectations. The individual does this by leaving the group, by redefining its value to him or her, or by making it irrelevant to the conflict situation. One can always quit, walk away, or lower the level of commitment.

Individual Determinants of Choice Resolution

Universalist versus particularist bias   Where affective or cognitive adjustments fail to resolve a conflict, people may respond in several other ways.[29] They may delay in making a decision. They may reject responsibility for the decision, either by withdrawing from the position or shifting responsibility. We have all been victims of stalling tactics on the part of another person faced with conflicting role expectations. In most instances, however, role conflict cannot be solved in this manner. Individuals must decide between conflicting demands.

As we noted in Chapter 13, much role enactment involves negotiation, or bargaining. Conflicting role demands are accommodated through such negotiation. Different individuals operate differently in negotiating roles, however. One way of characterizing the way they function is by whether they move toward a *particularist* solution, which favors an individual, frequently an acquaintance or friend, or toward a *universalist* solution, which favors widely shared societal norms.[30] Of course, whether a person resolves conflict in favor of particularist obligations or in favor of universalist obligations to abstract principles of society as a whole is also affected by features of the situation. Would you turn in someone who was about to let a smoke bomb off in chapel? A stink bomb? What if you were an usher in the chapel organization? What if the person with the smoke bomb was a friend of yours? An acquaintance? A total stranger? And what if the reporting of the smoke-bomber had to be public, so that everyone knew you were turning him in? A study asking just such a series of hypothetical questions indicated that when sanctions were weak, when the culprit was a friend, and when the reporting was private, the respondent chose a particularist response; he or she didn't report the culprit.[31] The opposite of these three conditions more frequently yielded the universalist responses.

[28] Goffman, 1961.
[29] Gullahorn and Gullahorn, 1963.
[30] Stouffer and Toby, 1951.
[31] Sutcliffe and Haberman, 1956.

Individual role hierarchies Where actors are faced with conflicting expectations arising from occupying several role categories, they are likely to resolve strain by choosing certain roles over others. This suggests that the individual has an established set of role hierarchies, or priorities. It has been suggested that there are two determinants of the relative position of a role in an individual hierarchy.[32] One is the need structure of the individual, and the other is the legitimacy of the role expectations. To illustrate the effects of need structure, a woman with strong achievement needs who is both a mother and a career woman might be expected to honor her career obligations over her maternal obligations, since the former will allow greater satisfaction of her achievement needs.

Legitimacy refers to the shared expectation that one role will take precedence over another. A professor at Air University who is both a teacher and a military officer places greater emphasis on his role as military officer, which is what he is at bottom, and what he will be after his three-year tour of duty at the university is completed. In this situation, added legitimacy is placed on the officer role over and above the teacher role.

A Theory of Role-conflict Resolution

Gross, Mason, and McEachern have proposed that individuals faced with conflicting expectations A and B may choose one of three alternatives: they may conform to expectation A or to expectation B; they may compromise by meeting both expectations *in part;* or they may try to avoid conforming to either expectation.[33] The choice an actor makes in such a situation will be a function of three variables: (1) the perceived legitimacy of the expectations, (2) the perceived strength of the sanction applied for nonconformity to each of the expectations, and (3) the orientation of the actor relative to legitimacy and to sanctions.

Legitimacy An expectation is perceived as legitimate if actors believe their role partners have a right to hold such expectations. If they have no such right, it is illegitimate. Instructors would consider it legitimate for their students to expect them to grade in a fair and impartial manner because they believe they have a moral right in our system to be treated equally. But for students to expect that they should be given preferential treatment would be illegitimate.

Actors are predisposed to conform to expectations that they perceive as legitimate and to avoid conforming to expectations that they perceive as illegitimate. If, for the moment, we consider legitimacy alone, we could make the following predictions: If one of the conflicting expectations is legitimate and the other illegitimate, actors will choose to honor the legitimate one. If both are

[32] Getzels and Guba, 1954.
[33] Gross, Mason, and McEachern, 1958.

legitimate, they will compromise. And if both are illegitimate, they will avoid meeting either.

Sanctions   A negative sanction is a response to a role player for not meeting the obligations of his or her role. It may consist of disapproval, criticism, deprivation of some privilege, or whatever. A second assumption in this theory of role conflict resolution is that actors are predisposed to act on the expectations they believe will result in the strongest negative sanctions if they fail to comply. Considering sanctions alone, we would expect that if one of the expectations carried strong negative sanctions and the other weak sanctions, actors would choose to honor the former. If both carried strong negative sanctions, then the actors would compromise. Where sanctions for both expectations were weak, no prediction is possible—unless there is a difference in legitimacy.

In everyday life, legitimate expectations generally carry stronger sanctions for nonobservance than do illegitimate ones. Sanctions and legitimacy, therefore, are likely to favor the *same* action for resolving a conflict. In fact, this marked association between sanctions and legitimacy is an important way in which social systems help in resolving role conflicts. On occasion, however, actors may find themselves in a situation in which legitimacy favors one action and sanctions favor another. Students in an examination are faced by the teacher's legitimate expectation that they will not aid other students by giving them answers to the questions. But because of friendship, another student may expect such help, even though both recognize that this is an illegitimate expectation. (Students do not have a legitimate right to ask another to help them to cheat.) In this instance, the sanctions imposed for nonobservance of the illegitimate expectations would be loss of regard from the student who expects help, which could be considerably stronger than the sanctions imposed by the instructor. To handle a situation of this kind, we need to introduce a third assumption.

Orientation or role disposition   The third assumption is that persons may be classified according to the strength of their orientation toward legitimacy or toward sanctions. This is a kind of disposition or tendency for an individual consistently to conform to expectations of a certain kind, but not to those of another kind. The notion is that individuals can be classified as having three possible kinds of orientation toward expectations: (1) a moral orientation that favors legitimate expectations, (2) an expedient orientation that favors enacting expectations that carry the heaviest sanctions for noncompliance, and (3) a moral-expedient orientation in which both legitimate and heavily sanctioned expectations are taken into account.

By examining role-conflict situations in the light of their theory, and taking into account an actor's orientation, these investigators were able to make theoretical predictions as to how the actor would behave. For example, actors are faced with two conflicting expectations, one of which is legitimate but carries only weak sanctions, and the other is illegitimate but carries strong sanctions.

Actors with a moral orientation would carry out the legitimate expectation. Actors with an expedient orientation would enact the expectation with strong sanctions for noncompliance. Actors with a moral-expedient orientation would compromise.

These theoretical predictions were checked against actual data obtained in a carefully structured interview with school superintendents, which presented a variety of potentially conflicting role situations (such as the hiring and promotion of teachers). On the basis of the extent to which each superintendent stressed the legitimacy of expectations, or the sanctions that might be applied, or, finally, some compromise or mixed posture, each was classed as having one of three orientations: moral, expedient, or moral-expedient (compromise). By comparing these orientations with the theoretical interpretations of how they actually acted, the usefulness and accuracy of the theory were determined. It correctly predicted over 90 percent of the cases studied.

In later studies, some by other investigators, of business executives, training directors, and labor leaders, the theory did not predict with such high accuracy, but still was accurate in roughly 3 out of every 4 cases.

Summary: Personality and Role Strain

Individuals can behave in various ways that reduce role strain arising from the social system. They can restructure the situation, establish their own priorities for expectations, or even leave the system. Individuals can also reduce role strain through bargaining or negotiation, and the various interpersonal strategies discussed in Chapter 8. People seem to vary in where they fall on a dimension ranging from a preference for particularistic expectations (for example, obligations to friends) to universalistic expectations (widely shared societal values). Another way of conceptualizing individual orientations toward role expectations is in terms of legitimacy, sanctions, or compromise. Legitimacy emphasizes the normative, obligatory aspect of an expectation—the moral aspect. Sanctions, of course, emphasize the consequences—the outcomes—that might follow from accepting the expectation. Individuals oriented toward legitimacy are considered to have a moral orientation; those oriented toward sanctions, an expedient one. Some individuals have mixed or compromise orientations.

CULTURE AND ROLE STRAIN

In recent years there has been an increasing awareness that where the system of beliefs or ideology shared by the actors in a situation runs counter to role expectations, strain results. Strong emphasis on equality, for instance, places strain on those role relations in American society that involve inequality.

In the military service, protocol involves a denial of equality. A subordinate in interaction with a superior in the military hierarchy is supposed to show deference by saluting first, by giving way to a superior should the latter wish to pass him, by standing when the superior enters the room, by using such terms of respect as "sir." People who have not internalized the nonegalitarian ideology of the military subculture find such role behavior uncomfortable, and the discomfort often leads to subterfuges to avoid acts of deference. A newly enlisted soldier may studiously look the other way to avoid saluting when an officer passes. A newly commissioned officer may feel sheepish about demanding deference and thus may not "notice" this intentional slight.

Such problems are not confined to the military. The egalitarian element in American ideology is pervasive, and almost any superior-inferior relation will suffer some strain, whether between supervisor and worker in industry, doctor and nurse in medicine, teacher and student in education, or parent and child in the family. Currently, the inequality between the traditional husband-wife and father-mother roles is changing, both because of societal changes and, more recently, because it is under attack by the women's liberation movement.

When the ideology itself contains conflicting elements, some conflict between it and role expectations is inevitable. Individuals in occupations such as medicine, social work, the ministry, and teaching are exposed to a number of ideological elements that emphasize service to humanity. At the same time, they share with other members of our society the ideals of materialistic success. Attempts on the part of the members of such professions to bolster their economic position are consistent with the latter elements of the ideology of the culture, but are in conflict with the former.

Where many actors in the same role position find themselves subject to similar role strains, mutual support is present for finding a common means of resolution. This often results in the development of a shared system of beliefs concerning appropriate forms and methods of resolution. Each individual troubled by the conflict supports others in moving toward a modification of the expectations involved.

Gunnar Myrdal's analysis of the historical development of the false dogma supporting racial inequality provides an illustration of how a false set of beliefs develops and becomes widely shared when many people in a population face a conflict.[34] The belief that blacks were biologically different from, and inferior to, whites served to resolve the conflict between the American creed that "all men are created equal" and both the practice of slavery and later forms of racial discrimination. Slaveholders and other deeply prejudiced people denied to blacks their status as human beings. In this way they could still believe that "all men are created equal" but not include blacks as part of mankind, or "men," because they were biologically different from whites, and therefore not human beings. Still earlier in the pioneer days of America, Indians were often treated in the same fashion. And, of course, the most recent historical example of a similar use of ideology is the Nazi destruction of 6 million Jews on the grounds that they

[34] Myrdal, 1944.

were "non-Aryan"—a supposedly inferior and undesirable type of human being. Shared belief systems may also add legitimacy to a particular role. When actors are not in agreement on the legitimacy of the expectations associated with that role, they may collectively develop a series of beliefs that help to rationalize the legitimacy. An analysis of a marginal social role—that of chiropractor—suggests that the ideology of an oppressed minority reduces strain.[35] Chiropractors explain their marginal position in the healing profession by blaming the selfishly motivated persecution of medical doctors. This general thesis suggests that most occupational groups of questionable acceptance would have shared beliefs that reduce role strain.

Albert Cohen has shown that, in subgroups that experience role strain, norms emerge to reduce that strain.[36] For instance, many situations in our society call for competition. We compete in the school room, on the job, in sports, and in courtship. Unlimited competition, however, is intolerable and can have disastrous side effects, creating feelings of inadequacy and interpersonal hostility. Because of the strain, then, groups often attempt to restrict competition by developing role expectations that control competitive output or, through codes of sportsmanship, restrict the kinds of tactics that an individual may use.

Assume that an instructor, toward the end of the semester, assigns a term paper and says that grades will be determined in large part by the length of the paper. The traditional norms would prescribe that each should do his or her best in competition with others. But this is not very comfortable because there is pressure to prepare for finals, to finish other term papers, and to maintain participation in extracurricular activities. Under these circumstances, each student may tentatively check with others about what they are planning to do. "How long is your paper going to be?" "How much time are you going to spend?" Such questions will be asked, more or less directly, and along with them there will be expressions of opinion about the injustice of the assignment.

Through these exchanges, the students encourage each other to move toward a reorientation of the situation of which each approves and which will allow them to agree not to submit more than a certain number of pages. This solution, which would have found little support at the beginning of the process, may become established because it fits in with norms that have emerged from the discussion and from the machinery of mutual help.

[35] Wardwell, 1955.
[36] Cohen, 1955.

FIFTEEN

PERSONALITY AND SITUATION

t is possible to classify the origins of behavior into two categories: the person and the situation. But as we do so, we must face a troublesome question: What is the relative importance of individual characteristics as compared with situational factors? The question has provoked widely varying answers, the range of which is worth illustrating with views from opposite extremes.

INDIVIDUAL VERSUS SITUATIONAL DETERMINANTS OF BEHAVIOR

One view of the question posed above is that people's behavior springs entirely from structured dispositions within the person; the other is that their behavior is determined by the situation in which they find themselves. As social psychologists, we have mostly emphasized social conditions under which people in general behave. We have paid more attention to situations than to individual characteristics. But social psychologists also have much to contribute to the understanding of individual differences, and this contribution depends in part on how the difference between the two extreme views is resolved.

Behavior as Individual Disposition

According to Fritz Heider, the lay view is that people are the origins of actions.[1] It is much simpler to interpret hostile acts as natural expressions of evil persons than to understand the situational and circumstantial factors that led them to commit the act. The average person exaggerates the role of the individual as causal agent, failing to see the social forces that make people act as they do in various situations (see Chapter 6). But this lay view is also maintained in more sophisticated form by many clinical psychologists, personality theorists, and other students of individual behavior. Essentially the idea is that the behavior patterns that characterize a person reflect intraindividual structures, or mechanisms, such as needs, cognitive structures, or, most frequently, personality traits. Traits are thought to provide the basis for predicting the behavior of an individual. The predisposition to anxiety, for instance, has been considered a general trait, with scores on anxiety tests being used to predict capacities for getting along in school, getting along socially, and even for controlling physical movements.

Behavior as a Function of the Situation

Sociologists, anthropologists, and many social psychologists have taken an opposite view from the one stated above, arguing that people's behavior is mostly a reflection of the situation they are in at the moment. Inherent in the situation are the social forces that shape and fix their behavior at any given moment, although it is recognized that their previous experience with such situations may dispose them to react in certain ways in the particular circumstances.

This view looks at the great diversity of people's behavior in various situations throughout the day—their moves from role to role as they interact with their families, their fellow workers, their superiors and subordinates—and finds the flexibility of response to situational demands to be more remarkable and more interesting than personal consistency. Remember the humble Uriah Heep, from Charles Dickens' novel *David Copperfield*, who was fawning and meek with superiors, but a tyrant at home.

Dispositional and Situational Factors in Moral Behavior

In this book, we have taken a middle position between these extreme views, admitting individual differences, but also admitting that the same individual may behave differently in different situations. It is perhaps instructive to consider an intensive study of the role of dispositional and situational factors in moral behavior that was undertaken nearly fifty years ago.[2] Honesty would seem to be an individual characteristic, or disposition. An honest person, after all, is ex-

---

[1] Heider, 1944, 1958.
[2] Hartshorne and May, 1928; Hartshorne, May, and Shuttleworth, 1930.

pected to behave honestly in many situations; a dishonest person, we should expect, would similarly behave dishonestly.

In this study, large numbers of children were exposed to a variety of situations in which they could lie, cheat, and steal. They were also asked to describe their feelings about moral issues in several different settings. The greater the difference in the situations compared, the less consistently the children responded. Moral behavior was surprisingly specific to the particular situation, so that cheating on one speed test was only moderately associated with cheating on another speed test. Cheating on different kinds of tests had only a low association, and if the tests were given in different settings—one inside a classroom, say, and the other outside—the correlations were even lower. The conclusion, supported by later, more sophisticated statistical techniques and factor analysis, was that children are only partially consistent in lying, cheating, and stealing, and that the greater the difference in situations, the less likely they are to be consistent.[3]

Later work bears out these findings.[4] Little consistency has been found between expressed willingness to postpone small rewards for the sake of getting larger ones later, and actual postponement when given the opportunity. A review of research in three areas of moral behavior suggested that judgments of standards of right and wrong, resistance to temptation in the absence of external restraint, and feelings of guilt after a guilt-arousing act, are almost entirely independent of one another. Thus a characterization of someone as *moral* turns out to be vague, ambiguous, unspecific—if, indeed, it means anything at all.

Individual-in-situation

These findings do not settle the issue of individual disposition versus situational determinants. The question about their relative importance may even be misleading. We know that people behave consistently at times and inconsistently at other times. We need to conceptualize the problem of behavioral determinants in a different way. Let us start with the assumption that *virtually every action is shaped partly by individual characteristics and partly by the situation.* This leads us to think in terms of *individual-in-situation* units. Here is a certain kind of individual in a certain kind of situation. Knowing both, we can correctly predict the behavior. If every individual were unique and every situation were specific, we would have an infinite number of units to deal with. So it is best to think of types of individuals and categories of situations—certain kinds of persons in certain kinds of situations.

Suppose we look at a study which examines the sources that contribute to behavior.[5] We will see clearly that one source is the characteristics of each indi-

[3] Burton, 1963.
[4] Mischel, 1968.
[5] Argyle and Little, 1972.

**TABLE 15-1 Variance Attributable to Individuals, Situations, and
Individuals-in-Situations**

NATURE OF INTERACTION	PERCENT VARIANCE		
	INDIVIDUALS	SITUATIONS	INDIVIDUAL-IN-SITUATION
1. Gossip and chat versus little gossip and chat	10	23	67
2. Discussion of personal problems versus no such discussion	12	53	35
3. Formal and rule-governed behavior versus informal behavior	4	62	34
4. Relaxes versus is tense	12	56	32
5. Swears versus never swears	16	34	50
6. Often refers to sex versus never refers to sex	7	56	37
7. Takes great care with personal appearance, etc., versus takes less care	38	19	43
8. Is concerned about whether the other thinks well of him versus is unconcerned	13	52	35
9. Openly shows emotional states versus conceals emotional states	17	35	48
10. Conceals anger and irritation versus shows them freely	36	13	51
11. Freely expresses love, admiration, etc., versus conceals them	15	46	39
12. Openly reveals ambitions and financial situation versus does not reveal them	6	62	32
13. Doing things for the other depends on reciprocity	19	37	44
14. Looks the other person in the eye versus avoids looking him in the eye	30	27	43
15. Sits or stands very close versus stays at a distance	15	52	33
16. Has a relaxed posture versus has a rather tense posture	19	38	43
17. Enjoys being with the other person versus does not enjoy it	6	68	26
18. Is very much at ease versus is very ill at ease	15	52	33
Mean percent variation	16	44	40

SOURCE: Adapted with permission from Basil Blackwell, Ltd., Oxford, and Argyle, M., & B. R. Little. Do personality traits apply to social behavior? *Journal for the Theory of Social Behavior,* 1972, 2, 1–36.

vidual, and another is the situation in which the behavior occurs. And a curious third source emerges, which looks suspiciously like our individual-in-situation category. In this study, the situation was defined primarily in terms of whom the individual was interacting with—a mother, a husband, a friend, and so on. While this is not a complete definition of a situation, the study is nevertheless instructive.

Individuals made quantitative estimates of their own behavior when in interaction with various other people they knew, rating kinds of behavior (gossiping and chatting, discussing personal problems, swearing, expressing love and admiration). By a statistical procedure that is beyond the scope of our discussion here, it was possible to estimate the amount of variation in the ratings that could be attributed to the individual raters, to the different situations, and to the individuals-in-situation source. These estimates are shown in Table 15-1.

Even though we cannot explain the statistical procedure here, it is possible to get an intuitive understanding of these sources of behavior by examining the table. All figures show the extent (in percentages) to which each source accounts for the behavior. Look at the first row. Only 10 percent of the variation in gossiping or chatting is attributable to individual differences. Apparently, gossiping or chatting is not a trait of *individuals* that remains constant when a person

Individual-in-situation: the type-category unit of mother-child.

talks with different types of other persons (here called situations). Evidently, among the people studied, hardly anyone could be called a gossip, and hardly anyone could be considered close-mouthed.

What about *situations* as a source of variability in gossiping? Close to a quarter of the variation (23 percent) in gossiping and chatting is explained by the situation—by whom people are talking to. As a group, for example, they may talk somewhat more to a spouse or a friend than to a boss. So we find here that variation from one person to another accounts for 10 percent of the gossiping, and that situations account for another 23 percent. But that still leaves 67 percent of the variation unexplained. What could possibly account for this large remainder?

It turns out that fully two-thirds (67 percent) of the variation in gossiping and chatting is attributable to the *individual-in-situation* source! This means that individuals differ in the amount of talking they do according to the class of person to whom they talk. One individual talks most to a spouse and least to a boss. Another talks most to a male friend and least to a coworker. The amount of talking depends primarily on the talker-*and*-the-person-to-whom-he-is-talking, *taken as a unit.*

Look at the other rows. The amount of variation due to an individual source, or due to the situation, is different for different behaviors. People are somewhat more consistent in whether or not they take care of their personal appearance. And more than half of the time that people talk about sex it is because of the situation—whom they are talking to. We can get an idea of the relative contribution of the three sources by looking at the last row of the table, which gives the average percent variation. We see that, on the average, individual actions account for only 16 percent of the variation in behavior, while situations and individual-in-situation each account for about 40 percent.

The point of this study is not to prove that individual variance is unimportant, or to provide firm quantitative estimates of each type of variance. As evidence, the study is of limited value because estimates of behavior are made from self-ratings rather than from ratings by other persons or other behavioral measures, which might give different results. We discuss it to suggest alternative conceptualizations to the idea that individuals are the source of most variation in behavior, and to emphasize the importance of situations and of the idea of individuals-in-situations.

Summary: Individual versus Situation

One way of getting a better understanding of the determinants of human behavior is to look at extreme views. One such view is the idea that all behavior depends upon the situation that an individual is in—whatever the situation, one behaves accordingly. The other is that all behavior depends upon the nature of the individual—his personality. No one subscribes to these extreme positions, but sociologists and social psychologists place more emphasis on the situation, and clinicians and personality theorists place more emphasis on the individual. It is obvious that both are important. One way of resolving the problem is to consider three sources: the individual, the situation, and the individual-in-situation. Perhaps a few behaviors would result from the first two sources, each taken alone. But most behavior seems to stem from individual-in-situation. This unit would mean that people are classed into certain types, and situations similarly classed into categories. Given a type-situation of a particular kind, certain behavior would be expected to invariably occur. Although this is a theoretical solution to the problem, virtually no research has yet been done along these lines.

NATURE OF THE SELF CONCEPT

One of the curious aspects of the human condition is that we become objects to ourselves. Because of our possession of language and our gift of intelligence, we have a unique capacity for thinking about our bodies, our behavior, our appearance to other persons. Each of us has a set of cognitions and feelings toward ourselves—for which the most commonly used terms are *self,* or *self concept.*

Self-attitudes are similar to other attitudes (see Chapter 9), except that they have a different object—oneself. So it is convenient to think of one's attitudes about oneself as having three aspects, the cognitive, the affective, and the behavioral. The *cognitive* component is the *content* of the self, as illustrated by such thoughts as, "I am intelligent, honest, sincere, ambitious, tall, strong, a little overweight," and so forth. The *affective* component is one's *feelings* about oneself, and is more difficult to illustrate. Feelings are not usually expressed in words. But affective component would include a rather general feeling of self-worth—or worthlessness—as well as evaluations of more specific cognitive aspects of self. One might dislike one's nose, or one's freckles. The *behavioral* component is the tendency to *act* toward oneself in various ways—self-deprecating, self-indulgent, or with oversensitivity about certain of one's characteristics.

Appearance is one aspect of the self concept.

Social Nature of the Self

While all attitudes are rooted in social experience, self-attitudes are particularly a product of interaction. Theories of self-development emphasize people's perception of how other people see them. They also focus attention on the process by which they compare their ideas about themselves with social norms, that is, with the expectations they believe others share concerning what they *should* be like. These features have been called the "looking-glass self." C. H. Cooley's description is worth quoting:

> As we see our face, figure, and dress in the glass, and are interested in them because they are ours, and pleased or otherwise with them according as they do or do not answer to what we should like them to be; so in imagination we perceive in another's mind some thought of our appearance, manners, aims, deeds, character, friends, and so on, and are variously affected by it.

Young woman in two role identities: teaching assistant and artist.

A self-ideal of this sort seems to have three principal elements: the imagination of our appearance to the other person, the imagination of his judgment of that appearance, and some sort of self-feeling, such as pride or mortification. The comparison with a looking-glass hardly suggests the second element, the imagined judgment, which is quite essential. The thing that moves us to pride or shame is not the mere mechanical reflection of ourselves, but an imputed sentiment, the imagined effect of this reflection upon another's mind.[6]

The looking-glass self, then, has three components: (1) what we think our person and our behavior looks like to the other person, (2) how we think the other person judges that appearance, and (3) our feeling about the judgment—pride, indifference, embarrassment, and so on. We often refer to the second element above as the *reflected self*—how we think the other person sees us.

[6] Reprinted with permission from C. H. Cooley. *Human nature and the social order.* New York: Charles Scribner's Sons, 1902. Reprinted: New York: The Free Press of Glencoe, Inc., 1956. P. 152.

Self and role   Cooley's idea of self as emerging out of reflected views held by other persons was later elaborated by George Herbert Mead, Erving Goffman, and others.[7] They saw the self as developing through social interaction by the individual's enactment of a series of social roles which society assigns to a person. As individuals move through the social structure, they are first a baby, later a small boy or girl. They are a dull pupil, John's little brother or sister, Juliet's best friend. As they perform these roles, their self concept is influenced by the ways in which their role partners see them and by the manner in which they enact all these roles. They learn the expectations that other persons associate with the category, and they form a role identity corresponding to each. In a sense, the picture one has of oneself is one with many facets, each corresponding to a particular identity. But these facets do not remain entirely independent of one another. Certain processes modify them. There begins to be a *me* upon which each role category can draw, a core identity, the still, small self of the dark room in the lonely night.

The view that people have of themselves is influenced by the reflected impressions other people have of them. This has been extensively documented by correlational, longitudinal, and experimental studies, all of which generally show a relation between one's perceptions of how others judge one, and one's self-conception. Also related to the self-conception is how others actually judge one. Often, the observed relations are small and suggest that the looking-glass conception of the self is an oversimplified scheme of the process of development of the self concept. Some of the additional elements that contribute to self will be brought out in the remainder of the chapter.

Role identities   Most people develop positive self-esteem because they are favorably regarded and loved by others (see Chapter 7). This positive evaluation accounts for the somewhat ideal character of our role identities. When we examined role performance, we saw that people's role portrayals are strongly influenced by their idealized conception of themselves in that role—how they like to think of themselves as being or acting in a given role. In part, these identities are shaped by the culturally prescribed expectations and attributes other persons hold for any particular social position. In part, though, role identity consists of unique elaborations that individuals have been able to work out in their interactions with others during the course of their lives. Thus, individuals actively enter into the creation and maintenance of the self. Their self-conceptions are not by any means entirely a reflection of the definitions of them by other persons.

Summary: Nature of the Self Concept

The self is acquired from the views that other persons have toward an individual, and from his or her active reconstructions of their views as they occur in the

[7] Mead, 1934; Goffman, 1959, 1961.

process of interaction. The concept of the looking-glass self has three elements: (1) one's opinion of how one appears to the other person, (2) one's estimate of how that person judges one's appearance, and (3) one's reaction and feelings concerning that imagined judgment. The self concept emerges and develops further through enactment of a progressive series of roles as one moves through various life stages. Using the expectations that other persons hold for one's role, one constructs a series of role identities that help to define what one is and what one believes about oneself.

RESISTING CHANGE IN SELF AND BEHAVIOR

An individual is not a passive object to be socialized by the molding and shaping of others who are older, more powerful, and more experienced. Even casual observation of small children reveals that they often stubbornly refuse parental influence. In part, this resistance is due to biological characteristics, including temperament and energy level. Furthermore, once the self concept is established and certain behavior patterns have been adopted, the individual is less readily subject to influence and more actively resistant to change. The present section will show *how the person may be immersed in a social environment of interacting forces and still behave in a distinctive manner that is at many points opposed to these forces.*

This view recognizes stability over time in an individual's self concept and behavior but attempts to explain it in terms of stabilities in his relations to other persons. In part, consistencies in behavior result from a person's participation in various social systems. In addition, however, they are due to individual mechanisms that stabilize the interpersonal environment. This section looks at the *individual* mechanisms and shows how they maintain unchanged behavior. A later section will examine forces in the *social system* that create stability and maintain behavior, and that also lead to changes of self and behavior.

An Interpersonal Theory of the Self

The individual is not passive, but is an *active agent* in maintaining a stable interpersonal environment. The theory of the writers is that, while circumstances may put pressure on one to change, one's own active efforts tend to maintain stability of self and behavior.[8] One's concept of oneself, one's individual ways of perceiving other persons, and one's learned behavior patterns, are instrumental in this process.

Consider the following three elements:

1 An aspect of Jack's self: he thinks he is smart.
2 Jack's interpretation of his behavior relevant to that aspect: he thinks he behaves intelligently.
3 Jack's beliefs about how another person (Jane) behaves toward him and

[8] Secord and Backman, 1961, 1965.

feels toward him with regard to that aspect: he thinks that Jane thinks he's smart.

The assumption is that a person attempts to maintain a *state of congruency* among these three elements. There are three kinds of congruency: congruency by implication, congruency by validation, and congruency by comparison. In *congruency by implication,* Jack may perceive that Jane sees him as possessing a particular characteristic corresponding to an aspect of his own self concept. He thinks he's smart and perceives that Jane also thinks he's smart. In *congruency by validation,* the behavior of the other person calls for behavior that confirms a concept of self. Jane asks him to help her with her homework so he gets a chance to demonstrate, or exercise, his smartness. In *congruency by comparison,* the behavior or attributes of another person suggest by comparison that one possesses a particular self-component. Jane praises and thanks Jack, and either is or seems to be a little less sharp than he is.

Maintaining Self, Behavior, and Social Environment

According to interpersonal congruency theory, people actively use techniques for maintaining their interpersonal environment so as to maximize congruency. These techniques use one or more of the three forms of congruency. In this way, pressures to change one's self concept or one's behavior are avoided. These techniques, or mechanisms, include cognitive restructuring, selective evaluation, selective interaction, and evocation of congruent responses.

Cognitive restructuring   The interpersonal environment enters into congruency only as it is seen by the individual. In instances where the actual expectations of other persons are not congruent with the person's self concept or behavior, pressures for change which incongruency would create can be avoided by not seeing the incongruent state. If you think you are intelligent, but someone points out that you made a stupid mistake, you may avoid seeing this as incongruent by noting that you were misinformed, fatigued, or careless. It is sometimes possible simply to *misperceive how others see oneself.* If you think you are witty, but others don't laugh much at your jokes, you may avoid incongruency by not noticing how they respond. One may also *misinterpret one's own behavior* so as to achieve maximum congruency between behavior and an aspect of one's self concept. If you think you are a pretty good skier, but actually ski down a particular slope rather sloppily, you may simply evaluate your performance as better than it is. Finally, one may restructure the situation to change the evaluation of one's behavior. Studies have reported that the correspondence between self and the way one *thinks* others see one is greater than the *actual* correspondence between the self concept and the views really held by others. If you consider yourself generous, you are apt to believe that a friend considers you generous, even though he or she really believes you are less generous than you think you are.

One experimental study illustrates some of the forms that restructuring can take.[9] College students were presented with fictitious but apparently valid ratings of a variety of their traits, some of them unfavorable. They were led to believe that the ratings came from an authoritative source, from a friend, or from a stranger. There were some shifts toward less favorable self-evaluations after seeing these fictitious sheets (the subjects rated themselves both before and after they saw the sheets). In addition, when asked to recall them, they distorted the evaluations in a favorable direction. Given the opportunity, they also dissociated the devaluations from the source by denying that they had actually been made by the other persons. By and large, their reactions were more marked where the devaluation was the greatest and where the ratings were perceived as coming from an authoritative source or from a friend rather than a stranger. This and other studies support the general idea that individuals process information about the self in a manner that supports congruency.

Restructuring is frequently involved in achieving congruency between self and behavior. Most people view themselves favorably, as good and moral persons. When they perform a questionable act, or a wrong one, there is incongruency which they reduce by redefining the behavior. One way of doing this is to perceive the situation as one in which the person was not fully responsible or had no choice. Thus, the behavior is not "bad" because it was unintentional. Finally, people may use congruency by comparison as a means of restructuring. Individuals having an undesirable trait may exaggerate the extent to which other people have it, thus minimizing its importance in themselves by comparing themselves with these other people. After having harmed someone, people may deny responsibility, or perceive the act as wrong but in accordance with some higher loyalty. There are reinterpretations of behavior to make them congruent with a favorable self concept.

The avenues for achieving congruency in experimental situations are frequently limited and blocked. In everyday situations, there is a wider variety of resolutions to the dilemma of having behaved contrary to one's self-conception. How an actor maximizes congruency will depend on the characteristics of the actor, the act, and the victim, as well as on features of the situation that allow the chance to misperceive. Characteristics of the actor include not only personality traits but also constraints and possibilities inherent in the role expectations and role identities that come into play in a given situation. Thus, males may claim nonresponsibility for behavior by saying they were drunk. For females, this is less acceptable in certain circles, but a woman may plead irrationality or illness and find her claims more readily accepted by herself and others than if she were male. In such ways, both men and women can maintain their usual views of self and behavior.

Selective evaluation   In the process of selective evaluation, an individual maximizes congruency or minimizes incongruency by altering the *evaluation* of self, of

[9] Harvey, Kelley, and Shapiro, 1957.

behavior, or of the other person in a positive or negative direction. Behaviors of people who are unimportant to an individual are not considered incongruous even though they may be at variance with one's self concept or one's behavior. Thus, persons may maximize congruency and maintain their usual self and behavior by favorably evaluating those who behave congruently toward them and by devaluating people who behave incongruently. Similarly, where one's behavior toward another person is incongruent with one's self concept, one may minimize incongruency by devaluing the other person (such as a victim to whom one has done harm). This devaluation may take many forms. For example, one may believe the other deserved his or her fate, that the other's evaluation of oneself is of no account, or one may minimize the harm by not taking or feeling the other's viewpoint.

Studies of sorority girls found that those who were liked most by a member were those the member both perceived as having the most congruent views of her, and who actually did have the most congruent views.[10] This liking may well have come about through the process of selective evaluation: people like others who validate self. In experiments, when individuals were negatively evaluated by another, they reduced their liking for that person—discrediting the source of the negative evaluation and eliminating the incongruency.

One study, involving devaluating victims after harming them, is particularly interesting for congruency theory.[11] Self concepts were changed by giving participants personality evaluations designed temporarily to enhance or to lower their self-esteem. Some participants were given the choice of delivering or not delivering a series of electric shocks to a victim, while others were given no choice. Having choice would increase responsibility for the incongruent behavior and increase the pressure to resolve incongruency. Where individuals had a choice, those with a more positive self-conception felt less friendly to the victim after they had administered the shocks. Thus, devaluing the victim is a way of resolving incongruency, and the positive self concept is not weakened. Those with no choice did not modify their feelings of friendliness, because they felt no responsibility for their behavior. And those with low esteem did not change their friendship rating either.

Congruency is also a function of the importance of the aspect of self that is relevant to behavior or to interaction with another person. If an insignificant aspect of self is at variance with a person's perception of his or her behavior or someone else's behavior, incongruency is minimized. Conversely, incongruency may be minimized by adjusting the values placed on various aspects of self, putting great stress on perceptions of behavior that fit, and less on those aspects of self that don't fit. For instance, a girl in junior high choosing activities realizes that some must be sacrificed so that others may be pursued.[12] She has equally

[10] Backman and Secord, 1962.
[11] Glass, 1964.
[12] McCandless, 1961.

strong and valued conceptions of herself as a scholar and an athlete, but must choose between debating and playing basketball. She chooses debating. It might be expected that she will devalue the importance of basketball, and perhaps of all sports, and upgrade the importance of intellectual activity. The actual *direction* of her conception of herself as an athlete may not change, but the *value* to her of this facet of her self concept will shift downward. Conversely, the value of intellectual activities will become even greater, and the importance of the intellectual facet of her self concept will increase.

Selective interaction   Another important means by which one may maintain interpersonal congruency without changing one's self concept or behavior is through selectively interacting with certain persons and not with others. One elects to interact with those with whom it is easiest to establish a congruent state. People who think of themselves as smart will interact frequently with other people who respect their intelligence and allow them to use it (congruency by validation). They will avoid those who are much smarter than they are, or so much dumber that they cannot even use their smartness.

In our discussion of role strain in Chapter 14, we mentioned studies that indicated that strain arises when a role category is incompatible with a person's characteristics. This suggests that one is likely to avoid entering such positions and to seek more compatible role categories. This idea is supported by a study of teachers who have been in the profession for different lengths of time.[13] Experienced teachers had smaller discrepancies between their self concepts and their perceptions of the teacher role than did inexperienced teachers. This did not appear to result from change in self, or in perception of the teacher role, but apparently resulted from the tendency of those with larger discrepancies between self and role to become dissatisfied and to drop out of the teaching role. In this way they could avoid pressures to change self to fit the role.

A longitudinal study of college roommates provides further support for selective interaction.[14] Views of self, reflected self, and actual views held by one's roommate were obtained in October of one year and in May of the following year. More initial and subsequent congruency between self and reflected self was found for those roommates who stayed together *when given a choice*. For the satisfied roommates, there was also more consensus between one's self-rating and the roommate's actual rating. The possibility that these findings might be due to a difference in similarity between satisfied and dissatisfied pairs of roommates was ruled out by a statistical analysis.

Another form of selective interaction uses congruency by validation. Individuals choose to interact with people whose behavior allows them to behave in a congruent way. In one study, the needs of pairs of friends were compared, and the needs matched according to congruency requirements.[15] For example, indi-

---

[13] Hoe, 1962.
[14] Doherty and Secord, 1971.
[15] Secord and Backman, 1964.

viduals who saw themselves as high on the need for succorance (emotional support and help) viewed their close friends as high on the need for nurturance (giving help and support to others).

Individuals may also reduce incongruency by selecting certain people as objects of comparison. In an experiment, participants were given information leading them to believe they were rated as quite hostile.[16] Then they were allowed to compare themselves with one person by looking at that person's score. They had the option of choosing that person from one of several groups known to be different in hostility. For the most part, they chose a person from the most hostile group, thus making themselves appear less hostile by comparison.

Response evocation and self-presentation A person also maintains congruency by developing techniques that evoke congruent responses from other people. Erving Goffman has suggested that in everyday interaction, people present themselves and their activities so as to guide and control the impressions they give of themselves.[17] These actions may be deliberately calculated, or the actors may be quite unaware of the effects they produce. Among the strategies that people use to elicit congruent responses, or to block incongruent ones, are: the *preapology*, which prevents the questioning of one's accuracy or expertise (*"Off the top of my head*, I'd say . . ."); and a phrase which confirms a preferred identity, as in name dropping or experience dropping ("Back at Harvard . . .").[18]

A number of lines of research have concerned self-presentation. One line involves studies of embarrassment, which has been conceptualized as a reaction to a loss of self-esteem through perception of negative reactions from others. Behavior designed to avoid or restore loss of self-esteem has been called *facework*. People react by attempting through facework to restore a favorable impression of themselves. Facework (the saving of face) is favorable self-presentation.

Affective congruency versus self-enhancement The concept of congruency may be applied to feelings as well as to cognitive elements. A state of affective congruency exists when a person (P) believes that another (O) feels toward him as P feels toward himself, either in regard to himself as a whole or in regard to some aspect of self. Especially relevant here is the positive or negative quality of the feeling—is it approval or disapproval, love or hate, admiration or contempt? In another form of affective congruency, P has comparable feelings toward an aspect of self and his or her corresponding behavior. Affective congruency is maintained by the same mechanisms as those previously described for cognitive congruency. People may misperceive how others feel about them; they may selectively associate with, and selectively evaluate, other persons; they may attempt to evoke congruent feelings from other persons.

Experiments have demonstrated that people like to be positively evaluated,

[16] Hakmiller, 1966.
[17] Goffman, 1959.
[18] Weinstein, 1966, 1969.

and also that they like others who like them, as noted in Chapter 7. People also use protective mechanisms to defend themselves from a person who evaluates them unfavorably. For example, in various studies, persons were not believed, were disliked and discredited; their evaluation was distorted in a favorable direction, or they were avoided. These are familiar mechanisms, already discussed, which restore congruency.

But it is seldom clear whether these behaviors result from a desire for self-enhancement or from the principle of affective congruency. If we assume that most people have positive feelings about themselves, then affective congruency would require that they prefer positive evaluations from other persons. But we also know that people prefer to be evaluated favorably by others—they need to be respected and liked. So the experimental results obtained with positive evaluations—or reactions to negative ones—would be consistent with affective congruency but also with the idea or principle that people have a need to be admired and liked.

Theoretically, a critical test of these two principles could be conducted by dealing with people who, at least temporarily, have *unfavorable* views of themselves. For such people, the principle of affective congruency predicts that they should like people who agree with their negative evaluation. But the idea that all people have a need to be respected and liked would predict that even these people would prefer and like people who evaluate them positively, not negatively. A number of investigators, including the authors, have attempted to create crucial experiments to test this proposition. Results have been mixed, with some support and some contradictions.

One of the difficult problems is that congruency processes themselves work against doing such experiments. Attempts by experimenters to create a temporary condition among participants in which they have unfavorable views of some aspect of their self or behavior are resisted by invoking all the congruency processes we have talked about. Moreover, even the manipulations designed to convince participants that other persons evaluate them negatively can be fouled up by congruency processes. Participants can distort the supposedly negative evaluation, seeing it as neutral or even positive. They can discount or devaluate the evaluator, and so on. Finally, there is evidence that the evaluation is difficult to confine to the negative aspect of self that is focused on in the experiment.[19] If individuals consider themselves poor at both tennis and baseball, they may view themselves as poor *athletes*. But even if participants in an experiment could be led to believe that the negative evaluation by another person was valid for a given negative aspect of self, it is not enough. For, if they apply the same evaluation to other *positive* aspects of self, the evaluation will be both congruent and incongruent at the same time (with different aspects of self). These effects could cancel each other out. Suppose, for example, that another person thinks you are a rather weak chess player. And you also believe you are a weak player. The

[19] Maehr, Mensing, and Nafzger, 1962.

other's view and yours are congruent. But suppose the other's view of you as a weak player also gives you the impression that he or she thinks you are not too smart. If you believe you are intelligent, the other's view of you is incongruent with that aspect of yourself. So negative views that others have of you may easily be congruent with a negative aspect of your self but incongruent with related positive aspects. Because of this tendency of negative views to spread to several aspects of self, definitive experiments are hard to conduct. So, at present, whether one chooses to explain reactions to negative evaluations by other persons in terms of self-enhancement or in terms of congruency is a matter of interpretation, not experimental evidence.

Stabilizing Effects of the Social Structure

We have been emphasizing that the stability and consistency of an individual's self and behavior rest on consistencies in his interpersonal environment. But we have also stressed that the individual contributes much to these environmental constancies, mainly through the operation of the variety of interpersonal processes we have been describing. Another source of stability lies in the social structure which helps to maintain a constant interpersonal environment in several ways.

Consistency in the interpersonal environment   So far, we have been discussing congruency in terms of an individual and one other person, and with regard mostly to a single aspect of behavior. But our relations with people are not independent of each other. If they were, then, chameleonlike, we could change our selves and our behavior each time we interacted with a different person, or each time a different aspect of self was involved. There is some variability from situation to situation, but there is also much consistency in a person's behavior in different situations. To the extent that different situations support similar aspects of self and behavior, these aspects may be said to support each other. Resistance to change in such components of self or behavior is especially great, and change is unlikely to be achieved by changes in relation to a single person—unless that person is of great importance.

An experiment was conducted to see if it was true that the greater the number of significant persons supporting an aspect of self, the more resistant that aspect would be to change.[20] College students were asked to rank themselves on a series of fifteen characteristics and also to estimate how they thought each of five persons important to them would rank them on these characteristics. They were given several personality tests for the ostensible purpose of determining how much insight they had into their own personalities. For each individual, the experimenter selected two traits for special analysis and treatment. Both traits were ranked among the highest five applying to self by each person, but one represented high perceived agreement among the five significant other persons

[20] Backman, Secord, and Peirce, 1963.

while the other represented low perceived agreement. The hypothesis was that, of the two traits selected, the one with greater consensus would be more resistant to change than the one with lower consensus.

On a later occasion, to test resistance to change, a false report purportedly based on personality tests was given to each individual. Actually, the reports were based on the initial self-rankings and contained descriptive statements very similar to those on which the individuals had previously ranked themselves. The rank order of the traits on this report was the same as the individuals' previous rankings except that the two traits selected for special treatment were reported as being eight ranks lower than the individuals themselves had put them. Thus, by being presented with deviant views from another source, individuals were confronted with an incongruency which could be resolved by lowering their self-rankings on these two traits.

After the participants had had time to study this report, and presumably to note discrepancies between it and their rankings of themselves, they were asked to rank themselves again. On this second ranking, most participants were influenced by the false report to lower the ranking of these two traits. But *the trait with low consensus was lowered more than the trait with high consensus.* Thus, the greater the number of significant other persons who are seen as defining one in a manner compatible with one's own definition, the more resistance there is to change in that self-definition.

Continuity in environment   Many factors help to stabilize the interpersonal environment. First, belonging to a group and holding particular positions in its affect, status, power, and leadership structures ensures that other members will treat one in a *regular* fashion. Inconsistent behaviors toward one are discouraged by other members. Second, the institutional structure of culturally defined role expectations that guide interaction help to stabilize both the personnel with whom one interacts, as well as the interactions themselves. People are seen by others and they see themselves in ways dictated by the various role categories they occupy. People not only learn behavioral expectations belonging to a role category, but also the personal attributes associated with it. By occupying certain positions—age-sex roles, for instance—they are consistently defined by others and consequently define themselves in terms of traits associated with their role category.

We have suggested that an individual is likely to enter groups and participate in social systems if the probability of establishing congruent relations is high, and have reported some evidence for this in discussing selective interaction. Once in such a group, participation in these congruent relations is in part determined by the conditions and processes that control the group. For long periods in life a person is surrounded by the same family members, the same playmates, the same friends. Even if some of the actual individuals change, those who replace them are likely to have certain similarities to the previous ones because of the constraining effects of the social structure (occupation, or region, or socioeconomic class).

Summary: Resisting Change in Self and Behavior

The individual is active in maintaining a particular kind of self and personality. One responds actively to situational factors in a manner that maintains the distinctive character of one's behavior. This activity is conceived of in terms of interpersonal congruency theory, in which the unit of analysis has three components: an aspect of one's self, one's interpretation of one's behavior relevant to that aspect, and one's beliefs about how another person behaves toward one and feels toward one with regard to that aspect. An individual attempts to maintain a state of congruency among the three components. Congruency exists when the behaviors of an individual and another person imply definitions of self compatible with one's self concept.

There are three kinds of congruency. In congruency by implication, one may perceive that another sees one as possessing a particular characteristic corresponding to an aspect of one's self concept. In congruency by validation, the behavior or other characteristics of another allow, or call for, behavior on the part of one that confirms a component of one's self. In congruency by comparison, the behavior, or attributes, of another suggest by comparison that one possesses a particular self-component. Congruency may also involve feelings, as when one has the same feelings toward oneself that one perceives another has toward one.

A number of activities on the part of the individual contribute to stability of self by creating for one an interpersonal environment which is likely to be congruent with one's self concept and behavior. These include: (1) misperceiving the attitudes, attributes, or behavior of other persons, or misinterpreting one's own behavior, (2) selectively interacting with persons who have congruent attitudes or who behave congruently toward one, (3) positively evaluating persons who have congruent attitudes or behavior toward one, (4) evaluating most highly the aspects of self that one perceives as congruent with the attitudes and behavior of other persons, (5) evoking congruent responses from others by presenting oneself in an appropriate manner or by casting the other in a congruent role.

Both institutional and interpersonal forces help to maintain one's self-conception and one's behavior, and also to maintain the personnel, the attributions, and the behaviors of others in one's interpersonal environment. Stability is at a maximum where consensus exists among significant others, particularly consensus on those statuses that exert a powerful organizing influence on the perception and attributions of others as well as oneself.

CHANGES IN SELF AND INDIVIDUAL BEHAVIOR

The social structure is not only a source of stability, but under certain conditions it also induces changes in the interpersonal environment. As one moves through the social structure, systematic changes occur in the ways one is categorized and the ways that other persons behave toward one. Features of the social structure also induce changes in the personnel of one's environment. In addition, various fortuitous events can produce changes. To illustrate changes arising from the social structure, the discussion below will treat the positional changes that occur with increasing age and with occupational socialization.

Life-cycle Changes

Each society has laid out for individuals of both sexes a series of role categories that they occupy at various stages of their lives. Every person occupies such categories as infant, small child, older child, adolescent, young adult, middle-aged adult, elderly adult. In addition, people have a certain place in their family, depending on its structure and composition. They are the youngest child, or the eldest, or have several siblings, or one, or none. Family activities may be limited to the immediate family or may extend to grandparents, uncles, aunts, and cousins.

Outside the family, people occupy certain roles in their peer groups. They go to school. A male may enter military service. Males and females usually marry, acquiring the roles of spouse, parent, and so on. Occupational roles play an important part in people's lives. All these roles contribute to their self concept. To the extent that they are discontinuous and sequential, they require movement and behavior changes and are instrumental in bringing about changes in the self. Simone de Beauvoir and R. S. Cavan write about the terrible wrenching that comes with the onset of old age, the discontinuity of the role category forced upon people at retirement, and how all those things that they had valued in themselves and that had been valued by others come to an abrupt halt. As Cavan has written:

> First, the means of carrying out the social role disappears: the man is a lawyer without a case, a bookkeeper without books, a machinist without tools. Second, he is excluded from his group of former co-workers; as an isolated person he may be completely unable to function in his former role. Third, as a retired person, he begins to find a different evaluation of himself in the minds of others from the evaluation he had as an employed person. He no longer sees respect in the eyes of former subordinates, praise in the faces of former superiors, and approval in the manner of former co-workers. The looking glass composed of his former important groups throws back a changed image: he is done for, an old timer, old-fashioned, on the shelf.[21]

Several studies of occupational socialization document the formative effects on self concept as an individual passes through the social structure. A study of nursing students asked them to give twenty answers to the question, "Who am I?"[22] Only a third of the students at the end of their freshman year identified themselves as nurses in one of the first three statements, but more than seven out

---

[21] Reprinted by permission from R. S. Cavan. Self and role in adjustment during old age. In A. M. Rose (Ed.), *Human behavior and social processes: An interactionist approach.* Boston: Houghton Mifflin Company, 1962.
[22] Kuhn, 1960.

of ten did so by the end of their junior year. This demonstrates the incorporation of the image of "nurse" into the self. A similar trend has been noted in medical students.[23] Thirty-one percent of first-year students reported they felt more like doctors than like students when dealing with patients. This figure rose to 83 percent for students finishing their fourth year of training. Whether or not they saw themselves primarily as doctors also depended on which role partner they were interacting with. With fellow students, faculty members, or nurses, the percentage of those who saw themselves as physicians was considerably lower than when they were dealing with patients.

This finding is consistent with the theoretical position that the expectations of role partners are an important determinant of how actors see their roles. More students see themselves as doctors when they are interacting with patients, who do not know the difference in meaning between red and blue name tags, see only the white coats, and depend on them for help.[24] Thirty-nine percent of the 117 first-year students who thought their patients regarded them as doctors defined themselves as such, while only 6 percent of the 35 students who believed their patients defined them as students saw themselves as doctors.

Learning to view oneself in a new manner involves considerably more than applying a new role identity to oneself. One learns to see oneself in terms of the range of physical, social, and personal attributes which are characteristic of actors in the same role, even including those attributes that are not directly concerned with the performance of the role. Thus, because doctors frequently play golf, a young doctor may also take it up.

Occupying a new position in the social structure may also involve radical changes in the personnel in one's environment. New persons become significant, old associations fade in significance or disappear. The person who is inducted into the service, or who takes a position in a strange community, is suddenly surrounded by new associates. To the degree that these people define the person in an unfamiliar way, and to the extent that the effects of the new definitions are not countered by the various means of maintaining congruency previously discussed, strong forces are created toward change in self and behavior.

Changes in Group Structures

Some sources of change need not be societal or institutional but may come from smaller groups or even from interaction with one other person. An abrupt change in one's group position in the status, power, or leadership structure, may lead to a change in self-conception, in behavior, and in the behaviors and attributions of others. The phrase "I knew him when . . ." suggests that the transformations that accompany sudden elevations are frequent indeed.

Changes in one's affectionate relations with other persons—a new and close friendship, a love relationship, the development of a relationship with a thera-

[23] Huntington, 1957.
[24] Scanlon, Hunter, and Sun, 1961.

pist—can cause drastic changes in a person's affective or cognitive components, or in both. If one is modified, the other is likely to be changed in order to reestablish affective cognitive consistency. Cognitive changes in self that have been observed after psychotherapy provide a good example.[25] Psychotherapy, a very intense experience, often involves the therapist's being warm and accepting toward the patient until the patient gradually increases the positive affect he has toward himself, which, in turn, is followed by the adoption of more positive self-cognitions to achieve consistency.

Once individuals have acquired a deviant identity—like that of criminal or mental patient—it is difficult for them to change it. Other people won't let them. But there are exceptional people who deviate in their attitudes toward deviance and see good in everyone. Sometimes these people are religious and believe that all are sinners and that all are capable of redemption. These people have been called *normal-smiths*, and often play a crucial role in returning individuals to the status of normality and in breaking the vicious circle that supports a deviant identity.[26] They are sometimes ex-deviants themselves—reformed alcoholics, drug addicts, or felons—and their definitions and examples therefore carry additional credibility. Their power to change may be further amplified through organization into groups such as Alcoholics Anonymous or Synanon (see Chapter 9). In one sense, psychotherapists are normal-smiths, too, because they believe the patient can change.

Often, significant others become the source and support for elements of the ideal self which, in turn, can exert pressure toward change of self-conception and role identity. Where there is an appreciable discrepancy between the ideal self and the actual self, another person with a loving and supportive attitude can help one to move toward these ideals (see Chapter 7). These others share with the actors their interest in realizing their ideal selves and support them in moving toward what they want to be. Through this kind of pressure, the individuals can be seen as actively creating new dimensions of the self.

Once a component of an interpersonal system changes, other components in the system are likely to change in the direction of congruency. This can be illustrated by a number of research findings. In one study, one group whose self-esteem had been lowered by giving them false information cheated on an exam to a greater extent than did the control group, whose self-esteem had not been lowered.[27] Thus, they changed their behavior to make it congruent with their newly lowered self-esteem. Another study, however, revealed that such behavioral changes are not likely to occur when an aspect of self is strongly believed. But they do occur if individuals are not too certain about an aspect of self.[28] In this investigation, participants with low self-esteem who were certain of their low

[25] Rogers and Dymond, 1954.
[26] Lofland, 1969.
[27] Aronson and Mettee, 1972.
[28] Maracek and Mettee, 1972.

self-appraisal were led to believe they were personally responsible for having done well in the early trials of a task, a performance incongruent with their self concept. They failed to improve in response to this feedback concerning success, maintaining instead a poor performance congruent with their low self-appraisal. But others who were either unsure of their low self-appraisal or were led to attribute their success to luck *did* improve in line with their perceived success.

The way in which the views of other people may lead to a *self-fulfilling prophecy* has been demonstrated by showing the effects of teachers' expectations for the performance of school children. Although there has been some controversy about the methodology of these studies, later reports confirm that self-fulfilling prophecies do have significant effects under some conditions.[29]

In this study, nonverbal IQ tests were administered in eighteen classrooms ranging from the first to the sixth grades, and the test scores were presented to teachers as measures that could predict academic "blooming" (that is, an improvement with time, due to latent capacities which need development). Names of 20 percent of the children were chosen *at random without regard for their IQ scores* and reported to the teachers as being likely to make considerable gains during the coming year. Some eight months later, these children were found to have made greater gains than children not named. This was especially true of those in the lower grades. A reasonable assumption is that the expectations and behavior of the teachers toward these randomly selected children raised their evaluation of their own intellectual competence and evoked a more intelligent performance from them, making all three components of the interpersonal system congruent.

While no measure of the self-concept of the children was taken, other investigations would lend support to this interpretation. One study of more than 500 children of grades seven through twelve found that the students' self-conception of their ability, the definitions of significant others (parents and, to a lesser degree, peers), and the performance in school, were appreciably related.[30]

Summary: Changes in Self and Individual Behavior

As one moves through the social structure, systematic changes occur in the ways one is categorized and the ways that other persons behave toward one. Features of the social structure also induce changes in the personnel of one's environment. In addition, chance events can produce changes. Each society has laid out for its members a series of role categories that they will occupy at various stages of their lives. Moreover, as they occupy new role categories, they sometimes encounter a whole new set of persons who will treat them differently from the way their earlier companions did. The self-fulfilling prophecy illustrates the force that expectations of other persons may have for shaping one's behavior in a new direc-

---

[29] Rosenthal and Jacobson, 1968; Rosenthal, 1973.
[30] Brookover, et al., 1967.

tion. If some event leads significant others to predict a new direction for an individual's life, they may help to create such changes by their treatment of that individual.

Changes in group structure also occur, as when one acquires a new position in the group. New friendships and loves sometimes create significant changes in one, which can have ramifications throughout one's life. Sometimes a change in feelings toward oneself leads to comparable cognitive changes in order to maintain consistency between these two facets of self. And often a chance event may have profound consequences. Performing a deviant act, for example, may put one into a new, deviant category in which one is systematically labeled by others as deviant, and from which it becomes difficult for one to return to a former status. We take up this topic of the establishment of deviant identity in the next chapter.

SIXTEEN

CRIME, DEVIANCE, AND IDENTITY

This final chapter will apply social psychological principles to an analysis of deviant behavior and its relation to social problems confronting contemporary society. We have chosen to concentrate primarily on delinquency and crime, although the discussion will, on a few occasions, refer to other problem areas such as mental illness. Delinquency and crime have been given more attention by social psychologists than any other form of deviant behavior, and we can gain the best understanding of deviance by concentrating on those topics.

WHAT IS A SOCIAL PROBLEM?

What conditions make up a social problem? Americans asked by pollsters to name some of the major problems confronting the nation have little trouble in responding. Many of the same problems are named, although their importance varies from person to person and group to group. Inflation, crime on the streets, urban blight, and inequality of opportunity are commonly mentioned. Presumably their importance varies depending on the respondent's location in society and his group identity.

These judgments underscore an idea about the nature of social problems that was introduced many years ago and which is currently being emphasized:[1] that social problems have two aspects, an *objective* and a *subjective* one.

The objective aspect is what we typically think of when we describe a social problem. Some condition of human existence, some facet of social behavior, is described in terms of a *statistic* considered excessive and undesirable: crime rate, divorce rate, or unemployment rate. The subjective aspect of a social problem is less obvious because it is not something "out there" but is part of ourselves. In part it concerns our judgment of the rate as satisfactory or undesirable, but several elements of this subjective aspect require comment.

First, persons must believe that a condition is a threat to their values. Whether it is actually a threat is not crucial. What people believe is what is important. The practice of witchcraft was a serious social problem in colonial America and still is in some societies. Yet today in most sectors of American society it is not, since we no longer believe that witches cause disease and other ills. Or, if people in a modern city believe that crime in the streets is so rampant that they are afraid to venture out at night, a social problem exists, even if their belief is incorrect.

Second, as the values in a culture change, the kinds of social conditions that are regarded as social problems also change. At one time religious heresy was considered a major social problem. As religious tolerance became more highly valued, however, and religious orthodoxy less valued, this social problem was no longer a national issue.

Third, values often are implicated in the maintenance of a particular social problem, because attempts to remedy the problem may do violence to some other value. Greatly increasing the powers of our police forces, our prosecuting attorneys, and our courts, might possibly reduce the current crime rate, but it might at the same time endanger other values, for instance, our civil and political rights. Often we are forced to live with a social problem because the available cures are worse than the disease.

Fourth is the extent to which a condition threatening a group's values is believed to be changeable.[2] Only if it is believed to be remediable can it be considered a social problem. Behaviors or conditions that are unalterable are not likely to be so viewed. As we learned in Chapter 11, on social norms, people give up trying to change others who are hopelessly deviant. That discussion also noted that behaviors which are intrinsically rewarding or driven by powerful needs, as well as behaviors difficult to control through surveillance and through sanctions, often do not become subject to normative control. Thus, we commonly hear such statements as: "War will always be with us, because human beings have an aggressive instinct," or, "There will always be crime because some people are evil." Or, before the advent of modern economic theory, and especially Marxist

[1] Fuller and Meyers, 1941; Becker, 1963; Lemert, 1967.
[2] Merton, 1971.

A threat to values: collaboration with the enemy in wartime. Woman with shorn head is being taunted by crowd for collaborating with the Nazis. (Robert Capa, "Images of War," copyright © 1964)

theory, "The poor will always be with us." To the extent that such beliefs are firm, the condition they refer to will not be considered changeable, and thus will not be considered a social problem.

At times in its history, mental illness appeared to be a hopeless condition, with no effective treatments known. Before the eighteenth century, mental patients were simply locked up, and often chained if they were considered dangerous. Attempting to change their behavior was considered hopeless. Later, during the nineteenth century, at places like the famous Worcester State Hospital in Massachusetts, the attitude was one of firm belief in the possibility of rehabilitation.[3] But again, in the several decades before the mid-twentieth century, when the population of patients in mental hospitals expanded markedly, a custodial attitude developed—at least in many state hospitals. Patients were simply housed and fed, but few received treatment. Then, once again, the advent of tranquilizing and antidepressant drugs created new hope for treating mental patients.

Fifth, the distribution of power in a society determines which value threats become defined as social problems. This works in two ways. One is that conditions which threaten values held by the more powerful are more likely to be

[3] Grob, 1966.

defined as social problems. The other is that behaviors engaged in by the more powerful are less likely to be defined as deviant. With respect to the first, in our discussion of social norms, we noted that what becomes normative depends upon what affects the outcomes of the more powerful. They shape the system of rules and values so that their satisfactions are maximized. This principle, developed in the context of small groups, also applies to the larger society. With respect to the second point, we saw in Chapter 6 that the behaviors of high-status people are more likely to be seen in a favorable light. What they do is less likely to be considered deviant.

Comparing cigarette smoking, which is not considered a major social problem, with marijuana using, which is, illustrates the role of power in the definition of social problems. The fact that the production of tobacco products is a major industry and that the consumption of these products is found among the rich as well as the poor contributes to the failure to define the use of tobacco as a social problem. That the use of marijuana was until recently confined largely to groups having minimal power in our society—the young and other minority groups—undoubtedly made it easier to define its use as problem behavior. But, more recently, as more and more higher-status people have taken up marijuana smoking, the penalties for its use are being weakened.

These subjective aspects of a social problem help to explain why so much controversy arises in dealing with social problems. Different segments of the population may disagree on whether a condition is a threat to their values. Or a solution which achieves one value may do violence to other values. People may disagree on whether a condition is changeable or not, or on whether it threatens other values. Or they may disagree on whether a particular solution in fact realizes a particular value. Does school segregation threaten the value of equal opportunity for all? Does busing of students to reduce segregation mean the end of neighborhood identity and cohesion? Can racial differences in performance be eliminated by education? These are illustrative themes in the current controversy over race relations in the United States. The answers to these questions are frequently biased by outcomes that people expect to get from taking different actions. These expected outcomes may or may not have a basis in reality: it is how persons define situations rather than the objective facts that influence their behavior.

Finally, social problems frequently persist not because we lack the knowledge and the technology to change an objective condition but because of socially structured value conflicts. These conflicts have emerged because society has developed so that what maximizes the outcome of some people minimizes the outcomes of others, and because the life experiences of people at different points in the social structure differ dramatically. These conditions produce different views of what is good and desirable, different values, and these differences become the basis for social conflict. Ultimately, the manner in which social problems are defined and resolved depends on these value conflicts. They play a major part in social change. Basic to this process of change is the power structure.

As the proportions of people with differing power adopt a new behavior, definitions of the behavior change. Similarly, as changes in the power structure occur, behavior once defined as a problem because of its perceived implication for the outcomes of more-powerful groups becomes defined otherwise when the relative power of these groups declines.

LABELING DEVIANT BEHAVIOR

Our emphasis on the subjective aspects of social problems is consistent with a similar emphasis in the *labeling,* or *social-control* approach to, deviant behavior. Howard Becker contrasts this view of deviant behavior with an earlier one that concentrated on the objective aspect of social problems. He points out that this older sociological view defined deviance as the infraction of some agreed-upon rule. It then asked who breaks these rules, and examined their personalities and searched for factors in their life situations that might explain the infractions of society's rules. This approach implicitly assumes that those who have broken a rule are all alike in certain respects, because they have engaged in the same deviant act. Thus, homosexuality was commonly considered a form of deviance, and intensive research efforts examined individual personality characteristics and childhood socialization of homosexuals in an effort to explain why they became homosexual.

Becker points out the limitations of this view, and the arbitrariness of labeling behavior as deviant:

> Such an assumption seems to me to ignore the central fact about deviance: it is created by society . . . social groups create deviance by making the rules whose infraction constitutes deviance, and by applying those rules to particular people and labeling them as outsiders. From this point of view, deviance is not a quality of the act the person commits, but rather a consequence of the application by others of rules and sanctions to an "offender." The deviant is one to whom the label has successfully been applied; deviant behavior is behavior that people so label.[4]

Social Power and the Labeling of Deviant Behavior

This approach to deviance raises a number of questions which are often ignored. Why does some behavior become defined as deviant or problematic while other behavior does not? Our previous discussion suggests that this is the outcome of social conflict. One outcome is that the behavior which interferes with, or challenges, the values of those who hold social power is apt to be labeled deviant. An increasing number of studies have been made of the process by which new cate-

[4] Reprinted by permission from H. S. Becker. *Outsiders: Studies in the sociology of deviance.* New York: Free Press, 1963. Pp. 8–9.

A clash of values: society uses its police power against strikers. (United Press International Photo)

gories of deviance emerge and are changed over time. Several studies illustrate the role of the economically powerful in determining what kinds of behavior are labeled deviant. A study of the emergence of vagrancy laws in England during the fourteenth century suggests that these emerged in response to an extreme labor shortage on the manors. This shortage occurred as a result of the Black Death, which wiped out an estimated half of the English population, and from the breakdown of serfdom as peasants began to flee from the manors.[5] Laws that then appeared making it a crime to give alms to any unemployed person of sound mind and body were obviously intended to force persons to work. This problem is still with us, apparently. Frances Piven and Richard Cloward reviewed the relations among the labor supply in the United States during the twentieth century, the economic conditions, and the amount of welfare money

[5] Chambliss, 1964.

made available.[6] They offer some evidence that, as the labor supply tightens up and becomes scarce, welfare payments are reduced in order to provide more cheap labor. And with a labor surplus, accompanied by demonstrations or even riots, welfare payments are increased.

Status and Deviant Labels

We have noted that the kinds of behavior enacted by high-status people are usually viewed favorably. This means that such behaviors are less apt to be seen as deviant and so labeled by others. Conversely, people with low status are apt to have questionable motives and undesirable characteristics attributed to them.

The amount of financial loss in most so-called white-collar crimes (for example, cases of financial fraud, restraint of trade, false and misleading advertising) far exceeds that incurred in a typical burglary, yet society's sanction in terms of the sentences imposed on the perpetrators of these two different types of crimes in no way reflects this difference. Burglars typically receive considerably more punishment than embezzlers. This tendency to attribute favorable characteristics to high-status persons has affected the development of criminal law through acts of legislatures and the interpretation and administration of justice through the courts.

In discussing the general nature of a social problem, we noted this attribution principle in connection with marijuana using. This principle is also borne out by the early legislation in the United States that was concerned with the use of opiates, and which appeared to be prompted by the association of opium first with low-status Chinese immigrants and later with the underworld and groups perceived as marginal to the underworld. A further illustration is found in the failure of laws prohibiting the use of alcohol. After the passage of prohibition laws, alcohol continued to be consumed by all strata of society, including the rich and powerful. For the most part, drinking was not labeled as deviant and morally wrong.

Of course the consequences of deviant acts for society, the actor, and the victim also affect the labeling process. Murder is labeled a more heinous crime than is assault. Nevertheless, the resolution of value conflicts so as to label some behaviors as deviant and to ignore others means that the consequences of deviant behavior are by no means directly proportional to the extent to which it is labeled as serious and subject to institutional sanctions. We have just seen this in the comparison of so-called white-collar crimes with others, such as burglary. Hence, the effects of labeling are very powerful.

Specialists in Labeling Behavior

Labeling theory also emphasizes the role of what have been called *moral entrepreneurs.*[7] These are persons who have taken it upon themselves to fight against a

[6] Piven and Cloward, 1971.
[7] Becker, 1963.

particular condition or form of behavior that they perceive as a threat. By arousing public opinion, lobbying before legislatures, and engaging in other political action these moral entrepreneurs are often successful in changing society's definitions in a manner that creates a new class of deviants. An early figure in the temperance movement, Carrie Nation, is an excellent example of a moral entrepreneur. Her actions, along with those of many others, eventually brought about the outlawing of alcoholic beverages in the 1920s and set the stage for such deviant categories as the rumrunner, the moonshiner, and the speakeasy operator. Similarly, the efforts of Senator Joseph McCarthy helped produce a new category of deviance in the 1950s—the communist subversive. Finally, one can point to a contemporary example, Ralph Nader. To the extent that he and his organization are successful in stimulating new legislation to protect the consumer, new categories of white-collar crime will be created (such as selling unsafe merchandise).

Moral entrepreneurs are frequently aided by another category of persons called *imputational specialists*.[8] These are professionals and others whose task is to seek out, classify, or diagnose persons as being of a particular type. Thus, psychiatrists played a major role in the formation of the sexual psychopath laws that appeared in many states during the late 1930s.[9] These laws, for example, placed the child molester and exhibitionist in special categories of crime, emphasizing the need for psychiatric treatment. Mental illness in general especially involves the use of imputational specialists.

A study of the growth of legislation governing the use of marijuana in America suggests that professionals and others in government agencies that were established to control a given form of deviance may function as moral entrepreneurs in extending the agency's control to new forms of behavior. Thus the U.S. Bureau of Narcotics, originally created to control the use of opiates, played a significant role in bringing about state and federal legislation to control marijuana use.[10]

While the term *moral entrepreneurs* called attention to those who work to create new rules or laws which result in new classes of deviants, an adequate designation is lacking for those who eliminate or change the meanings of various earlier forms of deviance. Recent years have seen the transformation of certain categories of deviance toward more social acceptance. The category of the insane, with its earlier negative connotation of demonic possession, has been transformed to the idea of mental illness that can be dealt with like any physical illness. Similarly the category of alcoholic, with its connotation of moral weakness, has been transformed into a category of mental or physical illness. A similar transformation of the addict appears to be gaining general support.

In these instances, the change is a matter of degree rather than of elimination of a deviant category. It may be that eventually homosexuality in the con-

[8] Lofland, 1969.
[9] Sutherland, 1950.
[10] Becker, 1963.

text of relations between consenting adults will provide an example of full transformation. The definitions of this category have been changed from one emphasizing perversion to one of illness, and, more recently, at least in certain circles, to one where this behavior is viewed as a nondeviant, alternative life style. Frequently in these types of transformations members or ex-members of the deviant categories themselves have played a major role in changing society's views, and in a number of instances they have also been helped by sympathetic professionals.

Labeling and Mental Illness

Contemporary controversies among imputational specialists over the labeling of the mentally ill are particularly prominent. Thomas Szasz, a psychiatrist, has forcefully asserted that there is no such entity as "mental" illness; there are only problems in living.[11] He argues that, except for a few disease-based cases, like *paresis* (a behavioral disorder caused by brain damage following a syphilitic infection), the application of the medical, or disease, concept to disturbances of behavior is a *mistake*. Labeling people with behavior problems as ill, he believes, overemphasizes the helplessness of the patient, detracts from his own responsibility for recovery, and places stress on the wrong forms of remedial action. The medical view of behavioral disorders favors placement in hospitals or other institutions, the use of drugs or other physical treatments, and minimizes the contribution of social psychological factors to the disorder. The attack on the medical model has led to less emphasis on long-term hospitalization, and more emphasis on returning the individual to his familiar environment as soon as possible, along with outpatient care through community "half-way" houses or mental health centers.

More recently, opinion has shifted back toward accepting at least some aspects of the medical model as applied to behavioral disorders. Evidence is continuing to mount in favor of the view that *schizophrenia,* the most common form of serious mental disturbance, has both a biochemical and a genetic basis. Children with one schizophrenic parent, but who are raised from infancy on by foster parents, have been shown to be much more likely to develop schizophrenia than foster children whose natural parents were not afflicted with schizophrenia.[12] The increasing success of drugs in controlling anxiety or in alleviating depression, thus enabling the patient to function more adequately, continues to sustain interest in the physical aspects of mental illness. Current theory and practice favor a combination of medical treatment and careful consideration of the social psychological aspects of the patient's condition and setting. Not the least of these is the provision of an accepting, favorable social environment which will facilitate recovery.

[11] Szasz, 1961.
[12] Rosenthal, et al., 1971.

Our discussion of labeling theory has not made a strong distinction between the role of labeling in making an initial attribution of deviance to some act, and the later labeling processes which help to maintain the initial attribution. This important aspect of labeling theory will be discussed at some length in the next section, which deals with crime and delinquency as forms of deviant behavior.

Summary: Labeling Deviant Behavior

Society creates deviance by making the rules whose infraction constitutes deviance, and by applying these rules to people and labeling those who commit infractions as deviant. So what is considered deviant is purely arbitrary. Behaviors which interfere with, or challenge, the values of those persons who hold social power are apt to be labeled deviant. Moreover, acts engaged in by people with high status are likely to be favorably seen, and, thus, less apt to be considered deviant. The reverse is true of acts performed by people with low status. Two kinds of specialists in labeling behavior contribute further to this process: moral entrepreneurs and imputational specialists. The former take it upon themselves to lead the fight against a particular condition or form of behavior that they consider a threat to society and to themselves. The latter are professionals who develop "scientific" bases for selecting, classifying, and diagnosing persons as being of deviant types. Finally, at different periods in a society's history, labeling takes somewhat different forms, according to which values are most dominant at that time.

CRIME AS DEVIANT BEHAVIOR

Theories of crime abound. Some theorists emphasize that criminal behavior, like noncriminal behavior, is largely a product of learning from others to define certain situations in a law-abiding or a law-breaking fashion.[13] Others view crime largely in terms of the acting out in a symbolic fashion of unconscious conflicts,[14] and still others emphasize the role of defective controls, the failure to develop a strong and effective conscience or superego.[15] These theories are not necessarily in conflict. All three could provide part of the explanation for criminal behavior. This also reveals the grossness of the category of "criminal behavior," for, to some extent, different theories refer to partially different behaviors.

But the matter is even more complicated. To have a complete explanation, it seems essential to bring in social psychological factors as well. While these other theories could partly be recast in social psychological terms, social psychology is especially relevant to a fourth set of theories which stress the role of the

[13] Sutherland and Cressey, 1974.
[14] Aichorn, 1955; Alexander and Staub, 1956.
[15] McCord and McCord, 1956.

self-concept and of situational conditions in the causation of crime. These theories help to answer three questions important to understanding crime.

The first question is: How can we account for the social distribution of various forms of crime? America has the highest crime rate among modern nations—twice the rate of its nearest competitor for this dubious distinction. Depending on the crime, the distribution is concentrated in certain subgroups in American society distinguished by age, sex, class, race, and ethnic origin.

The second question is: How can we account for a specific criminal act? While criminal acts are concentrated at certain points in the social structure, they are nevertheless widespread in our society, from the streets of the ghetto to the board rooms of our corporations and the offices of our highest government officials. Given the right circumstances, most persons could be involved in a criminal episode. What are the situational ingredients?

The third question is: How can we account for a career of crime among some individuals, and its nonpersistence among others? Many persons commit acts at some time or other in their lives that could be labeled criminal, but most do not persist in such activity. They do not develop a distinctive set of criminal attitudes and a conception of themselves as criminals. Engaging in crime continuously or periodically does not become a central part of their activities for a significant portion of their lives. For others, however, it does.

Self and Identity

Several themes emphasized by John Lofland and which revolve around self, identity, and situational conditions, will occur repeatedly in our attempts to answer our three questions.[16] These are threats to identities, creation of deviant identities, and transformations of identities. We will discuss these briefly here, and they will be repeatedly illustrated later.

Threats to identity We saw in the initial chapters of this book, and later in Chapter 13, on social roles, that the development of an identity, or set of identities, is crucial for each individual. Most of us know who we are and what we are, to varying degrees. And for most of us, society provides favorable settings for the development of these identities. But some categories of people—the poor, the racial and ethnic minorities—grow up and live under conditions where the development of identities valued by society as a whole is difficult. Their life situation makes such identities precarious, and subject to considerable threat from time to time. Threats to masculine identity often occur in the inner city because of the frequent resort to violence which requires a young male to respond in kind to defend his masculine image.

Favorable deviant identities Challenges or threats to one's tentative identities may be met by the further developing of various styles of behavior that create

---

[16] Lofland, 1969.

identities which are favorably regarded within one's own group, but which are at odds with middle-class values. One of the most common of these styles is machismo—the exaggerated presentation of self as tough, strong, aggressive, defiant, and independent. Everyone who has seen movies of youth gangs has seen this swaggering, tough-talking, threatening style depicted in vivid terms. Essentially, this is one kind of defense against threats to the male ego, an attempt to bolster a precarious identity.

Transformations of identity   Transformations of identity involve the social system as well as the individual, and occur over a longer period of time. Essentially, they amount to a passage from one identity to another. Much of our discussion in the previous chapter, explaining change in terms of interpersonal congruency processes, is relevant here. In this chapter we will try to pinpoint the processes that account for the transformation of the initially deviant behaviors into a permanent way of life, perpetuating a new identity.

THE INITIAL LABELING PROCESS

The processes and effects of labeling can be considered in two stages. In the first stage, individuals are recognized for the first time as having engaged in deviant acts. Such actions may be associated with arrest and possible prosecution, activities which publicly label an individual's actions as deviant. The second stage, to be discussed in the last part of the chapter, consists of a consolidation of the deviant status and its consequences for relating with other persons and fitting into society as a deviant.

Distribution of Crime in Our Society

Our first question concerns the issue of who engages in criminal behavior. What are the demographic characteristics of people who commit crimes, and why are there different rates for various types of crime among different segments of the population? The answer to this question, in outline form, goes something like the following.

Almost all Americans, at least initially, define success in terms of a materialistic life-style associated with a regular income, a car, and other possessions. For some subgroups, legitimate paths to achieving these goals are blocked. Under some conditions this leads to the adoption of illegitimate means in attaining them. Further, some subgroups may abandon or radically modify these dominant values, and substitute others as a group solution to their life situation. Finally, these social conditions have certain effects on individuals that deserve attention at the individual level. As we saw in the last chapter, everyone needs to develop a sense of self, a feeling of who one is—a sense of identity. Individuals from these subgroups are faced with the problem of establishing an identity that can be supported. Life conditions are such that identities available to most

Americans may not be possible to achieve. But some identities that are favorably regarded among these various subgroups may be available. While they may be viewed as deviant by the dominant society, their favorable regard in one's own group leads to their adoption. This outline discussion will be expanded upon in the remainder of this section.

The American crime rate and anomie   The high rate for certain types of crimes and their concentration in disadvantaged groups have been explained in terms of a theory of *anomie* advanced by Robert Merton.[17] Anomie, or a state of normlessness, emerges at points in a society that lack a fit between the outcomes, or values, that persons are led to strive for, and the approved or legitimate means available for the achievement of these ends. In America, with its democratic ethos, everyone is expected to strive for success, which is defined largely in terms of the accumulation of money and the kind of materialistic life style that money can provide. Yet, for some people, access to the means for such an accumulation—the capital to start a business or the chance for a good education leading to a position that pays well—is largely blocked.

Members of disadvantaged groups living at or below the poverty level, faced with a variety of handicaps to the attainment of an education, and blocked from entry to any but the most dead-end jobs, have little chance of realizing the American dream of affluence. Under such conditions strain and pressure emerge to achieve this end by other means. In other historical periods and places the barriers have often been more stringent, the gap between the disadvantaged and the advantaged greater, and the level of poverty more grinding. In such times the barriers were seen as impassable. But if a barrier remains extremely difficult to cross, and yet seems passable, the strain should be even greater. Certain features of contemporary American culture and society make the barrier seem less impenetrable and thus heighten this strain. First, through mass advertising, particularly on television, people at all social levels are exposed to the vision of success. Second, American culture, with its strong egalitarian spirit, deemphasizes individual differences in intelligence, abilities, and learned skills. Thus, Americans cling to the belief that anyone can be successful if he works hard enough.

Under these conditions, it has been suggested, people are motivated either to adopt illegitimate means to success or to redefine the nature of success by creating a world with success goals that are attainable. Since such cultural innovations are apt to be new, different, and associated with the activities of those regarded as morally suspect by those in power, these forms of innovation often become defined through the legislative process as criminal behavior—if they are not already beyond the law.

Whether the person faced with the prospect of continued failure—the young adolescent male falling steadily behind in school, the young adult unable to find employment, the older worker facing again an indefinite period of unemploy-

[17] Merton, 1957.

Residential section of New York City's Harlem. (Photograph by Bruce Davidson, Magnum Photos, Inc.)

ment—resorts to illegitimate means to maintain an identity of adult competence will be influenced in part by the availability of illegitimate means.[18] If the person lives in an area where gambling, prostitution, and various forms of petty crime flourish, the opportunity to learn and participate in these activities is much greater than would be the case for someone living elsewhere.

Thus, persons from disadvantaged groups are more subject than average to both the motivation and the opportunity to adopt illegitimate means to achieve favorable identities. In fact, some of the favorable identities available appear to be subcultural creations that have arisen in response to failure, or anticipated failure, in the competitive activities in school and business that characterize the dominant culture. The adolescent with a reputation for toughness, the adult hustler, or "cat," the identity of being "cool," all appear to have emerged in part as attempts to construct favorable identities on the part of those blocked from identities associated with the accumulation of wealth. On the other hand, middle-class people have opportunities to acquire wealth in illegitimate ways that are not available to disadvantaged groups. Thus, such crimes as bribery, illegal payoffs and kickbacks, and embezzlement are much more common among middle-class groups.

[18] Cloward, 1959.

Denial of dominant values and the emergence of subgroup values Albert Cohen has emphasized the group nature of these identities in a theory designed to account for the emergence of subcultures in general and that of the lower-class gang delinquent in particular.[19] He suggests that many lower-class males suffer status anxiety as a result of repeated failures to meet the middle-class standards of the school and the community. The result is the emergence of new values through a process of social facilitation where the tentative behavior of each in turn provides support for a movement away from conventional middle-class values, or ideas of what constitutes desirable behavior. Cohen's analysis of this process, emphasizing the importance of support from others with the same problem in aiding the move from the old norms and values to new ones, not only is consistent with our discussion of conformity in Chapter 11, but applies particularly to the present formulation in terms of identity, because these facets of the self are so dependent on the perceptions and evaluations of one's peers.

In his analysis of the emergence of delinquent subcultures, Cohen emphasized that the values that emerged as part of these subcultures were just the opposite of middle-class values. The nonutilitarian, negativistic activities characterized by short-run hedonism are in sharp contrast to the emphasis on the sanctity of property, on working toward long-term goals, and on conformity to rules. This turning upside-down of middle-class values not only allows for the expression of aggression toward the source of their frustration—middle-class values that they are unable to achieve—but also serves to deny the legitimacy of these values.

While studies of the values of gang delinquents do not provide unqualified support for the idea that they have values opposite to those of the middle-class,[20] an examination of various other deviant subcultures suggests that they do deny some middle-class values. The rejection of the "working stiff" found on the part of many professional and semiprofessional criminals, the emphasis on getting by on one's wits through successfully manipulating others that is a part of the role of the hustler, or cat, and the idealization of the role of the pimp in the ghetto, all reflect this element.[21]

Deviance and identity Few favorable identities are available for the economically deprived, particularly for males. Those identities available are precarious, subject to frequent attack, and difficult to defend. A number of important and positively valued identities for a male in American society depend on his occupation. How a male appears to see himself and how he is able to present himself as a husband, as a father, as head of a household, and as a valued person in the community, hinge on whether he can get and keep a job that provides sufficient income as well as a sense of dignity and respect from others.

Given the chronic situation of high unemployment, as well as underemployment in menial and marginal jobs, males from disadvantaged groups find that

[19] Cohen, 1955.
[20] Short and Strodtbeck, 1965.
[21] Finestone, 1957.

Homeless boys in New York City in the early 1900s. (Photograph by Jacob A. Riis, the Jacob A. Riis Collection, Museum of the City of New York)

these related identities are difficult to achieve and maintain. The fact that employment opportunities are often better for the female in these groups (even though low paid), creates an added strain and threat, because the male is placed in a dependent and subordinate position.

The male role is marginal in many ghetto families.[22] A male child in such a family has a less useful role in the household economy than his sisters, who are generally expected to help their frequently overburdened mothers with household chores and the care of younger children. As an adolescent he is more frequently a source of trouble to the family because of his activities on the street, which may lead to an intrusion in their lives of police and social agency personnel. As an adult he frequently is unable to perform the major male function of breadwinner because of unemployment. Unemployment rates among teenagers or young adults are often three times as high as rates for more experienced workers. So this major route to establishing identity and independence is often blocked at a time when it is needed most.

These characteristics of the male identity in the ghetto often lead to behav-

[22] Schultz, 1969.

iors that result in arrest and public labeling as a criminal. Gambling, pimping, and other forms of the hustle are forms of petty crimes; and the emphasis on machismo and the somewhat precarious nature of male identities contribute to the high potential for assault and homicide.

Defensive identities A variety of identities may develop in response to the precarious situation faced by the young male in disadvantaged areas. These include the young man with a reputation for toughness—emphasizing machismo—as well as the pimp, the hustler, and the cat. We will refer back to machismo in the next section, but here will describe the role of the cat. This identity mirrors certain elements in the dominant culture. The emphasis on making life a gracious work of art reflects a leisure-class theme. This, along with elements that are the antithesis of the values of the dominant culture, is evident in Finestone's description of a composite picture of this identity as presented by the black drug user in the Chicago ghetto.

> In contrast with the "square," the cat gets by without working. Instead he keeps himself in "bread" by a set of ingenious variations on "begging, borrowing, or steal-

Machismo as an element in identity.

ing." . . . One of the legendary heroes of the cat is the man who is such a skillful con-man that he can sell "State Street" to his victim. Concretely, the cat is a petty thief, pick-pocket, or pool shark, or is engaged in a variety of other illegal activities of the "conning" variety . . .

The main purpose of life for the cat is to experience the "kick." . . . A "kick" is any act tabooed by "squares" that heightens and intensifies the present moment of experience and differentiates it as much as possible from the humdrum routine of daily life. Sex in any of its conventional expressions is not a "kick" since this would not serve to distinguish the cat from the "square," but orgies of sex behavior and a dabbling in the various perversions and byways of sex pass muster as "kicks." Some "cats" are on an alcohol "kick," others on a marijuana "kick," and others on a heroin "kick" . . .

In addition to his "kick" the cat sets great store on the enjoyment of music and on proper dress. . . . The cat places a great deal of emphasis upon clothing and exercises his sartorial talents upon a skeletal base of suit, sport shirt, and hat. The suit itself must be conservative in color. Gaiety is introduced through the selection of the sport shirt and the various accessories, all so chosen and harmonized as to reveal an exquisite sense of taste. . . . He demonstrates his ability to "play it cool" in his unruffled manner of dealing with outsiders such as the police, and in the self-assur-ance with which he confronts emergencies in the society of "cats." . . .

It can be seen now why heroin use should make such a powerful appeal to the cat. It was the ultimate "kick." No substance was more profoundly tabooed by conventional middle-class society. Regular heroin use provides a sense of maximal social differentiation from the "square." The cat was at least engaged, he felt, in an activity completely beyond the comprehension of the "square." No other "kick" offered such an instantaneous intensification of the immediate moment of experience and set it apart from everyday experience in such spectacular fashion. Any words used by the cat to apply to the "kick," the experience of "being high," he applied to heroin in the superlative. It was the "greatest kick of them all."[23]

An additional source of some of the elements in the life style of the cat and his corresponding identity are the grim realities of life in the ghetto. The Machi-avellian orientation (see Chapter 8) implicit in the hustle with its emphasis on the use of lying and deception to manipulate others, the pervasive suspiciousness and wariness, reflect the basic facts of inadequate resources and the resultant competition and conflict for what little there is. The emphasis on luck and the popularity of gambling reflect both the hopelessness and the hope of those who have little control over life or fortune.

Initial Deviant Acts

Our second question asked how we could account for a specific criminal act. John Lofland has suggested that individual deviant acts can be explained in terms of a convergence of a whole set of factors, which include the role of other

[23] Reprinted by permission from H. Finestone. Cat kicks and color. *Social Problems,* 1957, 5, 3–13.

persons and the creation of a threat, the shaping of defensive deviant acts by certain psychological processes, such as encapsulation, the facilitating role of places and hardware, and the "subjective availability" of a deviant act. [24] For the most part, deviant acts that are defenses against threatening situations are discussed. But Lofland also calls attention to a different kind of deviant act—the adventurous deviant act, involving challenge, excitement, or pleasant fearfulness. Each of these factors are discussed below.

Other people and threat   Most homicides and assaults involve persons who are at least slightly acquainted, and frequently the bonds are much closer than that. The closer the bond, the more intensely a threat to one's identity from that individual is felt. It is not surprising that a high proportion of victims of homicide are relatives, friends, spouses, and lovers of the perpetrator. Many homicides are accidental outcomes of attempts to settle disputes by resort to physical violence. Such disputes frequently involve both physical and psychological threats. The latter in particular threaten identity. These threats may range from an especially galling remark, such as a slight on one's manhood, to an act of infidelity or rejection on the part of a spouse or lover. Often the situation is complicated by the escalation of disputes, where each party feels the obligation to retaliate in kind, and where any backing down amounts to losing the encounter and accepting humiliation.

Lack of ties between individuals may also be an aggravating cause. People who are strangers may also invite attack if they fall in the category of outsiders— members of another racial or ethnic group, or those whose characteristics, behavior, or background invite justification for attack because they "deserve" it. People can also contribute to victimization by making it easy to commit a crime against them. Obvious examples are those who leave their cars unlocked with the keys in the ignition. Less obvious are current merchandising practices that not only make products extremely attractive and tempting, but which increase the opportunity to steal by using self-service facilities instead of salespeople.

The invitation may be more direct, as to participate jointly in crime with one's companions. Many individuals commit their first criminal act as a member of a youth gang or other such group. Other people provide the occasion, suggest how the act is to be done, what to expect, and decide such matters as whether the act is to involve drug use, burglary, larceny, or financial fraud. Others are also a principal source of the beliefs and rationalizations that make a criminal act subjectively available in a given situation. A person not only must have the knowledge and skills involved in the commission of the act, but it must become subjectively available, the actors must be aware that it will solve their problems, and it must be compatible with their attitudes, future life plans, and, in particular, conception of themselves.

[24] Lofland, 1969.

Defensive deviant acts   John Lofland, in an attempt to account for the occurrence of an initial act of deviance—an assault, a homicide, a mugging, a check forgery—suggests that such acts can be classified as either defensive deviant acts or adventurous ones.[25] They are a response to some physical or psychological threat or a searching for the pleasantly fearful in an escape from boredom. We will discuss defensive acts here and adventurous ones later.

Studies of victim-precipitated crimes suggest that the victims could frequently just as easily have been the perpetrators, since it was they who initiated the act by threatening the persons accused of the offense. Like the gunslinger of the old West, the killer happened to be the fastest or perhaps the luckiest. Members of disadvantaged groups, much more frequently than middle- and upper-class people, encounter considerably more physical and psychological threats. With respect to physical threats, a study of violent crimes—homicide, aggravated assault, and rape—covering seventeen cities reports that two-thirds of the victims of homicide and aggravated assault and three-fifths of the victims of rape were black.[26] In one study of blacks arrested for carrying concealed weapons, 70 percent gave as their reason for carrying a weapon their expectation that they would be attacked by someone in their environment.[27]

Lofland suggested that a condition of threat often gives rise to a mental state which he calls *encapsulation*.[28] By this he means that there is an increasing focus on a narrow range of alternative actions and perceptions. The focus arises as a kind of fixation on a threat which evokes considerable anxiety. This emotional state narrows down the possible alternatives and intensifies the present moment at the expense of the future. The pressure to take some impulsive, short-term, violent act that removes the threat becomes unbearable. The explosive violence, the resort to the quick and easy as a solution, can be understood in terms of attempts to protect what little a person has of favorable images of the self. The man who shoots another who has challenged his manhood is understandable if his identity as a man is the only identity that he has left.

Such acts are frequently criminal or deviant. People often describe their feelings at the time of encapsulation in retrospect in such terms as, "I went nuts," "I lost my head, I didn't think," "I was desperate." Two conditions appear to encourage this psychological state. One is the lack of opportunity to learn ways of coping with life's emergencies, along with limited access to help in dealing with such situations. To be young, to be uneducated, to be a recent migrant to a city and unaware of community resources that are available to those in trouble, can all increase the chances of encapsulation. The other condition, also related to position in the social structure and to a heightened tendency toward encapsulation, is the absence of close ties with others who can suggest more adequate long-range solutions to the immediate threat, or who can at least slow the process by urging the person to stop and think.

[25] Lofland, 1969.
[26] *The Report of the National Commission on the Causes and Prevention of Violence,* 1969.
[27] Schultz, 1962.
[28] Lofland, 1969.

Perhaps not so readily recognized is that other types of crimes, more common among middle-class whites than among disadvantaged groups, may also be a defensive response to threat. A study of check forgery indicated that the actor often became entangled in an increasingly compelling web of circumstances, leading to one forgery after another, in order to escape the consequences of the initial act.[29] It is especially important to note that these individuals are nearly always alone with their problem—they have no one with whom they can share it and no alternative action by which they could escape the consequences.

In a similar way, the initial act of embezzlement may be an attempt to safeguard a favored identity as a successful executive or a pillar of the community. Such people are not expected to engage in unsound speculations, keep a mistress, gamble excessively, or engage in behaviors that might lead to blackmail. Thus, they strive to avoid the ruinous consequences of exposure by engaging in a desperate, deviant act. That this is the case is borne out through studies of embezzlers.[30] In every instance it was found that the act of embezzlement was preceded by what was regarded as an unshareable problem, a financial problem which could not be relieved by turning to other people for help, and which had to be dealt with in a solitary, private way.

Places and hardware   The characteristics of places either facilitate or inhibit deviant acts, depending on how they affect the likelihood that an actor's behavior is under surveillence, and the possible imposition of sanctions. Just as most accidents occur at home, so do most crimes of violence. In part, this is the result of the amount of time spent at home by most people, but in part it is also because homes are private places. Because of this privacy, deviant acts are not only more frequent, but the kinds of behavior that lead to such acts are more apt to occur. People are much more apt to avoid arguments and physical violence in public, for example, and behavior that escalates into assault or homicide occurs far more often in the privacy of the home.

Recent years have seen an increasing awareness of how features of the urban environment contribute to crime. Poorly lighted streets and dark alleys provide havens for illegitimate activities. The designers of high-rise, low-rent housing developments have inadvertently contributed to the high rates of crime in such settings by providing many places where assaults, muggings, and rape can occur with relative impunity. Dark stairwells, long, dimly lit halls, and elevators are frequent locations of criminal acts.

By the term *hardware*, Lofland means the wide variety of material elements in people's environments which they either own or have access to as they carry out their daily activities. Their clothes, furniture, car, occupational and recreational equipment, weapons, and any ideological artifacts that they may have— badges, diplomas, certificates of competence—are included in this category.

[29] Lemert, 1953.
[30] Cressey, 1953.

While some crimes may require special hardware, most crimes are committed by using the things that most people already have. For example, a butcher knife may well be as effective as a switch blade. Some widely distributed forms of hardware and their concentration in certain subgroups contribute particularly to the high incidence of certain crimes in the United States. A prime example of this is the handgun, although the wide distribution of other types of guns is also implicated. In most modern countries the possession of firearms in general and handguns in particular is closely controlled. This is not true in the United States. Millions of families have ready access to guns.

While it is quite true that homicides involving other forms of hardware— knives or other cutting instruments, for instance—are frequent, guns much more frequently stand out as the cause of death because they are so deadly. Attacks involving firearms result in death far more often than do those involving knives. Unfortunately, the widespread ownership of guns and the practice of carrying them as well as other weapons coincides with the pattern of settling disputes by a resort to fighting, and these two tendencies account in good part for the distribution of homicides—most of which occur when interpersonal disputes get out of hand, as we described earlier. The two tendencies are not unrelated. Undoubtedly many cases of homicide would have been cases of assault had not some piece of lethal hardware been readily available.

While Lofland and others argue that homicide occurs because of the simple availability of a weapon during a violent dispute, our discussion of aggression in Chapter 4 suggested that weapons may serve as cues to elicit or heighten aggression in situations where persons are exposed to them, and thus increase the chances of a fatal outcome.

Subjective availability of a deviant act Both Howard Becker and John Lofland have noted processes that make certain deviant acts easier to perform.[31] Lofland has referred to such acts as being *subjectively available.* More specifically, he identifies these acts as those which the individual feels to be moral or morally neutral. Those defined as immoral, or of dubious morality, are not available.

Becker notes that the normal development of people in our society may be seen as a series of progressively increasing commitments to conventional norms and institutions. With these commitments, most people are able to control deviant impulses by thinking of the consequences that acting on them would have. A deviant action, such as indulging in narcotics, might interrupt one's career, shame one's family, and ruin one's reputation. Often these deviant acts are considered not only foolish and ruinous, but also immoral.

As Becker notes, however, not everyone has an entangling set of commitments to society. Individuals who do not have reputations to maintain or conventional jobs to keep are freer to follow their impulses. Even when people are sensitive to conventional codes of conduct, however, they may use "techniques of neutralization" to weaken the effect of these moral controls. Sykes and Matza

[31] Becker, 1963; Lofland, 1969.

note that delinquents often have strong impulses to be law-abiding, but manage to exempt certain deviant acts by building a subjective justification for them or by exempting them from the moral code.[32] For example, individuals may see themselves as in the grip of impersonal forces that compel them to commit a deviant act—they have no responsibility for it. An act may be excused as not hurting or harming anyone, as when gang fighting is considered a private quarrel that does not involve society. Or harming another person may be considered a form of retaliation. The victim may be regarded as "deserving" what he suffers from the deviant act. The moralists may be seen as hypocrites. Or personal loyalty may be placed above abstract morality.

Lofland provides other examples, using somewhat different terms. An act, which is acknowledged to be wrong, may be transferred from the deviant class to a neutral or even moral category. For example, embezzling may be viewed as temporary borrowing. Studies of embezzlers have noted that they usually view themselves as perfectly honest—a view that is only possible through some such device as this.[33] Lofland also calls attention to the widespread availability of moral platitudes, which can often be adapted to justify an initial deviant act. Deviant acts that do not hurt anyone are frequently condoned, and the idea that individuals cannot control all their behavior is widespread in many societies. One may be either led astray by evil friends or unbearably pressed by circumstances to commit a deviant act.

Adventurous deviant acts   People are attracted to situations of challenge, mild threat, and excitement, which lead to a state of pleasant fearfulness. Lofland has suggested that this seeking for challenge and excitement is a fundamental trait that human beings share with other species. Others have suggested that such situations are sought out to demonstrate coolness, poise, and stability under stress.[34]

In any case, deviant acts may be involved in the expression of this trait. In part, these acts may occur because a particular form of deviance is inherently exciting—such as gambling or the use of hallucinatory or stimulating drugs. In part, however, they may occur because engaging in them involves the person in a contest. Thus, some shoplifting, vandalism, and joy riding in stolen cars often appears motivated by the sheer fun and excitement of having committed a daring act. Also, although not criminal in themselves, the games involved in sexual conquest on the part of adults may be similarly motivated, and these occasionally result in rape or homicide. People whose lives are otherwise humdrum, dull, and monotonous may be particularly attracted to situations and activities of this sort, and this again throws light on the social distribution of crime. The young unemployed or underemployed, in a monotonous, menial job, may especially seek excitement.

[32] Sykes and Matza, 1957.
[33] Cressey, 1953.
[34] Goffman, 1969; Lyman and Scott, 1968.

Summary: The Initial Labeling Process

Crime rates vary markedly among different segments of the population. A partial explanation lies in *anomie,* a state of normlessness arising at points in a society where there is no fit between its values and the legitimate means of achieving these values. Those segments of a society where people are handicapped in achieving these values because of lack of employment and educational opportunities, lack of personal contacts or capital, are encouraged by their circumstances to turn to illegitimate means of achieving satisfying states, and thus have higher crime rates. This process is supported by the emergence of values and norms peculiar to these subgroups, or segments, which support various illegitimate means of achievement.

The conflict between the dominant society values and subgroup values means that personal identities are continually subject to challenge. Economically deprived males in particular are apt to have difficulty in establishing favorable identities. Under these circumstances, defensive styles are apt to develop. These may emphasize machismo, or they may take the role of the pimp, the hustler, or the cat. The styles of acting are often reactions to the precarious nature of existence in impoverished areas, and help to protect against recurrent threats to one's identity.

A second question asks how we can account for the occurrence of specific criminal acts. First, some interpersonal situations are provocative. Where bonds of affection or kinship are strong, strong emotions are often felt. Thus it is in such relationships that violence and assault often occur. Another kind of interpersonal provocation comes from the identification of some strangers as outsiders, as fair game, as targets for robbery or violence. People can also make it easy for others to commit crimes by leaving valuable property unattended. And companions can introduce individuals to an initial criminal act. Some deviant acts are defensive. They take place under a condition of high threat or danger. A mental state called encapsulation may make it difficult to focus on anything but the threat, leading to an impulsive, violent act. Various psychological processes may remove the moral inhibitions against performing a deviant act, thus facilitating its initial occurrence. Other deviant acts may result from a sense of adventure—mild threat, excitement, or pleasant fearfulness. Finally, places and hardware may contribute to a deviant act. Some places are difficult to defend or to observe, and thus encourage crime. The availability of dangerous or lethal hardware also makes crime easier to commit.

PERSISTENCE OF CRIMINAL BEHAVIOR

So far we have dealt with our first two questions, concerning the distribution of criminal behavior among the population, and the initiation of deviant acts. It remains to deal with our third question: Once deviant behaviors have been enacted by an individual, why do they persist? Why do so many convicted and imprisoned people, when released, return to a life of crime?

Studies of both adolescents and adults suggest that a great many people have engaged in behavior that could have led to their being convicted of a criminal offense or adjudged delinquent.[35] Yet they were never regarded by other people or by themselves as anything but normal, law-abiding persons, and they continued to function as such. Those people, however, who do get caught and who get processed by society's machinery for dealing with deviants are much more likely to persist in this behavior.

Consequences of Initial Deviant Labels

Persistence of deviant behavior becomes increasingly understandable when one realizes the *consequences* of having been defined as deviant—changes occur within individuals so defined, and in their relationships with others. (Sociologists refer to this process as *secondary deviation*.)[36] These effects, or processes, resulting from the initial label, branch out into the future along several lines:

1 The initial label becomes a *master status*—other people define such individuals—and come to see them—as different kinds of persons, occupying a morally inferior status (such as that of a *felon,* an *alcoholic,* an *addict*).[37]

2 Strong constraints are placed upon the individuals' opportunities—many paths of activity available to others are now denied to them (for example, many kinds of jobs, the right to hold political office, and even the opportunity to become a respectable citizen in good standing).

3 The individuals learn to accept and to cope with their new status and its associated activities. They learn to see themselves as stigmatized citizens, and from others like themselves they learn how to manage a life of crime.

These changes and processes account for the fact that many people, once publicly labeled as criminals, continue in their activities almost irrespective of society's official actions. *Our most enlightened and humane ways of dealing with offenders appear to be about as effective in maintaining criminal behavior as our most backward and punitive methods.* Labeling or social control theories of crime have emphasized that this is the case because society's reaction has consequences which make crime preferable to the alternatives available to people who have been labeled as criminals. Each of these processes is worth discussing in more detail.

Deviance as a master status   The terms *defendant, felon, criminal,* like other deviant labels, such as *addict, alcoholic, mental patient,* are *master statuses.* Not only does

[35] Porterfield, 1946; Wallerstein and Wyle, 1947.
[36] Lemert, 1967.
[37] Hughes, 1958; Becker, 1963.

categorization as a deviant imply the possession of certain characteristics that are consistent with this morally inferior status, but other people react to these individuals first in terms of this status, and only later, if at all, in terms of their other statuses. The master status dominates the total impression.

It is quite possible for a known thief to be a loving parent, a faithful spouse, an apparently respectable citizen—and a scrupulously honest partner in crime! Yet his master status as a thief leads others to expect the opposite. The primacy of master statuses can be illustrated by public reaction when someone thought *not* to be deviant—such as our above-mentioned thief—suddenly and dramatically enters this status. Other examples are the respectable business person suddenly accused of fraud, or, even worse, of indecent exposure; the popular young person sent to a mental hospital after an unsuccessful suicide attempt; or the quiet, well-mannered young person accused of shooting and wounding a number of passing motorists. This not only leads to the attribution of a new set of traits to these people, more consistent with their new status, but also to new assessments of their *past* and probable *future* behaviors. The individuals whose previous behavior was characterized as reserved and quiet are now viewed in retrospect as preoccupied, brooding, or secretive. Often the individuals' biographies are suitably revised or reinterpreted. Childhood illnesses, accidents, and injuries long forgotten suddenly acquire significance as possible determinants of some organic malfunctioning that has contributed to the current status. Minor misdeeds or peculiarities of behavior are reinterpreted as forerunners of later deviant development.

Predictions as to the persons' future behavior are also affected once they are assigned a deviant status. Deviants can never entirely outlive their status. Felons become ex-felons, addicts become ex-addicts and mental patients become ex-mental patients. Such designations serve as a reminder to all that these people may revert to their earlier, deviant condition. These features of a master status are a product of a general human tendency, noted in our discussion of person perception in Chapter 5, to perceive others in a global fashion and to perceive consistency in the behavior and attributes of others even when it does not exist.

In contemporary society this tendency is also enhanced by the activities of imputational specialists, whom we described earlier as persons specially trained to identify and to provide a rationale for the behavior of various types of individuals, particularly deviants. Psychologists, psychiatrists, sociologists, social workers, judges, probation officers, and other specialists provide a degree of scientific and legitimate credibility for categorizations of deviant people. Other nonspecialists contribute further to the new status: police, prison guards, employers, and even acquaintances, friends, and relatives. While fellow deviants may play a role in helping the newcomers to cope with their new identities, it is primarily society at large and its various functionaries of control who create the identities and bring about the transformation in the individuals' attitudes toward themselves and others, and in their relations with those others.

The pervasiveness of such categorization and its stereotypic character ensures that deviants are confronted with a high degree of consistency in the definitions that other people apply to them. Our earlier discussion of the processes underlying the maintenance and change of an individual's self-conception noted that one is frequently able to resist incongruent definitions of self by misperceiving how others see one, by challenging the credibility of others, or by avoiding or reducing one's attraction toward those with incongruent views of self. These devices become ineffective when one is faced with the same attributions no matter where one turns, and when they are received from highly credible sources or from close friends and relatives.

Attempts at self-presentation that deny deviant status are also difficult in a society where record keeping is widespread and where persons are frequently required to state their past history when applying for a job, for admission to a school, for public benefits, and so forth.

There are some exceptions to this overpowering effect of deviance as a master status, and they help further to explain the distribution of crime as well as conviction and punishment among different segments of society. Other powerful statuses, which only a small number of people have, may counteract the effect of initial labeling and in some instances overcome it. This is one of the reasons that white-collar criminals are often perceived in a more favorable light and dealt with in a much more lenient fashion. Juries have greater difficulty in convicting them and judges in sentencing them, because perceiving and treating them as criminals is so inconsistent with their other statuses. Further, to the degree that the individuals labeled as deviant have other favorably regarded statuses firmly supported by a number of significant other people, as is usually the case for white-collar criminals, they are more able to resist the impact of the labeling.

Frequently, middle- and upper-class persons are also spared many of the experiences that underscore the validity of their deviant status. They are less apt than members of a disadvantaged group to undergo the experience of such "degradation ceremonies"[38] as formal arrest procedures, long incarceration before and during trial, and the like, which serve to emphasize to themselves and to others their deviant status. Finally, they are less apt than the typical blue-collar criminal to experience lengthy imprisonment and to encounter subsequent barriers to returning to a normal life on discharge. Again, the poor pay more.

Opportunity constraints   Constraints on the deviant individual's behavior operate to produce the kinds of behavior consistent with the deviant identity imputed by other persons. Blocked or discouraged from conventional activities by employers' reluctance to hire people with a record of deviancy, or of school officials to admit them, the individuals are frequently forced into marginal occupations or, at best, types of work with rewards that are so low that they provide little competition for the attraction of illicit—but more rewarding—pursuits.

Having a conventional job is a major prop for other adult identities, such as those of spouse and parent. These, along with occupational identity and other

[38] Garfinkel, 1956.

conventional identities, tie persons into a network of conventional activities and relationships. The lack of them, however, leads to isolation or increasing association with others with similar backgrounds and problems, and heightens the possibility of encountering opportunities to participate in criminal activities.

It has been fashionable to explain recidivism in terms of the inadequacies of our prisons and other forms of rehabilitation. But it is becoming increasingly evident that *society's* reaction to the convicted offenders makes it very difficult for them to reestablish themselves in that society, and that this is a major force in explaining why, once caught and labeled as a criminal, many individuals persist in criminal pursuits for a significant portion of their young adult years. When imprisonment does occur, it contributes to secondary deviation as well. As total institutions, prisons, to a far greater degree than normal environments, surround their occupants with consistent definitions of their deviancy while at the same time providing them with the learning opportunities for coming to terms with this new status.

Learning the Deviant Role

The final step in the making of a confirmed deviant consists of integration into deviant subgroups who help their members to cope with the problems entailed in their new status.[39] Learning to cope, or at least to make do, with a deviant status involves learning how to deal with recurring problems associated with deviance, such as learning how to locate sources of drug supplies, or how to safely fence stolen articles, or how to handle the problems associated with occasional arrests. Also learned is how to justify one's life so as to maintain a certain self-respect, a positive view of self. Most deviant groups share a special view of the world and of their various role partners—victims, police, the public—as well as of those they view as their own kind. This view provides a justifying rationale.

Not only do persons differ in the degree to which they perceive that their futures depend on conforming to the law and other social rules, but they also differ in the degree to which they find available a variety of techniques which neutralize the impact of conventional rules and values on conduct. We have already encountered these in our discussion of the ways in which people can maintain favorable views of themselves as good and moral persons and yet behave incongruently by violating norms in which they believe. There we noted that delinquents often use a variety of devices called techniques of *neutralization*.[40] These include denial of responsibility, where one argues that one was forced by circumstances to commit the act, or some form of justification, such as denying or minimizing the harm done, or arguing that the victim deserved it, that others do worse things, or that the act is not wrong because it was done for some higher purpose, such as helping out a friend.

[39] Becker, 1963.
[40] Sykes and Matza, 1957.

While such definitions are widely used throughout our society to justify behavior contrary to moral mandates, they appear to be particularly available to groups with high crime rates. Members of disadvantaged groups can more readily claim with some justification that their behavior is beyond their control. They live in settings where other people around them are engaging in many criminal or deviant acts, and can readily see victims as having contributed to their own fate—he would have done it to me—or as being rightful targets of revenge: many blacks feel that the white store owners in ghetto areas have been "ripping them off" for years.

Summary: Persistence of Criminal Behavior

A third question was: Once deviant behaviors have been enacted by an individual, why do they persist? This outcome can often be explained in terms of the consequences of having performed such acts. The initial label becomes a master status for the individual. Possessing the label leads others to consider the individual as morally inferior, and they put this status first, above all others. Imputational specialists and others help to consolidate the individual's assignment to the category of felon, addict, or whatever, and thus help to extend the status into the future. Only in a small percentage of cases do individuals have some other powerful status which helps to counteract the effects of initial labeling, and which biases authorities toward favorable treatment (for example, as with white-collar criminals).

Once individuals have acquired a deviant master status, their opportunities become severely limited. Most employers will not hire them, they may not be admitted to schools, and they will not even be accepted as citizens in good standing. Blocked from establishing an adequate identity, they may turn to others who share their flawed identity, and learn from them ways of coping with their problems. These others help to provide solutions that are often outside the law. They also help to develop justifications for their identity as deviants, and techniques of neutralizing the harsh judgments of society.

GLOSSARY

achievement motivation The degree to which an individual sets high standards, strives to achieve them, and responds with feeling to failures or successes in such efforts.

action instructions Information given to the recipient of a fear-arousing communication about ways of coping with the danger.

actor (See *role player.*)

adventurous deviant act An act violating social norms which is performed because of a challenge, mild threat, excitement, or pleasant fearfulness.

advocating a contrary position A way of changing attitudes; individuals are induced to advocate positions contrary to those in which they believe, which often leads them to move toward the position advocated.

affect display A category of movement in which feelings or emotions are conveyed by facial expressions.

affect structure The pattern of attraction and repulsion of a group of individuals to one another. (See *sociometry.*)

affectional system A set of patterned behaviors displaying liking between two organisms.

affective congruency A state of consistency among actors' feelings about elements of their self-concept, their related behavior, and the feelings toward these system components held by other persons.

aggression Action which is intended to harm or injure someone either physically or mentally.

alienation A psychological condition in which individuals feel unable to influence or predict future outcomes, have doubts concerning the effectiveness of socially approved means to goal achievement, of the validity of widely held values, and experience a lack of intrinsic satisfaction in daily activities.

altercasting The process by which another person (an alter) is placed in an identity or a role that requires him or her to behave in a manner advantageous to the manipulator.

anomie A condition of society in which the use of normatively approved means does not result in obtaining culturally valued goals for all or a portion of the population, giving rise to pressures toward norm violation and social change.

anxiety An internal state of apprehension or anticipation of punishment.

authoritarian personality A

pattern of traits with an important relation to prejudice. Individuals with such a personality have unrecognized hostility toward authority figures and strong repressive measures for controlling their own impulses, are rigid in interactions with others, and emphasize power, status, and dominance in relating to other persons.

autokinetic effect The phenomenon that a stationary point of light shown briefly and repeatedly in a dark room will appear to move.

background expectations Those aspects of interactions that are taken for granted by everyone, and are so well accepted that their violation often produces incredulity and bewilderment.

bargaining In exchange theory, a process in which each of two or more persons attempts to negotiate a definition of the situation and of the resultant relationship that will maximize the outcomes for all involved.

behavior modification The form of psychotherapy that makes use of behavioristic learning principles.

behaviorism An approach to psychology emphasizing the observation and manipulation of overt behavior under laboratory conditions and the restriction of concepts and theory to what can be inferred from such procedures.

belief component One of the two parts of an attitude, consisting of the content of the attitude, typically expressed in verbal statements. (See *evaluative component*.)

boomerang effect A change of attitude by the recipient of a persuasive communication in a direction opposite to that intended by the communicator.

brainstorming A process in which group members are encouraged to list all the ideas which come to mind, even the most ridiculous, and to avoid evaluating their quality.

career The sequence of movements which persons normally make from one position to another as in an occupation or any other way of life, including becoming a deviant.

career contingencies Those factors on which sequential movement from one position to another depend.

cat An identity which recognizes some elements in the dominant culture, such as being affluent and living in style, especially in more deviant or extreme forms, but which involves achieving this without working. Instead, the cat lives by his wits outside the law. Central here is a lifestyle that emphasizes the "kicks" the cat gets from his exploits.

cathartic effect A supposed reduction in the tendency of a viewer to perform aggressive behavior, brought about by a vicarious release of aggressions through viewing the aggressive behavior of other persons in fictional media or other events.

chronic personality characteristics Characteristics of an individual that are relatively enduring—present at different times and in different situations.

clique A subgroup whose members have many mutual choices and few choices of persons outside of the clique. Identified by means of sociometric measurement.

coalition formation Development of an alliance between two members of a three-person group.

coercive persuasion Use by communicators of complete control over respondents, with respect to both communication and sanctions, to bring about desired attitudes or behaviors.

coercive power The ability to punish another person.

cognitive controls Constraints on behavior resulting from an individual's acceptance of norms or standards as guides.

cognitive element A single unit of knowledge, a single belief, or an evaluation held by people about some object in their environment, about their behavior, or about themselves.

cognitive restructuring Restoring a state of congruency by misperceiving how other persons see one, by misinterpreting one's own behavior, or by restructuring the situation to change the evaluation of the relevant behavior.

cognitively complex Using many dimensions in evaluating people.

cohesiveness The net force acting on the members of a group to keep them in it. It is a product of (1) the attractiveness of the interaction with group members, (2) the inherent value to the individual of the group activities themselves, (3) the extent to which membership achieves other ends, and (4) the extent to which attractive outcomes are available in alternative relations outside the group.

commitment A personal decision to engage in a line of behavior.

commitment A process in which the actor adheres to normative behaviors because the disruptive consequences of not conforming would interfere with the achievement of socially approved ends or values.

commitment In interpersonal attraction, a tacit agreement to give priority to, and maintain an intimate relationship with, a particular individual.

common fate A situation in which individuals or groups will win or lose together; it encourages working together and often increases attraction or reduces prejudice.

communication structure The pattern of information access and transmission characterizing a set of positions in a group.

comparison level In exchange

theory, a plane of expectation or expected outcome which is influenced by an individual's past experiences in a relationship, past experiences in comparable relationships, judgment of what outcomes other persons similar to oneself are receiving, and perception of outcomes available in alternative relations.

competition In role expectations, a condition in which the actor cannot adequately honor conflicting expectations because of limitations of time or energy.

complementary needs A state in which each member of a dyad has a need which is expressed in behavior that is rewarding to the other member.

compromise process In forming attractions, a process in which a group moves toward an equilibrium in which each individual's position in the affect structure is the best that he or she can obtain in terms of reward-cost outcomes. The end result is that individuals form relationships with other persons whose worth or desirability matches their own.

concreteness-abstractness A pervasive quality on which individuals may be characterized. Concrete individuals make extreme distinctions, depend on authority and other extrapersonal sources, and have a low capacity to act "as if." Abstract persons behave in the opposite of these ways.

conflict In role expectations, a condition which arises when one expectation requires behavior of the actor which in some degree is incompatible with the behavior required by another expectation.

congruency (See *interpersonal congruency.*)

congruency by comparison A condition that occurs when the behavior or attributes of O suggest that P possesses a particular self-component.

congruency by implication A condition that occurs when P perceives that O sees him or her as possessing a particular characteristic corresponding to an aspect of his or her self-concept.

congruency by validation A condition that occurs when the behavior or other characteristics of O allow or call for behavior on the part of P that confirms a component of P's self.

conscience A system of norms that individuals apply to their own acts or contemplated acts to arrive at a judgment about whether they are right or wrong.

consensual validation A process by which individuals check their ideas or beliefs against those of other people in order to determine their validity. (See also *social reality.*)

contingencies of reinforcement In behaviorism, a relation among the following three elements: (1) the occasion on which a response occurs, (2) the response itself, and (3) the action of the environment on the organism after a response has been made.

coping with danger Overcoming a problem—one way of reacting to a fear-arousing communication (e.g., stopping smoking after being warned of the hazard of lung cancer).

cost In exchange theory, the undesirable consequences of carrying out an activity or taking an action.

counternorm effects Those aspects of the influence process which produce resistance to the influence attempt.

credibility The degree to which a communicator is believable. One's credibility is a function of one's personal characteristics, one's position or status, the nature of the communication, the context in which it is delivered, one's relation to the listener, and the listener's characteristics.

cue trait A quality of a stimulus person which is used as a basis for making further judgments about the person.

debt management In a social sense, the process by which individuals keep their social debts to a minimum. The social debt depends not only on the rewards and costs experienced by both donor and recipient but also on the degree to which the donor's acts are perceived by the recipient as voluntary, intentional, and without ulterior or sinister motives.

defensive attribution Placing blame for a serious and frightening accident on the victim, in order to avoid thinking that a similar accident might happen to oneself (e.g., a responsible person would not have such an accident).

defensive deviant act An act violating social norms which is a response to some physical or psychological threat.

defensive identity A conception of self and one's social roles created to withstand living under conditions of constant threat.

degradation ceremonies Formal procedures which emphasize and legitimize an individual's deviant status, such as arrest and imprisonment.

deintensification An attempt to underplay an emotion, as when a fearful person attempts to look less afraid.

demand characteristics The features of an experiment or of an experimenter's behavior that convey to the participant the desired outcome of the experiment.

dependency A determinant of social power by virtue of an individual's need for *resources* that another person possesses.

descriptiveness The degree to which an item yields information about the person as an individual.

desocialization The process of removing persons from the role categories which they have previously occupied.

differentiating item In the description of persons, a word, phrase, or statement about the abilities, interests, or beliefs of persons.

discriminative stimulus In behaviorism, a special feature of a situation which has been associated with making a particular response.

display rules Various movements by which an emotion differing from the real feelings of the individual is presented. There are four kinds: *deintensification, overintensification, masking,* and *neutralization.*

disposition The tendency of an individual to behave in a particular way across a wide variety of situations.

dispositional item In the description of persons, a word, phrase, or statement that labels how the person behaves in a broad class of situations.

dissonance An inconsistency between two or more elements. Two elements are in a dissonant relation if, considering these two alone, the opposite of one would follow from the other.

distributive justice A condition in which the outcomes of each individual—rewards minus costs—are directly proportional to the investments.

dyad A two-person group.

dyadic Of or pertaining to two persons.

egocentrism A form of personal involvement in which the other person is described in subjective, self-oriented terms representing the observer's personal frame of reference.

emotional inoculation Repeated exposure to an anxiety-arousing series of communications which leads to development of resistance to attitude change. (Same as *immunization.*)

encapsulation An emotional state in which possible alternatives are narrowed down perceptually, and in which the present situation is intensified at the expense of the future.

evaluative component One of the two parts of an attitude, which refers to the positive or negative character of an individual's orientation toward an aspect of his or her world. (See *belief component.*)

exchange theory A set of propositions relating interaction of persons to the level of satisfying outcomes they experience and specifying the consequences of these outcomes for maintenance or change of the interaction.

expectations An individual's anticipations that he or she and other people will behave in certain definite ways. In entertaining such expectations, the individual anticipates the nature of interaction in particular situations. Further, his or her expectations and those of the other party are generally shared.

expert power A form of potential influence over another person by virtue of the special knowledge that an individual possesses.

external sanction A form of social control in which the environment or other persons punish an individual for an act.

facework Behavior designed to repair a particular presentation of self.

forming alternative relations Establishing a satisfying relation with a person other than P, resulting in reduced dependency on P and a shift toward equalization of the relative social power of P and O.

group-decision process A procedure in which a group is exposed to a persuasive communication or presented with a problem, followed by discussion and a decision on whether to adopt the recommended behavior.

hierarchy of role obligations An arrangement of role obligations according to priorities. Those with the highest priority represent the strongest obligations, and should be enacted in preference to those lower in the hierarchy whenever there is a problem of enacting the role. (See *role obligations.*)

icon In interpersonal strategy, a linguistic device for confirming a preferred identity; in an attempt to impress others, the individual mentions names of important persons he has known or places that he has been or refers to significant experiences.

identification Choosing a person as a model for one's own behavior.

illustrators Movements which illustrate what is being communicated verbally.

immanent justice The idea that rule violations are followed by accidents or misfortunes willed by God or by some inanimate object.

implicit personality theory The system of terms that an individual uses in thinking about and describing other persons.

imputational specialists Professionals and others whose task is to seek out, classify, or diagnose persons as instances of a particular type of individual.

independence The freedom with which an individual may function in a group, derived from his or her position in the communication structure, from the actions of other members, from situational factors, and from the individual's own perceptions and cognitions of the situation.

individual-in-situation A unit of analysis in which a particular person's behavior under particular conditions is the focus of study.

induced-compliance paradigm An experimental setting in which a participant is caused to behave in a manner contrary to his attitude.

induction A form of parental discipline in which the parent gives explanations or reasons why he or she wants the child to change behavior, particularly in terms of the consequences of the child's behavior for the parent or other persons.

informational influence A process in which an individual accepts information from an outside source as evidence about reality. (Contrasted with *normative influence*.)

ingratiation tactics A set of behaviors for obtaining the support or approval of other persons. Such tactics include giving compliments, behaving in a pleasing manner, and agreeing with or conforming to the expressed opinions of the other person.

inoculation (See *emotional inoculation*.)

institutionalization A relationship that has become socially recognized and approved. Shared expectations have emerged recognizing the rightness or legitimacy of the relation. The rights and obligations are shared and enforced not only by the participants but by other parties as well.

interactional context A function of the characteristics of the situation and the actors which determines the role categories to be enacted, the role expectations to be applied, and the range of permissible behavior.

internal controls Norms or standards of conduct that one accepts as one's own and which place limits on the expression of various behaviors.

internal sanction A form of social control in which the individual experiences anxiety, guilt, or shame as a consequence of an act.

internalization The process by which individuals acquire norms or standards of conduct from other persons and make them their own.

interpersonal congruency A system state prevailing when the behaviors of P and O imply definitions of self consistent with relevant aspects of P's self concept.

interpersonal system A set of elements consisting of: (1) an aspect of S's self, (2) S's interpretation of his or her behavior relevant to that aspect,

and (3) his or her beliefs about how another person behaves and feels toward him or her with regard to that aspect.

intruding role A position that generates expectations which are superimposed upon the main role being enacted.

investments Characteristics of an individual or features of his or her past history or background that have become associated with the expectation of a certain level of outcomes. For example, seniority on a job becomes associated with the expectation of additional pay.

isolate In sociometry, a group member who is rarely chosen by other members.

isolation In *alienation*, a kind of detachment in which the individual assigns a low value to goals and beliefs that typically are highly valued in society.

justifiability Excusability; may be interpreted in terms of loci of cause. An action performed because of powerful external pressures is likely to be seen as justifiable.

justification The act of thinking of cognitive elements that reduce the uncomfortable dissonance felt after making a decision and engaging in a contrary behavior.

kinetic information Gestures, expressive movements, posture, observable tension or relaxation, and similar items which are used to make judgments about persons.

labeling theory An explanation of deviant behavior which emphasizes the reaction of other persons to the individual labeled deviant.

leader-follower relation Complementary behavior occurring between leaders and their followers.

legitimacy (in a relationship) The recognition by the parties to a relationship and by

outside parties that a relationship based on shared agreement concerning patterns of exchange has been developed. (See also *institutionalization*.)

legitimacy (of a role expectation) The recognition by actors that their role partners are justified in holding a particular expectation.

legitimacy of leadership A condition in which group members accept an individual as their leader and share this acceptance with each other.

legitimate power The ability to modify another person's behavior by virtue of the fact that both accept certain norms and values which prescribe behaving in a particular fashion.

locus of cause Where an act originates. The locus of cause is viewed as internal if the act seems to originate in the actor and as external if it seems to originate in compelling circumstances.

Machiavellianism The degree to which an individual is motivated to manipulate and does manipulate other persons to gain his or her own ends. A personality test for measuring this trait is called the Mach V.

masking Giving the appearance of experiencing a certain feeling in order to conceal one's true feelings.

master status A classification which dominates the evaluation of a person. Each individual has many statuses, but master statuses (e.g., status as a criminal or a mental patient) have a compelling effect on how one is evaluated.

mixed-motive situation A gamelike situation in which both cooperation and competition are part of the process of negotiation.

model The concepts used to describe a process and an explication of the way in which the process works. A person, fictional or real, whose actions are imitated.

modeling Learning to perform the behavior of a person whom one has observed.

moral entrepreneurs Individuals who take it upon themselves to fight against a particular condition, or form of behavior, that they perceive as being a threat to society's values. They are instrumental in creating new classes of deviant persons.

mutual need gratification A form of complementarity in which each member of a dyad has an inner urge which is expressed in behavior that is rewarding to the other member.

need for nurturance An inner urge to give help and support to other persons.

need for succorance An inner urge to receive emotional support and help from other persons.

negative reference group A group used by an individual as a standard to deviate from.

negative referent power A condition where an individual is influenced to behave in a manner opposite to that of the power figure.

negative reinforcement The reinforcement of a response that successfully avoids an aversive or punishing stimulus.

negative sanctions Actions by other persons that negatively reinforce or punish an individual.

neutralization One of the rules for displaying emotion, in which an agitated person tries to appear unperturbed.

neutralization, techniques of Elaboration of various ideas, beliefs, and feelings to deny responsibility for one's actions, or to defend or to justify them.

norm of altruism The widely shared idea that a person in need is entitled to receive help. (Compare *norm of social responsibility*.)

norm of fairness or justice The idea that in a social exchange where each party receives something from the other, the amount received by each party should be in accord with his contribution.

norm of reciprocity The idea that when an individual does a favor for another person, the other person is obligated to do something in return.

norm of social responsibility The generally accepted idea that an individual should help other persons in need. (Compare *norm of altruism*.)

norm-sending processes The operations by which norms are communicated and enforced.

normal-smith A type of individual who sees good in everyone and believes that all persons are capable of change. The term comes from the function of the normal-smith in eliminating deviant behavior.

normative influence A process in which an individual conforms to the expectation of another person or a group because of a desire to maintain the relationship. (Contrasted with *informational influence*.)

normative judgments Judgments shared by a group which are believed by members of the group to be appropriate or expected.

opportunity constraints The blocking of career and other paths ordinarily open to everyone but denied to deviant individuals.

orientation (toward role obligations) An actor's preferred attitude toward certain expectations, particularly when faced with role strain. Three possible orientations are: (1) a moral orientation, which favors doing the legitimate thing, (2) an expedient orientation, which favors doing what will be rewarded and not punished, and (3) a moral-expedient orientation, a compromise attitude which takes both morality and expediency into account.

other-oriented In personal involvement, seeing the other person as an entity separate from the self.

outcome In exchange theory, the net effect of carrying out an activity, expressed in terms of rewards less costs.

overintensification A display rule, involving the expression of more emotion than one feels.

paradigm A particular method of research based upon a specific set of concepts.

parallel model explanation An attempt by Leventhal to explain the persuasive effects of communications which arouse fear. The model proposes two parallel and independent reactions: (1) to control the fears aroused by the threat and (2) to cope with the danger. The two reactions have different consequences for attitude change.

partial withdrawal Activity reducing O's dependence on P and resulting in a shift toward equalization of the relative social power of P and O.

particularistic orientation The tendency to behave toward other persons in terms of their unique characteristics or their special relationship to oneself rather than in terms of some abstract category (e.g., honesty or morality). (See also *universalistic orientation*.)

personal involvement The way in which observers bring themselves into a description of another person.

personal stereotype The attributes an individual personally believes should be assigned to a category of persons.

personality The set of attributes which represent an individual's nature and characteristic behavior.

physical reality That which is believed to be true based on the direct evidence of one's senses. (Contrasted with *social reality*.)

position A form of *role category* designating a class of persons in a social system.

positive sanctions Actions by other persons that gratify or reinforce an individual's behavior.

power assertion A form of parental discipline in which the parent, by virtue of his or her power over the child, punishes the child either physically or by deprivation.

preapology A preface to remarks, designed to prevent other persons from questioning one's expertise or accuracy.

primary group Any small, intimate group in which members are highly dependent on each other for the satisfaction of their emotional needs (e.g., nuclear family, friendship groups, small groups dealing with enduring stresses and problems).

principle of equity The idea that the more one puts into an activity, as compared with the input of another person, the more one should get in return.

prisoner's dilemma A game situation in which each party has a cooperative choice or a competitive choice but in which the outcome is dependent on the choice made by the other party. The competitive choice will yield either the best outcome or the worst outcome, depending on the other party's choice.

private stereotype (See *personal stereotype.*)

public commitment In coercive persuasion settings, the confession of wrong thinking and profession of "proper" attitudes.

public stereotype The adjectives an individual thinks would be attributed to a person category by the general public.

radical behaviorism An extreme form of behaviorism, identified with B. F. Skinner, in which all learned behavior change is accounted for in terms of contingencies of reinforcement.

reciprocal In person perception, seeing a mutual, two-way relationship between oneself and another person.

reference group A group that the individual takes as a standard for self-evaluation and attitude formation.

referent power The influence which one has over another person who uses one as a model for identification. Often the prolonged use of reward power transforms it into referent power. (See also *reward power.*)

reinforcement In radical behaviorism, any action of the environment that changes the response (changes the probability that it will occur again).

resource In social power, a property or conditional state of an individual—a possession, an attribute of appearance or personality, a position held, or a certain way of behaving—which enables him or her to modify the rewards and costs experienced by another person.

response evocation In congruency theory, behaving so as to evoke congruent responses from other persons.

responsibility The amount of personal volition involved in a particular act. When the cause of an act is seen as external, the individual is seen as having minimal responsibility for it. When the cause of the act is seen as internal, the actor is seen as having responsibility for the act.

reward In exchange theory, any activity by an individual that contributes to the gratification of another person's needs.

reward power The ability to provide rewards for another person.

risky shift The phenomenon that a group decision is generally less cautious than the average of the decisions of the individual members before the group discussion.

rites of passage The ceremonial recognition given to important status passages (movements from one role category to another).

role (See *social role.*)

role bargaining (Same as *role negotiation.*)

role behaviors The acts of a person in a role category that are relevant to expectations for that role.

role category A grouping of persons whose behavior is subject to similar expectations.

role demands (See *situational demands.*)

role differentiation The development and assumption by group members of specialized functions.

role expectations Anticipations that are associated with a role category. Actors in a role category are expected to behave in a certain way.

role identity The view that individuals have of themselves as actors in a particular position.

role learning Learning to behave, feel, and see the world in a manner similar to that of other persons who are in the same role category.

role negotiation The process by which an actor and his or her role partners work out to their mutual satisfaction how each will behave in particular encounters and situations, and decide on what the general character of their relationship will be. Usually this process is less explicit and more subtle and indirect than ordinary negotiation; the partners may be unaware that they are negotiating. (Also known as *role bargaining.*)

role obligations Behavior expected of role partners because of the positions they occupy in relation to each other. (See also *role rights,* which are the complement of role obligations.)

role partner An actor occupying a role category which specifies particular behaviors toward actors in related role categories.

role player The individual in a role category or position. (Also referred to as an *actor.*)

role rights Privileges expected of role partners because of the positions they occupy in relation to each other. (See also *role obligations,* which are the complement of role rights.)

role strain Difficulties in attempting to enact a role.

sanctions Rewards for conforming to social norms or punishments for not conforming.

secondary deviation The social processes that bring about changes in individuals and in their relationships with others as a consequence of their having initially been defined as deviant.

selective avoidance A process by which individuals refrain from exposing themselves to communications that are dissonant with their attitudes.

selective evaluation A process in which individuals maximize congruency or minimize incongruency by altering their estimation of self, behavior, or the other person in a positive or negative direction.

selective exposure The process by which individuals choose to notice communications that are consonant with their attitudes and choose not to notice communications that are dissonant with them.

selective interaction A process in which individuals choose to be involved with those persons who behave congruently toward them and avoid involvement with those who behave incongruently toward them.

self (See *self concept.*)

self-commitment Making a judgment or decision in a manner that makes one feel obligated to carry out the act.

self concept The set of cognitions and feelings that individuals have about themselves.

self-enhancement, need for The idea that individuals have an urge to behave so as to receive positive evaluations from others and to evaluate themselves positively.

self-estrangement In *alienation,* a lack of intrinsic satisfaction in one's activities.

self-fulfilling prophecy The idea that strong expectations concerning an individual's behavior will eventually lead him or her to fulfill those expectations by behaving in accord with them.

self-presentation Acting so as to guide and control the impressions that other persons form of oneself.

significant other A term for persons whose opinions are especially important to individuals, particularly with respect to their self-concept.

simple differentiating item In the description of persons, a level of descriptiveness that refers to the individuals described but does not provide much information about them as people. Simple differentiating items include appearance items, behavior items denoting specific acts but not implying a disposition or trait, global dispositions or categories, expressions of liking or disliking, and role category items.

situational demands The expectations imposed upon an actor by the nature of the circumstances. These include not only role expectations, but also any special features of the situation that generate expectations.

situational personality characteristics Traits of an individual which are temporary or which occur only under certain conditions (e.g., anxiety about failing at the time of taking a test). Often such characteristics are created experimentally to determine their effects on individuals in combination with other conditions.

social accommodation A normative process consisting of conforming behavior resulting from a desire to maintain positive relations with liked people.

social comparison The process of evaluating one's inputs and outcomes in relation to those obtained by other persons in order to see whether they are equitable.

social contract An unwritten pact which takes the form of a rule or norm on which both parties have agreed.

social-emotional leader An individual who helps to boost group morale and to release tension when things are difficult.

social motive A set of behaviors that have a common goal as their object.

social norm An expectation shared by group members which specifies behavior that is considered appropriate for a given situation.

social power A property of a relationship between two or more persons such that the power of person P over person O is a joint function of P's capacity for affecting the outcomes of person O relative to his or her own outcomes.

social reality Perception of the attitudes and opinions of other people as a major resource for checking opinions or beliefs. (Contrast with *physical reality.*)

social role A social role consists of a category of persons and the expectations for their behavior. (Also referred to as *role.*)

social stereotype (See *stereotyping.*)

social system A set of interlocking social roles (e.g., the roles in a family).

socialization A process of change occurring throughout the life career of an individual as a result of interactions with other persons.

sociometry A method of studying structures based on affection or attraction. The basic data collected consist of choices of the most preferred (and sometimes the least preferred) members of the group made by each individual member. The choices are then tallied and patterns discernable in them are identified.

state of congruency A condition in which the behaviors of

P and O imply a definition of self that is consistent with relevant aspects of P's self-concept.

state of egocentrism The assumption by a child that other persons view events in the same way that he or she does.

state of equity A condition in which the ratio of inputs and outcomes of individuals is equal to that of the persons with whom they compare themselves.

state of realism A condition in which children confuse objective and subjective reality (e.g., they think of their dreams as actually occurring).

status The worth of a person as estimated by a group or class of persons.

status congruence A condition in which all the status attributes of a person rank higher than, equal to, or lower than the corresponding attributes of another person. (See *status.*)

status conversion processes A series of changes that lead to status congruence. Individuals behave so that other persons will judge them similarly on the various dimensions of status. (See *status.*)

status envy Jealousy of a person who occupies a powerful and coveted position. Status envy has been proposed as one of the sources of identification with a role.

status passage Change from one role category to another during the course of an individual's life.

status structure The pattern formed by the statuses of positions in a group. (See *status.*)

status symbol An attribute which initially has no intrinsic value but which through regular association with a particular level of worth comes to be seen as indicative of that level.

stereotyping A sociocultural phenomenon in which people identify a category of persons, agree in attributing sets of traits or characteristics to the category of persons, and attribute the characteristics to any person belonging to the category.

stimulus or target person The individual who is the object of a persuasive attempt.

structural information Relatively unmodifiable elements, such as physiognomy and body build or type, which are used to make judgments about persons.

synanon A group session aimed at changing the attitudes and behavior of group members and characterized by extreme candor and honesty. Such sessions involve considerable attack and criticism, but also are conducted in a larger supportive context. Emphasis is placed on getting members to admit their faults and weaknesses. These sessions are usually held in Synanon houses, residences of an organization of former drug addicts who live together in a communal style.

tactics, interpersonal Strategies deliberately adopted to influence another person.

target act The deed (e.g., a confession, a purchase, a favor, an opinion change) which is to be performed by the recipient of an influence attempt.

target person The recipient of an influence attempt.

task leader An individual who supplies ideas and guides the group toward a solution.

trust An attitude reflected in behavior that would allow another person to take advantage of an individual.

type-category unit A unit of analysis in which one class of individuals in one class of situations is the focus of study.

undifferentiating item In the description of persons, the lowest level of descriptiveness; refers to an individual's material possessions or social setting.

universalistic orientation A tendency to behave toward other persons in terms of widely shared societal norms. (See also *particularistic orientation.*)

values Ideas about desirable states of affairs shared by members of a group or culture.

withdrawal of love A form of parental discipline in which the parent explicitly or implicitly implies dislike for the child because of a specific action performed by the child.

BIBLIOGRAPHY

Abelson, R. P. Psychological implication. In R. P. Abelson et al. (eds.), *Theories of cognitive consistency: A sourcebook.* Chicago: Rand McNally & Company, 1968. Pp. 112-139.

Adams, J. S. Inequity in social exchange. In L. Berkowitz (ed.), *Advances in experimental social psychology.* Vol. 2. New York: Academic Press, Inc., 1965. Pp. 267-299.

————, **and W. B. Rosenbaum.** The relationship of worker productivity to cognitive dissonance about age inequities. *Journal of Applied Psychology,* 1962, **46**, 161-164.

Aichorn, A. *Wayward youth.* New York: Meridian Books, 1955.

Alexander, F., and H. Staub. *The criminal, the judge, and the public: A psychological analysis.*

Rev. ed. Chicago: The Free Press of Glencoe, 1956.

Allen, V. L., and R. S. Crutchfield. Generalization of experimentally reinforced conformity. *Journal of Abnormal and Social Psychology,* 1963, **67**, 326-333.

Alston, W. P. Comments on Kohlberg's "From is to ought." In T. Mischel (ed.), *Cognitive development and epistomology.* New York: Academic Press, Inc., 1971. Pp. 269-284.

Altman, I., and W. W. Haythorn. Interpersonal exchange in isolation. *Sociometry,* 1965, **28**, 411-426.

Argyle, M. Non-verbal communication in human social interaction. In R. Hinde (ed.), *Non-verbal communication,* New York: Cambridge University Press, 1972.

Argyle, M., and J. Dean. Eye contact, distance, and affiliation. *Sociometry,* 1965, **28**, 289-304.

Argyle, M., and B. R. Little. Do personality traits apply to social behavior? *Journal for the Theory of Social Behavior,* 1972, **2**, 1-35.

————, **V. Salter, H. Nicholson, M. Williams, and P. Burgess.** The communication of inferior and superior attitudes by verbal and non-verbal signals. *British Journal of Social and Clinical Psychology,* 1970, **9**, 222-231.

Aronfreed, J. Punishment learning and internalization: Some parameters of reinforcement and cognition. Paper presented at the Biennial Meeting of the Society for Research in Child Development, Minneapolis, March, 1965.

————. *Conduct and conscience: The socialization of internalized control over behavior.* New York: Academic Press, Inc., 1968.

Aronson, E. Dissonance theory: Progress and problems. In Robert P. Abelson et al. (eds.), *Theories of cognitive consistency: A sourcebook.* Chicago: Rand McNally & Company, 1968. Pp. 5-27.

————. The theory of cognitive dissonance: A current perspective. In Leonard Berkowitz (ed.), *Advances in experimental social psychology.* Vol. 4. New York: Academic Press, Inc., 1969. Pp. 1-34.

————, and D. R. Mettee. Dishonest behavior as a function of differential levels of induced self-esteem. *Journal of Personality and Social Psychology,* 1968, 9, 121-127.

Asch, S. E. Studies of independence and conformity. A minority of one against a unanimous majority. *Psychological Monographs,* 1956, 70 (9). (Whole no. 416.)

Atkinson, J. W., and N. T. Feather. *A theory of achievement motivation.* New York: John Wiley & Sons, Inc., 1966.

————, and G. H. Litwin. Achievement motive and test anxiety conceived as motive to approach success and motive to avoid failure. *Journal of Abnormal Social Psychology,* 1960, 60, 52-63.

————, and P. O'Connor. Neglected factors in studies of achievement-oriented performance: Social approval as an incentive and performance decrement. In J. W. Atkinson and N. T. Feather (eds.), *A theory of achievement motivation.* New York: John Wiley & Sons, Inc., 1966.

Azrin, M. H., R. R. Hutchinson, and D. F. Hake. Extinction-induced aggression. *Journal of the Experimental Analysis of Behavior,* 1966, 9, 191-204.

Back, K. W. Influence through social communication. *Journal of Abnormal and Social Psychology,* 1951, 46, 9-23.

————, and K. E. Davis. Some personal and situational factors relevant to the consistency and prediction of conforming behavior. *Sociometry,* 1965, 28, 227-240.

Backman, C. W., and P. F. Secord. Liking, selective interaction, and misperception in congruent interpersonal relations. *Sociometry,* 1962, 25, 321-335.

————, and ————. The compromise process and the affect structure of groups. *Human Relations,* 1964, 17 (1), 19-22.

————, ————, and J. R. Peirce. Resistance to change in the self concept as a function of perceived consensus among significant others. *Sociometry,* 1963, 26, 102-111.

Bales, R. F., and P. E. Slater. Role differentiation in small decision-making groups. In T. Parsons and R. F. Bales (eds.), *Family, socialization and interaction process.* Chicago: The Free Press of Glencoe, 1955.

Bandura, A. Influence of models' reinforcement contingencies on the acquisition of imitative responses. *Journal of Personality and Social Psychology,* 1965, 1, 589-595.

————. Social learning theory of identificatory processes. In D. A. Goslin (ed.), *The handbook of socialization theory and research.* New York: Rand McNally & Company, 1969.

————. *Social learning theory.* New York: McCaleb-Seiler, 1971.

————, J. E. Grusec, and F. L. Menlove. Observational learning as a function of symbolization and incentive set. *Journal of Personality and Social Psychology,* 1967, 5, 16-23 (a).

————, ————, and ————. Some determinants of self-monitoring reinforcement systems. *Journal of Personality and Social Psychology,* 1967, 5, 449-455 (b).

————, and A. C. Huston. Identification as a process of incidental learning. *Journal of Abnormal and Social Psychology,* 1961, 63, 311-318.

————, and C. J. Kupers. Transmission of patterns of self-reinforcement through modeling. *Journal of Abnormal and Social Psychology,* 1964, 69, 1-9.

————, and W. Mischel. Modification and self-imposed delay of reward through exposure to live and symbolic models. *Journal of Personality and Social Psychology,* 1965, 2, 698-705.

————, D. Ross, and S. A. Ross. Vicarious reinforcement and imitative learning. *Journal of Abnormal Social Psychology,* 1963, 67, 601-607.

————, and R. H. Walters. *Social learning and personality development.* New York: Holt, Rinehart and Winston, Inc., 1963.

————, and C. Whalen. The influence of antecedent reinforcement and divergent modeling cues on patterns of self-reward. *Journal of Personality and Social Psychology,* 1966, 3, 373-382.

Bartos, O. J. Concession making in experimental negotiations. In J. Berger, M. Zelditch, and B. Anderson (eds.), *Sociological theories in progress.* Boston: Houghton Mifflin Company, 1965.

Bateson, N. Familiarization, group discussion, and risk taking. *Journal of Experimental Social Psychology,* 1966, 2, 119-129.

Bayton, J. A., L. B. McAlister, and J. Hamer. Race-class stereotypes. *Journal of Negro Education,* 1956, Winter, 75-78.

Bechtel, R. B., and H. M. Rosenfeld. Expectations of social acceptance and compatibility as related to status discrepancy and social motives. *Journal of Personality and Social Psychology,* 1966, 3, 344-349.

Becker, H. S. *Outsiders: Studies in the sociology of deviance.* New York: The Free Press, 1963.

————, B. Geer, E. Hughes, and A. L. Strauss. *Boys in White.* Chicago: The University of Chicago Press, 1961.

Bem, D. Self-perception theory. In L. Berkowitz (ed.), *Advances in experimental social psychology.* Vol. 6. New York: Academic Press, Inc., 1972. Pp. 2-62.

Benedict, R. Continuities and discontinuities in cultural conditioning. *Psychiatry,* 1938, **1**, 161-167.

Benoit-Smullyan, E. Status, status types and status interrelations. *American Sociological Review,* 1955, **9**, 151-161.

Berelson, B. R., P. F. Lazarsfeld, and W. N. McPhee. *Voting: A Study of opinion formation in a presidential campaign.* Chicago: The University of Chicago Press, 1954.

Berkowitz, L. Sharing leadership in small, decision-making groups. *Journal of Abnormal and Social Psychology,* 1953, **48**, 231-238.

――――. The frustration-aggression hypothesis revisited. In L. Berkowitz (ed.), *Roots of aggression.* New York: Atherton Press, Inc., 1969.

――――. The contagion of violence: An S-R mediational analysis of some effects of observed aggression. In W. J. Arnold and M. M. Page (eds.), *Nebraska Symposium on Motivation.* Lincoln, Neb.: University of Nebraska Press, 1970. Pp. 95-136.

――――, and D. R. Cottingham. The interest value and relevance of fear arousing communications. *Journal of Abnormal Social Psychology,* 1960, **60**, 37-43.

――――, and A. Le Page. Weapons as aggression-eliciting stimuli. *Journal of Personality and Social Psychology,* 1967, **7**, 202-207.

Berscheid, E., K. Dion, E. Walster, and G. W. Walster. Physical attractiveness and dating choice: A test of the matching hypothesis. *Journal of Experimental Social Psychology,* 1971, **7**, 173-189.

――――, and E. Walster. Physical attractiveness. In Leonard Berkowitz (ed.), *Advances in experimental social psychology.* Vol. 6. New York: Academic Press, Inc., 1972.

――――, and ――――. A little bit about love. In T. L. Huston (ed.), *Foundations of interpersonal attraction.* New York: Academic Press, Inc., 1974. Pp. 356-381.

Bettelheim, B. Individual and mass behavior in extreme situations. *Journal of Abnormal Social Psychology,* 1954, **38**, 417-452.

Birdwhistell, R. L. *Introduction to kinesics.* Louisville, Ky.: University of Louisville Press, Foreign Service Institute, 1952.

Blake, R. R., H. Helson, and J. S. Mouton. The generality of conformity behavior as a function of factual anchorage, difficulty of task, and amount of social pressure. *Journal of Personality,* 1956, **25**, 294-305.

――――, and J. S. Mouton. Conformity, resistance, and conversion. In I. A. Berg and B. M. Bass (eds.), *Conformity and deviation.* New York: Harper & Brothers, 1961. Pp. 1-37.

Blau, P. M. *The dynamics of bureaucracy.* Chicago: The University of Chicago Press, 1955.

――――. *Exchange and power in social life.* New York: John Wiley & Sons, Inc., 1964 (a).

――――. Justice in social exchange. *Sociological Inquiry,* 1964, **34**, 193-206 (b).

Bloch, H. A., and A. Niederhoffer. *The gang: A study in adolescent behavior.* New York: Philosophical Library, Inc., 1958.

Blumstein, P. W. *An experiment in identity bargaining.* Unpublished doctoral dissertation. Nashville, Tenn.: Vanderbilt University, 1970.

Brayfield, A. H., and W. H. Crockett. Employee attitudes and employee performance. *Psychological Bulletin,* 1955, **52**, 396-424.

Brecher, E. M., and Editors of Consumer Reports. *Licit and Illicit drugs: The Consumers Union Report on narcotics, stimulants, depressants, inhalants, hallucinogens and marijuana including caffeine, nicotine and alcohol.* Boston: Little, Brown and Company, Inc., 1973.

Brigante, T. R. Adolescent evaluations of rewarding, neutral, and punishing power figures. *Journal of Personality,* 1958, **26**, 435-450.

Bronfenbrenner, U. Early development in mammals: A cross species analysis. In G. Newton and S. Levine (eds.), *Early experience and behavior.* Springfield, Ill.: Charles C Thomas, 1968.

Brookover, W. B., et al. Self concept ability and school achievement. III. Third report on the continuing study of the relations of self concept and achievement. Educational Research Series 36, Cooperative Research Project 2831, February, 1967.

Brown, M., J. Jennings, and V. Vanik. The motive to avoid success: A further examination. *Journal of Research in Personality,* 1974, **8**, 172-176.

Brown, R. W. *Social psychology.* New York: The Free Press, 1965.

Broxton, J. A. A test of interpersonal attraction predictions derived from balance theory. *Journal of Abnormal and Social Psychology,* 1963, **66**, 394-397.

Bruner, J. S., and H. V. Perlmutter. Compatriot and foreigner: A study of impression formation in three countries. *Journal of Abnormal Social Psychology,* 1957, **55**, 253-260.

Bryan, J. H., and M. A. Test. Models and helping: Naturalistic studies in aiding behavior. *Journal of Personality and Social Psychology,* 1967, **6**, 400-407.

Buchanan, W. Stereotypes and tensions as revealed by the UNESCO international poll. *International Social Science Journal,* 1951, **3**, 515-528.

Burchard, W. W. Role conflicts of military chaplains. *American Sociological Review,* 1954, **19**, 528-535. Pp. 532, 534.

Burton, R. V. Generality of honesty reconsidered. *Psychological Review,* 1963, **70**, 481-499.

Byrne, D. *The attraction paradigm.* New York: Academic Press, Inc., 1971.

Campbell, D. T. Stereotypes and the perception of group differences. *American Psychologist*, 1967, **22**, 817–829.

Canon, L. Self-confidence and selective exposure to information. In L. Festinger (ed.), *Conflict, decision, and dissonance.* Stanford, Calif.: Stanford University Press, 1964. Pp. 83–96.

Carlsmith, J., B. E. Collins, and R. Helmreich. Studies in forced compliance: I. Attitude change produced by face-to-face role playing and anonymous essay writing. *Journal of Personality and Social Psychology*, 1966, **4**, 1–13.

Cartwright, D. The nature of group cohesiveness. In D. Cartwright and A. Zander (eds.), *Group dynamics: Research and theory.* 3d ed. New York: Harper & Row, Publishers, Incorporated, 1968.

Cavan, R. S. Self and role in adjustment during old age. In A. M. Rose (ed.), *Human behavior and social processes: An interactionist approach.* Boston: Houghton Mifflin Company, 1962. P. 80.

Chambliss, W. J. A sociological analysis of the law of vagrancy. *Social Problems*, 1964, **12**, 67–77.

Church, R. M. The varied effects of punishment on behavior. *Psychological Review*, 1963, **70**, 369–402.

Clark, J. W. A preliminary investigation of some unconscious assumptions affecting labor efficiency in eight supermarkets. Unpublished doctoral dissertation. Cambridge, Mass.: Harvard University, 1958.

Clarke, P., and J. James. The effects of situation, attitude intensity and personality on information-seeking. *Sociometry*, 1967, **30**, 235–245.

Cloward, R. Illegitimate means, anomie, and deviant behavior. *American Sociological Review*, 1959, **24**, 164–176.

Coch, L., and J. R. P. French, Jr. Overcoming resistance to change. In E. E. Maccoby, T. M. Newcomb, and E. L. Hartley (eds.), *Readings in social psychology.* 3d ed. New York: Holt, Rinehart and Winston, Inc., 1958. Pp. 233–250.

Cohen, A. K. *Delinquent boys, the culture of the gang.* Chicago: The Free Press of Glencoe, 1955.

Coleman, J. S., E. Q. Campbell, and C. J. Hobson, et al. *Equality of educational opportunity.* Washington, D. C.: U.S. Office of Education, 1966.

Collins, B. E. The effect of monetary inducements on the amount of attitude change produced by forced compliance. In A. C. Elms (ed.), *Role playing, reward, and attitude change.* New York: D. Van Nostrand Company, Inc., 1969. Pp. 209–223.

———, R. D. Ashmore, F. W. Hornbeck, and R. Whitney. Studies in forced compliance: XIII and XV. In search of a dissonance-producing forced compliance paradigm. *Representative Research in Social Psychology*, 1970, **1**, 11–23.

———, and R. H. Raven. Psychological aspects of structure in small groups: Interpersonal attraction, coalitions, communication and power. In G. Lindsey and R. Aronsen (eds.), *Handbook of social psychology.* Vol. 4. Reading, Mass.: Addison-Wesley Publishing Company, Inc., 1969. Pp. 102–204.

Committee on Government Operations, U.S. Senate, 84th Congress, 2d Session. Hearings on "Communist interrogation, indoctrination and exploitation of American military and civilian prisoners." June 19, 20, 26, and 27, 1956.

Cook, T. D. Competence, counterarguing, and attitude change. *Journal of Personality*, 1969, **37** (2), 342–358.

Cooley, C. H. *Human nature and the social order.* New York: Charles Scribner's Sons, 1902. Reprinted: Chicago: The Free Press of Glencoe, Inc., 1956.

Cooper, J., and S. Worchel. Role of undesired consequences in arousing cognitive dissonance. *Journal of Personality and Social Psychology*, 1970, **16**, 199–206.

Crandall, V. C., W. Katkovsky, and U. J. Crandall. Children's beliefs in their own control of reinforcements in intellectual-academic achievement situations. *Child Development*, 1965, **36**, 91–109.

Cressey, D. R. *Other people's money.* Glencoe, Ill.: The Free Press of Glencoe, Inc., 1953.

Crockett, H. J., Jr. The achievement motive and differential occupational mobility in the United States. *American Sociological Review*, 1962, **27**, 191–204.

Curry, T. J., and R. M. Emerson. Balance theory: A theory of interpersonal attraction? *Sociometry*, 1970, **33**, 216–238.

Dabbs, J. M. Self-esteem, communicator characteristics, and attitude change. *Journal of Abnormal and Social Psychology*, 1964, **69**, 173–181.

Darley, J. J., and B. Latane. Bystander intervention in emergencies: diffusion of responsibility. *Journal of Personality and Social Psychology*, 1968, **8**, 377–383.

Davis, A., and J. Dollard. *Children of bondage.* Washington, D.C.: American Council on Education, 1940.

Davis, K. Final note on a case of extreme isolation. *American Journal of Sociology*, 1947, **52**, 432–437.

Dennis, W., and P. Najarian. Infant development under environmental handicaps. *Psychological Monographs*, 1957, **71** (7). (Whole no. 436.)

Deutsch, M., Y. Epstein, D. Canavan, and P. Gumpert. Strategies of inducing cooperation: An empirical study. *Journal of Conflict Resolution*, 1967, **11**, 345–360.

———, and H. B. Gerard. A study of normative and informational influence upon individual judgment. *Journal of*

Abnormal and Social Psychology, 1955, **51**, 629–636.

———, and R. M. Krauss. The effect of threat upon interpersonal bargaining. *Journal of Abnormal and Social Psychology,* 1960, **61**, 181–189.

Dicks, H. V. German personality traits and Nazi ideology. *Human Relations,* 1950, **3**, 111–154.

Dion, K. K., and E. Berscheid. Physical attractiveness and peer perceptions among children. *Sociometry,* 1974, **37**, 1–12.

———, ———, and E. Walster. What is beautiful is good. *Journal of Personality and Social Psychology,* 1972, **24**, 285–290.

Dion, K. L., R. S. Baron, and N. Miller. Why do groups make riskier decisions than individuals? In L. Berkowitz (ed.), *Advances in experimental social psychology.* Vol. 5. New York: Academic Press, Inc., 1970. Pp. 306–377.

Dittes, J. E. Attractiveness of group as a function of self-esteem and acceptance by group. *Journal of Abnormal and Social Psychology,* 1959, **59**, 77–82.

———, and H. H. Kelley. Effects of different conditions of acceptance on conformity to group norms. *Journal of Abnormal Social Psychology,* 1956, **53**, 100–107.

Doherty, E. G., and P. F. Secord. Change of roommate and interpersonal congruency. *Representative Research in Social Psychology,* 1971, **2** (2), 70–75.

Dollard, J., L. W. Doob, N. E. Miller, Jr., O. H. Mowrer, and R. R. Sears. *Frustration and aggression.* New Haven, Conn.: Yale University Press, 1939.

Dornbusch, S. M. The military academy as an assimilating institution. *Social Forces,* 1955, **33**, 316–321.

Douvan, E. M. Social status and success strivings. *Journal of Abnormal Social Psychology,* 1956, **52**, 219–223.

Ekman, P., and W. V. Friesen. The repertoire of nonverbal behavior: Categories, origins, usage, and coding. *Semiotica,* 1969, **1**, 49–98.

Ellis, R. A., and T. C. Keedy, Jr. Three dimensions of status: A study of academic prestige. *Pacific Sociological Review,* 1960, **3**, 23–28.

Elms, A. C. Role playing, incentive, and dissonance. *Psychological Bulletin,* 1967, **68**, 132–148.

Emerson, R. M. Power-dependence relations. *American Sociological Review,* 1962, **27**, 31–41.

Epstein, R. Aggression toward outgroups as a function of authoritarianism and imitation of aggressive models. *Journal of Personality and Social Psychology,* 1966, **3**, 574–579.

Evan, W. M. Role strain and the norm of reciprocity in research organizations. *American Journal of Sociology,* 1962, **68**, 346–354.

———, and E. G. Levin. Status-set and role-set conflicts of the stockbroker: A problem in the sociology of law. *Social Forces,* 1966, **45**, 73–83.

Exline, R. V., D. Gray, and D. Schuette. Visual behavior in a dyad as affected by interview content and sex of respondent. *Journal of Personality and Social Psychology,* 1965, **1**, 201–209.

Exline, R. V., and L. C. Winters. Affective relations and mutual glances. In S. S. Tompkins and C. E. Izard (eds.), *Affect cognition and personality.* New York: Springer Publishing Co., Inc., 1965.

Fast, J. *Body language.* Philadelphia: M. Evans and Company, 1970. Distributed by Lippincott.

Feather, N. T. Valence of outcome and expectation of success in relation to task difficulty and perceived locus of control. *Journal of Personality and Social Psychology,* 1967, **7**, 372–386.

Feierabend, I. K., and R. L. Feierabend. Aggressive behaviors within politics,

1948–1962: A cross-national study. *Journal of Conflict Resolution,* 1966, **10**, 249–271.

Feld, S. C. Longitudinal study of the origins of achievement strivings. *Journal of Personality and Social Psychology,* 1967, **7**, 408–414.

Festinger, L. Laboratory experiments: The role of group belongingness. In J. G. Miller (ed.), *Experiments in social process.* New York: McGraw-Hill Book Company, 1950. Pp. 31–46.

———. A theory of social comparison processes. *Human Relations,* 1954, **7**, 117–140.

———. *A theory of cognitive dissonance.* Evanston, Ill.: Row, Peterson & Company, 1957.

———, and J. M. Carlsmith. Cognitive consequences of forced compliance. *Journal of Abnormal Social Psychology,* 1959, **58**, 203–210.

———, S. Schachter, and K. Back. *Social pressures in informal groups: A study of human factors in housing.* New York: Harper & Brothers, 1950.

Fiedler, F. E. A contingency model of leadership effectiveness. In L. Berkowitz (ed.), *Advances in experimental social psychology.* Vol. 1. New York: Academic Press, Inc., 1964. Pp. 149–190.

Finestone, H. Cat kicks and color. *Social Problems,* 1957, **5**, 3–13.

Flanders, J. P., and D. Thistlethwaite. Effects of familiarization and group discussion upon risk taking. *Journal of Personal and Social Psychology,* 1967, **4** (1), 91–97.

Foskett, J. M. Role conflict: The concept. Paper presented at a meeting of the Pacific Sociological Society, Spokane, Washington, April, 1960.

Freedman, J. L. Preference for dissonant information. *Journal of Personality and Social Psychology,* 1965, **2**, 287–289.

French, J. R. P., Jr., H. W. Morrison, and G. Levinger. Coercive power and forces affecting conformity. *Journal of Abnormal Social Psychology,* 1960, **61**, 93–101.

————, **and B. Raven.** The basis of social power. In D. Cartwright (ed.), *Studies in social power.* Ann Arbor, Mich.: The University of Michigan Press, 1959.

Freud, A. *The ego and mechanisms of defense.* New York: International Universities Press, Inc., 1946.

Frisch, D. M., and M. S. Greenberg. Reciprocity and intentionality in the giving of help. Paper presented at the American Psychological Association Convention, San Francisco, August, 1968.

Fromm, E. *Escape from freedom.* New York: Farrar & Rinehart, Inc., 1941.

Fuller, R. C., and R. R. Meyers. Some aspects of a theory of social problems. *American Sociological Review,* 1941, **6,** 24–32.

Garfinkel, H. Conditions of successful degradation ceremonies. *American Journal of Sociology,* 1956, **61,** 420–424.

————. *Studies in ethnomethodology.* Englewood Cliffs, N.J.: Prentice-Hall, Inc., 1967.

Geen, R. G., and L. Berkowitz. Some conditions facilitating the occurrence of aggression after the observation of violence. *Journal of Personality,* 1967, **35,** 666–667.

Gerard, H. B. Deviation, conformity, and commitment. In I. D. Steiner, and M. Fishbein (eds.), *Current studies in social psychology.* New York: Holt, Rinehart and Winston, Inc., 1965.

Getzels, J. W., and E. G. Guba. Role, conflict, and effectiveness. *American Sociological Review,* 1954, **19,** 164–175.

Gibb, C. A. Leadership. In G. Lindzey and E. Aronson (eds.), *The handbook of social psychology.* (2d ed.) Vol. 4. Reading, Mass.: Addison-Wesley Publishing Co., Inc., 1969. Pp. 205–282.

Gilbert, G. M. Stereotype persistence and change among college students. *Journal of Abnormal and Social Psychology,* 1951, **46,** 245–254.

Glass, D. C. Changes in liking as a means of reducing cognitive discrepancies between self-esteem and aggression. *Journal of Personality,* 1964, **32,** 531–549.

Goffman, E. On cooling the mark out: Some aspects of adaptation to failure. *Psychiatry,* 1952, **15,** 451–463.

————. The moral career of the mental patient. *Psychiatry,* 1959, **22,** 123–142.

————. *Encounters.* Indianapolis, Ind.: The Bobbs-Merrill Company, Inc., 1961.

————. *Where the action is.* London: Allen Lane The Penguin Press, 1969.

Goldfarb, W. The effects of early institutional care on adolescent personalities. *Journal of Experimental Education,* 1943, **12,** 106–129 (a).

————. Infant rearing and problem behavior. *American Journal of Orthopsychiatry,* 1943, **13,** 249–265 (b).

Goldstein, M. The relationship between coping and avoiding behavior and response to fear arousing propaganda. *Journal of Abnormal and Social Psychology,* 1959, **58,** 247–252.

Goode, W. J. Norm commitment and conformity to role-status obligations. *American Journal of Sociology,* 1960, **66,** 246–258.

Gouldner, A. W. The norm of reciprocity: A preliminary statement. *American Sociological Review,* 1960, **25,** 161–178.

Greenberg, M. S. A preliminary statement on a theory of indebtedness. Paper presented to Western Psychological Association, San Diego, March, 1968.

Greenwald, G. When does role playing produce attitude change? Toward an answer. *Journal of Personality and Social Psychology,* 1970, **16,** 214–219.

Grob, G. N. *The state and the mentally ill: A history of Worcester State Hospital in Massachusetts, 1830-1920.* Chapel Hill, N.C.: The University of North Carolina Press, 1966.

Gross, E., and G. P. Stone. Embarrassment and the analysis of role requirements. *American Journal of Sociology,* 1964, **79,** 1–15.

Gross, N., W. S. Mason, and A. W. McEachern. *Explorations in role analysis.* New York: John Wiley & Sons, Inc., 1958.

Gullahorn, J. T., and J. E. Gullahorn. Role conflict and its resolution. *Sociological Quarterly,* 1963, **4,** 32–48.

Hakmiller, K. Need for self-evaluation, perceived similarity and comparison choice. *Journal of Experimental Social Psychology,* 1966, **1,** Supplement 1 (September), 49–54.

Harlow, H. F., and M. K. Harlow. The affectional systems. In A. M. Schrier, H. F. Harlow, and T. Stollnitz (eds.), *Behavior of nonhuman primates.* Vol. 2. New York: Academic Press, Inc., 1965. Pp. 287–334.

————, ————. Learning to love. *American Scientist,* 1966, **54** (3), 244–272.

Harsanyi, J. C. Measurement of social power, opportunity costs, and the theory of two-person bargaining games. *Behavioral Science,* 1962, **7,** 67–80.

Hartley, E. L. *Problems in prejudice.* New York: King's Crown Press, 1946.

Hartshorne, H., and M. A. May. *Studies in the nature of character.* Vol. 1. *Studies in deceit.* New York: The Macmillan Company, 1928.

————, **and F. K. Shuttleworth.** *Studies in the nature of character.* Vol. 3. *Studies in the organization of character.* New York: The Macmillan Company, 1930.

Harvey, O. J., and Consalvi, C. Status and conformity to pressures in informal groups. *Journal of Abnormal Social Psychology,* 1960, **60,** 182–187.

————, **D. E. Hunt, and H. M. Schroder.** *Conceptual systems and personality organization.* New York: John Wiley & Sons, Inc., 1961.

————, **H. H. Kelley, and M. M. Shapiro.** Reactions to unfavorable evaluations of the self made by other persons.

Journal of Personality, 1957, **25**, 398-411.

———, and H. M. Schroder. Cognitive aspects of self and motivation. In O. J. Harvey (ed.), *Motivation and social interaction: Cognitive determinants.* New York: The Ronald Press Company, 1963. Pp. 95-133.

Hastorf, A. H., W. R. Kite, A. E. Gross, and L. J. Wolfe. The perception and evaluation of behavior change. *Sociometry,* 1965, **48**, 400-410.

Heider, F. Social perception and phenomenal causality. *Psychological Review,* 1944, **51**, 358-374.

———. *The psychology of interpersonal relations.* New York: John Wiley & Sons, Inc., 1958.

Heinicke, C., and R. F. Bales. Developmental trends in the structure of small groups. *Sociometry,* 1953, **16**, 35-36.

Hicks, D. J. Imitation and retention of film-mediated aggressive peer and adult models. *Journal of Personality and Social Psychology,* 1965, **2**, 97-100.

Higbee, K. L. Fifteen years of fear arousal: Research on threat appeals: 1953-1968. *Psychological Bulletin,* 1969, **72**, 426-444.

Hoe, B. H. Occupational satisfaction as a function of self-role congruency. Unpublished master's thesis. Reno, Nev.: University of Nevada, June, 1962.

Hoffman, M. L. Moral development. In P. H. Mussen (ed.), *Carmichael's manual of child psychology.* (3d ed.) Vol. 2. New York: John Wiley & Sons, Inc., 1970. Pp. 261-360.

———, and H. D. Saltzstein. Parent discipline and the child's moral development. *Journal of Personality and Social Psychology,* 1967, **5**, 45-57.

Hollander, E. P. Conformity, status, and idiosyncrasy credit. *Psychological Review,* 1958, **65**, 117-127.

Homans, G. C. *The human group.* New York: Harcourt, Brace and Company, Inc., 1950.

———. The cash posters: A study of a group of working girls. *American Sociological Review,* 1954, **19**, 724-733.

———. *Social behavior: Its elementary forms.* New York: Harcourt, Brace & World, Inc., 1961.

Hornstein, H. A., E. Fisch, and M. Holmes. Influence of a model's feeling about his behavior and his relevance as a comparison other on observers' helping behavior. *Journal of Personality and Social Psychology,* 1968, **10**, 222-227.

Hovland, C. I., I. L. Janis, and H. H. Kelley. *Communication and persuasion.* New Haven, Conn.: The Yale University Press, 1953.

Hughes, E. C. *Men and their work.* New York: The Free Press of Glencoe, 1958.

Huntington, J. The development of a professional self-image. In R. K. Merton, G. G. Reader, and P. Kendall (eds.), *The student-physician.* Cambridge, Mass.: Harvard University Press, 1957. Pp. 179-187.

Inkeles, A., and D. J. Levinson. The personal system and the sociocultural system in large-scale organizations. *Sociometry,* 1963, **26**, 217-229.

Iverson, M. A. Attraction toward flatterers of different statuses. *Journal of Social Psychology,* 1968, **74**, 181-187.

Izard, C. E. Personality similarity and friendship: A follow-up study. *Journal of Abnormal and Social Psychology,* 1963, **66**, 598-600.

Jackson, D. N., and S. Messick. Individual differences in social perception. *British Journal of Social and Clinical Psychology,* 1963, **2**, 1-10.

Jakubczak, L. F., and R. H. Walters. Suggestibility as dependency behavior. *Journal of Abnormal and Social Psychology,* 1959, **59**, 102-107.

Janis, I. L. *Air war and emotional stress.* New York: McGraw-Hill Book Company, 1951.

———. *Victims of groupthink: A psychological study of foreign-policy decisions and fiascoes.* Boston: Houghton Mifflin Company, 1972.

———, and S. Feshbach. Effects of fear-arousing communications. *Journal of Abnormal Social Psychology,* 1953, **48**, 78-92.

———, and J. B. Gilmore. The influence of incentive conditions on the success of role playing in modifying attitudes. *Journal of Personality and Social Psychology,* 1965, **1**, 17-27.

———, and B. T. King. The influence of role playing on opinion change. *Journal of Abnormal Social Psychology,* 1954, **48**, 211-218.

———, A. A. Lumsdaine, and A. I. Gladstone. Effects of preparatory communications on reactions to a subsequent news event. *Public Opinion Quarterly,* 1951, **15**, 487-518.

———, and C. N. Rausch. Selective interest in communications that could arouse decisional conflict. A field study of participants in the draft-resistance movement. *Journal of Personality and Social Psychology,* 1970, **14** (1), 46-54.

Jennings, H. H. *Leadership and isolation.* 2d ed. New York: Longmans, Green, and Company, Inc., 1950. P. 203. Copyright by David McKay Company, Inc., New York.

Jessor, R., T. D. Graves, R. C. Hanson, and S. L. Jessor. *Society, personality, and deviant behavior: A study of a tri-ethnic community.* New York: Holt, Rinehart and Winston, Inc., 1968.

Jones, E. E. *Ingratiation: A social psychological analysis.* New York: Appleton-Century-Crofts, Inc., 1964.

———, and R. deCharms. The organizing function of interaction roles in person perception. *Journal of Abnormal Social Psychology,* 1958, **57**, 155-164.

———, R. G. Jones, and J. Gergen. Some conditions affecting the evaluation of a conformist. *Journal of Personality,* 1963, **31**, 270-288.

Karabenick, S. A., and Z. I. Youssef. Performance as a function of achievement motive level and perceived difficulty. *Journal of Personality and Social Psychology,* 1968, **10,** 414-419.

Karlins, M., T. L. Coffman, and G. Walters. On the fading of social stereotypes: Studies in three generations of college students. *Journal of Personality and Social Psychology,* 1969, **13,** 1-16.

Katz, D., and K. W. Braly. Racial prejudice and racial stereotypes. *Journal of Abnormal Social Psychology,* 1933, **30,** 175-193.

———, **and R. L. Kahn.** Some recent findings in human relations research in industry. In G. E. Swanson, T. M. Newcomb, and E. L. Hartley (eds.), *Readings in social psychology* (rev. ed.). New York: Holt, Rinehart & Winston, Inc., 1952. Pp. 650-665.

Kelley, H. H. The warm-cold variable in first impressions of persons. *Journal of Personality,* 1950, **18,** 421-439.

———, **and J. W. Thibaut.** Group problem solving. In G. Lindzey, and E. Aronson (eds.), *The handbook of social psychology.* 2d ed. Vol. 4. Reading, Mass.: Addison-Wesley Publishing Company, Inc., 1969.

Kidd, J. W. An analysis of social rejection in a college men's residence hall. *Sociometry,* 1951, **14,** 226-234.

Kiesler, S. B. The effect of perceived role requirements on reactions of favor-doing. *Journal of Experimental Social Psychology,* 1966, **2,** 198-210.

Killian, L. M. The significance of multiple-group membership in disasters. *American Journal of Sociology,* 1952, **57,** 309-313.

Kintsch, W. *Learning, memory, and conceptual processes.* New York: John Wiley & Sons, Inc., 1970.

Kirkpatrick, C. *The family as process and institution.* New York: The Ronald Press Company, 1955.

Klausner, S. Z. Choosing a new reference group. Paper presented at the meeting of the American Sociological Associ-

ation, St. Louis, Mo., September, 1961.

Kleinberg, O. *Social psychology.* Rev. ed. New York: Henry Holt and Company, Inc., 1954.

Kogan, N., and M. A. Wallach. Effects of psychical separation of group members upon group risk-taking. *Human Relations,* 1967, **20,** 41-48.

Kohlberg, L. Stage and sequence: The cognitive-developmental approach to socialization. In D. A. Goslin (ed.), *Handbook of socialization theory and research.* Chicago: Rand McNally & Company, 1969. Pp. 347-480.

Komoritu, S. S., and A. R. Brenner. Bargaining and concession making under bilateral monopoly. *Journal of Personality and Social Psychology,* 1968, **9,** 15-20.

Kornzweig, N. D. Behavior change as a function of fear arousal and personality. Unpublished doctoral dissertation, Yale University, 1967. Cited in H. Leventhal, Findings and theory in the study of fear communications. In L. Berkowitz (ed.), *Advances in experimental social psychology.* Vol. 5. New York: Academic Press, Inc., 1970. Pp. 119-186.

Kuhn, M. H. Self attitudes by age, sex, and professional training. *Sociological Quarterly,* 1960, **1** (1), 39-55.

Kurtines, W., and E. B. Greif. The development of moral thought: Review and evaluation of Kohlberg's approach. *Psychological Bulletin,* 1974, **8,** 453-471.

Langer, W. *Mind of Adolph Hitler.* New York: Basic Books, Inc., 1972.

Latané, B., and J. M. Darley. Group inhibition of bystander intervention in emergencies. *Journal of Personality and Social Psychology,* 1968, **10,** 215-221.

———, **and J. Rodin.** A lady in distress: Inhibiting effects of friends and strangers on bystander intervention. *Journal of Experimental Social Psychology,* 1969, **5,** 189.

Laumann, E. E. Friends of urban men: An assessment of accuracy in reporting their socioeconomic attributes, mutual choice and attitude agreement. *Sociometry,* 1969, **32,** 54-69.

Lazarsfeld, P. F., B. Berelson, and H. Gaudet. *The people's choice.* New York: Columbia University Press, 1948.

Leavitt, H. J. Some effects of certain communication patterns on group performance. *Journal of Abnormal Social Psychology,* 1951, **46,** 38-50.

Lee, A. M. The social dynamics of the physicians' status. *Psychiatry,* 1944, **7,** 371-377.

Lemert, E. *Human deviation, social problems and social control.* Englewood Cliffs, N.J.: Prentice-Hall, Inc., 1967.

Lesser, G. S. Maternal attitudes and practices and the aggressive behavior of children. Unpublished doctoral dissertation, Yale University, 1952.

Lester, J. T. Acquaintance and compatibility. *Technical Report No. 2.* Berkeley, Calif.: Berkeley Institute of Psychological Research, 1965.

Leuptow, L. B. Need for achievement and occupational preferences: Some operations with value-orientations as intervening variables in need-goal relationships. *Sociometry,* 1968, **31,** 304-312.

Leventhal, H. P., R. P. Singer, and S. Jones. Effects of fear and specificity of recommendation upon attitudes and behavior. *Journal of Personality and Social Psychology,* 1965, **2,** 20-29.

Leventhal, G. S. Self-deprivation as a response to unprofitable inequity. Research proposal (renewal) #S7 0474 R submitted from North Carolina State University to the National Science Foundation. Proposed renewal date: September 1, 1967.

Leventhal, H. Findings and theory in the study of fear communications. In L. Berkowitz (ed.), *Advances in experimental social psychology.* Vol. 5.

New York: Academic Press, Inc., 1970. Pp. 179–186.

——, and G. Trembly. Negative emotions and persuasion. *Journal of Personality,* 1968, 36, 154–168.

——, and J. C. Watts. Sources of resistance to fear-arousing communications on smoking and lung cancer. *Journal of Personality,* 1966, 34 (2), 155–175.

——, ——, and P. Pagano. Effects of fear and instructions on how to cope with danger. *Journal of Personality and Social Psychology,* 1967, 6, 313–321.

Levinger, G. A three-level approach to attraction: Toward an understanding of pair relatedness. In T. L. Huston (ed.), *Foundations of interpersonal attraction.* New York: Academic Press, Inc., 1974. Pp. 100–120.

——, D. J. Senn, and B. W. Jorgensen. Progress toward permanence in courtship: A test of the Kerckhoff-Davis hypothesis. *Sociometry,* 1970, 33, 427–443.

Levy, D. *Maternal overprotection.* New York: Columbia University Press, 1943.

Lewin, K., R. Lippitt, and R. K. White. Patterns of aggressive behavior in experimentally created social climates. *Journal of Social Psychology,* 1939, 10, 271–299.

Lewis, L. D., J. M. Darley, and S. Glucksberg. Stereotype persistence and change among college students: One more time. Princeton, N. J.: Princeton University, unpublished manuscript, 1972.

Lewis, O. *Children of Sanchez.* New York: Random House, Inc., 1961.

Lofland, J. *Deviance and identity.* Englewood Cliffs, N.J.: Prentice-Hall, Inc., 1969.

Longstreth, L. E. A cognitive interpretation of secondary reinforcement. *Nebraska Symposium on Motivation,* 1971, 19, 33–80.

Loomis, J. L. Communication, the development of trust and cooperative behavior. *Human Relations,* 1959, 12, 305–315.

Lott, A. J., and B. E. Lott. The role of reward in the formation of positive interpersonal attitudes. In T. L. Huston (ed.), *Foundations of interpersonal attraction.* New York: Academic Press, Inc., 1974. Pp. 171–192.

Luce, R. D., and H. Raiffa. *Games and decisions.* New York: John Wiley & Sons, Inc., 1957.

Lyman, S. M., and M. B. Scott. Coolness in everyday life. In M. Truzzi (ed.), *Sociology and everyday life.* Englewood Cliffs, N.J.: Prentice-Hall, Inc., 1968.

McCandless, B. R. *Children and adolescents.* New York: Holt, Rinehart and Winston, Inc., 1961.

Maccoby, E., and J. C. Masters. Attachment and dependency. In P. H. Mussen (ed.), *Carmichael's manual of child psychology.* 3d ed. Vol. 2. New York: John Wiley & Sons, Inc., 1970.

McCord, W., and J. McCord. *Psychopath and delinquency.* New York: Grune & Stratton, Inc., 1956.

McDavid, J., Jr. Personality and situational determinants of conformity. *Journal of Abnormal Social Psychology,* 1959, 58, 241–246.

McGuire, W. J. The relative efficacy of active and passive prior defense in immunizing beliefs against persuasion. *Journal of Abnormal and Social Psychology,* 1961, 63, 326–332.

——. Persistence of the resistance to persuasion induced by various types of prior belief defenses. *Journal of Abnormal and Social Psychology,* 1962, 64, 241–248.

——, and D. Papageorgis. The relative efficacy of various types of prior belief-defense in producing immunity against persuasion. *Journal of Abnormal and Social Psychology,* 1961, 62, 327–337.

McWhirter, R. M., and J. D. Jecker. Attitude similarity and inferred attraction. *Psychonomic Science,* 1967, 7 (6), 225–226.

Maehr, M. L., J. Mensing, and S. Nafzger. Concept of self and the reaction of others. *Sociometry,* 1962, 25, 353–357.

Mahone, C. H. Fear of failure and unrealistic vocational aspiration. *Journal of Abnormal Social Psychology,* 1960, 60, 253–261.

Maier, N. R. F., and A. R. Solem. The contribution of a discussion leader to the quality of group thinking: The effective use of minority opinions. *Human Relations,* 1952, 5, 277–288.

Maracek, J., and D. R. Mettee. Avoidance of continued success as a function of self esteem, level of esteem, certainty, and responsibility for success. *Journal of Personality and Social Psychology,* 1972, 22, 98–107.

Martin, H. W. Structural sources of strain in a small psychiatric hospital. Paper read at American Sociological Association, St. Louis, Mo., September, 1961.

Mead, G. H. *Mind, self and society.* Chicago: The University of Chicago Press, 1934.

Merton, R. K. The role set. *British Journal of Sociology,* 1957, 8, 106–120.

——. Epilogue: Social problems and sociological theory. In R. K. Merton and R. A. Nisbet (eds.), *Contemporary Social Problems.* New York: Harcourt Brace Jovanovich, Inc., 1971.

——, G. G. Reader, and P. L. Kendall (eds.). *The student-physician.* Cambridge, Mass.: Harvard University Press, 1957.

Middleton, R. Alienation, race and education. *American Sociological Review,* 1963, 28 (6), 973–976.

Milgram, S. Behavioral study of obedience. *Journal of Abnormal and Social Psychology,* 1963, 67, 371–378.

——. Some conditions of obedience and disobedience to authority. *Human Relations,* 1965, 18, 57–76.

Miller, N., and R. S. Baron. On measuring counterarguing. *Journal for the Theory of Social Behavior*, 1973, **3**, 101-118.

Milstein, F. A. Ambition and defense against threats of failure. Unpublished doctoral dissertation. Ann Arbor, Mich.: University of Michigan, 1956.

Mischel, W. Theory and research on the antecedents of self-imposed delay of reward. In B. A. Maher (ed.), *Progress in experimental personality research*. Vol. 2. New York: Academic Press, Inc., 1965.

———. *Personality and assessment*. New York: John Wiley & Sons, Inc., 1968.

———, and R. M. Liebert. Effects of discrepancies between observed and imposed reward criteria on their acquisition and transmission. *Journal of Personality and Social Psychology*, 1966, **3**, 45-53.

Mitchell, W. C. Occupational role strains: The American elective public official. *Administrative Science Quarterly*, 1958, **3**, 219-228.

Mixon, D. Instead of deception. *Journal for the Theory of Social Behavior*, 1972, **2**, 145-177.

Moreno, J. L. *Who shall survive?* 2d ed. Beacon, N.Y.: Beacon House, Inc., 1953.

Moulton, R. W. Effects of success and failure on level of aspiration as related to achievement motives. *Journal of Personality and Social Psychology*, 1965, **1**, 399-406.

Myrdal, G. *An American dilemma*. New York: Harper & Brothers, 1944.

Newcomb, T. M. *The acquaintance process*. New York: Holt, Rinehart & Winston, Inc., 1961.

Norman, W. T., and L. R. Goldberg. Raters, ratees, and randomness in personality structure. *Journal of Personality and Social Psychology*, 1966, **6**, 681-691.

Nunnally, J. C., and H. M. Bobren. Variables governing the willingness to receive communications in mental health.

Journal of Personality, 1959, **27**, 38-46.

Osborn, A. F. *Applied imagination*. New York: Charles Scribner's Sons, 1957.

Osgood, C. E. Suggestions for winning the real war with communism. *Journal of Conflict Resolution*, 1959, **3**, 295-325.

———. *An alternative to war or surrender*. Urbana, Ill.: The University of Illinois Press, 1962.

Papageorgis, E., and W. J. McGuire. The generality of immunity to persuasion produced by pre-exposure to weakened counterarguments. *Journal of Abnormal Psychology*, 1961, **62**, 475-481.

Parke, R. D. The role of punishment in the socialization process. In R. A. Hoppe, G. A. Milton, and E. C. Simmel (eds.), *Early experiences and the processes of socialization*. New York: Academic Press, Inc., 1970. Pp. 81-108.

Passini, F. T., and W. T. Norman. A universal conception of personality structure. *Journal of Personality and Social Psychology*, 1966, **4**, 44-49.

Patchen, M. A conceptual framework and some empirical data regarding comparisons of social rewards. *Sociometry*, 1961, **24**, 136-156.

Pearlin, L. I., M. Yarrow, and H. A. Scarr. Unintended effects of parental aspirations: The case of children's cheating. *American Journal of Sociology*, 1967, **73**, 73-83.

Peevers, B. H., and P. F. Secord. Developmental changes in attribution of descriptive concepts to persons. *Journal of Personality and Social Psychology*, 1973, **27**, 120-128.

Pepitone, A. Attributions of causality, social attitudes, and cognitive matching processes. In R. Tagiuri and L. Petrullo (eds.), *Person perception and interpersonal behavior*. Stanford, Calif.: Stanford University Press, 1958. Pp. 258-276.

———, and J. Sherberg. Cognitive factors in interpersonal

attraction. *Journal of Personality*, 1957, **25**, 757-766.

Perry, S. E., and L. C. Wynne. Role conflict, role redefinition, and social change in a clinical research organization. *Social Forces*, 1959, **38**, 62-65.

Piaget, J. *The moral judgment of the child*. New York: Harcourt, Brace and Company, Inc., 1932.

Piliavin, I. M., J. Rodin, and J. A. Piliavin. Good samaritanism: An underground phenomenon? *Journal of Personality and Social Psychology*, 1969, **13**, 289-299.

Piven, F. F., and R. A. Cloward. *Regulating the poor: The functions of public welfare*. New York: Random House, Inc., 1971.

Pope, L. *Millhands and preachers*. New Haven, Conn.: Yale University Press, 1942.

Porter, L. W., and E. E. Lawler, III. *Managerial attitudes and performance*. Homewood, Ill.: Richard D. Irwin, Inc., 1968.

Porterfield, A. L. *Youth in trouble*. Fort Worth, Tex.: The Leo Patishman Foundation, 1946.

Pratt, M. Learning the why of others: The development of conceptions of social causality. Unpublished doctoral dissertation. Cambridge, Mass.: Harvard University, 1975.

Pritchard, R. D. Equity theory: A review of critique. *Organizational Behavior and Human Performance*, 1969, **4**, 176-211.

Ransford, H. E. Isolation, powerlessness, and violence: A study of attitudes and participation in the Watts riot. In E. F. Borgatta (ed.), *Social psychology: Readings & perspectives*. Chicago: Rand McNally & Company, 1969.

Raynor, J. O. Relationships between achievement-related motives, future orientation, and academic performance. *Journal of Personality and Social Psychology*, 1970, **15**, 28-33.

Riley, M., and R. Cohn. Control networks in informal

groups. *Sociometry*, 1958, **21**, 30–49.

Roethlisberger, F. J., and W. J. Dickson. *Management and the worker.* Cambridge, Mass.: Harvard University Press, 1939.

Rogers, C. R., and R. F. Dymond (eds.). *Psychotherapy and personality change: Coordinated studies in the client-centered approach.* Chicago: The University of Chicago Press, 1954.

Rommetveit, R. *Social norms and roles: Explorations in the psychology of enduring social pressures.* Minneapolis: The University of Minnesota Press, 1955.

Rosen, B. C. The achievement syndrome. *American Sociological Review*, 1956, **21**, 203–211.

————. Race, ethnicity, and the achievement syndrome. *American Sociological Review*, 1959, **24**, 47–60.

————, **and R. D'Andrade.** The psycho-social origin of achievement motivation. *Sociometry*, 1959, **22**, 185–217.

Rosenberg, M. J. The experimental parable of inauthenticity: Consequences of attitudinal performance. In J. S. Antrobus (ed.), *Cognition and affect.* Boston: Little, Brown and Company, 1970. Pp. 179–201.

Rosenberg, S., and R. Jones. A method of investigating and representing a person's implicit theory of personality. Theodore Dreiser's view of people. *Journal of Personality and Social Psychology*, 1972, **22**, 372–386.

————, **and A. Sedlak.** Structural representations of implicit personality theory. In L. Berkowitz (ed.), *Advances in experimental social psychology.* Vol. 6. New York: Academic Press, Inc., 1972.

Rosenfeld, H. Social choice conceived as a level of aspirations. *Journal of Abnormal and Social Psychology*, 1964, **68**, 491–499.

Rosenthal, A. M. *Thirty-eight witnesses.* New York: McGraw-Hill Book Company, 1964.

Rosenthal, D., P. Wender, S. S. Kety, J. Weiner, and F. Schulsinger. The adopted-away offspring of schizophrenics. *American Journal of Psychiatry*, 1971, **128**, 336–343.

Rosenthal, R. The Pygmalion effect lives. *Psychology Today*, 1973, **7**, 56–59.

————, **and L. Jacobson.** *Pygmalion in the classroom: Teacher expectation and pupils' intellectual development.* New York: Holt, Rinehart and Winston, Inc., 1968.

Rubin, Z. *Liking and loving: An invitation to social psychology.* New York: Holt, Rinehart and Winston, Inc., 1973.

Sarbin, T. R., and V. L. Allen. Role theory. In G. Lindzey and E. Aronson (eds.) *The handbook of social psychology.* (2d ed.) Vol. 1. Reading, Mass.: Addison-Wesley Publishing Co., Inc., 1968. Pp. 488–567.

Scanlon, J. C., B. Hunter, and G. Sun. Sources of professional identity in medicine. Unpublished manuscript, 1961.

Schachter, S. Deviation, rejection, and communication. *Journal of Abnormal and Social Psychology*, 1951, **46**, 190–207.

Scheff, T. J. A theory of social coordination applicable to mixed motive games. *Sociometry*, 1967, **30**, 215–234.

Scheflen, A. E. Quasi-courtship behavior in psychotherapy. *Psychiatry*, 1965, **28**, 245–257.

Schein, E. H. The Chinese indoctrination program for prisoners of war: A study of attempted "brainwashing." In E. E. Maccoby, T. M. Newcomb, and E. L. Hartley (eds.), *Readings in social psychology.* 3d ed. New York: Holt, Rinehart and Winston, Inc., 1958.

Schelling, T. C. *The strategy of conflict.* Cambridge, Mass.: Harvard University Press, 1960.

Schopler, J., and V. D. Thompson. Role of attribution processes in mediating amount of reciprocity for a favor. *Journal of Personality and Social Psychology*, 1968, **10**, 243–250.

Schulman, G. I. Asch conformity studies: Conformity to the experimenter and/or to the group? *Sociometry*, 1967, **30**, 26–40.

Schultz, L. Why the Negro carries weapons. *Criminal Law, Criminology, and Police Science*, 1962, **53**, 476–483.

Schwartz, G. Problems for psychiatric nurses in playing a new role on a mental hospital ward. In M. Greenblatt, D. J. Levinson, and R. H. Williams, *The patient and the mental hospital.* Chicago: The Free Press of Glencoe, 1957.

Schwartz, S. H. Words, deeds, and the perception of consequences and responsibility in action situations. *Journal of Personality and Social Psychology*, 1968, **10** (3), 232–242.

Sears, R. R. Identification as a form of behavioral development. In D. B. Harris (ed.), *The concept of development.* Minneapolis: The University of Minnesota Press, 1957. Pp. 147–161.

————, **E. Maccoby, and H. Levin.** *Patterns of child rearing.* Evanston, Ill.: Row, Peterson & Company, 1957.

————, **L. Rau, and R. Alpert.** *Identification and child rearing.* Stanford, Calif.: Stanford University Press, 1965.

Secord, P. F. The role of facial features in interpersonal perception. In R. Tagiuri and L. Petrullo (eds.), *Person perception and interpersonal behavior.* Stanford, Calif.: Stanford University Press, 1958. Pp. 300–315.

————, **and C. W. Backman.** Personality theory and the problem of stability and change in individual behavior: An interpersonal approach. *Psychological Review*, 1961, **68**, 21–32.

————, **and** ————. Interpersonal congruency, perceived

similarity, and friendship. *Sociometry*, 1964, **27**, 115-127.

————, and ————. Interpersonal approach to personality. In B. H. Maher (ed.), *Progress in experimental personality research*. Vol. 2. New York: Academic Press, Inc., 1965. Pp. 91-125.

————, and ————. *Social psychology*. 2d ed. New York: McGraw-Hill Book Company, 1974.

————, W. Bevan, and B. Katz. The Negro stereotype and perceptual accentuation. *Journal of Abnormal and Social Psychology*, 1956, **53**, 78-83.

————, W. F. Dukes, and W. Bevan. Personalities in faces: 1. An experiment in social perceiving. *Genetic Psychology Monographs*, 1954, **49**, 231-279.

————, and J. E. Muthard. Personalities in faces: IV. A descriptive analysis of the perception of women's faces and the identification of some physiognomic determinants. *Journal of Psychology*, 1955, **39**, 269-278.

Seeman, M. On the meaning of alienation. *American Sociological Review*, 1959, **24**, 783-791.

Shaver, Kelley G. Defensive attribution: Effects of severity and relevance on the responsibility assigned for an accident. *Journal of Personality and Social Psychology*, 1970, **14**, 101-113.

Sheldon, W. H., and S. S. Stevens. *The varieties of temperament: A psychology of constitutional differences*. New York: Harper & Brothers, 1942.

————, ————, and W. B. Tucker. *The varieties of human physique: An introduction to constitutional psychology*. New York: Harper, 1940.

Sherif, M. *An outline of social psychology*. New York: Harper & Brothers, 1948.

Shils, E. A., and M. Janowitz. Cohesion and disintegration in the Wehrmacht in World War II. *Public Opinion Quarterly*, 1948, **12**, 280-315.

Short, J., Jr., and F. L. Strodtbeck. *Group process and gang delinquency*. Chicago: The University of Chicago Press, 1965.

Siegel, S., and L. E. Fouraker. *Bargaining and group decision making: Experiment in bilateral monopoly*. New York: McGraw-Hill Book Company, 1960.

Simmons, C. H., and M. J. Lerner. Altruism as a search for justice. *Journal of Personality and Social Psychology*, 1968, **9**, 216-225.

Skinner, B. F. *Contingencies of reinforcement*. New York: Appleton-Century-Crofts, Inc., 1969.

Snoek, J. D. Role strain in diversified role sets. *American Journal of Sociology*, 1966, **71**, 363-372.

Solomon, R. L. Punishment. *American Psychologist*, 1964, **19**, 239-253.

Sorrentino, R. M., and J. A. Short. Effects of fear of success on women's performance at masculine versus feminine tasks. *Journal of Research in Personality*, 1974, **8**, 277-290.

Spitz, R. A. Hospitalism. An inquiry into the genesis of psychiatric conditions in early childhood. *The psychoanalytic study of the child*. New York: International Universities Press, Inc., 1945, **1**, 53-74.

————. Hospitalism. A followup report. *The psychoanalytic study of the child*. New York: International Universities Press, Inc., 1946, **2**, 113-117.

————, and K. M. Wolfe. Anaclitic Depression: An inquiry into the genesis of psychiatric conditions in early childhood. *The psychoanalytic study of the child*. New York: International Universities Press, Inc., 1946, **2**, 313-342.

Stein, A. H. Imitation of resistance to temptation. *Child Development*, 1967, **38**, 157-169.

————, and M. M. Bailey. The socialization of achievement orientation in females. *Psychological Bulletin*, 1973, **80**, 335-366.

Stern, G. G., M. I. Stein, and B. S. Bloom. *Methods in personality assessment: Human behavior in complex social situations*. Chicago: The Free Press of Glencoe, 1956.

Stoner, J. A. F. A comparison of individual and group decisions involving risk. Unpublished master's thesis. Cambridge, Mass.: Massachusetts Institute of Technology, School of Industrial Management, 1961.

Stotland, E. Identification with persons and groups. Final report on Grant M-2423 to National Institute of Mental Health. U.S. Public Health Service, October, 1961.

Stouffer, S., and J. Toby. Role conflict and personality. *American Journal of Sociology*, 1951, **56**, 395-406.

Strauss, A. L. *Mirrors and masks*. New York: The Free Press of Glencoe, 1959.

Stritch, T. M., and P. F. Secord. Personality in faces: VI. Interaction effects in the perception of faces. *Journal of Personality*, 1956, **24**, 270-284.

Stroebe, W., C. A. Insko, V. A. Thompson, and B. D. Layton. Effects of physical attractiveness, attitude similarity, and sex on various aspects of interpersonal attraction. *Journal of Personality and Social Psychology*, 1971, **18**, 79-91.

Sutcliffe, J. P., and M. Haberman. Factors influencing choice in role conflict situations. *American Sociological Review*, 1956, **21**, 695-703.

Sutherland, E. H. *The professional thief*. Chicago: The University of Chicago Press, 1937.

————. The sexual psychopath laws. *Journal of Criminal Law and Criminology*, 1950, **40**, 543-554.

————, and D. Cressey. *Criminology*. 9th ed. Philadelphia: J. B. Lippincott Company, 1974.

Suttles, G. D. *The social order of the slum*. Chicago: The University of Chicago Press, 1968.

Swingle, P. G. The effects of the win-loss difference upon cooperative responding in a "dangerous" game. *Journal of Conflict Resolution,* 1967, **11,** 214–222.

Sykes, G., and D. Matza. Techniques of neutralization: A theory of delinquency. *American Sociological Review,* 1957, **22,** 664–670.

Szasz, T. S. *The myth of mental illness.* New York: Harper & Row, Publishers, Incorporated, 1961.

Teasdale, S. Effigy of a nun. *Collected poems of Sara Teasdale.* New York: Collier Books, The Macmillan Company, 1966.

Tedeschi, J. T., B. R. Schlenker, and T. V. Bonoma. Cognitive dissonance: Private ratiocination or public spectacle? *American Psychologist,* 1971, **26,** 685–695.

Tesser, A., R. Gatewood, and M. River. Some determinants of gratitude. *Journal of Personality and Social Psychology,* 1968, **9,** 233–236.

The Report of the National Commission on the causes and prevention of violence. Violent crime: Homicide, assault, rape, robbery. New York: George Braziller, 1969.

Thibaut, J. W., and H. H. Kelley. *The social psychology of groups.* New York: John Wiley & Sons, Inc., 1959.

———, and H. W. Riecken. Authoritarianism, status, and the communication of aggression. *Human Relations,* 1955, **8,** 95–120.

Tolman, E. C. *Purposive behavior in animals and men.* New York: Appleton-Century Company, Inc., 1932.

Turner, R. H. Role-taking process versus conformity. In A. Rose (ed.), *Human behavior and social processes: An interactionist approach.* Boston: Houghton Mifflin Company, 1962.

Verba, S. *Small groups and political behavior: A study of leadership.* Princeton, N.J.: Princeton University Press, 1961.

Vroom, V. H. *Work and motivation.* New York: John Wiley & Sons, Inc., 1964.

Waller, W., and R. Hill. *The family.* New York: The Dryden Press, Inc., 1951. Pp. 186–187.

Wallerstein, J. L., and C. J. Wyle. Our law-abiding law breakers. *Federal Probation,* 1947, **25,** 107–112.

Walster, E. Assignment of responsibility for an accident. *Journal of Personality and Social Psychology,* 1966, **3,** 73–79.

———, V. Aronson, D. Abrahams, and L. Pottman. Importance of physical attractiveness in dating behavior. *Journal of Personality and Social Psychology,* 1966, **4,** 508–516.

———, E. Berscheid, and W. Walster. New directions in equity research. *Journal of Personality and Social Psychology,* 1973, **25,** 151–176.

———, and B. Walster. Effect of expecting to be liked on choice of associates. *Journal of Abnormal and Social Psychology,* 1963, **67,** 402–404.

Walters, R. H., M. Leat, and I. Mezei. Inhibition and disinhibition of responses through empathetic learning. *Canadian Journal of Psychology,* 1973, **17,** 235–240.

———, and R. D. Parke. Influence of response consequences to a social model on resistance to deviation. *Journal of Experimental Child Psychology,* 1964, **1,** 269–280.

Wardwell, W. A. The reduction of strain in a marginal social role. *American Journal of Sociology,* 1955, **61,** 16–25.

Ware, R., and O. J. Harvey. A cognitive determinant of impression formation. *Journal of Personality and Social Psychology,* 1967, **5,** 38–44.

Warr, P. B., and C. Knapper. *The perception of people and events.* London: John Wiley & Sons, Inc., 1968.

Watts, W. A. Relative persistence of opinion change induced by active compared to passive participation. *Journal of Personality and Social Psychology,* 1967, **5,** 4–15.

Weiner, B., and A. Kukla. An attributional analysis of achievement motivation. *Journal of Personality and Social Psychology,* 1970, **15** (1), 1–20.

Weinstein, E. A. Toward a theory of interpersonal tactics. In C. W. Backman, and P. F. Secord (eds.), *Problems in social psychology.* New York: McGraw-Hill Book Company, 1966.

———. The development of interpersonal competence. In D. A. Goslin (ed.), *Handbook of socialization theory and research.* Chicago: Rand McNally & Company, 1969. Pp. 753–778.

———, and P. Deutschberger. Some dimensions of altercasting. *Sociometry,* 1963, **26,** 454–466.

Weinstein, M. S. Achievement motivation and risk preference. *Journal of Personality and Social Psychology,* 1969, **13,** 153–172.

White, M. M. Role conflict in disasters: Not family but familiarity first. Research report. Washington: Disaster Study Group, National Academy of Sciences, National Research Council, August, 1962.

White, T. H. *The making of the President 1960.* New York: Atheneum Publishers, 1961.

Whiting, J. W. M. Resource mediation and learning by identification. In I. Iscoe, and H. W. Stevenson (eds.), *Personality development in children.* Austin, Tex.: University of Texas Press, 1960. Pp. 112–126.

Whittaker, J. O. Parameters of social influence in the autokinetic situation. *Sociometry,* 1964, **27,** 88–95.

Whyte, W. F. *Street corner society.* Chicago: The University of Chicago Press, 1943.

Wiggins, N., and P. J. Hoffman. Types of judges and cue utilization in judgments of intelligence. *Journal of Personality and Social Psychology,* 1969, **12,** 52-59.

Wilson, R. S. Personality patterns, source attractiveness, and conformity. *Journal of Personality,* 1960, **28,** 186-199.

Winterbottom, M. R. The relation and need for achievement to learning experiences in independence and mastery. In J. W. Atkinson (ed.), *Motives in fantasy, action, and society.* Princeton, N.J.: D. Van Nostrand Company, Inc., 1958. Pp. 453-478.

Wright, P. H., and A. C. Crawford. Agreement and friendship: A close look and some second thoughts. *Representative Research in Social Psychology,* 1971, **2,** 52-69.

Yablonsky, L. *Synanon: The tun-*nel back. New York: The Macmillan Company, 1965.

Zipf, G. Resistance and conformity under reward and punishment. *Journal of Abnormal and Social Psychology,* 1960, **61,** 102-109.

Zurcher, L. A., Jr., D. W. Sonenschein, and E. L. Metzner. The hasher: A study of role conflict, *Social Forces,* 1966, **44,** 505-514.

NAME INDEX

Hoffman, M., 42, 43, 46*n.*, 47, 49*n.*
Hoffman, P. J., 89*n.*
Hollander, E. P., 217*n.*
Holmes, M., 225*n.*
Homans, G., 192, 193, 195*n.*, 217*n.*, 218, 249*n.*
Hoppe, R. A., 34*n.*, 35
Hornbeck, F. W., 160*n.*
Horner, M., 68, 69
Hornstein, H. A., 225*n.*
Hovland, C. I., 170*n.*
Hughes, E., 212*n.*, 351*n.*
Hunt, D. E., 89*n.*
Hunter, B., 322*n.*
Huntington, J., 322*n.*
Huston, A. C., 21*n.*
Hutchinson, R. R., 58*n.*

Inkeles, A., 293*n.*
Insko, C. A., 185*n.*
Iverson, M. A., 101*n.*

Jackson, D. N., 88*n.*
Jacobson, L., 324*n.*
Jakubczak, L. F., 23*n.*
James, J., 168*n.*
Janis, I. L., 158, 159*n.*, 168*n.*, 170*n.*, 241, 242, 245
Janowitz, M., 176*n.*
Jecker, J. D., 116*n.*
Jennings, H. H., 182*n.*
Jennings, J., 69*n.*
Jessor, R., 228*n.*
Jessor, S. L., 228*n.*
Johnson, L. B., 242
Jones, E. E., 101*n.*, 102*n.*
Jones, R., 90*n.*
Jones, R. G., 101*n.*
Jones, S., 173*n.*
Jorgensen, B. W., 114*n.*

Kahn, R. L., 249*n.*, 256*n.*
Karabenick, S. A., 66*n.*
Karlins, M., 77*n.*, 78*n.*
Katkovsky, W., 70*n.*
Katz, B., 77*n.*
Katz, D., 77*n.*, 249*n.*, 256*n.*
Keedy, T. C., Jr., 293*n.*
Kelley, H. H., 83*n.*, 135*n.*, 170*n.*, 194, 215, 247*n.*, 313*n.*
Kennedy, J. F., 190
Kety, S. S., 335*n.*
Kidd, J. W., 182*n.*
Kiesler, S. B., 102*n.*
Kimmel, Admiral, 242
King, B. J., 158*n.*
Kintsch, W., 18*n.*
Kirkpatrick, C., 290*n.*
Kite, W. R., 103*n.*

Klausner, S. Z., 216*n.*
Kleinberg, O., 61, 62*n.*
Knapper, C., 84*n.*
Kogan, N., 246*n.*
Kohlberg, L., 42–44, 45, 50, 51
Komoritu, S. S., 150*n.*
Kornzweig, N. D., 173*n.*
Krauss, R. M., 149*n.*
Kuhn, M. H., 321*n.*
Kukla, A., 70*n.*
Kupers, C. J., 23*n.*, 46*n.*
Kurtines, W., 45*n.*

Langer, W., 61*n.*
Latané, B., 222*n.*, 223*n.*
Laumann, E. E., 112*n.*
Lawler, E. E., III, 257*n.*
Layton, B. D., 185*n.*
Lazarsfeld, P. F., 168*n.*, 175*n.*
Leat, M., 46*n.*
Leavitt, H. J., 238*n.*
Lee, A. M., 281
Lemert, E., 328*n.*, 347*n.*, 351*n.*
LePage, A., 59*n.*
Lerner, M. J., 225*n.*
Lesser, G. S., 60*n.*
Lester, J. T., 113*n.*
Leuptow, L. B., 70*n.*
Leventhal, G. S., 142*n.*
Leventhal, H., 170, 171, 172*n.*, 173*n.*, 174*n.*
Levin, E. G., 281*n.*
Levin, H., 17*n.*, 56, 60
Levinger, G., 114*n.*, 121, 122*n.*, 214*n.*
Levinson, D. J., 293*n.*
Levy, D., 7*n.*
Lewin, K., 248*n.*
Lewis, L. D., 77*n.*, 79*n.*
Lewis, O., 211
Liefert, R. M., 46*n.*
Lippitt, R., 248*n.*
Little, B. R., 303*n.*, 304*n.*
Litwin, G. H., 66*n.*
Lofland, J., 323*n.*, 334*n.*, 337*n.*, 344–349
Longstreth, L., 55
Loomis, J. L., 149*n.*
Lott, A. J., 115
Lott, B. E., 115
Low, J., xiv
Luce, R. D., 148*n.*
Lumsdaine, A. A., 168*n.*
Lyman, S. M., 349*n.*

McAlister, L. B., 79*n.*
McCandless, B. R., 314*n.*
McCarthy, J., 334
Maccoby, E. E., 17*n.*, 38*n.*, 56, 60
McCord, J., 336*n.*
McCord, W., 336*n.*
McDavid, J., Jr., 219*n.*

McEachern, A. W., 281n., 295n.
McGuire, W. J., 169n.
McNamara, R., 242
McPhee, W. N., 168n.
McWhirter, R. M., 116n.
Maehr, M. L., 317n.
Mahone, C. H., 67n.
Maier, N. R. J., 250n.
Maracek, J., 323n.
Martin, H. H., 291n.
Mason, W. S., 281n., 295n.
Masters, J. C., 38n.
Matza, D., 348, 349n., 354n.
May, M. A., 302n.
Mead, G. H., 308
Menlove, F. L., 21n., 46n.
Mensing, J., 317n.
Merton, R. K., 227, 285n., 328n., 339
Messick, S., 88n.
Mettee, D. R., 323n.
Meyers, R. R., 328n.
Mezei, I., 46n.
Middleton, R., 229n.
Milgram, S., 136, 224n.
Miller, N., 169n.
Miller, N. E., 58n.
Milstein, F. A., 67n.
Milton, G. A., 34n., 35
Mischel, W., 46n., 303n.
Mitchell, W. C., 282n.
Mixon, D., 136n.
Moreno, J. L., 181n.
Morrison, H. W., 214n.
Moulton, R. W., 66n.
Mouton, J. S., 205n., 217n.
Muthard, J. E., 93n.
Myrdal, G., 298

Nader, R., 334
Nafzger, S., 317n.
Najarian, P., 36n.
Namath, J., 23
Nation, C., 334
Newcomb, T. M., 112, 114, 115, 184n.
Nicholson, H., 95n.
Niederhoffer, A., 288n.
Nixon, R., 104
Norman, W. T., 85n.
Nunnally, J. C., 170n.

O'Connor, P., 66n.
Ofshe, L., 149
Ofshe, R., 149
Osborn, A. F., 243n.
Osgood, C. E., 150n.

Pagano, P., 174n.
Papageorgis, D., 169n.
Parke, R. D., 14n., 17n., 34n., 35, 46n.
Passini, F. T., 85n.

Patchen, M., 193n.
Pearlin, L. I., 229n.
Peevers, B. H., 74n.
Peirce, J. R., 318n.
Pepitone, A., 103, 104n.
Perlmutter, H. V., 81n.
Perry, S. E., 286n.
Petrarch, 121
Piaget, J., 42, 45, 50, 51
Piliavin, I. M., 223n.
Piliavin, J. A., 223n.
Piven, F. F., 332n., 333n.
Pope, L., 213n.
Porter, L. W., 257n.
Porterfield, A. L., 351n.
Pottman, L., 185n.
Pratt, M., 75n.
Previn, D., 121
Pritchard, R. D., 255n.

Raiffa, H., 148n.
Ransford, H. E., 229n.
Rau, L., 21n., 46n.
Rausch, C. N., 168n.
Raven, B., 135
Raynor, J. O., 70n.
Riecken, H. W., 103n.
Riley, M., 217n.
River, M., 144n.
Rodin, J., 223n.
Roethlisberger, F. J., 217n.
Rohers, C. R., 323n.
Rommetveit, R., 207n.
Rosen, B. C., 67n., 69n.
Rosenbaum, W. B., 255n.
Rosenberg, M. J., 161
Rosenberg, S., 84n., 90n.
Rosenfeld, H., 185n.
Rosenthal, A. M., 220n.
Rosenthal, D., 335n.
Rosenthal, R., 324n.
Ross, D., 46n.
Ross, S. A., 46n.
Rubin, Z., 121, 123n., 124n.

Salter, V., 95n.
Saltzstein, H. D., 47, 49n.
Sarbin, T. R., 270n.
Scanlon, J. C., 322n.
Scarr, H. A., 229n.
Schachter, S., 213n., 214n., 216n.
Scheff, T. J., 149n.
Scheflen, A. E., 96n.
Schein, E. H., 177n.
Schelling, T. C., 147n.
Schlenker, B. R., 162n.
Schopler, J., 144n.
Schrier, A. M., 41n.
Schroder, H. M., 89n., 90n.
Schuette, D., 123n.

SUBJECT INDEX

Change:
    groups as agents of, 164–167
    groups as agents for resistance to, 174–175
    individual resistance to, 167–177
    social influence and resistance to, 153–178
    in stereotypes, 79
Characteristics, observer, in describing persons,
    89–90
Childhood antecedents of the motivation to
    achieve, 69–70
Childrearing practices, moral development and,
    47–50
Classical conditioning, 54
Cognitive element in dissonance, 155
Cohesiveness, high degree of, and productivity,
    244–245
Commitment, personal, and attitude change, 160
Communication, interference with, and
    productivity, 244
Communicator, credibility, 175
Compliance, forced, 154
Concepts, person, 74
Concreteness vs. abstractness in describing
    persons, 89
Conditioning:
    classical, 54
    instrumental, 54
    operant, 54
Conflict, avoidance-avoidance, 222
Conformity:
    distribution of, 209, 216
    extent of, 209
    focus of, 209
    power and, 217
    as result of socialization, 12
    status and, 217
Conformity to norms:
    on part of leaders, 218
    of social responsibility, 220–227
Confrontation and privacy and attitude change,
    159–160
Congruency, interpersonal:
    affective, 317
    affective congruency vs. self-enhancement,
        316–318
    behavior, changes in individual behavior, 320
    change: in group structures, 322
        in life-cycle, 321
        resistance to, 319
        in self and individual behavior, 320
    cognitive, 317
    cognitive restructuring, 312
    consistency in interpersonal environment, 318
    continuity in environment, 319
    environment: continuity in, 319
        interpersonal, 318
    group structures, changes in, 323–324
    life-cycle changes, 321

Congruency, interpersonal:
    misinterpretation of one's own behavior, 312
    misperception, of how others see oneself, 312
    reflected self, 308
    resistance to change, 319
    response evocation and self-presentation, 316
    selective interaction, 313–315
    self, change in, 320
    self-presentation, and response evocation, 316
    social structure, stabilizing effects of, 318
Consensus:
    on attributed traits, 76–77
    degree of, in role expectations, 28
Consistent behavior toward other persons and
    dissonance theory, 162
Contingencies of reinforcement, 13
Control of behavior, 33–34
Controls:
    cognitive, 31–51
    internal, 12, 33
    moral, development of, 41–46
Copers, definition of, 172
Coping with danger in fear appeals, 171–173
Counternorm effect, 207
Credibility of communicators, 175
Crime, 327–355
    anomie and, 339–340
    as deviant behavior, 336–338
    distribution of, 338–344
    opportunity constraints and, 353–354
    persistence of, 350–355
    recidivism in, 354
    subgroup values and, 341
Criminal behavior:
    learning deviant role, 354–355
    persistence of, 350–355
    and techniques of neutralization, 354–355
    theories of, 336
Critical period in infancy, 37
Cultural system(s), 5–8
    anthropology and, 7
    psychology and, 7
Culture:
    analysis of, 7
    role strain and, 297–298

Danger, coping with, 171
Debt management, as counterstrategy, 143–145
Decision, as group process, 251
Decision matrix or payoff, 148
Defensive attribution, 104
Defining the situation, 221–222
Deintensification of emotional expression, 97
Delayed response to fear appeals, 171
Dependency, 37
Deprivation and isolation, effects of, 35–38
Depth items in person perception, 75

Describing people, social setting or possessions, 74
Desocialization, process of, 29
Determinants, situational, of aggression, 70
Deterrent strategy, 150
Development:
  childrearing practices and moral development, 47–50
  of moral controls, 41–46
Deviance, 327–355
  norms in society and, 226–227
Deviant acts, initial, 344–350
  adventurous acts, 349
  defensive acts, 346–347
  encapsulation, role of, 346
  other people, 345
  places and hardware, 347–348
  subjective availability of, 348–349
  techniques of neutralization, 348
  threat, role of, 345
Deviant behavior:
  labeling of, 331–336
  imputational specialists in, 334
  moral entrepreneurs in, 333–334
  schizophrenia in, 335
  social power and, 331–333
  specialists in, 333–335
  status and, 333–335
  lack of fit between means and values, 227
Differential monetary rewards and productivity, 256
Differentiation in describing persons, 74
Dilemma:
  of leadership, 239
  prisoner's, 147
Diplomacy, international, games of strategy and, 150
Direct tuition, 60
Discriminative stimulus, 13
Display:
  affect, in impression formation, 96
  rules, in impression formation, 96
Dispositional items in person perception, 75
Dissonance:
  explanation for, 158
  formula for, 156
  theory, 154
  reinterpretations of, 160–163
Distribution of conformity in the group, 216
Drives, acquired, 54
Dyad, 107

Effectiveness of threats, 147
Egocentrism, 42
  in describing people, 75
Emotional inoculation and resistance to change, 168
Emotional support, low, 124

Employee absence and satisfaction, 256
Employment stability and satisfaction, 256
Engagement of self and dissonance theory, 162
Environment, restricted, 37
Envy, status, in modeling, 30
Equilibrium and role differentiation in groups, 234
Equity theory, 253
  input, 253
  norms of, 226
  outcome, 253
  overcompensation in, 226
  overpayment, 253
  principle of, 254
  restoration of, 253
  state of, 253
  undercompensation in, 227
  underpayment in, 253
Essay situations and attitude change, 160
Estimation and sampling in initial interaction, 118
Evaluation:
  of persons in ongoing interaction, 100–104
  in ratings of persons, 84
Exchange theory, 108–110, 117
  alternatives, comparison level for, 128
  changes: in comparison level, 127–128
    in costs and rewards, sources of, 126–127
  comparison level, 108, 109, 124
    changes in, 127–128
    low, 124
  comparison level for alternatives, 128
  cost, 108, 109
  costs and rewards, sources of change in, 126–127
  exclusiveness, in attraction, 120
  expectation of success, 58
  expectations: anticipatory nature of, 262
    normative quality of, 263
    role, 260
  transactions in, 114
Expert power, 136
Exposure, effects of group structure on, 174

Face-to-face interaction in social influence, 160
Failure:
  fear of, 64
  incentive value attached to, 63
  motive to avoid, 65
  negative value attached to, 65
  probability of, 64
  tendency to avoid, 63
Fairness, norm of, 142
Favorable traits in describing people, 80
Fear:
  control of, in attitude change, 170
  of failure, 64
  persuasion and, 170
  of success, 68
Fear appeals in attitude change, 169–170

Kinetic information in impression formation, 91, 95

Labeling:
consequences of, 351–354
initial process in deviance, 338–350
and master status, 351–353
secondary deviation, 351–354
Labeling theory, deviant behavior, 331–336
Laissez-faire, style of leadership, 248
Leader-follower relationship, 232
Leadership, 217–218
activities, social-emotional and task, 235
authoritarian style, 250
authority, and normative structure, 239
balance between task and social-emotional
activities, 235
behavior, 231–233
conditions favoring role differentiation, in
groups, 235
democratic style of, 248, 250
dilemma of, 239
esteem vs. liking, distinction between, 236
group structure and, 237
productivity and, 250
role differentiation in, 233–237
satisfaction and, 249
specialization, task and social-emotional, 233
styles of, 248
task and social-emotional specialization, 233
task leader, hostility toward, 235
task performance and, 248–252
Learning:
imitation, 18
modeling, 18
observational learning, 18
socialization and, 12
theories of, 13
Legitimacy:
in attraction, 120
of leadership, 236
Legitimate power, 136
Legitimization in leadership, 239
Life situations, applications of animal experiments
to, 15
Liking, 107–129
anticipation of, and attraction, 116
vs. esteem, for leaders, 236
perceived mutual liking, 123
Locus of cause, attribution of, 102–104
Love, 107–129
romantic, 121–124
withdrawal of, 48–50
Loveless marriage and comparison level for
alternatives, 128

Machiavellianism, 274
Management:
of debt, as manipulative strategy, 143–145
of impression, 101–102

Manipulating power, strategy and tactics, 141–151
Marriage, loveless, and comparison level for
alternatives, 128
Masking of emotional expression, 97
Master status, 89
Mechanism of advocacy, 158
Member satisfaction in groups, 252
Mental illness:
labeling of, 335–336
as a social problem, 329
Minority of one and social pressure, 204
Minority opinions, protection of, in problem-solving
groups, 244
Mixed motive in games of strategy, 147
Modeling, 18
status envy, 30
Models, selection of, 22
Monetary rewards, differential and productivity,
256
Money, as secondary reinforcer, 54
Moral:
absolutism, developmental stage of, 51
behavior, dispositional and situational factors in,
302
controls, development of, 41–46
development and childrearing practices, 47–50
entrepreneurs, in labeling deviant behavior,
333–334
prohibition, 33
Morale of groups, 256
Mother, absence of, 37
Mother-infant affectional system, 39
Mother substitute, absence of, 37
Motivation:
achievement, 63
social, 53–71
Motive to avoid failure, 65
Motives, strength of motive to succeed, 63
Multidimensional analysis, 84–85
Mutual attraction, 121
Mutual commitment in a love relation, 122
Mutual distrust and tension, 150
Mutual liking, perceived, 123
Mutuality, balance of, in attraction, 122

Nazi concentration camps and social power, 214
Negotiation:
games of strategy and, 147–151
of role obligations and rights, 26–27
in roles, 271–274
(See also Bargaining)
Neutralization of emotional expression, 97
Nonverbal information:
in impression formation, 91
kinetic, in impression formation, 95
Norm formation:
of altruism, 143
forces toward, 204
of reciprocity, 137, 143, 225